ECONOMICS
AN ALTERNATIVE TEXT

By the same author

THE ORIGIN OF ECONOMIC IDEAS
OCCUPATION AND PAY IN GREAT BRITAIN, 1906–79
DEVELOPMENT PATHS IN AFRICA AND CHINA (*co-editor*)
THE TEACHING OF ECONOMICS IN AFRICA (*co-editor*)

ECONOMICS
AN ALTERNATIVE TEXT

Guy Routh

Palgrave Macmillan

© Guy Routh 1984

All rights reserved. No part of this publication may be reproduced or transmitted, in any form or by any means, without permission.

First published 1984 by
THE MACMILLAN PRESS LTD
*London and Basingstoke
Companies and representatives
throughout the world*

ISBN 978-0-333-35300-4   ISBN 978-1-349-17348-8 (eBook)
DOI 10.1007/978-1-349-17348-8

*Filmset by Vantage Photosetting Co. Ltd
Eastleigh and London*

Contents

Acknowledgements	ix
List of Tables	xi

1 Economic Viewpoints — 1
  1.1 What this book tries to do — 1
  1.2 How many worlds? — 2
  1.3 Background information — 3

2 Pre-capitalist Societies — 4
  2.1 As it was in the beginning — 4
  2.2 Hunters and gatherers — 5
  2.3 Herdsmen and cultivators — 9
  2.4 States and empires — 10
  2.5 Religion and magic — 11
  2.6 Written history — 14
  2.7 Other ancient societies — 15
  2.8 The feudal system — 19

3 Merchant Capitalism — 24
  3.1 Feudalism to despotism — 24
  3.2 Immediate causes — 25
  3.3 The Reformation — 28
  3.4 Private enterprise — 29

4 Triumph of the Bourgeoisie — 34
  4.1 The absolute monarchs — 34
  4.2 The industrial revolution — 37
  4.3 Costs and benefits — 40
  4.4 Imperialism — 44

5 Capitalist Systems and How They Work — 54

6 The Profit-seekers — 62

6.1	Growth of the giants	62
6.2	The nature of businesses	67
6.3	Business in action	85
6.4	Interpretations	103

7 Work and Pay — 115
7.1	The nature of work	115
7.2	Classification	121
7.3	Job design and assessment	137
7.4	Pay	144

8 Consumers and Distributors — 164
8.1	Perfect competition?	164
8.2	Household expenditure	165
8.3	The appetites of men ... and of women	168
8.4	Shopkeepers	183
8.5	The art of persuasion	197
8.6	Consumer protection: beware the unseen hand!	201

9 Money and Banking — 207
9.1	Notes, coins, shells and oxen	207
9.2	The value of money	210
9.3	Banks	211
9.4	Other financial institutions	218
9.5	Lights that failed	226
9.6	Inflation	234

10 Government — 251
10.1	*Vadere sicut vult*	251
10.2	The public purpose	253
10.3	The environment	260
10.4	Protecting investors from businesses, and businesses from each other	262
10.5	The management of economies	264

11 Socialism — 272
11.1	Preparations	272
11.2	First five-year plan	274
11.3	Developments in planning	276
11.4	Planning today	278
11.5	Achievements	281

		Contents	vii
12	**The Third World**		**285**
	12.1	Problems of poverty	285
	12.2	Causes	288
	12.3	The nature of Third World countries	291
	12.4	Development programmes	293
	12.5	Case studies	298
	12.6	Secrets of success?	300
	12.7	Aid	302
	Conclusion		**304**
Index			309

Acknowledgements

There is hardly anyone from whom a teacher of economics cannot learn. My teachers have included all sorts of people in all sorts of countries. I could not possibly list all those to whom I am indebted, but present this book in acknowledgement.

There are some influences about which I must be more specific. An important part of my education took place in my years of teaching at the University of Sussex. There are no departments at Sussex, only schools of study, in which great effort has been made to remove disciplinary boundaries. Thus I have taken classes together with anthropologists, historians, psychologists and others: an intensive and often strenuous way of extending my own intellectual boundaries. Thus I have been led, for example, to explore African and Asian cultures, some of which are vanishing, while others withstand the European and North American impact and exert counter-influences on Europe and North America.

I was helped in my writing by a six-months' fellowship from the Institute of Development Studies at the University of Sussex, a venue that manages to combine the studious calm of a monastery with the strenuous endeavour of a railway station. There I could work in solitary peace or consult with development specialists venturing into distant fields or returning from them.

Assisted by a grant from the University of Sussex, I studied federal institutions in the United States under whose control and guidance American business operates. I am grateful for the help given in the preparation of my programme by Peter Carr, Labour Counsellor at the British Embassy in Washington, and Rosetta E. Worley and Lorraine D. Turner of the Division of Professional and Governmental Exchange of the US Department of Labor.

There is now a sizeable battalion of economists working on the reform of economics, by whose endeavours I have been encouraged and sustained. One manifestation of this has been the volume edited by Daniel Bell and Irving Kristol, *The Crisis in Economic Theory* (New York: Basic Books, 1981). What may be viewed as a companion volume is being produced in the United Kingdom as a result of a conference held at New College, Oxford, in December 1982. The editor is Peter Wiles of the London School of Economics (*In Search of a Better Economics*, Oxford: Basil Blackwell, forthcoming). I hope that my book may be of some help in the search.

It is usual for a writer of books to mention members of the family in acknowledgement of the sufferings they endure as a result of his monomania. My wife and youngest son (last of the family to remain at home) have long since developed immunity and have used their talents to improve the product. They cannot be blamed for its defects, not all of which I have been modest enough to eliminate, but their criticisms, delivered without fear, favour or prejudice, have often given me pause and made me think again.

GUY ROUTH

List of Tables

4.1	The industrial revolution in Britain	39
4.2	A household weekly budget of 1833 and what it would cost in 1980	43
6.1	Share of the 100 largest enterprises in manufacturing net output, UK and USA, 1909–70	65
6.2	Percentage of shipments accounted for by the 4 largest manufacturing companies in various industries in the USA, 1963–72	66
7.1	Participation rates by sex in 15 OECD countries, 1969 and 1979	124
7.2	Employment in 9 industrial orders, GB, 1871 and 1921	126
7.3	Employment in 23 industrial orders, GB, 1921, 1971 and 1981	128
7.4	Employment by industry in 4 countries, mid-1979	130
7.5	Occupations of greatest growth or decline in the USA, 1972–7	134
7.6	The civilian labour force in four classes, USA, 1972 and 1977	135
7.7	The civilian labour force in 10 occupational groups, USA, 1972 and 1977	136
7.8	Percentage of occupied population in occupational groups, USA (1910 and 1970) and GB (1911 and 1971)	136
7.9	Pay structure by occupation in the USA in 1969, men and women aged 25 to 64	146
8.1	Percentage distribution of consumer expenditure in the USA, 1929, 1933 and 1979	166
8.2	Proportion of those in civil employment in wholesale and retail trade, restaurants and hotels, OECD countries, 1979	186
8.3	Retail trade in the UK, 1979	187
8.4	Gross margin as percentage of purchase price in divisions of the retail trade, GB, 1980	189

9.1	Barclays Bank plc, consolidated balance-sheet, 31 December 1981	214
9.2	Price indices of UK imports, 1970 = 100	244
9.3	Summary of changes, UK	248
10.1	Public consumption and social protection, various countries	256

1 Economic Viewpoints

1.1 WHAT THIS BOOK TRIES TO DO

You will find this book unlike other books on economics. It arises from a long-felt discontent with orthodox texts that require students to spend an undue time mastering the models that have been thought up by past generations of theorists, and an inadequate time in exploring the world in which they live. I have discarded theories that have no basis in reality, or that give those that learn them an illusion of understanding, which is worse than no understanding at all. I have tried to ensure that the data and ideas substituted are well-founded. They are drawn from many sources, much discussion and many years of observation and research. When, in the absence of adequate knowledge, I state what I *imagine* to be so, I have given a warning to that effect.

In the belief that you cannot understand the present without a knowledge of the past, I include three chapters of socio-economic history before coming to the study of present-day capitalist economies. A great deal of what is wrong in standard economics derives from a misevaluation of the human species. In the last hundred years the complexities of human psychology have begun to be revealed, whereas Economic Man is a stereotype carried through from the eighteenth century. But it is not only from the psychologists that we must seek understanding in human behaviour: we can see it in action in the history of societies past and in their present-day survivals, each of which puts enormous effort into shaping its inhabitants to accord with their needs of survival.

Students are curiously modest about incorporating the evidence of their own eyes and experience into the corpus of economic knowledge: the result is that they find it difficult to evaluate the theorems that they are required to learn, and to judge what, if anything, they really mean. Most students, nowadays, have worked for a living, even if only during vacations: this gives them knowledge of great importance for the understanding of economics. It is still more important for them to undertake formal research into the economy of which they are part: to learn what questions to ask and how to interpret the answers. If groups of students work together so that enough data are collected to tabulate and test, all the better. They will never forget what they learn in this way about consumer behaviour, methods of costing and pricing, management decision-making, pay-bargaining and so on.

The methodology I am promoting is historical, empirical and interdisciplinary. To understand economics we cannot do without the help of historians, anthropologists, sociologists, psychologists and the rest of the social scientists. At the end of it all they will still know more about their subjects than we do; so will managers about managing, bankers about banking, trade unionists and personnel managers about industrial relations. But it is only the economists who have the task of surveying and understanding the workings of the economy as a whole, and it is as a contribution to this process that this book is designed.

1.2 HOW MANY WORLDS?

In 1873 Jules Verne astounded his readers by sending Phileas Fogg around the world in 80 days; in 1980 David Springbett, a Lloyd's underwriter, did it in 44 hours and 6 minutes, travelling on scheduled flights from Los Angeles to Los Angeles via London, Singapore, Tokyo and Honolulu. So the passage of goods has been speeded up, by air-freight and sea, and banks, merchants, brokers and travel agents are in instant communication with each other, and in this respect are made inhabitants of one quite small world.

Barbara Ward and René Dubos chose *Only One Earth* as the title of their report on the UN Conference on the Human Environment held in Stockholm in 1972. On the other hand the Brandt Commission, in their programme for survival (*North–South: A Programme for Survival*, London: Pan Books, 1980), note the paradox of two worlds, of rich and poor countries, whose disparities exist, and are in some respects widening, 'just when human society is beginning to have a clearer perception ... of how North and South depend on each other in a single world economy'.

Rich and poor countries are today connected by many bonds: the debt of the latter to the former at the end of 1982 stood at more than $600 000 million, a third of which was overdue; in the industrial quarters of the poor countries are plants displaying the same names that one sees in Europe and North America (net private foreign direct investment in 1980 was about $10 000 million); the cities of those countries are thronged with *experts* bringing technology and counsel from the rich countries; in the olden days cattle-raiders or bandits would attack or be repelled with sticks and stones, arrows or spears – now machine-guns, automatic rifles, rockets and grenades are used, by-products of the wars and military coups that have occurred in many areas. Sales of arms by the OECD countries and the Soviet bloc to the rest of the world are now in excess of $80 000 million per year (*South*, July 1982, p. 11).

The process of unification, by fair means and foul, appears irreversible; does it make sense, then, to devote as much space as I do to industrialised capitalist economies? They occupy 23 per cent of the world's land surface, are inhabited by 18 per cent of the world's population, but produce nearly two-thirds of the world's wealth. What happens inside them, and what they do to the rest of the world, will be decisive for the foreseeable future. In Chapter 11, when I turn attention to the socialist countries, it is so that we may learn from their achievements and failures. We have much to learn, too, from the experiences of the Third-World countries that form the subject-matter of Chapter 12 – in some ways, as much as they have to learn from us.

1.3 BACKGROUND INFORMATION

There are some reference books that every student of economics should possess. One is the report prepared by the Council on Environmental Quality and the Department of State of the United States, *The Global 2000 Report to the President*. In Britain it is published by Penguin Books, 1982. It is concerned with the world's wealth, population and resources, as they have been in the last ten or twenty years, as they are now and as they are likely to be in the year 2000.

Another is the *World Development Report*, published annually for the World Bank by the Oxford University Press. The third, the *World Bank Atlas*, published by the World Bank in Washington, D.C.

Finally, I mention *North–South: A Programme for Survival*, the Report of the Independent Commission on International Development Issues under the Chairmanship of Willy Brandt (London: Pan Books, 1980). It identifies world problems and helps to get them into focus. A great debate has followed, and in February 1983 the Commission published a progress report.

2 Pre-capitalist Societies

2.1 AS IT WAS IN THE BEGINNING

Of the three thousand million years since the origin of life on earth, hominids, or man-like creatures, have been around for about two million. But of these man-like species, only one remains – *homo sapiens*: *wise* man. Two million years, on the galactic scale of time, is a very short period. As a species we are in our early childhood. Fossilised coelecanths are to be found in deposits of 400 million years ago. Even the African ape goes back for 20 million.

We may study the origin of man by examining his bones, more especially his skull from which the development of the brain may be deduced. Archaeologists lovingly sort through deposits of rubbish in search of messages from the past, and from these we may hear whispers of the life-style of our remote ancestors, what they ate and how far they went to get it and, of prime importance, the tools they used to perform their tasks. But what words they used and what they said to each other remain unknown until the fourth millennium B.C., for it is only from then that written records have survived, first in pictograph, then in cuneiform. Between 5000 and 4000 B.C., farming villages had appeared in western and northern Europe. In the next millennium, towns and cities were built in Mesopotamia, potters used kilns and wheeled vehicles came into use.

Comparatively, our period of written history is a moment in time. But it is in moments in time that cultural changes can take place: by contrast the physiological differences that characterise species take hundreds of thousands of years to emerge. Time is the one ingredient of which evolution is not short. It is this ingredient that gives surviving species their most distinctive qualities: the methods by which they survive and propagate themselves. Across the spectrum from insect to man there is one characteristic that all living creatures have in common: they are all obsessed with sex, the result of elimination trials spread over the eons: a law that says, 'Any species not obsessed with sex shall be eliminated'.

Again there is a striking similarity across the species in the ties between parents and children. The young look to the parent for food and protection. Crocodiles, despite their unprepossessing looks, display solicitude for their young, while birds, despite their feebleness, will protect them with heroism and to the death against the fiercest predators. Why is this so? Because if it were not so, the species would not have survived.

People have the distinction, amongst species, of periodically making war on one another. By our own cleverness we have, too, achieved exemption from various natural laws. We control other species of plants or animals to produce our food; we can regulate both birth and death. In all sorts of ways we have extended our boundaries of choice by amending the laws of nature that have bound us in the past. We do this in the main through communal efforts that have enabled us to store and perpetuate knowledge.

2.2 HUNTERS AND GATHERERS

Some millions of years ago man-like creatures (hominids) came down from the trees and took to walking on their hind legs. This left the arms and hands free for other purposes than locomotion – an advantage if you are not a very powerful creature and need to defend yourself with sticks and stones. So the upright stance went with the prehensile thumb, good for holding things and for manipulation, and with binocular vision, better for judging distances and identifying objects than the monocular vision of other creatures. The production and use of tools required sensitive hands, and a power of thought and memory absent even in other primates. *Homo erectus* had a brain more than twice the size of that of a chimpanzee, while Neanderthal Man had one half as big again.

L. S. B. Leakey presents the following time-scale for human development: near-man became man and produced the culture discovered in the Olduvai Gorge in Tanzania – 1 200 000 years: single culture, devoid of material progress. Then, over half a million years, twelve main stages of hand-axe cultures. Then 75 000 years of major cultures and many stages, each of which disappeared. In the next 40 000 years, change accelerated, and the Stone Age moved into the Metal Age. The next 5000 years, with the advent of recorded history, was marked by still more rapid development, but still of minor significance compared with the next five hundred years, while the scale of change in the past fifty years of the twentieth century has exceeded them all. (L. S. B. Leakey, *The Progress and Evolution of Man in Africa*, London: Oxford University Press, 1961, pp. 22–3.) During this period the other hominids, who had been around for some millions of years, disappeared; a million years ago only *homo sapiens* remained.

For all but the last 10 000 of the two million years of human existence people have lived by hunting and gathering. Natural selection operates as a long-drawn-out aptitude test, or series of aptitude tests if conditions change; species that pass the test flourish, those that fail pass away. Richard Leakey and Roger Lewin put it well: 'The forces of evolution that ... moulded the human mind and shaped our psychology and our social responsiveness are those embedded in the hunting and gathering way of life. So much so that today we look out on a technologically sophisticated and socially divided world with the brains of hunter-gatherers in our heads.' (*People of the Lake–Man; His Origins, Nature and Future*, London: Collins, 1979.)

So, if we are to understand the nature of the human constitution we should do well to study the features of hunter-gatherer society. Fortunately, there are some hunter-gatherers left in the world today, and from them we can get an idea of the life-style by which mankind was shaped.

The San of South-West Africa have been well-documented: Laurens van der Post, *The Lost World of the Kalahari* (London: Hogarth Press, 1958; Penguin Books, 1962); Elizabeth Marshall Thomas, *The Harmless People* (Harmondsworth: Penguin Books, 1969); Richard Borshay Lee, *The !Kung San: Men, Women, and Work in a Foraging Society* (Cambridge University Press, 1979).

The San, as they are now called rather than Bushmen, are not at all like our ethnocentric stereotype of the savage. Elizabeth Thomas describes them:

> Bushmen have long slender arms and legs, and the men are built for running, all lean muscle and fine bone, and consequently they often seem younger than they are. They are delicate of proportion, too, and they speak very softly. ... They are handsome because of the extreme grace in their way of moving, which is strong and deft and lithe; and to watch a Bushman walking or simply picking up something from the ground is like watching part of a dance. (*The Harmless People*, p. 18.)

Richard Lee estimated in 1964 that the !Kung San (the exclamation mark denotes a click) worked from 12 to 21 hours a week for subsistence, and a total of 40 to 44 hours a week if tool manufacture, maintenance and housework are included (The *!Kung San*, p. 440). Thus they have plenty of leisure time. This they devote to conversation, dancing, singing, playing games and story-telling, all things that they do with great finesse.

The San once inhabited the mountains that divide the plateau from the coastal lowlands of southern Africa, and their beautiful paintings are still to be found in the caves of this area. But for some thousands of years they have occupied the much-less-hospitable scrublands of South-West Africa. There they live in family groups of between 20 and 40 people. I quote Elizabeth Thomas again:

> Although Bushmen are a roaming people and therefore seem to be homeless and vague about their country, each group of them has a very specific territory which that group alone may use, and they respect their boundaries rigidly. Each group also knows its own territory very well; although it may be several hundred square miles in area, the people who live there know every bush and stone, every convolution of the ground, and have usually named every place in it where a certain kind of veld food may grow, even if that place is only a few yards in diameter, or where there is only a patch of tall arrow grass or a bee tree, in this way each group of people knows many hundred places by name. Even if you are travelling randomly with Bushmen and ask at any time on the journey for the name of the place where you happen to be standing they will probably be able to tell you. They themselves always like to know exactly where they are. (*The Harmless People*, pp. 21–2.)

As is the case in most African tribal societies, patterns of behaviour are instilled in the young from the earliest age. They consist of customs and usages that have been formed and proved over long periods of time, without which those concerned could not have survived. There are no police or legal authorities to enforce them; they are observed because the decorum of doing so is unquestioned.

Groups respect one another's territory, though people may change groups, or two groups may combine or visit each other. Van der Post quotes a traditional San greeting: 'Good day. I saw you from afar and I am dying of hunger'. And the reply, 'Good day! I have been dead but now that you have come, I live again.' (*The Lost World*, p. 205.)

From this harsh land, in which other peoples could not survive, the

San make a good living. They do so because they know it intimately, and because they live with it, not destroying it in the process. They are trained to read every sign, for underground water or roots, insects or berries. Likewise they have an intimate knowledge of the animals they hunt.

The men are the hunters, armed with bows and arrows whose poison will paralyse even a large animal. It is extracted from the pupa of three forms of chrysomelid beetles (Lee, *The !Kung San*, p. 134). Leakey and Lewin describe the allocation of meat from a kill, carefully shared by the hunter among all the people in the band. 'Not that one person divides the prey into, say, 25 pieces and then hands these out to each of the 25 people in the band. Instead, the person who killed the beast gives large portions to his closest relatives and to others to whom he may have a special obligation of some sort. ... And so it goes on: the meat is shared in waves along lines of kinship and obligation.' (*People of the Lake*, p. 88.) Elizabeth Thomas elaborates:

> It seems very unequal when you watch Bushmen divide a kill, yet it is their system, and in the end no person eats more than any other. That day Ukwane gave Gai still another piece because Gai was his relation, Gai gave meat to Dasina because she was his wife's mother. After the meat had been divided again in this way and cooked, the cooked food was shared. No one, of course, contested Gai's large share, because he had been the hunter and by their law that much belonged to him. No one doubted that he would share his large amount with others, and they were not wrong, of course; he did. It is not the amount eaten by any person but the formal ownership of every part that matters to Bushmen. (*The Harmless People*, pp. 57-8.)

The women are the gatherers. In the area of the !Kung there are 105 species of edible wild plants, the chief of which is the mongongo, whose fruit and nuts provide up to half their vegetable diet. '... some foods are adversely affected by drought, but others are drought-resistant; some foods are damaged by heavy rainfall; but other foods (like tsama melon) actually thrive on it' (Lee, *The !Kung San*, p. 438.)

The balance of nature requires a stable population, or a population growing no faster than land and other resources can be brought into use. In the case of the San this is done by birth-spacing. Mothers continue breast-feeding their children until they are 3 or 4 years old, a practice that retards fertility. This is just as well, for they also carry their children round with them, foraging or migrating, until the child is 4.

They have little in the way of material possessions, not even huts, for it is only in the brief rainy seasons that they trouble to thatch a shelter to keep out the rain. Sticks for digging, bows and arrows for hunting, musical instruments and ornaments that they make themselves. Even in the reservation of their territories there is flexibility, with members joining or leaving the group, and access being allowed to the preserves of other groups according to established rules of courtesy. Thus it is possible for conflict to be avoided or resolved – a co-operative rather than a competitive society.

If economic man exists he does not derive from 'human nature' but from something grafted on to human nature very late in human development. The inhumanity of the modern world is our own invention, not an inheritance from a savage past. (Lewin and Leakey assemble the evidence in the final chapter of *People of the Lake*.)

2.3 HERDSMEN AND CULTIVATORS

I have dealt at length with the hunter-gatherers, for they accounted for two million years of human life on earth, whereas herdsmen and cultivators appeared some time after the last Ice Age, only 10 000 years ago. Brian M. Fagan reviews the hypotheses that have been put forward to account for the change. (*People of the Earth – An Introduction to World Prehistory*, Boston: Little, Brown, 1977.)

The millennia pass, the range of domesticated animals and plants increases, villages are established, with houses built of mud-brick in Asia Minor and clay on wooden frames in Europe. Ornamented pottery becomes common. The wheel originates, probably in Mesopotamia in the middle of the fourth millennium B.C., and copper tools, ornaments and weapons appear. Early in the following millennium, Mesopotamian smiths were alloying copper with tin to make bronze. In the first millennium B.C. the Iron Age began.

We may turn again to Africa for examples of these societies for, until the arrival of the Europeans, Africa was less disturbed by conquest and cultural upheavals than Europe and Asia. Old moral modes have survived to the present day, demonstrated in rules of hospitality and the extended family.

Traditional African societies had certain features in common: an absence of private property in land, and thus of landlords; the use of cattle as depositories of wealth and as media of exchange, rather than as a source of meat (in some pastoral societies, their blood is drawn and drunk, a form of interest on their capital); the absence of civil authority in the form of police or armies. Disputes were argued out before the elders of the tribe until the issues were so plain that the solution was obvious. Marriage and family life were governed by strict rules, instilled in children from their earliest days. Evil-doers were restrained by the fear that their victims would bewitch them. The spirits of the dead could take revenge on the living for any wrongs they might have suffered.

One may still see these traditions in operation in the Africa of today, with rules of behaviour so firmly implanted, and according so well with what is expedient for survival, that it takes a catastrophe to undo them. Colin M. Turnbull reports on, though I fear misinterprets, such a catastrophe in *The Mountain People* (New York: Simon & Schuster, 1972). See, too, the admirable accounts in James L. Gibbs, ed., *Peoples of Africa* (New York: Holt, Rinehart & Winston, 1965).

Basil Davidson identifies pastoralists before 3000 B.C. in what was then a well-watered Sahara. 'These peoples engraved and painted beautifully on stone and have left great galleries of pictures of themselves, their gods, their cattle and the game they knew.' Then, before 2500 B.C., the Sahara began to dry out and its inhabitants dispersed north and south. (*Africa – History of a Continent*, London: Weidenfeld & Nicolson, 1966, p. 21.) The organised States that appeared in Asia, the Near East and Egypt in the third and second millennia B.C. did not show themselves in the rest of Africa until much later.

But even when organised governments did appear, private property in land was not instituted, and would have seemed as curious an idea as private property in the sea would seem today. Two thousand years ago the population of Africa was probably about three or four million, but even today, with a population of 450 million, agricultural land remains vested in the tribe, and is only exceptionally bought and sold by individuals. Jacques Maquet gives an account of the history and development of African societies in *Civilizations of Black Africa*, revised and translated by Joan Rayfield (New York: Oxford University Press, 1972).

2.4 STATES AND EMPIRES

Six or seven thousand years ago farming villages appeared in Europe, and a thousand years later peoples of southern Mesopotamia began to build urban centres.

The 'mass production' of food that came from agriculture, horticulture and the domestication of animals enabled farmers both to produce a surplus and to find a use for it. The towns and cities were markets, linked by trade routes, and there farmers could exchange their surpluses for goods brought from places far away. The domestication of the donkey, horse and camel transformed the possibilities of trade. They were an aid to mobility that was complementary to the curtailment of mobility resulting from sedentary farming, and these features combined to permit something that had not existed before: the maintenance of a class of parasites. Farmers could not run away; even herdsmen could be overtaken by horsemen. From this great innovation there arose the states and empires that remained so conspicuous a feature of the next 5½ thousand years. Another characteristic of this era was the institution of slavery. An army could be run at a profit by enslaving subject people and/or extracting tribute from them. If you extract even quite a little from each of a large number of people you can be very rich (an effect illustrated by the popular writers and recorders of today). So the princes of Church and State were able to lead lives of luxury and splendour and, from their bounty, scholars, craftsmen, artists, writers and entertainers have been maintained.

2.5 RELIGION AND MAGIC

In modern industrial societies, other than Japan, a person's private life, social life and working life are clearly separated from one another. In previous societies these elements were bound together in patterns of thought, formed and sanctified over the ages. Work, recreation, religion, procreation, birth and death were integrated: 'in particular in "primitive" and archaic societies, the economy is always more or less "embedded" in society and all its institutions; it is not a separate sphere, experienced and organized as such . . .' (M. M. Austin and P. Vidal-Naquet, *Economic and Social History of Ancient Greece: An Introduction*, London: Batsford, 1977, p. 8.)

It is this that helps to explain why, in the sedentary societies that we are now examining, classes of exploiters and exploited could co-exist for centuries, even though the exploited were numerically superior, and had to offer not only passive submission but active co-operation in the system of exploitation. For a society to function requires that the mass of those involved must accept the role in which they are cast, and perform it, for most of the time, without question. The safest way of trying to influence those within whose power you happen to be is to please them, and this is at the base of the religions to which people have subscribed from their earliest days.

Once one ceases to take natural processes for granted, that is to say, once one begins to *think*, the mind becomes active in the production and maintenance of fantasies. (See Sir James George Frazer, *Adonis Attis Osiris: Studies in the History of Oriental Religion*, London: Macmillan, 1906.)

As far back as records go, and in the mythologies that preceded the records, we observe an independent class of priests and sorcerers. But they did not wish their ideas on the people: the people wished their ideas on to them. In fact, to get the people to change their minds was extremely difficult, requiring messiahs, prophets, martyrs, zealots, plus a popular need to escape from a situation that had become intolerable. In the clash of two cultures the conquerors and the conquered sometimes exchanged gods, but generally the religions of the richer culture ousted those of the poorer.

These beliefs performed useful services: they explained the unexplainable, predicted the unpredictable, gave power to the impotent, help to the helpless and coherence to the disparate elements of a tribe or State. There were now authorities to which the weak could appeal against the strong, or the strong against each other, and rules of conduct that removed much of the uncertainty from human relations. 'Rational behaviour' in such circumstances required one to consult the entrails of a hen before going into battle, to fulfil one's contractual obligations rather than have the wrath of Osiris brought down upon one's head, to be a dutiful slave, wife, tax-collector, landlord, and so on.

The authority of the priesthood was considerable. They were able to extract tribute from the lay community and maintain themselves against governments and tyrants. Further, they constituted the only organised trans-national political force whose support or opposition was powerful enough to make or break kings and governments. Even the rich, whose wealth required and occasioned love of material things, gave alms and benefices by way of insurance against the wrath to come. Plato puts these words into the mouth of a rich man:

> when the prospect of dying is near at hand, a man begins to feel some alarm about things that never troubled him before. He may have

laughed at those stories they tell of another world and of punishments there for wrongdoing in this life; but now the soul is tormented by a doubt whether they may not be true.... If he finds that his life has been full of wrongdoings, he starts up from his sleep in terror like a child, and his life is haunted by dark forebodings; whereas, if his conscience is clear, that 'sweet Hope' that Pindar speaks of is always with him to tend his age. (The Republic of Plato, ed. F. M. Cornford, Oxford: Clarendon Press, 1941, p. 6.)

The later Christians and the Muslims were much occupied with the rightful torments that God had devised for those who displeased him. Ignorance was no defence: even if you had never heard of God and could thus neither fear nor obey him, you were *ipso facto* damned.

Most systems of belief included codes of conduct for application in everyday life, the most elaborate being devised by Confucius (*c.* 551–479 B.C.). It is noteworthy that Confucius (K'ung Ch'iu) relied on an appeal to good sense for his authority rather than supernatural terrors or promises.

It is wonderful that the humble practitioner of *li* should have become ultimately the greatest teacher of morality: but what is even more wonderful is that that morality, though 2500 years old, is in its fundamental concept strikingly up to date and still aspiring.... But what impresses us most is his lofty conception of the basic virtues of *chung* (faithfulness to oneself and others), *shu* (altruism), *jen* (human-heartedness), *yi* (righteousness), *li* (propriety), *chih* (wisdom), *hsin* (realness or sincerity), all of which the Master preached so forcibly and exemplified in himself so worthily that they have since become an ethical creed of the Chinese people.... As he himself had constantly asserted, he was all his life championing a way of life, or truth, which he called *tao*; and he would not be satisfied until it had been adopted by mankind. (Liu We-Chi, *A Short History of Confucian Philosophy*, Harmondsworth: Penguin Books, 1955, p. 25.)

The Confucian code applied to business as to all other forms of social life. Sse Ch'ien records: 'After Confucius had conducted the government of the state for three months, the sellers of lambs and of suckling pigs no longer falsified their prices, and men and women walked on different sides of the road. Lost objects were not picked up on the streets. Strangers who came from all sides did not need to turn to the officials when they entered the city, for all were received as if they were returning to their own homes.' (Richard Wilhelm, *Confucius and Confucianism*, London: Routledge & Kegan Paul, 1972, p. 23. First published by Harcourt Brace Jovanovich, 1931.)

Confucius was concerned with good government, music, ceremony and decorum, all things pertaining to the gregarious existence of mankind. His contemporary, Buddha, by contrast, was preoccupied with the perfection of the individual, which would be achieved through many lifetimes of purification, until the final release from identity and reunion with the infinite. This required disciples to renounce material possessions and the appetites of the flesh. That not everyone did so is evidenced by the continued presence of people on earth, especially in those regions where Buddhism is most prevalent, since the survival of those who have renounced depends on the bounty of those who have not. But even so, it resulted in respect being accorded to those who did turn their backs on worldly things, and may have reduced the greed of those who, possessing them, had acquired an appetite for more.

Jesus of Nazareth, too, preached a doctrine that prescribed the renunciation of wealth as the price of salvation. The lilies of the field toiled not neither did they spin, yet outdid Solomon in all his glory. The rich man went sorrowfully away when told that if he wished to be saved he must give his wealth to the poor, 'for where a man's purse is, there shall his heart be also'. There seemed to be singularly little hope for the rich, it being easier for a camel to go through the needle's eye than for a rich man to enter the Kingdom of Heaven. (I have heard it explained that 'the Needle's Eye' was the name of a small gate in the walls of Jerusalem that camels, having been unloaded, had to go on their knees to get through.)

Later, the Church took discretion to relax these restraints, and for those of the rich who recognised its authority and relinquished to it at least a part of their fortunes, interceded to gain admission to the heavenly realms. We shall deal in the next section with the elaborate codes of conduct that were laid down in feudal times for the regulation of economic affairs.

2.6 WRITTEN HISTORY

The earliest writing has been discovered in Mesopotamia, and appears to have been used for keeping accounts. This in itself suggests a certain level of affluence that was attained first by riverine states. (See D. D.

Kosambi, *The Culture and Civilisation of Ancient India in Historical Outline*, London: Routledge & Kegan Paul, 1965, p. 58.) Irrigation, natural and contrived, assured regularity of food supply, and the ability to maintain people engaged in pursuits other than agriculture. John Gray quotes from an Egyptian papyrus relating to the travels in Canaan of Sinuhe, a political refugee from Sesostris at the beginning of the second millennium B.C.:

> It was a good land. Figs were in it and grapes. It had more wine than water. Plentiful was its honey, abundant its olives. Every kind of fruit was on its trees. Barley was there, and emmer wheat. There was no limit to any cattle.... Bread was made for me as daily fare, wine as daily provision, cooked meat and roast fowl, besides the wild beasts of the desert, for they hunted for me and laid [game] before me, besides the catch of my own hounds. (*The Canaanites*, London: Thames & Hudson, 1964, p. 32.)

In Egypt, too, enough was produced to support the kings and their courts, an army, a public service of governors, judges and tax-collectors, a powerful and wealthy priestly establishment, architects and engineers, artists and craftsmen.

King Solomon was rich enough to support seven hundred wives and three hundred concubines, though it is hard to imagine what use he found for so many. For the building of the temple in Jerusalem he raised a levy in Israel of more than 180 000 men. When his son Rehoboam became king, all the congregation of Israel complained of the level of taxation, but promised to obey him provided he reduced it. The elders advised him to agree, but his reckless young friends advised him to extract even more. 'My father hath chastised you with whips, but I will chastise you with scorpions.' This, of course, was his undoing. The moral drawn by the historian is clear to see: however powerful the king, he could not chastise his subjects with whips and scorpions for very long and get away with it.

2.7 OTHER ANCIENT SOCIETIES

In India, by 1500 or 1000 B.C., the class structure is clearly defined, with priests, warriors, peasants and serfs. The Aryans (perhaps from north-east Europe) overran the country, conquering the indigenous peoples. The Aryans had been pastoral people, whose groups of families formed clans, who now settled into villages. As in Africa today, they had strong social as well as economic ties with their cattle, that constituted a standard of value as well as a source of food and object of religious sacrifice. They used horse-drawn chariots, were addicted to inebriating drinks, lovers of music and dancing, while the discovery of numerous dice suggests a fondness for gambling. (See A. L. Basham, *The Wonder that was India*, London: Sidgwick & Jackson, 1954, p. 35.)

The ties between religion and economics are demonstrated by the rites that priests were called upon to perform: for putting bulls and oxen to the plough, for sowing, honouring the Goddess of Agriculture and the Lord of the Field, partaking the first fruits of harvest, threshing, reaping and putting crops in the barn. (R. C. Majumdar, ed., *The Vedic Age*, London: Allen & Unwin, 1951, p. 523.)

The *Arthasastra* of Kautilya appears to have been a sort of early 'Wealth of Nations' – 'an instructive thesis on the art and technique of government . . .'. (Benoy Chandra Sen, *Economics in Kautilya*, Calcutta: Sanskrit College, 1967, p. 1.)

His rules on price are very similar to those of the medieval Schoolmen in Europe. A capricious price cannot be proper or just. Traders are not permitted to raise prices by cornering the market, but if they do, the excess profit shall be expropriated by the State. 'The distinction between inferior and superior grades of merchandise is strictly kept in view in the settlement of price. Incidental expenses are to be rigidly controlled as these are to be counted in the composition of the price which will rise without an effective restraint over costs.' Supply must aim at meeting the requirements of consumers, while proper price is composed of the costs incurred at different stages, plus controlled profits (10 per cent on imports and 5 per cent on internal goods) and the toll exacted by the State. (*Economics in Kautilya*, p. 33.)

Over the centuries castes developed religious, ceremonial and behavioural characteristics that were superimposed on their foundations of occupation and status. (See André Béteille, *Castes: Old and New*, Bombay: Asia Publishing House, 1969, pp. 230–1.)

The classical Greek States present contrasting models of social organisation, demonstrating the immense range of patterns to which people are able to adapt themselves. In Sparta the Spartiates administered a strict military regime, being forbidden any kind of economic activity, while the perioikoi (free men) and helots did the work. With the help of the gods, revolts of the helots were put down despite their numerical superiority. (Austin and Vidal-Naquet, *Economic and Social History of Ancient Greece*, pp. 255–7.)

The Spartiates engendered in their young men a mentality to which an expedition to war was no more daunting than, to us, a business trip across the Atlantic. They were taken from their mothers at the age of seven, schooled in the martial arts and embued with a mystic devotion to their fellows in their age-cohort.

Fortunately for the helots and the rest of the world, there was one fatal flaw in the design: as time went by, they appear to have lost their taste for heterosexual activity. At the battle of Plataea (479 B.C.) they were able to field a force of 5000. At the battle of Leuctra, a century later, they had only 1000. They never recovered from the ensuing defeat. (Ibid. pp. 82 and 134.)

Liberal Athens is in marked contrast with the regimentation of Sparta, though, there too, there was a clearly defined class structure: the citizens on the one side, the slaves on the other and, in between, the metics. The metics were equivalent to what, in North America, are called 'landed immigrants', except that their chances of ever becoming citizens were remote. We do not know how many there were of each. Estimates range from 25 000 to 100 000 slaves, 25 000 to 40 000 metics and 100 000 to 160 000 citizens. (Maurice Pope, *The Ancient Greeks: How They Lived and Worked*, London: David & Charles, 1976, p. 82.)

Only citizens were allowed to own land, but there were great differences in the amount of land they owned: the small farmers led a quiet life in the countryside, and the big ones lived in the city while their estates were run by tenants or slaves. The metics could not own land or houses, but were active in manufacture, trade and commerce. In contrast to the helots of Sparta, slaves in Athens were of diverse ethnic origin, captives brought home from a multitude of successful wars. Mining was, in the main, performed by slaves, but otherwise they might be found doing the same work as free men.

It is strange to find the most profound philosophers accepting the institution of slavery without question. Plato confines himself to suggesting that Greeks should be exempt. 'Then they would be more likely to keep their hands off one another and turn their energies against foreigners.' (*The Republic of Plato*, ed. F. M. Cornford, Oxford: Clarendon Press, 1941, p. 168.) Aristotle, in his *Politics*, argued that the art of war was a natural way to acquire property. 'Hunting should be employed not only against animals in the wild state but also against human beings intended by nature to be ruled by others, and who refuse to obey that intention. War of this kind is naturally just'. (Quoted by John Scarborough, *Facets of Hellenic Life*, Boston: Houghton Mifflin, 1976, p. 53.) But the Greek slave-traders were quite ready to sell other Greeks into slavery. Herodotus, in his *Histories*, VIII, cites one Panionius who specialised in supplying Greeks to the courts of the Near East. 'He bought boys of great beauty, and castrated them and sold them in Sardis and Ephesus for enormous sums. The barbarians value eunuchs more than other slaves because of their perfect faithfulness.' (Scarborough, op. cit. pp. 51-6.)

There were, perhaps, 12 million Roman citizens and 4 million slaves in Italy about 28 B.C. (Tenney Frank, *An Economic Survey of Ancient Rome*, Paterson: Pageant Books, 1959, vol. I, pp. 314-15.) They had established a legal system that became a model for the rest of the world, while their five social classes were determined on the basis of wealth. They also organised their armies with enormous industry and efficiency. Conquests were supposed to be self-financing and to make a profit for the victors. At worst, cities would be looted and then destroyed, the inhabitants slaughtered or enslaved; at best, the defeated peoples would be subdued, captives sold back to their families, and tribute exacted.

The same quality of energy and enterprise displayed in their conquests was applied to their engineering. Some of their bridges are still in use in southern Europe. As affluence increased, so did the extremes of wealth and poverty. The response was dictatorship, beginning in 59 B.C. with the triumvirate of Caesar, Pompey and Crassus. A procession of emperors followed, of contrasting quality, until the empire was dismantled and overrun by barbarians and, in A.D. 306, Constantine, the first Christian Emperor, prudently withdrew to Constantinople. There the Eastern Empire flourished as a centre of art, science and commerce until its fall to the Turks in 1453.

In 1206, while Christians and Muslims were at war in the Holy Land, Jenghiz was elected Khan of the Mongols. Within two generations the Mongols (or Tartars) had conquered most of Asia and a large piece of northern Europe. We know a good deal of the nature of their empire from the record that Marco Polo made of his travels. (I refer to the translation by Ronald Latham of *The Travels of Marco Polo*, Harmondsworth: Penguin Books, 1958.)

Kublai Khan had been ruling for forty-two years when Marco and his brother visited his capital of Khan-balik in 1298. They describe a splendid city, with fine mansions, inns, dwelling-houses, shops and booths, good roads, ample courtyards and gardens. The volume and value of imports and internal trade exceeded those of any other city in the world. (Ibid. pp. 128-30.)

To the great encouragement of international trade, Kublai celebrated the feasts and ceremonies of Christians, Saracens, Jews and idolaters (Hindus and Buddhists). He explained, 'There are four prophets who are worshipped and to whom all the world does reverence.... And I do honour and reverence to all four, so that I may be sure of doing it to him who is greatest in heaven and truest; and to him I pray for aid.' (Ibid. p. 119.)

Fiat money was employed (that is, without intrinsic value, but having legal tender by government edict). 'The procedure of issue is as formal and as authoritative as if they were made of pure gold or silver.' (Ibid. p. 147.) It was 600 years before paper money began to be used in Europe. Here Marco first came upon coal – 'stones that burn like logs' – and a remarkable system of communications, with roads radiating from the capital to the provinces, each one bearing the name of the province to which it led. Posting stations were located every twenty-five miles, with luxurious accommodation and an abundant supply of horses, so that messages could be sent about the country at great speed. (Ibid. pp. 150–1.)

There was an elaborate system of social security. When a family was impoverished by misfortune or illness, they could go to the appropriate officials for food and clothing. It was the idolaters, in particular the Bakhshi, who had persuaded the Great Khan that it was good to provide for the poor and that their idols would be greatly pleased by it. (Ibid. pp. 157–8.)

Marco was much impressed with the good manners of the people of Cathay, but warned that among the people of the eight kingdoms of Persia, 'there are many who are brutal and bloodthirsty. They are for ever slaughtering one another; and were it not for fear of the government, that is, the Tartar lordship of the Levant, they would do great mischief to travelling merchants.... And I can assure you that they all observe the law of Mahomet their prophet.' (Ibid. p. 61.)

The Mogul Empire merits study, partly because of its intrinsic interest, partly as a corrective to the ethno-centrism of European accounts of economic history, and partly because it was the disintegration of the great trading area of the empire that brought about the explorations of the fifteenth century and the rise of capitalism.

2.8 THE FEUDAL SYSTEM

With the collapse of the Roman Empire the manorial system became the form of organisation in Europe. The manors constituted the molecules of feudal society. In the words of Marc Bloch:

European feudalism should therefore be seen as the outcome of the violent dissolution of older societies. It would in fact be unintelligible without the great upheaval of the Germanic invasions which, by forcibly uniting two societies originally at very different stages of development, disrupted both of them and brought to the surface a great many modes of thought and social practices of an extremely primitive character. It finally developed in the atmosphere of the last barbarian raids. It involved a far-reaching restriction of social intercourse, a circulation of money too sluggish to admit of a salaried officialdom, and a mentality attached to things tangible and local. (*Feudal Society*, London: Routledge & Kegan Paul, 1961, p. 443.)

Much of Europe had been laid waste and population greatly reduced by fire, sword and plague. A population of perhaps 27.5 million in A.D. 500 had fallen to 18 million in 650. (J. C. Russell, 'Population in Europe 500–1500', in Carlo M. Cipolla, ed., *The Middle Ages*, Glasgow: Fontana, 1972, p. 36.) The resulting abundance of land made it both necessary and possible for people to group themselves into isolated, self-sufficient clusters. Warrior-chiefs established themselves in houses surrounded by farming populations who looked to them for protection, in return for which they paid tribute.

Clovis, king of the Franks, had been converted to Christianity in A.D. 496 and, along with the manors, one sees the establishment of the Catholic Church. Indeed, the churches and monasteries themselves enjoyed feudal rights and became great landowners. How could these men of God, with their gentle gospel of love and forgiveness, survive and flourish in such barbarous climes? They were the one element that gave coherence to Europe, with a unity of faith and organisation and the common use of the Latin tongue and script.

We have already observed the role of the supernatural in human societies, from the hunter-gatherers onwards. In the Middle Ages it achieved peculiar power in both Islam and Christianity. Both were proselytising religions offering the reward of Paradise to those who believed and the punishment of eternal damnation to those who would not. They were close rivals, using the same biblical stories, which may help to explain why their struggles were so bitter. By contrast, the Jews discouraged conversion and thus, perhaps, bred into their stock a strain of steadfastness that may account for their survival. A convert is someone who has changed his mind, and it is the propensity to change the mind that must be avoided if identity is to be preserved.

In our sceptical age it is difficult to understand why predatory barons and impoverished serfs and peasants should have been prepared to tolerate the existence of large numbers of priests and monks, to build and maintain cathedrals and churches, and enrich popes, cardinals and bishops by tithes and bequests. In part this was because, no doubt, the Church had a moderating influence on what would otherwise have been a lawless society, where the weak had no protection against the strong nor the strong against each other. In these circumstances it is to everybody's advantage to subscribe to the same set of beliefs, though the beliefs must appeal if they are going to offer some guarantee of continued observance. Perhaps the Christian faith, with its Marian concept of gentleness and mercy in an otherwise brutal (and masculine) world may have offered this appeal.

Gibbon offers a further explanation: the universal belief that the end of the world, and the kingdom of Heaven, were at hand. (*The Decline and Fall of the Roman Empire*, vol. II, chap. xv.)

Carlo Cipolla remarks, 'The clergy and the warlords ruled society and controlled most of its wealth.' The merchants were of modest status. No one would have thought, to look at them, that they carried the seeds of a class that would, in due season, dominate the world. They ranged from petty pedlars who went from village to village to sell their wares, to those working on a grander scale, conveying the products of distant lands. But all merchants had one common characteristic: their social status was low.

> They were itinerant, virtually rootless vagabond people, and they were looked upon suspiciously by everyone. The Church damned them because their lives were devoted to the pursuit of material gains, a sinful thing according to the clergy.... The common people also held suspect these strangers who often had no homes and no land, men who moved to and from strange places, often with strange merchandise, indulging in black marketeering, usury, and God knew how many other sinful activities. (*The Middle Ages*, pp. 12–13.)

The second millennium A.D. inaugurated a great rural expansion and an urban revival. 'The dissymmetric plough, an improved harness, the use of horses for ploughing and three-course rotation, all spread to the rhythm of urban growth. The medieval town ate the grain of the countryside and also bought wine and the plants it needed for industry, especially dyestuffs.' (Jacques Le Godd, 'The Town as an Agent of Civilisation 1200–1500', *The Middle Ages*, ed. Cipolla, p. 81.) Townspeople (burghers or bourgeoisie) guarded the reputation of their products and their right to manufacture them. Each industry had its guild, governed by the journeymen who had passed through an apprenticeship to learn the mysteries of their craft.

Religion was intimately concerned with the conduct of business affairs, a concern against which the economists of the seventeenth and eighteenth centuries were in due time to lead an intellectual revolt. Thomas Aquinas was one of the first medieval Schoolmen to apply his mind to the rules that should govern economic life, with particular reference to wages, price and interest. (See Dino Bogongiari, *The Political Ideas of St. Thomas Aquinas*, New York: Hafner, 1953, p. vii.)

On price he begins from the scriptural text, 'In all things whatsoever you would that men should do to you, do you also to them.' (Matthew, vii. 12.) It was thus altogether sinful to resort to deceit to sell something for more than its just price, because this injures one's neighbour.

> But, apart from fraud, we may speak of buying and selling in two ways. First, as considered in themselves, and from this point of view buying and selling seem to be established for the common advantage of both parties, one of whom requires that which belongs to the other, and vice versa.... Now whatever is established for the common advantage should not be more of a burden to one party than to another, and consequently all contracts between them should observe equality of thing and thing. (*Summa Theologica*, II-II, question 77. Bogongiari, *St. Thomas Aquinas*, p. 144.)

A seller may not raise his price just because the buyer will derive great advantage from the purchase, although the purchaser 'may, of his own accord, pay the seller something over and above; and this pertains to his honesty'. The common desire to buy for a song and sell at a premium is not from nature but from vice, 'wherefore it is common to many who walk along the broad road of sin'. (*St. Thomas Aquinas*, pp. 144-6.)

A lender is not permitted to profit by the need of the borrower. It is not unjust for a landlord to accept rent for the use of his house, for the transaction does not involve the destruction of the house, but its continued usage. But money borrowed is spent and, for the borrower, ceases to exist, therefore, 'To take usury for money lent is unjust in itself, because this is to sell what does not exist, and this evidently leads to inequality which is contrary to justice.' (Ibid. p. 148.)

Similar precepts determine the just wage:

> a Just Wage is one which allows an employee of normal earning capacity – one who is not disabled by illness or mental defect – to earn enough to keep himself and his wife and children at the standard customary in his social class: also to meet any costs he incurs as a producer. The fourteenth century craftsman is to fix his price so that 'by selling his goods he may be able to maintain his state of life', taking account both of 'natural' needs such as food, drink, clothing, and housing and of productive needs such as the upkeep of his tools. (Michael Fogarty, *The Just Wage*, Westport: Greenwood Press, 1975, p. 267.)

In present-day inquiries in which people are asked to rank jobs and suggest rates of pay, wildly disparate answers are obtained, but in those days the status of everyone was immutably fixed in everyone's mind. I was surprised to discover in East Africa in the late sixties a similar knowledge and application of just-price and just-wage rules. It is one of the most objectionable features of inflation that it destroys people's orientation in respect of values. Indeed, it is possible that notions of justice in wages and prices arose from the deeply held convictions of ordinary people, to which the Schoolmen sought to give divine authority:

> These doctrines sprang as much from the popular consciousness of the plain facts of the economic situation as from the theorists who expounded them. The innumerable fables of the usurer who was prematurely carried to hell, or whose money turned to withered leaves in his strong box, or who (as the scrupulous recorder remarks) 'about the year 1240', on entering a church to be married, was crushed by a stone figure falling from the porch, which proved by the grace of God to be a carving of another usurer and his money-bags being carried off by the devil, are more illuminating than the refinements of lawyers. (R. H. Tawney, *Religion and the Rise of Capitalism*, Harmondsworth: Penguin Books, 1961, p. 49.)

These restraints on profits and interest were irksome for the merchants and bankers who, in due course, became the advance-guard of capitalism. It is to the advent of capitalism that we now turn.

3 Merchant Capitalism

3.1 FEUDALISM TO DESPOTISM

At the same time that feudalism was being transformed into absolute monarchy, events occurred that were to occasion the rise of capitalism by which absolute monarchy was to be destroyed. The distinguishing mark of capitalism, as Karl Marx emphasised, is the accumulation of capital. In all previous epochs the purpose of seeking wealth was the enjoyment of spending it; in the capitalist epoch it was to accumulate and possess. (The status of this proposition: it is an *assertion*, a way of looking at things, not an hypothesis, theory or statement of fact.)

Thus David Hume contrasted merchants with landlords. The merchant's special virtue was his passion for profit. He 'knows no such pleasure as that of seeing the daily increase of his fortune. And this is the reason why trade increases frugality, and why, among merchants, there is the same overplus of misers above prodigals, as, among possessors of land, there is the contrary.' (Eugène Rotwein, ed., *David Hume: Writings on Economics*, Edinburgh: Nelson, 1955, pp. 51–4.)

In all preceding millennia of sedentary society these seekers and possessors of wealth had been allotted a very menial role, below the soldiers, priests, administrators and landowners: how was it that they were now to conquer the earth? It was, I shall argue, because in the fifteenth and sixteenth centuries a formula was developed by means of which fortunes could be made with little physical risk or exertion. This discovery preceded the industrial revolution by some centuries, for it was capitalism that created the industrial revolution, not the other way round.

By the time the Dutch and British East India Companies were established, in 1602 and 1599 respectively, the capitalist system was already in operation, its magic formula pouring wealth into the coffers of the lucky participants. Love of money, that St Paul identified as the root of all evil (1 Timothy vi. 10) became the inspiration of a small class of people whose love accorded such gratification that they attracted a steady stream of recruits.

3.2 IMMEDIATE CAUSES

The origin of capitalism is to be found in the great explorations of the fifteenth and sixteenth centuries – what J. H. Parry has called 'The European Reconnaissance' (in a book, bearing that name, of selected documents published in New York by Harper & Row, 1968). It was a process in which seamen from Italy, Portugal and Spain, later England and the Netherlands, 'dis-covered', or drew back the curtains on, the world. Within a historically short time myth and rumour were replaced by exact measurement whose culmination is the system of satellite communication and space travel of the present day.

The chronology of events was as follows:

1348–9	The Black Death
1368	Overthrow of the Mongol Empire; expulsion of Toghon Timur from China; foundation of the Ming dynasty
1415	Portuguese capture Ceuta (across the Strait of Gibraltar) from the Moors
1419	Prince Henry becomes Governor of the Algarve and Ceuta
1420	The Portuguese begin their voyages to West Africa
1441	First slave cargoes brought back
1450	Johann Gutenberg prints with movable type
1453	Constantinople captured by the Turks
1460	Death of Prince Henry; Pedro da Sintra reaches Sierra Leone
1485	End of the Wars of the Roses
1487–8	Bartholomew Diaz goes to and from the Cape of Good Hope
1492	Colombus goes on first transatlantic voyage
1497–9	Vasco da Gama goes to and from Calicut
1499	Independence of Switzerland
1501	The Spanish take Granada from the Moors
1517	Publication of Luther's 95 theses on the value of indulgences
1520	Magellan discovers the Strait; Thomá Pires arrives in Peking
1521	Spanish capture Mexico
1531	Pizarro in Peru
1533	Henry VIII excommunicated
1534	Cartier's first voyage to the St Lawrence
1577	Drake leaves on voyage round the world

1579 The Netherlands proclaim their independence
1588 Defeat of the Spanish Armada
1599 Establishment of the British East India Company
1602 Establishment of Dutch East India Company
1609 The Pilgrim Fathers set off in the *Mayflower*

I begin with the Black Death and the overthrow of the Mongol Empire, for they signalled the violent disruption of the long-established trade routes between Europe and the East, thus inspiring the search for the sea-route to the East Indies.

In the Dark Ages, after the fall of the Roman Empire, the manors had of necessity to be largely self-sufficient. It was through trade, the Church and the Crusades that contacts were re-established.

The highest profits of the Levantine trade came from the luxuries of the fabulous East: spices, silks, ivory, precious stones, dyes, drugs, and condiments, brought by Arab merchants through the Persian Gulf or the Red Sea and deposited on the doorstep of Christian Europe. In addition, however, the Italian merchants imported many valuable products of the Levant itself: cotton, silk, the alum that was essential for the finishing of cloth, sugar, and a great variety of luxury articles from the workshops of Byzantine or Moslem artisans. In return they exported European products: olive oil, wine, woollen cloth, metals, armor and weapons.   (Wallace K. Ferguson, *Europe in Transition 1300–1520*, Boston: Houghton Mifflin, 1962, p. 10.)

After the death of Kublai Khan in 1294, the Mongol Empire declined, until, in the reign of Timur, his ninth successor, the empire was overthrown. The decline and fall had familiar features: 'the struggles between the Mongol factions completed the ruin of the dynasty's prestige and the erosion of the central power. Toghon Timur, a weak, vacillating person, found delight only in the company of his favourites and of Tibetan lamas. Dulled by debauchery, he took no interest in affairs of state and ignored the Chinese national rebellion now rumbling in the south.' (René Grousset, *The Empire of the Steppes*, New Brunswick: Rutgers University Press, 1970, p. 323. See, too, Michael Prawdin, *The Mongol Empire, its Rise and Legacy*, trans. Eden and Cedar Paul, London: Allen & Unwin, 1940. The poem with which poor Timur celebrated his misfortunes is on p. 387.)

For $2\frac{1}{4}$ years, beginning in 1348, bubonic plague swept across

Europe. It caused dark blemishes on the limbs of the afflicted (black death) and wiped out between a quarter and a half of the population, profoundly affecting trade and social and economic relations. Castles, churches, rural monasteries, hospitals, fell into ruin. People moved from inferior to superior land, serfs obtained freedom, wages rose by 50 or 100 per cent, rents dropped by ¼ or ⅓, offerings to churches decreased in similar proportion. (See Yves Renourd, 'The Black Death as a Major Event in World History', in William M. Bowsky, ed., *The Black Death: A Turning Point in History*, New York: Holt, Rinehard & Wilson, 1971, p. 30.) There were further outbreaks in 1360, 1369 and 1375, with substantial though diminishing mortality.

Trade routes were disrupted. Journeys by Europeans to the east came to an end, and the ascendancy of the Ottoman Turks, leading to the sack of Constantinople in 1453, ended hope that old contacts could be restored. Thus Prince Henry of the Algarve began his maritime experiments and earned his title of 'the Navigator'.

Gomes Eannes de Azurare, *The Chronicle of the Discovery and Conquest of Guinea*, described his motives: a strange mélange of religious zeal, superstition, animosity for the Muslims, and recognition of a good commercial proposition. If he was to know what 'lay beyond the isles of Canary' he would have to find out for himself, since 'no mariners or merchants would ever dare to attempt it – (for it is clear that none of them ever trouble themselves to sail to a place where there is not a sure and certain hope of profit) . . .'.

If populations of Christians or safe havens could be discovered many kinds of merchandise might be brought back, 'and also the products of this realm might be taken there, which traffic would bring great profit to our countrymen'. Another reason was to increase the faith of our Lord Jesus Christ, thus assuring his own salvation by the prayers of the converts. The final reason was that his astrologers had predicted that he would be an explorer, and he felt a duty to fulfil the prophecy. (Charles Raymond Beazley and Edgar Prestage, eds. and trans., *The Chronicle of the Discovery and Conquest of Guinea*, 2 vols., London: Hakluyt Society, 1896, vol. I, pp. 27–30. Quoted by Parry, 'The European Reconnaissance', pp. 54–7.)

By the end of the fifteenth century knowledge of chemistry and metallurgy was sufficiently advanced to permit the replacement of the bow-and-arrow by the gun, so the Europeans set off, inspired by religious and commercial zeal, well-equipped to conquer the unsuspecting world.

It is difficult to convert into terms understandable to modern people the value of the wealth brought back by the Portuguese and Spanish adventurers. However, an opportunity of doing so is provided by the recovery by Mel Fisher of the treasure carried by the *Santa Margarita*. I quote from the London *Sunday Times* of 13 July 1980:

> A massive gold chain 11 ft long is among the treasure that divers have brought up from a Spanish galleon which sank in a hurricane off Key West, Florida, in 1622. The total value of the booty is estimated at £10 million.
>
> Divers who entered the hold ... recovered 15 gold chains, two silver bars, each weighing 80 lbs, a bronze cannon, and rare artifacts including silver plates, scissors, an ivory-handled knife, a silver cross, a mortar and pestle and several thousand silver coins.
>
> Five unusual gold bands and a gold disc have also been brought up.

3.3 THE REFORMATION

At the same time that the Spanish and Portuguese royal houses were being enriched by the inflow of gold, silver, jewels, spices, silks and slaves, other features of the Renaissance were in evidence. Leonardo da Vinci, Michelangelo, Raphael and Titian flourished in Italy. The art of printing, long known in Asia, was established in Europe by Johann Gutenberg of Mainz, about 1450. William Caxton established the first press in England in 1476.

Without the art of printing it is doubtful if the Reformation could have succeeded. Luther translated the Bible into German, and produced the requisite handbooks for the conduct of a church: an Order of the Worship of God, a hymnal, an Order of Baptism, a prayer-book and a catechism. (Wilbur Cortez Abbott, *The Expansion of Europe*, London: Bell & Sons, 1919, vol. I, pp. 193–5.) Anyone who wished to set up an opposition to the Orthodox Church could go into business.

Max Weber suggested that the Reformation might have caused the rise of capitalism. (*The Protestant Ethic and the Spirit of Capitalism*, London: Allen & Unwin, 1930). But in fact Lutheran and Calvinist doctrines were, if anything, more rigorous than Catholicism in their condemnation of acquisitiveness, usury and the love of money. Indeed we can perceive a multitude of strands interacting with and supporting one another. The commercial disruption caused by the fall of the Mongol and the rise of the Ottoman Empires; the rise in material possessions per head resulting from the Black Death; the resulting breakdown of feudal restrictions; the accession of power that resulted from the great explorations; the resulting expansion of trade and profit; the stimulus given to investment by the inflow of gold and silver; the Reformation and the resulting breakdown of the grip of the Catholic Church; the consolidation of countries, and the concentration of power in the hands of the absolute monarchs.

To these last the Reformation brought an immediate dividend: the confiscation of monastic land and treasure.

Luther postulated the responsibility of the individual against the corporation of the Church, and this was no doubt congenial to the spirit of the merchant, while wealth, previously devoted to the glory of God or of Rome, now found its way into private hands. Protestantism also gave religious sanction to another highly remunerative activity: the plunder by the Dutch and English of the Spanish treasure fleets. This last seems to me to have been of key importance to the rise of capitalism. Fortunes were made in the two countries, part of which found their way into the East India Companies that became the leading joint-stock ventures of the age. It is the joint-stock company that marks the difference between capitalism and all previous systems: the possibility of people providing nothing but capital to an enterprise of which they become *ipso facto* part-owners, and from which they then share in the fruits of the labours of others.

3.4 PRIVATE ENTERPRISE

The Spanish excursions, conquests and settlements in the New World, like those of the Portuguese in the East, were the results of royal enterprise. The Dutch and English intervention, by contrast, was a manifestation of private enterprise, even though Queen Elizabeth had a share in Drake's ventures. The pirates, of whom Hawkins and Drake were the best-known, were even called 'privateers' to distinguish them from official vessels.

There was a curious mixture of national, religious and commercial alliances and rivalries as the sixteenth century wore on. The Protestant forces – French Huguenot, Dutch, English and, in due course, Scottish – and movements for national independence, mixed with commercial rivalries that sometimes brought the English into conflict with the Dutch.

The French Huguenots set an example in private enterprise by establishing a settlement in Florida, from which they made forays against the Spaniards. This was captured by the Spaniards, its leader flayed alive and his followers hanged, and a notice put up explaining that they had been given this treatment 'not because they were Frenchmen but because they were Lutherans'. When the settlement was recaptured and its garrison wiped out, the Huguenots in turn displayed a notice, 'that they had not been inspired by animosity against the Spaniards as such, but against treacherous thieves and murderers'. (George Malcolm Thomson, *Sir Francis Drake*, London: Secker & Warburg, 1972, pp. 18–19.)

John Hawkins, a businessman and shipowner of Plymouth, raised money in the City of London in 1562, bought four hundred slaves in Sierra Leone and sold them for gold in Hispaniola. His and the Portuguese versions differ somewhat: they claimed he had captured six of their ships and stolen their cargo of slaves and ivory. (Ibid. pp. 19/20.)

Hawkins's cousin, Drake, trained with him and, in 1572, set out in command of two ships, one of seventy tons, the other of twenty-five. He returned to Plymouth fourteen months later, having lost thirty-four of his seventy-four sailors. By a combined operation of French Huguenots and Cimarrons (a colony of escaped slaves) they had robbed the Spaniards of about 100 000 gold pesos. This was equivalent to about £20 000 at exchange rates then current, and more than £2 000 000 at today's prices. (Ibid. p. 96.)

Thomson gives an interesting account of the finances of Drake's voyage round the world (1577–80):

> The total cost of sending out four ships with crews numbering a hundred and sixty would be in the region of £5,000. It is known that each investor received £47 for every £1 he ventured. In other words, the shareholders divided a quarter of a million, a sum that corresponds reasonably well with the records of bullion declared to the customs (£307,000). But this, of course, does not take account of the Queen's share which, it seems, was probably as much again. In April 1581, six months after the return of the *Golden Hind*, it was reported that the total value of the treasure was £600,000 and that there was £263,000 in Spanish coin in the Tower of London. Finally, there were the jewels which Elizabeth took and which she could wear or sell or pawn as was convenient. . . .
>
> Let it be supposed that she got £300,000 out of the adventure. How did that compare with the current costs of government and

war? It was more than the total of Exchequer receipts for a year. It was nearly twice the cost of fighting the Spanish Armada in 1588. It was, in all likelihood, the reason why the Crown was free of debt in the year after Drake's return. (Ibid. p. 153.)

Thomson quotes from John Maynard Keynes, 'Indeed, the booty brought back by Drake may fairly be considered an origin of British Foreign Investment. Elizabeth paid off out of the proceeds the whole of her foreign debt and invested a part of the balance (about £42 000) in the Levant Company. . . .' Its profits went towards the finance of the East India Company, whose profits were the main foundations of England's foreign connections. (*A Treatise on Money*, London: Macmillan, 1932, pp. 156–7.)

When Spain and England were at war, nothing more was required for privateering than a licence from the Lord Admiral, who was entitled to 10 per cent of all plunder. It is recorded that, between 1589 and 1591, 'at least 235 English vessels made privateering voyages, ranging all the seas southward from the Channel to Cape Verde and westward to the Americas'. (Kenneth R. Andrews, ed., *English Privateering Voyages to the West Indies 1588–1595*, published for the Hakluyt Society, Cambridge University Press, 1959.)

By the beginning of the seventeenth century private enterprise had taken the initiative, and the pattern is laid for the capitalist conquest of the world. Even the class structure of business activity is clear: a small class of wealthy people risk their money, a much more numerous class of people do the work. In the Dutch Netherlands there is already the semblance of capitalist democracy, though in the rest of Europe it was some time before it attained that form.

Also in the seventeenth-century, money-lenders began to diversify into banking, discounting bills of exchange, and then settling international transactions not by transporting gold or silver, but by swopping bills of exchange. So banks developed in response to the growth of trade and began to play their part as auxiliaries to the business system.

Another of the characteristics of capitalism made its appearance at that time: its instability. In other economic systems there were years of dearth and years of plenty, but they were the results of the weather, war or pestilence. But capitalism is subject to those curious fluctuations that constitute the trade cycle. Booms are interrupted by crises and followed by slumps, prosperity followed by depression. These phases are associated with varying states of business confidence. William Robert Scott identifies fourteen business crises between 1550 and 1720. (*The Constitution and Finance of English, Scottish and Irish Joint-Stock Companies to 1720*, New York: Peter Smith, 1951, vol. I, p. 147.)

Another phenomenon that appeared in the seventeenth century and is still with us today is that combination of greed and credulity upon which con men flourish. There is something intoxicating about the idea of getting rich without working that, before the days of the joint-stock company, found expression only in wars of acquisition, piracy, robbery, legend and fairy story. But the joint-stock company brought this possibility into the reach of anyone with surplus wealth to invest. The South Sea Bubble was only one of many episodes in which investors risked their capital and lost.

The company was incorporated in 1711 as the 'Governor and Company of the merchants of Great Britain, trading to the South Seas and other parts of America and for the Encouragement of fishing'. In 1717 it accounted for nearly half of the share-capital of the twelve companies registered in England in that year. (Ibid. p. 394.)

Stocks fluctuated within reasonable limits until 1719, then came a stock market boom, followed in September 1720 by panic and collapse. Scott describes it thus:

> On Monday, Tuesday and Wednesday (26th–28th) the panic was at its worst, South Sea stock touched 180 (a fall of 600 in a month) ... East India stock fell from 210 to 150, York Buildings from 30 to 17, Royal Exchange Assurance from 65 to 40, London Assurance from 35 to 20. The breakdown of credit was felt universally. Loans, even on good security, were almost unobtainable; and those who had funds to lend considered that they had 'acted a charitable part in taking no more than five per cent. *for a month*'. Most credit-instruments were not negotiable – as it has been graphically described 'every note and bill, except those of the Bank, and some few others, is now become as mere piece of waste paper as if a prayer or a creed was writ on it instead of money'. It was 'unfashionable not to be a bankrupt', the consequences to trade were described 'as most miserable and ruinous' and merchants were said 'to be reduced to such misery as they had never felt before.' (Ibid. p. 429.)

It is interesting to see that even then crisis did not stop at national frontiers: in that same year John Law's great schemes were coming to grief in Paris, with the collapse of the Mississippi Company.

But so far capitalism had manifested itself in only a small corner of the world, and in only small corners of that small corner. Before its ultimate triumph it was going to have to depose the absolute monarchs, cutting off some heads in the process, substitute another morality for that of the Christian Churches, replace cottage industry by factory production, peasants by proletarians, and bombard and conquer every country in the world with its ideas and products. That will be the subject of the next chapter.

4 Triumph of the Bourgeoisie

4.1 THE ABSOLUTE MONARCHS

The absolute monarchs put down the feudal barons, unified countries through war and marriage, and created a civil service through which the unified countries could be governed. They also disposed of the parliaments that had given some protection to the individual citizens, and had first been instituted as an aid to taxation and to give the king some measure of popular support. For several centuries Europe was dominated by despots who ran countries, through cumbrous bureaucracies and armies, as if they were their personal property.

The population of Europe was much smaller then than it is today. In the middle of the seventeenth century it was probably between 100 and 120 million, about one-sixth of its present size. (See André Armengaud, *The Fontana Economic History of Europe: Population in Europe 1700-1914*, London: Fontana, 1970, p. 12.) Most of the populace was thinly spread over the countryside, so that organisation and concerted action were not practical propositions.

The monarchs pursued their territorial aims by intermarriage and consolidated their territories by inheritance. So Habsburgs and Bourbons intermarried in the most intricate ways, so that whenever a throne became vacant there were several claimants for it, each backed by a different branch of the family. Europe would be plunged into war, great armies hurled at one another, soldiers subjected to painful death, farms overrun, crops pillaged, while kings and courtiers watched the hideous spectacle from a safe distance.

The Hundred Years War (1337-1455) began with the claim of Edward III of England to the throne of France. The Thirty Years War (1616-48) was an unholy mixture of personal ambitions and religious intolerance. The eighteenth-century saw the Wars of the Spanish Succession (1701-13), Polish Succession (1733-8), Austrian Succession (1741-8). France was at war for thirty-six of the eighty-eight years between 1701 and 1789.

These wars were hideously expensive, and the kings were constantly in a state of insolvency, but the peace-time activities of the monarchs and their courts were hardly less expensive. Louis XIV spent about 80 million livres on his various palaces, of which over half went on the Palace of Versailles. (See Charles Woolsey Cole, *Colbert and a Century of French Mercantilism*, London: Frank Cass, 1964, p. 315.) At 5 livres to an ounce of silver (Richard Cantillon, *Essai sur la Nature du Commerce en Général*, London: Frank Cass, 1959, p. 245) and with silver at about $16 per ounce, this would equal $256 million in dollars of the present day.

André Alem comments that Louis XIV left an appalling confusion in the accounts. He quotes the preamble to the royal declaration of 7 December 1715:

> There were not the least funds either in the royal treasury nor in our receipts to satisfy the most urgent expenses; we found the royal estate mortgaged, state revenues practically destroyed by an infinity of charges and annuities, ordinary taxes consumed in advance, arrears of every variety accumulated over many years, and the flow of receipts reversed; a multitude of notes, orders and assignations made in advance, of so many varieties, and that amounted to such considerable sums, that it was hardly possible to calculate them. (André Alem, *Le Marquis d'Argenson et l'Économie Politique au Début de XVIIIe Siècle*, New York: Burt Franklin, 1968, pp. 25–6.)

In all the countries of Europe the curbing of the absolute monarchs was a long-drawn-out process. There had to be alternative sources of power: classes of people with common interests, who were capable of formulating and supporting agreed policies. These were constituted by the businessmen: merchants, bankers and manufacturers, who had both the wealth and the means of communication to perform this function. But there were too few of them to do it on their own and in France, in the conduct of the revolution, they had the support of the artisans and peasantry. When events got out of hand it took Napoleon to restrain the excesses of democracy and communism to which Babeuf and others aspired.

In England the nobility had depleted their own ranks in the Wars of the Roses. The new aristocracy established by Henry VIII and subsequent monarchs showed a willingness to participate in business ventures, while the new-rich amongst the mercantile class were equally ready to set themselves up as country gentlemen. Nevertheless, the range of political loyalties evident in the Civil War of 1642–51 was no less diverse than that later demonstrated in the French Revolution. Catholics, Anglicans, Puritans and Presbyterians fought for supremacy or survival. In the Commonwealth forces the Levellers demanded manhood suffrage; the Diggers were prototype socialists. Oliver Cromwell matriculated at Cambridge, inherited considerable wealth and married a merchant's daughter. He was a good, solid, middle-class man, with the simple but devout views of the Puritans, and most of his supporters no doubt shared these views.

The events that led to the execution of Charles I involved questions of immense importance to Presbyterians, Anglicans and Catholics as well as that of who should govern the country and, subsidiary to that, who should decide on the size and nature of taxes. Again, motives for the removal of James II were extraordinarily mixed: if he had not been a devout Catholic, with plans to convert the country to that faith, he might have survived.

In 1714, with the first of the long line of Georges, the country settled down to a solid bourgeois existence as a constitutional monarchy. It was not a capitalist democracy – manhood suffrage did not arrive until 1867. It was ruled by landlords, squires and businessmen. It was not until 1846, with the abolition of the corn laws, that townsmen and industrialists had triumphed over landlords and farmers.

How aware, I wonder, were those who participated, of the historical drama of which they were part? Monchrétien, Petty and the economists who succeeded them clearly had in mind the need for businessmen to be left alone and for property to be protected from arbitrary taxation and the depredations of the tax-farmers, just as it was from robbers. Boisguillebert, as the eighteenth century began, uttered a cry against the parasites who wielded political power or lived as satellites to those that did:

> crime and violence reached the stage, with the passage of time, when he who was strongest wanted to do nothing, and to enjoy the fruits of the labour of those more feeble, thereby rebelling entirely against the orders of the Creator; and this corruption has reached so great an extreme, that today people are completely divided into two classes, one doing nothing and enjoying all pleasures, while the other, working from morning till night, obtains necessities with difficulty, and is often entirely deprived of them. (Routh, *Origin of Economic Ideas*, pp. 56–7.)

What of the American colonists who rebelled against the British government in 1775 – were they engaged in a bourgeois struggle against feudalism? In Britain the struggle had already gone in favour of the bourgeoisie, while the colonists received valuable aid from the governments of France and Spain, still dominated by despots. History becomes somewhat confusing once one ceases to view it from a great height.

4.2 THE INDUSTRIAL REVOLUTION

The inventors, whose genius converted mercantile capitalism into industrial capitalism, had the greatest difficulty in putting their ideas across. The sequence was: machines for spinning and weaving; water, then steam, to drive these machines; coal to fire the boilers of the steam-engines, pumps to extract water from the coal-mines and lifts to raise the coal to the surface. Mass-production, of course, presupposed mass-sale, and the establishment of a world market over the past two centuries had made mass-sale possible.

William Lee had invented the stocking-frame in 1598. The time was plainly not ripe for stocking-frames, for the inventor was persecuted, fled the country, settled in Rouen, forced to leave again and died in poverty in Paris. (Paul Mantoux, *The Industrial Revolution in the Eighteenth Century*, New York: Harper & Row, 1961, pp. 191–2.)

John Kay, who patented his flying-shuttle in 1733, was also given a rough time, and it was not until 1760 that his invention was in general use (ibid. pp. 207–8). In 1738 Lewis Paul patented his spinning machine, which seems to have been conceived by John Wyatt almost simultaneously. Both went bankrupt in 1742. Only after Hargreaves had produced his spinning-jenny in 1765 did it begin to be generally used. Hargreaves died in 1778, and Mantoux records, 'Ten years after Hargreave's death it was reckoned that there were no fewer than twenty thousand of these machines in England, of which the smallest could do the work of six or eight spinners.' (Ibid. p. 218.)

Coked coal for iron smelting was developed in the 1760s; iron puddling in the 1780s; Thomas Newcomen had invented his steam-engine by 1698, and James Watt provided it with pistons and condenser and in 1774 went into partnership with Matthew Boulton for its production. It took more than half a century for the steam-engine to come into general use. But one can measure the progress of production by the rise of imports of raw cotton into Britain: one million pounds weight in 1771 and fifty-six million in 1800. (Henry de Beltgens

Gibbons, *Economic and Industrial Progress of the Century*, London and Edinburgh: Chambers, 1903, p. 21.)

So the various elements of the changes reinforced one another: an agricultural revolution was dispossessing tenants and forcing them into the towns, there to be absorbed by the new factories. James Brindley designed canals; Metcalfe, Telford and Macadam bridges and roads. Stationary steam-engines were adapted into locomotives, with George Stephenson producing his 'Puffing Billy' in 1813. On 23 April 1837 two steamships arrived in New York, the *Great Western* from Bristol and the *Sirius* from Cork (ibid. p. 33). Steam both speeded travel and greatly reduced the cost.

After railways the next great innovation was the Bessemer process of making steel. Sir Henry Bessemer patented the process in 1856, whereby 'a blast of air at high pressure is forced through pig-iron in a molten state, thereby driving out the carbon contained therein, and converting the iron into a cheap and useful kind of steel ...' (ibid. p. 427–8). The cost of steel fell from about £40 per ton in 1860 to between £4 and £5 in 1895.

Adam Smith appears to have been oblivious of the fact that a revolution was going on about him. The first edition of the *Wealth of Nations* was published in 1776, the last during Smith's lifetime, in 1789, but nothing in his work suggests that he was aware of the scope of the rise of the factory system or the great inventions on which it was based. In fact, although private fortunes were being made, some workers losing their jobs and others getting new ones, it was only in the nineteenth century that the massive changes took place. The pace of change is illustrated in Table 4.1.

Note that 'export industries' in Table 4.1 are those industries whose products made up the bulk of British exports. Their real output includes home consumption. Home industries, given as a control, are beer, leather, candles and soap. In textiles, metals and engineering Britain far outstripped the rest of the world, and it was not until the closing years of the nineteenth century that France, Germany and the United States began catching up. (See B. R. Mitchell, *The Fontana Economic History of Europe Statistical Appendix 1700–1914*, London: Fontana, 1971.)

Since the Second World War we have come to expect increases in output per capita of 2, 3, 4 or more per cent a year. Thus it is curious to find how very slow the rise was in Britain in the eighteenth century. Until mid-century, Deane and Cole estimate that the increase in real output per head ranged from 0.3 to 0.6 per cent per year, then

Table 4.1 *The industrial revolution in Britain*

1. Index numbers of real output

	Export industries	Home industries
1700	100	100
1750	176	107
1760	222	114
1770	256	114
1780	246	123
1790	383	137
1800	544	152

2. Retained imports of raw cotton

lb. m. yearly averages

1772–4	4.2
1798–1800	41.8
1815–17	99.7

3. Cloth milled in West Riding of Yorkshire

	yards (000s)	
	Broad	Narrow
1769	2772	2144
1779	3427	2660
1789	4716	4410
1799	8807	6377

4. Output of pig iron

	tons
1720	25 000
1788	68 300
1796	125 080
1806	243 851
1852	2 701 000

5. Steel output

	tons (000s)
1871	329
1881	1778
1891	3157

Sources: Phyllis Deane and W. A. Cole, *British Economic Growth 1688–1959*, Cambridge University Press, 1969. 1: p. 78; 2: p. 51; 3: p. 189. B. R. Mitchell and Phyllis Deane, *Abstract of British Historical Statistics*, Cambridge University Press, 1962. 4: p. 131; 5: p. 136.

remained stationary, then in the 1780s and the closing years of the century rose at an average of 0.9 per cent a year (*British Economic Growth*, p. 80). The phenomenon of rising expectations had not yet appeared: people were relieved if the present year was no worse than the one before.

4.3 COSTS AND BENEFITS

The industrial revolution has paused from time to time, and changed pace, but it has never stopped. Door after door of Nature has been unlocked, its mysteries taken for granted and now hardly noticed. You may catalogue the achievements as you look about you. I type this book instead of writing it by hand; I work by electric light instead of by candle. My journey from Brighton to London takes me an hour by train instead of 4¼ hours by stage-coach. *The Great Western* steamed from Bristol to New York in two weeks; now I can fly there in seven hours. My wheeled-box can carry me to the supermarket without intervention of horses, and as easily take me and my luggage on holiday, with a potential speed of 110 miles per hour though I am only allowed to go at 70. My food is grown with the aid of chemicals and machines; some of it comes from the other end of the earth. There are fabrics in an infinite choice of colours, artificial fibres mixed with cotton or wool and treated so that they drip-dry instead of having to be ironed. Housework has been mechanised and entertainment boxed and distributed electronically. The news is so up to date that we can watch events thousands of miles away as they happen. My house is heated by natural gas drawn from the bed of the cold and stormy North Sea. Setting aside the question of the quality of life (which is something that perhaps only an economist would want to do) can we make a guess at the rise in real income per head with which these changes have been accompanied?

For Britain, Deane and Cole suggest an increase for the eighteenth century of 60 per cent in output per head of population (*British Economic Growth*, p. 78), and a fourfold increase for the nineteenth century (ibid. p. 282) after which we may turn to Charles Feinstein's calculations that take us up to 1965. For consumers' expenditure per capita at constant prices, he shows an increase of 81 per cent between 1900 and 1965, and for gross domestic product per capita, also at constant prices, an increase of 118 per cent. (C. H. Feinstein, *Statistical Tables of National Income, Expenditure and Output of the U.K.*

1855–1965, Cambridge University Press, 1972, pp. 42–3.) There are differences in definition between these measures. *Output per head* includes the production of capital goods, *consumers' expenditure* excludes capital consumption, *gross domestic product* covers everything made in the country without making an allowance for capital depreciation (or consumption), hence the word 'gross', and without allowing for financial payments made to or received from people resident abroad. Between 1965 and 1983 there has been a further increase of about 27 per cent. These calculations combine to suggest that, per head of population, we are about sixteen times as rich today as were our ancestors in the year 1700.

Now let us pause to consider some of the costs of all this affluence. Because the transformation was the result of private enterprise the decision-makers did not have to consider the social costs. One result was that great stretches of the earth were desolated, and remain to this day as memorials to the industrial revolution. Millions of children are still brought up in slum houses that were originally built as speculative ventures to house the burgeoning hordes of factory workers. Surrounded by man-made squalor, generations of workers in Europe and the United States were born, lived and died.

As the great factories spread, so workers' dwellings clustered around them. The young and impressionable Friedrich Engels gave a memorable description of the city of Manchester of his day in *The Condition of the Working Class in England in 1844*.

It was perhaps the unsavoury conditions at home that led workers to tolerate such long hours of work. The factories were places of incessant toil, but at least were dry and warm. Laws to reduce hours of work and to improve working conditions came through the efforts of humane people and after publicity had been given to the outrages with which factory life was replete. The nineteenth century opened with the minds of the ruling class dominated by a belief in *laissez-faire*, so that the struggle was long and hard. (See J. L. and Barbara Hammond, *The Town Labourer, 1760–1832*, London: Guild Books, 1949, and Brian Inglis, *Poverty and the Industrial Revolution*, London: Hodder & Stoughton, 1971.)

The official reports of those times give abundant testimony to the horrors perpetrated on children, but these are no more appalling than the complacency in the evidence of some of the medical and other witnesses. The Factories Inquiry Commission of 1832 was told that a 69-hour week (five days of 12 hours and 9 on Saturday) was consistent with the full efficiency of the work people. Sir David Barry, Factory Commissioner in Scotland, reported to the Commission:

The masters are unanimous in asserting that girls, and they alone are trained to flax-spinning, never become expert artists if they begin to learn after eleven. I observed two girls... about thirteen each, in the same pass or space between two frames; one attended to sixty wet spindles... the other to fifty spindles. The first had 11d. the other 10d. per day. The range which each girl had to move over along her spindles, of the length of the pass, was about twenty-two feet. It is quite impossible to give an adequate notion of the quickness and dexterity with which these girls joined their broken ends of threads; shifted the pirns; screwed and unscrewed the flies, etc. To supply the place of such artists by new hands would be utterly impracticable, and difficult in the extreme to find a relay of hands equally expert, under present circumstances. There is no sameness of attitude – every muscle is in action, and that in quick succession. (*Second Report of the Central Board of His Majesty's Commissioners appointed to collect Information in the Manufacturing Districts, as to the Employment of Children in Factories, etc.* Sir David Barry's Medical Report, pp. 1–4. See the Irish University Press Series of British Parliamentary Papers, volumes on *Industrial Revolution and Children's Employment*, Shannon: Irish University Press, 1968.)

The most gruesome reports relate to the employment of children in coal-mines in 1842. It was for these working children that Sunday schools were instituted, as places for learning to read, write and count. (See *The Town Labourer*, vol. II, pp. 7–8.)

This happened a long time ago, in a world that has mercifully vanished, but not in all countries. In 1980 the Anti-Slavery Society gave evidence to the UN Working Group on Slavery on child labour in Italy. They claimed that in that country there are half a million children aged 9 and over at work, mainly in small workshops, with a 'wide network of corruption and protection which controls clandestine employment and prevents its detection'. They work between 6 and 9 hours a day for 5½ or 6 days a week, and are paid the equivalent of between £3.50 and £7.60 a week. 'The report cites examples of the extensive use of poisonous glues in small leather workshops resulting in cases among children of glue polyuritis... which can cause disability and death.' (*The Times*, 11 Aug. 1980, 'Mafia-type control of child labour in Italy'.)

The 13-year-olds in the flax mill earned 11d and 10d per day. Women in a textile factory in Leicester averaged 10s a week. In the mines 6-year-olds would get 3d or 5d a day. A woman of 20 would get

2s a day or less; a man 3s 6d. (*First Report of the Commissioners on the Employment of Children*, 1842, p. 26.) This means very little unless we know what could be got for a penny in those days and how much the same things would cost today. The Second Report for 1833 gives details of the weekly budgets of two families in that year. Table 4.2 shows the purchases for the first family – father, mother and two children – converting prices from shillings and old pence into new pence, at 5 pence per shilling and 2.4 old pence to a new penny, and show what the same amounts of each item cost in a Brighton supermarket in September 1980.

In terms of the 'basket of consumables' there specified, Table 4.2 shows that the penny of July 1833 was worth 33.6 pennies of September 1980 (*new* pence in each case). The value of the latter is $\frac{1}{33.6}$ of the former.

Table 4.2 *A household weekly budget of 1833 and what it would cost in 1980*
(Prices in new pence, 100 = £1)

	July 1833 p	September 1980 p	multiple of July 1833
30 lb. loaf bread	20.8	686	33.0
8 lb. beef	21.6	1200	55.6
20 lb. potatoes	4.2	121	28.8
3 lb. butter	15.0	215	14.3
3¼ lb. sugar	8.75	60	6.9
2 oz. tea	3.1	12	3.9
2 oz. coffee	1.0	14	14.0
3 lb. flour	2.5	37	14.8
7 quarts ale	14.6	770	52.7
7 quarts milk	7.5	272	36.3
1 lb. soap	2.5	39	15.6
¼ lb. candles	1.25	31	24.8
	102.8	3457	33.6

Source: Factories Inquiry Commission Second Report, 1833, p. 170.

So the thirteen-year-old girls would have been able to buy a portion of things from the basket that in 1980 would have cost £1.54 in the case of the one and £1.40 the other, and, in the case of the coal miners, the six-year-old, 42p or 70p; the woman of twenty would have £3.36 and the man, £5.88, all for a day's work. The average earnings of adult men manual workers in Britain in October 1980 was about £28 a day, 4¾ times that of the coal-miner of 1842, converted, that is, in terms of the 'basket' in Table 4.2.

4.4 IMPERIALISM

The industrial revolution replaced green fields by noisome cities and, out of the toil of children who sprouted like mushrooms from the mould, amassed fortunes for the few and a comfortable living for officials, administrators and the white-collar and professional workers who served them. From the sense of outrage of a small number of public-spirited people, reforms originated: Robert Owen and Francis Place, who had come from the ranks of the workers; or Lord Shaftesbury, promoter of the factories acts; William Cobbett, the farmer's son; Michael Thomas Sadler, linen-manufacturer as well as Member of Parliament; and many others. Trade unions were established and grew slowly and painfully, and a series of acts was passed in the British Parliament between 1871 and 1875 that went some way to rectify the imbalance of power between employers and workers. But, at the same time, the capitalist system itself entered a new phase of development where the inhabitants of pre-capitalist societies became its victims in a more calculated and intensive way than before. The East India Company showed the way in the last half of the eighteenth century; others followed.

There is no mention of imperialism in orthodox economic texts, for it is a method by which power is used to override what are regarded as legitimate market relations, and in which governments, who in the *laissez-faire* model are supposed to keep out of business, are conscripted to serve the purposes of businessmen.

From November 1884 to February 1885 delegates from fourteen industrialised countries met in Berlin for the purpose of carving up the African continent. Sir Henry Morton Stanley, the explorer, attended as advisor to the United States delegation. He also presented a memorandum on behalf of the Association Internationale du Congo, stating its intention to enable commerce to follow its advance into equatorial Africa, so that merchants might 'freely enter into commercial negotiation with the natives'. Their aims were of the highest propriety: promotion of civilisation and commerce, humanitarian purposes, free exercise of religion, rights of navigation, commerce, and industry, suppression of slavery.... Stanley describes this enterprise in

The Congo and the Founding of its Free State. (New York: Harper, 1885), and so does E. E. Morel in *Red Rubber* (London: Fisher Unwin, 1906.)

At the time even so humane a socialist as John Ruskin thought this a good idea, and propounded it in his inaugural lecture as Slade Professor of Art at Oxford:

> This is what England must do or perish. She must found colonies as fast and as far as she is able, formed of the most energetic and worthiest of men; seizing any piece of fruitful waste ground she can set her foot on, and then teaching her colonists that their chief virtue is to be fidelity to their country, and that their first aim is to advance the power of England by land and sea.

But things looked quite different to J. A. Hobson when he wrote his book, *Imperialism, a Study.* (London: Allen & Unwin, 1902; revised ed. 1938.) He examined the spectacular growth of empires, which by then were in some cases vastly larger than the metropolitan countries that governed them. The mania for geographical expansion Hobson ascribed to 'those conditions of modern capitalist production which compel an ever keener "fight for markets" '. (Ibid. p. 12.) From the point of view of nations, this struggle is misguided. 'There is no necessary limit to the quantity of capital and labour that can be employed in supplying the home markets, provided the effective demand for the goods that are produced is so distributed that every increase of production stimulates a corresponding increase of consumption'. Socialist measures could be used for relieving owners of property of their excesses of unearned income. (Ibid. p. 29.)

The new territories had not been effective in stimulating trade, for the major expansion of both imports and exports had been with foreign countries. Then why was the wealth of the nation jeopardised in imperialist adventures, that roused the strong resentment of other nations?

> The only possible answer is that the business interests of the nation as a whole are subordinated to those of certain sectional interests that usurp control of the national resources and use them for their private gain. This is no strange or monstrous charge to bring; it is the commonest disease of all forms of government. The famous words of Sir Thomas More are as true now as when he wrote them: 'Everywhere do I perceive a certain conspiracy of rich men seeking their

own advantage under the name and pretext of the commonwealth.' (Ibid. p. 46.)

Members of certain professions profited too: soldiers, sailors, diplomats, engineers, missionaries. '... our colonies still remain what James Mill cynically described them as being, "a vast system of outdoor relief for the upper classes".' (Ibid. p. 53.)

In 1916 Lenin wrote *Imperialism, the Highest State of Capitalism*. (I refer to the edition published by Progress Publishers, Moscow, 17th printing, 1978.) He follows Hobson closely, but in contrast to Hobson, does believe that a whole nation can benefit from imperialism, quoting a letter from Marx to Kautsky in 1882, 'the workers gaily share the feast of England's monopoly of the world market and the colonies'. The division of the world had been completed by a handful of states, who now enjoyed a 'colonial monopoly' by means of which they drew superprofits. (Ibid. pp. 101–2.) Further, 'The more capitalism is developed, the more strongly the shortage of raw materials is felt, the more intense the competition and the hunt for sources of raw materials throughout the whole world, the more desperate the struggle for the acquisition of colonies'. (Ibid. p. 78.) Marx, Engels, John Stuart Mill and Hobson made much of inadequate demand, manifest in times of depression, as a driving force in the search for new markets, but, strangely enough, Lenin mentions this only obliquely. On the other hand, his evaluation of the rise of giant enterprises is curiously prophetic. (Ibid. pp. 110–20.)

4.4.1 Case studies

Imperialist adventures have been spectacular enough to be identified, their effects measured. The British East India Company offers a clear example in its conquest of Bengal. They were faced with a problem: whilst Indian products were in high demand in Europe, it was difficult to find European products that were in high demand in India. The Company overcame the problem by military conquest of Bengal and subsequent extension of Company rule to the rest of the country. After that it raised its revenue not by trade, but by taxation. R. Palme Dutt described the result in *India To-day* (Bombay: People's Publishing House, 1947):

> The ceaselessly renewed demand for more and yet more spoils led to the most reckless raising of the land revenue demands to heights which in many cases even meant taking the seed corn and the

bullocks from the peasants. In the last year of administration of the last Indian ruler of Bengal, in 1764-5, the land revenue realised was £817,000. In the first year of the Company's administration, in 1765-6, the land revenue realised in Bengal was £1,470,000. In 1771-2 it was £2,341,000, and by 1775-6 it was £2,818,000. When Lord Cornwallis fixed the Permanent Settlement in 1793, he fixed it at £3,400,000. (Ibid. p. 91.)

£3,400,000 in 1793 would be equal to about £85 million in 1983.

Palme Dutt quotes Brooks Adams, *The Law of Civilisation and Decay*, to the effect that the industrial revolution in Britain was financed by the plunder of India. (Ibid. pp. 95-6.) It is ironic to reflect that the mechanisation of the British textile industry destroyed that of India, just as it ruined the hand-loom weavers of Britain. Sir Henry Cotton wrote, in retrospect: 'In 1787 the exports of Dacca muslin to England amounted to 30 lakhs [three millions] of rupees; in 1817 they had ceased altogether. The arts of spinning and weaving, which for ages afforded employment to a numerous and industrial population, have now become extinct.' (Quoted in Dutt, *Civilisation and Decay*, p. 102.)

Military means were used, too, to solve the problem occasioned by the tea trade with China. The Chinese, like the Indians, were curiously unenthusiastic in their response to European products, except for a certain traffic in mechanical instruments, known in China as 'sing-songs': clocks, watches and mechanical toys made in Birmingham. (Frederic Wakeman Jr, 'The Canton Trade and the Opium War', in the *Cambridge History of China*, Cambridge University Press, 1978, vol. 10, chap. 4, pp. 163-4; Edgar Holt, *The Opium Wars in China*, London: Putnam, 1964, pp. 36-8.) Then in 1829 Jardine, Matheson brought the first opium clipper into service. In the first decade of the nineteenth century China had a credit balance with the rest of the world of about $26 million; in the years 1828 to 1836 there was a debit balance of $38 million. It was opium, grown in India for this purpose, that caused the change. (Wakeman, 'The Canton Trade...', p. 173). By 1836, 1820 tons were entering China and the number of smokers was thought to be in excess of twelve million. (Arthur Waley, *The Opium War Through Chinese Eyes*, London: Allen & Unwin, 1958, p. 12.)

The Chinese banned the traffic and blockaded the port of Canton, with its English merchants. In October 1939 William Jardine, of the famous partnership, went to England to press the merchants' cause. To

Lord Palmerston, the Foreign Secretary, he suggested a blockade of China's ports, reparations for the opium that had been surrendered by British merchants, a commercial treaty, the opening of further ports and the occupation of several islands.

In the House of Commons Macaulay laid down a principle that governments are inclined to follow in such cases: Englishmen abroad, 'surrounded as they were by enemies, and separated by great oceans and continents from all help' knew that 'not a hair of their heads would be harmed with impunity'. Gladstone, for the opposition replied, 'A war more unjust in its origin, a war more calculated to cover this country with permanent disgrace, I do not know and I have not read of.' (Holt, *The Opium Wars*, pp. 98–100.)

But British frigates had already arrived in China. The Chinese surrendered in mid-1842, the Treaty of Nanking providing for an indemnity of $21 million, various trading concessions, and the cession to Britain of the island of Hong Kong.

The acquisition of the Congo by Belgium was begun as a bit of private enterprise by Leopold II, king of the Belgians. In 1865 he had written a 'Note on how useful and important it is for states to possess domains and provinces outside their European frontiers, especially when the extension of the latter is out of the question', and he began looking round for a suitable colony. Failing to buy the Philippines, or find anything in China or the Pacific, he turned his attention to Africa. He was unable to win the support of the Belgian Parliament, so called a conference of representatives of financial interests. This, too, disappointed him and in 1882, he proceeded on his own, operating under the title Association Internationale du Congo. (Ruth Slade, *King Leopold's Congo*, London: Oxford University Press, 1962, pp. 35–8.) This was blessed with success and, in the space of fifteen years, made him a profit of £5 million (or say about £150 million in pounds of 1983).

The *modus operandi* was to compel the inhabitants of the Congo to produce rubber and ivory. Officials were given bonuses in inverse proportion to the prices they had to pay for these commodities. Letters and reports soon began to accumulate giving evidence of the frightful depredations to which the country was being subjected. Officials would give a time limit by which village chiefs were required to produce a given number of tusks. If the chief failed, hostages would be held until the demands were met. Fearful punishments were meted out for continued failure. (Ibid. pp. 45 and 49.)

It was due mainly to the campaign conducted by E. D. Morel that the

Triumph of the Bourgeoisie   49

Belgian Government was compelled to intervene and, against spirited resistance from Leopold, take over the country. The king, as a last resort, attempted to retain his personal estate, the *Fondation de la Couronne*, on the grounds that profits therefrom would be used to finance public works in Belgium, but resistance from within was adding to his difficulties. (See L. H. Gann and Peter Duignan, *The Rulers of Belgian Africa 1884–1914*, Princeton University Press, 1979, p. 139.) The transfer was completed in November 1908, and a programme of reform initiated.

There are many examples of imperialist adventures, some of which are described in E. D. Morel, *The Black Man's Burden*, first published in Britain in 1920, reissued in New York: Modern Reader Paperbacks, 1969. I cite only one more: that which led to the South African War between Britain and the two Boer Republics, 1899–1902. The Boers had left the Cape Colony in the 1840s to escape British rule; the British followed them when, in 1868, diamonds were discovered on the banks of the Orange River near what became Kimberley. It was here that Cecil John Rhodes made his fortune that helped to develop the gold-mines of the Witwatersrand, and the activities of the British South Africa Company in what became Rhodesia and is now Zimbabwe.

News of the Witwatersrand gold began reaching Kimberley about 1885, but Rhodes, according to Dr Jameson, had formulated his imperial schemes some years before. Jameson had gone to Kimberley in 1878 to practise medicine, and he and Rhodes 'shared a quiet little bachelor establishment together'.

> Even at that early period, Cecil Rhodes, then a man of twenty-six or twenty-seven, had mapped out, in his clear brain, his whole policy just as it has since been developed. That policy consisted of the occupation of the *hinterland* of the Cape, by which he proposed to effect the ultimate federation of South Africa ... He had, for instance, even at that early date (1878–9) formed the idea of doing a great work for the over-crowded British public at home, by opening up fresh markets for their manufactures. He was deeply impressed with a belief in the ultimate destiny of the Anglo-Saxon race. He dwelt repeatedly on the fact that their great want was new territory fit for the overflow population to settle in permanently, and thus provide markets for the wares of the old country – the workshop of the world.
>
> ... This idea of the occupation of unoccupied Africa, both South and

Central, for England's benefit, was always in Cecil Rhodes's mind, from the time I knew him; and how long before I cannot, of course, say. (Leander Starr Jameson, *Cecil Rhodes: a Biography and Appreciation*, London: Macmillan, 1897, p. 392.)

President Kruger and his Volksraad put many obstacles in the way of the development of the Rand gold-mines and, quite early in the proceedings Rhodes and his allies decided he must be overthrown.

Jameson (Dr Jim) gave his name, and almost his life, to the Jameson Raid of 1895 which, to his disappointment, the *uitlanders* (foreigners) of the Rand failed to support. Rhodes's co-conspirators were Julius Wernher and Alfred Beit, who had appeared in Kimberley at the very outset and who became much richer and perhaps more influential than Rhodes himself. Julius Wernher was the son of a German general, Alfred Beit of a Hamburg merchant.

But imperialist conspiracies require a government as well as capitalists. The most sinister character involved in this story was the High Commissioner for South Africa and Governor of the Cape, Sir Alfred Milner. Like Beit and Wernher, he had been born in Germany, 'the son of a half-German medical student and an English gentlewoman who had come to Germany in straitened circumstances'. (Thomas Pakenham, *The Boer War*, London: Weidenfeld & Nicolson, 1979, pp. 12–13.)

Milner and the others set about a systematic mobilisation of support in Britain, while Milner, in negotiations with Kruger, engineered obstacles to the settlement of the miners' grievances. Milner sent a dispatch in April 1899 for inclusion in Chamberlain's Blue Book: 'The case for intervention is overwhelming.... The spectacle of thousands of British subjects kept permanently in the position of helots... calling vainly to Her Majesty's government for redress....' (Ibid. p. 59.)

The franchise question was prominently featured, but a different view is presented by 'A peaceful Citizen' whose letter was published in the *Standard and Diggers' News* of 27 May 1899:

> As regards the franchise, how many men, if full burgher rights were conceded, would accept? Not one in a thousand with their own free will, but the big houses no doubt would compel each and everyone to register, as to enable them (the capitalists) to run the men they wish for the constituency, and put pressure upon all hands in their employ to support their candidate. Of course, the men are supposed to vote freely, *but* – and a big but – if there was any opposition to their views the result would be 'voetsac'.

'Voetsak' (in its modern spelling) means 'push off'. (Diana Cammack, 'The Politics of Discontent: the Grievances of the Uitlander Refugees, 1899–1902', *The Journal of Southern African Studies*, vol. 8, no. 2, April 1982, p. 260.) The uitlanders, in fact, suffered greatly as a result of the war. Evacuated in mass and housed in camps in Durban or Cape Town, their principal concern was to get back to their comfortable jobs on the Rand.

Rhodes and his allies assured the British government there would be no war – if Britain called Kruger's bluff and sent out troops. 'Kruger's friends in the Cape and Orange Free State persuaded him to make concessions, but as fast as he made them, Milner raised his demands'. (Pakenham, *The Boer War*, p. 89.)

The predictions that Kruger was bluffing were proved wrong. So too the forecasts that the war would be over in a few weeks. 'In fact, it proved to be the longest (two and three-quarter years), the costliest (over £200 million), the bloodiest (at least twenty-two thousand British, twenty-five thousand Boer and twelve thousand African lives) and the most humiliating war for Britain between 1815 and 1914.' (Ibid. p. xv.) These costs may be compared with the £75 million invested in the Rand gold-mines and the £20 million paid in dividends by 1899. (S. Herbert Frankel, *Capital Investment in Africa*, London: Oxford University Press, 1938, p. 95.)

Cecil John Rhodes died in March 1902, his dying words, 'So little done, so much to do'. Alfred Beit died in July 1906, Jameson in 1917. All three had been born in 1853. Neither Rhodes nor Alfred Beit were given titles, but Jameson, Alfred's brother Otto and his associates Julius Wernher and Frederick Eckstein were all made baronets. Despite the ousting of Smuts's pro-imperial government of the Union of South Africa in 1924, and the advent to power of the purified National Party in 1948 with the subsequent declaration of the Republic of South Africa, the mining houses have lived on, the dynasties intact.

4.4.2 Imperialism assessed

Each of the cases I have examined featured wealthy, powerful, predatory companies who succeed in mobilising governments in their support. The cost to governments sometimes seems disproportionate to the business assets that they protect. The cost in public expenditure and human life has been immense, but the business interests have survived and flourished. Of course, the East India Company is no longer with us and King Leopold has long since returned to dust, but De Beers and Wernher Beit's Rand Mines still flourish. So does

Rhodes's creation, Consolidated Gold Fields, that made a profit (before interest and tax) of £99 million in 1979. Anglo-American who, amongst other things, manage De Beers, made profits of £168.7 million. At the end of 1980 Jardine, Matheson's capital value, as given by the price of their shares, was £800 million. The elephants of the Congo were almost exterminated, and its wild rubber superseded by the plantation rubber of Malaya, but copper was discovered there and yielded its wealth to the Belgian Société Générale and the Union Minière du Haut-Katanga. (See Greg Lanning, with Marti Mueller, *Africa Undermined*, Harmondsworth: Penguin Books, 1979, pp. 51-2.) There is ample evidence, too, of the enrichment of officials, officers and miscellaneous professional people.

How much of the colonial plunder reached the general populace of the metropolitan countries? As we have noted, the imports into Britain of the East India Company greatly exceeded their exports to India, the difference being made up of taxes exacted from the Indians. For instance, in the year 1797-8, imports were valued at £5 785 000 and exports at £1 640 000. At a time when imports from India constituted more than 10 per cent of all imports this made a substantial difference to the terms of trade (the ratio of exports needed to pay for imports). Cole and Deane (*British Economic Growth*) suggest that there was about £6¼ million of new investment in the iron industry in Britain between 1790 and 1806, to which Indian profits seeking investment could have made a substantial contribution.

Tea was the theme of the Opium War. Pepys had his first cup on 25 September 1661. Six years later the East India Company indented for a hundred pounds weight of it. In 1800 United Kingdom consumption amounted to 23 million pounds. (Gibbons, *Economic and Industrial Progress of the Century*, pp. 79-80.) Consumption per head was 1.58 lb. in 1802, down to 1.22 lb. in 1840 and, with the end of the war, back to 1.50 lb. in 1844 and, by 1854, had risen to 2.24 lb. By the 1960s it had reached 9 lb. The tea-drinking public of the British Isles had their supplies assured by the war. Again, the terms of trade benefited, for the tea was paid for not by the products of British labour, but by the poppy-growers of south-east Asia. It was not until 1931 that the League of Nations adopted a satisfactory convention for the suppression of production of and trade in opium for non-medical purposes. By then India and Ceylon had replaced China as the principal supplier of tea to the British public.

In Leopold's time the profits from the Congo Free State would not have made much impact on Belgian finances. On the other hand the profits of Union Minière in 1959, the year before the Belgian Government abruptly abandoned the Congo, were equivalent to 2 per cent of the import bill of Belgium and Luxembourg.

The South African War, by contrast, was a gigantic miscalculation. Excluding the cost in human suffering, British expenditure on the war amounted to three times the capital investment in the mines. The mine-owners could have got their concessions from the Boer Government without having to fight for them; they lost three years' production and, in an attempt to rebuild their labour force, went through a disastrous experiment of importing Chinese labourers.

Imperialist adventures seem to require three ingredients: one or more powerful business concerns that see an opportunity for considerable increases in profits; allies in government prepared to intrigue to that end; an apparent threat to national honour or the safety of fellow countrymen or the national interest or all three, in response to which popular enthusiasm can be invoked.

Hobson and Lenin may be seen to have rightly identified, as the most important politico-economic phenomenon of the age, the rise of what we now call multinational or transnational corporations, and international financial institutions, with close ties with governments and central banks.

But is there such a thing as an *imperialist system* in which capitalism, in its highest and final phase, is compelled to use metropolitan powers to acquire territories to absorb investment and provide raw materials? No, and this fact began to dawn on metropolitan governments once the imperialist fever had passed. In the 1950s and 1960s they divested themselves of their colonial empires, though the bonds of sentiment, culture and business mysteriously survived. Raw materials (commodities) are bought in world markets, the great increase in world trade has been between industrialised countries and so have flows in investment. (See C. C. Eldridge, *Victorian Imperialism*, London: Hodder & Stoughton, 1978, pp. 129-30.)

The ultimate paradox has been investment by the rich of Africa, Asia and Latin America in Europe and the United States, and the flow of migration not to the wide, open spaces of those continents, but to the congested cities of the industrialised countries. In those respects Hobson and Lenin got it wrong, but their errors of commission are venial compared with the errors of omission of economic orthodoxy, where power, beyond that of the market-place, is assumed away.

5 Capitalist Systems and How They Work

We have retraced the steps of *homo sapiens* over a couple of million years: hunter-gatherers, herdsmen and cultivators, citizens, soldiers and slaves; lords, churchmen and serfs; conquerors and vassals, absolute monarchs, landlords, farmers and bourgeoisie; through the age of imperialism down to the present day.

We learn about the past by studying history, or see in the world about us remnants of things past whose story we vaguely discern. But the history of *now* – how are we going to learn that? The flow of information has reached such proportions as to defy comprehension, with confusion worse confounded by the conflicting interpretations to which it is subject. Bourgeois and socialist, conservative and liberal, employer and worker, rich and poor, townsman and countryman, aesthete and philistine; each argue amongst themselves and with every one else. But the confusion adds excitement to our quest for understanding, and makes it all the more urgent that we should press on towards an understanding of modern capitalism.

Of course, if you live in a capitalist country, you will already know a great deal about it. But this knowledge has to be arranged and interpreted if it is going to yield the sort of insight that we seek. Let me hasten to emphasise that what I am about to say in this chapter contains nothing profound: it is a way of interpreting the obvious.

We have, ready-made, certain categories and terms that purport to distinguish the various parts of the system and identify the ways in which they interact. Though these sound like economic entities they refer in fact to people cast in various roles: the determinants in economic equations are human, not mathematical. Everybody plays at least two roles, and quite often a great many more.

One role that everyone must play is that of *consumer*, for he who does not consume does not live very long. In vulgar parlance consumption concerns what you eat and drink; not so in economics, where it involves everything you buy for purposes other than business. Even this distinction is not always observed, for 'capital consumption' is used to mean the wearing-out or depreciation of fixed capital in the process of production. Generally, though, the term is used to cover all personal or family purchases, including household durables, detergents and clothing was well as services: bus rides and the ministrations of hairdressers, entertainers and so on. We consume these things not by eating them, but by buying them. Does this make sense? Yes, because in capitalist systems, the decisive moment is that of purchase-and-sale. In the operation of the system this is the moment that counts.

The second role that most men and an increasing number of women also play is that of producer. But this term, too, is used in a restricted sense to cover the production of goods or services for sale. Who buys them does not matter. The services of teachers, soldiers and police are generally bought by governments, of preachers by their congregations, of pilots by airlines, of factory workers by manufacturers. Add up the costs of the producers, and you get the values of saleable goods and services. These are recouped by businesses through sales and by governments through taxation. By this definition services performed by members of the household for the household are not regarded as production, for they are not done for sale.

Producers get income in the form of salaries, wages, profits or fees, and with their incomes they must pay taxes (though they may seek to evade them) and are entitled to buy goods and services and share them with their dependants.

But it is not only producers who get income: the feature that distinguishes capitalism from socialism is that income can also be obtained by owning. The very term 'capitalism' points to the central role played by capital, ownership of which enables income to be obtained through investment. Investment takes many forms: ownership of stocks and shares, land and buildings, or simply the lending of money to those who want to borrow, pending the return of which one receives interest. We distinguish three categories of income: income from work (earned income); income from property or ownership (unearned income); and transfer income – income paid to dependants by parents or other relatives, charities, pension-funds or governments.

Production takes place in business units that we refer to as firms. If the firm is incorporated by registration with the appropriate government department, it becomes legally a person, with the right to sue or be sued, and is called a company or corporation. If a company owes you money that you have difficulty in recovering, you cannot sue the shareholders who own it, you can only sue the company; thus, it is called a limited-liability company, because the shareholders are not liable for the company's debts.

Now let us imagine the system in action. Firms have owners, managers and workers, and own capital in the form of land, buildings, machinery and raw materials or goods in process of production. Farms and mines produce primary products that are bought by factories. Factories are referred to collectively as secondary industry. Their finished products are bought by the distributive trade: wholesalers, chain stores, department stores or individual shops, whose profits come from the difference between what they pay their suppliers and what they charge their customers.

So, farmers farm and miners mine. They pay wages to their workers and ship their products to the factories, where workers process them. Eventually the finished products arrive in the shops, where they are bought by consumers. That is to say, that the recipients of income (earned, unearned or transfer) now assume their roles as consumers. What were wages and profits become the income of the distributive trade and the whole process is repeated. In the textbooks this is often depicted in a diagram, with goods and services flowing one way and incomes flowing the other (Fig. 5.1).

The households supply labour to the farms, mines and factories, in return for which they receive wages, salaries or fees. The farms and mines supply the factories with materials, from which they manufacture goods that they supply to the shops. The households buy goods from the shops, who in turn pay the factories who make more goods and pay out more to their employees. Of course, the shops also draw labour from households and pay them wages and salaries. And it is not only in shops that consumers spend their money: there are also hotels and hospitals, restaurants and railway-stations, theatres and tollgates.

The sales of the shops (using the term to cover all who sell goods or services for consumption) must defray all the costs incurred in the process of production – enough, that is, to pay all the wages of the workers, rent of the landlords, interest of the lenders and profits of the owners. If they are not high enough to do this, then the producers instead of making profits will suffer losses. And likewise the income of the households, derived from wages, rent, interest and profits will, by simple book-keeping, be equal to all the costs that go to make up the prices of the saleable products, for costs and incomes are simply the two sides to the transactions in buying and selling. But note well: salaries and wages, rent and interest and the costs of raw and intermediate materials are paid out *before* the end-products are sold. Profits

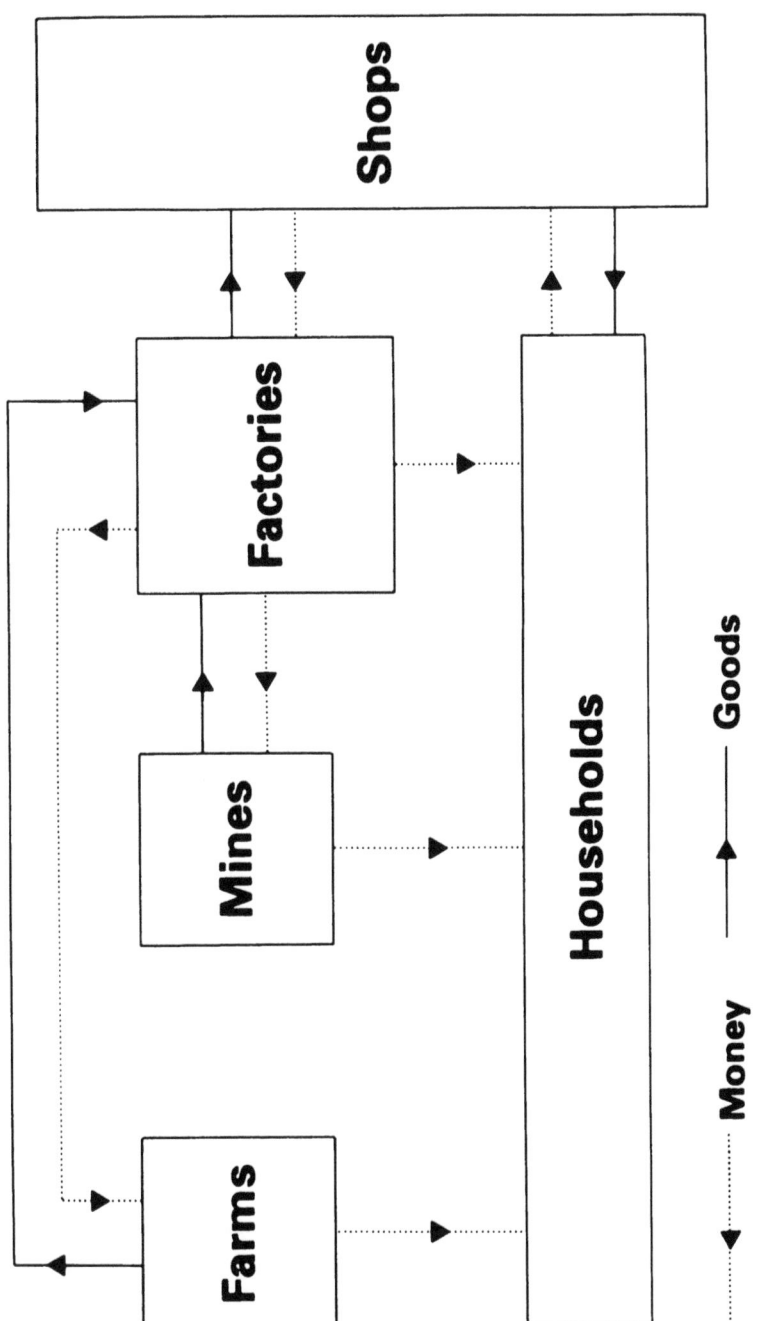

Figure 5.1 *Flows of goods and money in the macro economy*

are in a different position: profit *margins* are determined in advance and are fixed by convention in most trades. When a job is being costed, direct costs are estimated (labour, power, materials), a percentage added to look after overheads (rent, interest, management, office staff, capital depreciaton) and a further percentage added to look after profits (dividends to be paid to shareholders or added to company reserves). But there are all sorts of unpredictable occurrences that may add to or subtract from profits. This is referred to in greater length in the next chapter.

But now we must introduce a feature that distinguishes capitalism from all other systems. It is an obvious feature, but one whose existence was denied in orthodox economies from the time Adam Smith published his *Wealth of Nations* in 1776 until John Maynard Keynes published his *General Theory of Employment, Interest and Money* in 1936.

If the productive activities of the farms, mines, factories and shops are to follow their orderly course, the demand for their products must equal the supply. But there is no guarantee that this will be so, for the households can please themselves as to how quickly or slowly they spend their income. They can reduce the time between receiving their income and spending it and, through the credit system, can even spend it *before* they get it. Or they can extend the time, keep more of their income in cash about the house or in savings accounts. If all those who are paid by the week kept their wages for an extra day it would reduce the sales of the shops by one-seventh. If those paid by the month kept their salaries for an extra week it would reduce sales by nearly one-quarter. Since people are social animals, tending to conform and to emulate one another, these changes in behaviour are sometimes general and cumulative.

The young John Stuart Mill described this characteristic of capitalism rather well in a book written when he was 24 or 25 and first published in 1844. The orthodox doctrine proclaimed that general overproduction (a general glut of commodities) was impossible because no one produced anything except to exchange it for the other things he required. This would only be true, Mill argued, in a barter economy:

> Now the effect of the employment of money, and even the utility of it, is, that it enables this one act of interchange to be divided into two separate acts or operations; one of which may be performed now, and the other a year hence, or whenever it shall be most convenient.

Although he who sells, really sells only to buy, he needs not buy at the same moment when he sells; and he does not therefore necessarily add to the *immediate* demand for one commodity when he adds to the supply of another. The buying and selling being now separated, it may very well occur, that there may be, at some given time, a very general inclination to sell with as little delay as possible, accompanied with an equally general inclination to defer all purchases as long as possible. This is always actually the case, in those periods which are described as periods of general excess. . . .

For when there is a general anxiety to sell, and a general disinclination to buy, commodities of all kinds remain for a long time unsold, and those which find an immediate market, do so at a very low price. If it be said that when all commodities fall in price, the fall is of no consequence, since mere money price is not material while the relative value of all commodities remains the same, we answer that this would be true if the low prices were to last for ever. But as it is certain that prices will rise again sooner or later, the person who is obliged by necessity to sell his commodity at a low money price is really a sufferer, the money he receives sinking shortly to its ordinary value. Every person, therefore, delays selling if he can, keeping his capital unproductive in the meantime, and sustaining the consequent loss of interest. There is stagnation to those who are not obliged to sell, and distress to those who are. . . . In extreme cases, money is collected in masses, and hoarded; in milder cases people merely defer parting with their money, or coming under any new engagements to part with it. But the result is, that all commodities fall in price, or become unsaleable. (*Essays on some unsettled questions of political economy*, 2nd ed., 1874, pp. 70–2. Reprinted by Augustus M. Kelley, Clifton, 1974.)

Mill summarises this phenomenon in these terms:

In the present state of the commercial world, mercantile transactions being carried on upon an immense scale, but the remote causes of fluctuations in prices being very little understood, so that unreasonable hopes and unreasonable fears alternately rule with tyrannical sway over the minds of a majority of the mercantile public; general eagerness to buy and general reluctance to buy, succeed one another in a manner more or less marked, at brief intervals. Except during short periods of transition, there is almost always either great briskness of business or great stagnation; either the principal producers of almost all the leading articles of industry have as many orders as they can possibly execute, or the dealers in almost all commodities have their warehouses full of unsold goods. (Ibid. p. 68.)

All this is pretty obvious and was only made difficult because the economists who denied it were blinded with their own theories – a danger to which theoreticians are constantly exposed. In Chapters 8, 9 and 10 we deal, respectively, with consumer behaviour, the role of the banks and governments in promoting or reducing industrial fluctuations, the trade cycle, booms and slumps, prosperity and depression, as these oscillations in the workings of capitalism are variously termed. I think, though, that it will be useful to give a preview of some of the factors involved.

There are quite important limitations to the discretion that can be exercised by households in the variation of their expenditure: they must buy food, pay for transport and power and meet their contractual obligations. But the richer they are, the more discretion they have, and this adds up to quite a substantial potential for fluctuations in expenditure. Businesses, too, are sensitive to fluctuations in demand and add to them by varying their rates of new investment. If they are expanding their productive capacity, their expenditures add to the flow of purchasing-power, the force of which will be all the greater because it will be in advance of the increased flow of goods in which it will result.

The ride of the economy could be extremely bumpy if it did not have an elaborate system of shock-absorbers. These shock-absorbers are provided by the banking system, whose ramifications are described in Chapter 9. One of the services performed by banks concerns the flow of purchasing-power. They lend funds from households or businesses who spend less than they receive to households or businesses who want to spend more than they receive. Those households or businesses with credit balances in their current bank accounts are, unwittingly, making credit available to provide other households or businesses with overdrafts. But, as you will know, you can also lend money wittingly. This you do when you put money into a savings account and get paid interest on it. Other people will be borrowing this money and paying even higher interest, the difference in interest rates being the bank's profit.

In an affluent capitalist country this debtor-creditor system reaches enormous proportions, and the financial institutions busily ply their trade. They are ready to borrow from you, to lend to you, to insure you, to take from you now in return for guaranteeing you a pension when you retire. They will finance business ventures of whose soundness they are satisfied, and finance others when the money is repaid. They very successfully cushion the system against the little bumps that it regularly encounters; but against the much bigger disturbances, cumulative in their impact, they are powerless. For the unreasonable hopes and unreasonable fears upon which Mill remarked are self-justifying. When a system or whole group of systems is upset it seems prudent to postpone expenditure for, as Mill said, 'persons in general, at that particular time, from a general expectation of being called upon to meet sudden demands, liked better to possess money than any other commodity'. (Ibid. p. 72.) Stocks accumulate in the shops; shops reduce their orders from the factories, who in turn reduce their inputs of raw materials. Investment is reduced; workers lose their jobs, firms make losses and thus household income is reduced. The fears that led people to reduce expenditure are thus confirmed, and the resulting feed-back reduces purchases still more. Booms alternate with slumps: in times of optimism expenditure is increased. There is no shortage of sound business ventures; there is no shortage of jobs; optimism is confirmed. Again, the process is cumulative.

There is one other complication that deserves emphasis. Under capitalism production is undertaken for profit. No expectation of profit, no production. Profit entails selling goods and services for more than they cost. But how can the shops sell the goods and services produced in the productive process for *more* than has been distributed to households for their services? They can do so to the extent that *some* production takes the form of investment, in terms of which incomes are generated that add to purchasing-power but that will add to the flow of goods only at some subsequent time. Some workers will be working on goods that will be sold tomorrow; some, next week, some next month, some next year, but they all want today's food today and likewise (though not literally today) their clothes, and other goods for consumption. But when the new investment has increased the flow of goods to the shops, an increased flow of investment will be needed to generate the profit on them. This process, too, is cumulative, and adds to the inherent instability of the system. Can governments do anything to remove the instability? Keynes and his followers thought they could; the monetarists maintain that the Keynesian remedies are worse than the disease. We will look at these aspects of our subject in Chapter 10.

6 The Profit-seekers

6.1 GROWTH OF THE GIANTS

One of the distinguishing features of capitalism, as we have just noted, is its instability. Another is the paradox of deprived people co-existing with unsaleable goods. A third is its cumulative concentration of productive power in giant corporations. This is not a new phenomenon – the Anti-Trust Act was passed in the United States in 1890, promoted by John Sherman, a Republican senator.

The Sherman Act was an attempt to curb a tendency that Adam Smith had noted in 1776. 'People of the same trade seldom meet together, even for merriment and diversion, but the conversation ends in a conspiracy against the publick, or in some contrivance to raise prices.' (*The Wealth of Nations*, p. 145 of the Glasgow ed.) Section 1 of the Act states: 'Every contract, combination in the form of trust or otherwise, or conspiracy, in restraint of trade or commerce among the several States or with foreign nations, is hereby declared to be illegal.' And Section 2: 'Every person who shall monopolize, or attempt to monopolize, or combine or conspire with any other person or persons to monopolize any part of the trade or commerce among the several States, or with foreign nations, shall be deemed guilty of a misdemeanour.'

The Clayton Act of 1914 was more explicit and prohibited price discrimination (charging some of your customers more than others), exclusive dealing and tying contracts, acquisitions of competing companies and interlocking directorates (ostensibly competing companies controlled by the same directors). (See A. D. Neale, *The Antitrust Laws of the United States of America*, Cambridge University Press, 1970, p. 3. A third edition was published in 1981.)

The Anti-Trust Act achieved some notable effects including (in 1911) the dismemberment of Standard Oil into half a dozen separate companies. Those were the days when the chief product of the oil companies was kerosene. One of the labours of Hercules was to destroy the Hydra of Lerna that sprouted two heads for each one he cut off. Hercules found a solution to that problem, but the authorities in the United States have not discovered a way to curb the power of the business giants. Today the old Standard Oil of New Jersey, renamed Exxon, is at the top of *Fortune*'s list of the 50 largest industrial companies in the world. (*Fortune*, 10 August, 1981, p. 205.) In this same list of 50, one finds other pieces of Standard Oil of 1911: Standard Oil of California (number 7), of Indiana (12), and of Ohio (50).

In the great companies there are enormous concentrations of economic power, carrying with them power over politicians, governments and, through the mass media, people's minds. Commenting on its list, *Fortune* remarks (loc. cit.), 'Total sales of the 50 have grown to $1.2 trillion – greater than the gross national product of any of the countries represented here except the U.S.'

Prior to 1844, when the first Companies Act was passed in the United Kingdom, an organisation that wanted to turn itself into a corporation (thereby limiting the liability of its shareholders) had to have a special Act of Parliament passed for this purpose. The British East India Company was incorporated in this way in 1600. In the last quarter of the nineteenth century most states in the United States enacted similar laws enabling companies to incorporate by registration, a procedure that now applies to every country in the non-communist world. Companies so registered have an obligation to keep proper books of account that must be audited and certified correct by a firm of chartered accountants. They must have annual general meetings of shareholders and there present a report on the activities of the previous year, with balance-sheets and income and expenditure accounts. This is designed to protect the shareholders, and those who have business dealings with the company, from fraud. The balance-sheet shows the money values of the assets and liabilities of the company. The income and expenditure account, alternatively called the profit and loss account, summarises the results of the year's trading.

Of course, not all businesses are incorporated. In 1971 over a million people in Great Britain were in business on their own account. Of these, 118 000 were in the professions – self-employed lawyers, doctors, accountants, architects and so on. So were 350 000 skilled manual workers, engaged mainly on maintenance and repair, and including motor mechanics, plumbers, building workers and hairdressers. There were also 131 000 farmers and 194 000 shopkeepers working on their own account. There were in addition 725 000 employers who were proprietors of unincorporated businesses with one or more employees. (See Guy Routh, *Occupation and Pay in Great Britain 1906–79*, London: Macmillan, 1980, pp. 6–7 and 19.)

There is a strong trend towards incorporation because of the legal advantages it brings. In the United States the number of corporations rose from 629 000 in 1950 to 2 105 000 in 1976. Unincorporated businesses also increased, but not nearly so fast: from 6.9 million in 1950 to 11.4 million in 1976. (*Statistical Abstract of the United States*, 100th ed., Bureau of Census, 1979, tables 913–14, p. 553.)

In the United Kingdom the Department of Inland Revenue identified 306 700 companies in 1969, 375 600 in 1972 and 396 600 in 1975. In 1976 the numbers fell by 6200, but no doubt as the effect of recession rather than a change in the long-term trend.

It is strange that unincorporated businesses should survive and even increase, like midgets in the valley of the giants, for a much-remarked feature of modern capitalism is the increase in business concentration, in the course of which the giants absorb smaller firms and gobble up each other.

There are technical difficulties in identifying what it is we ought to try to measure in determining the growth of the giants. Is it concentration of ownership that is the key factor or the size of the productive unit? Economies of mass production give a very real reason for growth, but another feature of modern trends has been diversification. Horizontal integration signifies the amalgamation, into larger and larger units, of firms making the same sorts of product; vertical integration signifies the acquisition by the firm of resources at various stages of production from the supply of raw materials to the wholesale or even retail outlets. It may include transport and the design and production of machines. Diversification signifies the acquisition of interests in different industries, so that the company becomes a conglomerate.

In Britain the Census of Production regards a firm 51 per cent of whose stock is owned by another firm as part of that other firm. This makes sense from the viewpoint of the law, but effective control may be exercised by some firm or person owning only 20 per cent of the stock or even less if the rest of the stock is widely diffused. There is also the device of interlocking directorships; several companies may share a group of directors so that their policies are effectively co-ordinated, even though they are legally independent. There are other aspects that may be relevant to an assessment of the concentration of power, in particular the increasing importance of financial institutions that may own critical proportions of shares in a variety of companies that are none the less regarded as independent, because the statistical measures generally exclude banks and finance houses. These problems are discussed in Sam Aaronovitch and Malcolm Sawyer, *Big Business: Theoretical and Empirical Aspects of Concentration and Mergers in the United Kingdom* (London: Macmillan, 1975, Chap. 3.)

S. J. Prais has estimated figures for the share of the hundred largest enterprises in manufacturing net output in the United Kingdom and the United States from 1909 to 1970. These are shown in Table 6.1.

Table 6.1 *Share of the 100 largest enterprises in manufacturing net output, UK and USA, 1909–70*

	1909	1935	1958	1963	1970
			Percentages		
United Kingdom	16	24	32	37	41
United States	22	26	30	33	33

Source: S. J. Prais, *The Evolution of Giant Firms in Britain*, Cambridge University Press, 1981, pp. 4 and 213.

The US Bureau of Census *Annual Survey of Manufactures* shows that the share of the largest 100 remained at 33 per cent between 1963 and 1972, but by 1976 had risen to 34 per cent – not a very impressive rise. (See *Statistical Abstract of the U.S. 1980*, p. 568.)

Robert L. Heilbroner offers reasons for the slow-down in the rate of concentration. He suggests greater government opposition to policies by one corporation that are calculated to damage others; that concentration rises during depression but decelerates in prosperity; the greater emphasis on expansion by diversification, which exposes the big corporations to competition in new markets, in many cases with smaller but more specialised companies. 'There remains, however, a final reason that must not be omitted from our analysis. This is the possibility that big business is no longer expanding as rapidly as in the halcyon days of the early twentieth century because it is no longer being run by a group of executives who are as unabashedly aggressive as were the founding fathers and early corporate managers of these companies.' Perhaps a generation of acquisitors has been replaced by one of administrators, more interested in long-run survival and stability? (Robert L. Heilbroner, *The Limits of American Capitalism*, New York: Harper & Row, 1965, pp. 18–23.)

Before we move on to other aspects of our subject, let us look at another table kindly compiled for us by the US Bureau of Census. This shows, *inter alia*, the proportion of shipments originating in various industries from the four largest manufacturing companies within those industries. This I show for some of these industries in Table 6.2.

Table 6.2 *Percentage of shipments accounted for by the 4 largest manufacturing companies in various industries in the US, 1963–72*

Industry	1963	1967	1972
Motor-vehicles and car bodies	—	92	93
Motor-vehicle parts and accessories	—	60	61
Blast furnaces and steel mills	51	48	45
Radio and TV communications equipment	29	22	19
Pharmaceutical preparations	22	24	26
Aircraft	59	69	66
Petroleum refining	34	33	31
Photographic equipment and supplies	63	69	74
Bread, cake and related products	23	26	29
Refrigeration and heating equipment	25	31	40
Electronic computing equipment	—	66	51
Commercial printing, lithographic	6	5	4
Toilet preparations	38	38	38
Telephone, telegraph apparatus	92	92	—
Soap and other detergents	72	70	62

Source: *Statistical Abstract of the US 1980*, pp. 821–2.

We may learn one important lesson from Table 6.2: that there is no clear trend discernible. The big four of each industry are expanding their scope in some industries and reducing it in others, so we cannot predict future developments with any certainty. One feature of the modern world comes across very clearly, however: there is nothing in modern manufacturing that resembles the imaginary world of 'perfect competition'.

In the table of concentration compiled by the US Bureau of Census, 32 industries are distinguished. In 13 of these in 1972, the 50 largest accounted for 90 per cent or more of all shipments in the relevant industry. In another 5 industries, they accounted for between 80 and 89 per cent. In the vast territory of the United States 50 companies is very few to account for so high a proportion of the production of these great industries. There are few enough of them to be able to talk to each other, watch each other, lead or be guided by each other and combine to bring pressure on governments to promote their common interests.

6.2 THE NATURE OF BUSINESSES

In the capitalist world we have some millions of corporations, but a few thousand who overshadow all the rest. Then come the unincorporated businesses, some of which constitute the *black economy*, busily at work but unknown to the tax collectors or factory inspectorate. Their operators come and go, sometimes working on their own, sometimes re-entering the measurable labour force as employees. In the Third World especially they are of great importance, but at this point in the narrative I do not propose to deal with them. Let us concentrate our attention on the firms that have an entry in the yellow pages, who keep a set of books, pay value-added tax or its equivalent, and make returns to the department of inland revenue.

6.2.1 **Purchase and sale**
Does it make sense to study entities of such diversity as if they belonged to a single species? We may find that the generalisations we can make about them are too trivial to entertain, but let us try anyway. Let us begin with Thorstein Veblen, *The Theory of Business Enterprise*, first published in 1904. Veblen was a distinguished American economist who, like the founders of the American Economic Association, turned his gaze on the phenomena of the real world, in contrast to those economists who tried to deduce everything by logical process from the principle of competition.

> The motive of business is pecuniary gain, the method is essentially purchase and sale. The aim and usual outcome is accumulation of wealth. Men whose aim is not increase of possessions do not go into business, particularly not on an independent footing. (Ibid. New York: Mentor Books; London: New English Library, chap. III, p. 16.)

So businesses buy, try to sell for more than they have paid, and so make their profit. Their purchases of space, equipment, labour, raw materials, components and power will extend over a period that differs according to industry and product, but the takings, when they come rolling in, must exceed the costs if the firm is to show a profit.

I am presenting a fairly obvious way of looking at the world of business. Veblen stressed 'increase of possessions', but it is important to draw attention to a further distinction between capitalism and pre-capitalist societies. In the latter, wealth was sought for enjoyment. King Solomon grew very rich, but he spent his wealth on wives, concubines and temples: things to enjoy or, at any rate, to display. Profit, beyond the limit that was required to maintain the status of the recipient, was regarded with disfavour except by misers. Under capitalism the purest, most venerated form of profit is that that requires no effort on the part of the recipient other, perhaps, than anxiety as to whether he is going to get it. The effort may be by people unknown, unseen and far away. After they have been paid their wages there remains a surplus, if the venture has been a success, that is divided amongst the shareholders.

Many and ingenious were the theories devised by economists to prove that profit was necessary and morally justified, and that its amount was economically determinate: that is, predictable and calculable, given the terms of the equation upon which it depended. In the days when most businesses were operated by working proprietors, the theorists used to puzzle over what portion of their income was derived from ownership (interest on capital) and what part from their own work (wages). This is a question without an answer, for the two returns are not separable: no one works harder than the self-employed farmer, unless it be the self-employed farmer's wife. For the proprietor the business, if it is to succeed, must be an absorbing hobby, his capital much more intensively used, and therefore more productive, than if it were operated by employees.

6.2.2 Double entry

A characteristic of legitimate businesses is that their business transactions are recorded in a set of books of account. The double-entry system, in terms of which every debit has a credit and every credit a debit, means that the books should balance at any given moment: that the total of debits should exactly equal the total of credits. If they do not, it means that an error has been made in the book-keeping. The books should also reveal whether the firm is operating at a profit or a loss and, at least after a while, whether an employee is embezzling its funds. Public companies have to publish a summary of their accounts once a year.

Werner Sombart attached similar importance to double entry in the promotion of capitalism as Max Weber did to the Protestant ethic.

> By transforming assets into abstract values and by expressing quantitatively the results of business activities, double-entry bookkeeping clarified the aims of acquisitive business; moreover, it provided the rational basis on which the capitalist could choose the

The Profit-seekers

direction in which to employ his capital to best advantage; and finally, it made possible the separation of the business firm from its owners and hence the growth of large joint-stock businesses. (*Der Moderne Kapitalismus*, 6th ed., Munich and Leipzig, 1924. I quote from Basil S. Yamey, 'Accounting and the Rise of Capitalism: Further Notes on a Theme by Sombart', in K. A. Tucker, ed., *Business History Selected Readings*, London: Frank Cass, 1977, p. 319.)

The first printed exposition of the double-entry system, by Luca Pacioli, appeared in 1494. Yamey contests Sombart's thesis and, although double-entry must have helped capitalism along, it seems unlikely that either it or the Protestant ethic were causal factors. Despite which, common systems of accounting give a common framework to businesses in the way that skeletons do to vertebrate animals or filaments to cells.

6.2.3 Owners and managers

The puzzle mentioned above of distinguishing profit from the wages-of-management has ceased to be of importance in societies where the business process is carried on overwhelmingly by companies, for here ownership and management are divorced. The owners are the shareholders while the business is conducted by professional managers. Of course, businesses are still sometimes started by people with new ideas and the vision to market them. They pour their energies and whatever capital they can scrape together into promoting them. If they fail, they disappear and are heard of no more; if they succeed, they often 'go public' (that is, convert the business into a public company and offer shares for sale to the public) or are bought out by one of the giants. In either case, they become very rich.

In the modern world there is a tribe of top managers who grace the boards of directors of the great companies, appearing now here, now there, sometimes remaining with one company throughout their working lives, sometimes appearing promiscuously on the boards of a dozen or more. It is true that the directors generally own some shares in the company or companies they direct, but as a rule dividends on these shares constitute a minor part of their income. For instance, Sir David Orr, chairman of Unilever, owned 3011 shares in that company at the end of December 1979 and would have received a dividend of £724 for the year, compared with his salary for the year of £70 490. (Unilever, *50th Report and Accounts*, pp. 29, 51 and 52.)

While ownership and management were combined in one person, economists relied on the principle of self-interest to deduce that the aim of the owner-manager (or entrepreneur) would be to maximise the profits of the firm (but please note 'maximisation' means something special in economics that has no equivalent in the real world). This led John Stuart Mill to be pessimistic of what would result from the separation of ownership and control. (*Principles of Political Economy*, bk I, chap. IX, sec. 2. People's ed. 1883, pp. 85–6.) Accepting the principle of pecuniary self-interest he argued that the self-interest of the professional manager will diverge from that of the owner-manager. One does indeed come upon cases where professional managers sacrifice the shareholders for their own advantage, but one cannot say *a priori* that this is how they will behave. They may drive harder bargains for their companies than an owner-manager would, especially if he is a second- or third-generation owner-manager. Consider the contrasts in behaviour of Henry Ford I, Edsel Ford and Henry Ford II. But if you cannot deduce from the assumption of pecuniary self-interest what economic agents will do, there is no alternative but to investigate and observe. Orthodox economists have preferred to avoid this course, but fortunately for the improvement of our understanding, industrial psychologists and sociologists have done it for us.

There are also some quite important things that are instantly observable by anyone who has worked in business and been able to see higher managers in action. They are often addicted to the company in the way golf enthusiasts are to golf, sex maniacs to sex or fanatics to their causes. Junior managers who want to get on must display the same devotion. In fact, running a company can easily become addictive, for it is full of interest, psychic challenges and rewards.

Fortunately for the survival of mankind people are not really emotionally isolated, without attachment, in love only with themselves. It is precisely by their gregariousness, need for affection and ability to exist as members of a family, band or tribe that they have survived. The urge manifests itself in all sorts of ways, not least in the sense of belonging to the organisation from which one draws one's livelihood. The trainee manager is selected because of his evident potential to accommodate himself to the company, and, after selection, is trained and conditioned to do so, or eliminated if he cannot. Loyalty and ambition should impel him towards the top, and by the time he gets there the company has become an indispensable part of his life.

Sometimes managers' loyalty is so strong that they commit crimes for their companies; sometimes so weak that they commit crimes against them. Under some, companies flourish, under others languish or collapse. If we are to be able to generalise or differentiate, we can do so only by observing, by ourselves working for or with them, by participant-observation or by questionnaire and interview. This a number of industrial sociologists or psychologists have done.

W. Lloyd Warner and James C. Abegglen examined the social origins and education of American managers, as exemplified in the careers and backgrounds of more than 8000 business leaders. (*Big Business Leaders in America*, New York: Harper & Brothers, 1955.) Of these, 52 per cent were the sons of business executives or owners of businesses, 14 per cent were the sons of professional men, 8 per cent of clerks or salesmen and 9 per cent of farmers. Only 15 per cent were the sons of manual workers, though manual workers then constituted 56 per cent of the labour force. 57 per cent were college graduates, while a further 20 per cent had had some college education.

Warner and Abegglen identified various types amongst their businessmen and sought some insight into their psychic life. (Ibid. p. 68.) Each member of the business elite confronted a dual task: 'He must achieve and maintain his occupational position as an executive in the business hierarchy, and he must establish himself and his family as accepted and respected members of the social hierarchy of his community.' (Ibid. pp. 59–60.) Thus it is relevant to devote a chapter to 'The Wives of Ambitious Men' and another to 'The Kinds of Women Who Make Successful Wives'.

Also in 1955 Mabel Newcomer published *The Big Business Executive* (New York and London: Columbia University Press). Her study was narrower in scope but dealt with similar questions. She was concerned with the history of the president and chairman of big business corporations about the years 1900, 1925 and 1950, and obtained data relating to 284 such people for 1900, 319 for 1925 and 863 for 1950. She used published information, including obituaries for those deceased, and wrote to all living officers for whom important data were missing. She guessed that the 1950 sample included corporations owning at least one-third of all business assets, and the earlier ones a little less. Increasingly chairmen and presidents work full-time for their corporations. Either may be the chief executive officer (p. 14).

Miss Newcomer observes three historical phases in the development of big business. In the nineteenth century they were under the control of their founders or builders, who usually held sufficient stock to guarantee control. About the turn of the century affairs were dominated by 'corporate speculators and plungers', who established holding companies that traded in their subsidiaries. This was followed by the present era classified by Berle and Means as 'management control'. 'Most of the big corporations today have widely scattered stock ownership. This has led, as has often been emphasized, to the separation of ownership and control. The stockholders tend to sign proxies mechanically, since they have little information on which to base considered judgments. Even the directors, who actually elect the top executives, are likely to accept the recommendations of the chief executives themselves without thorough investigations.' (p. 5.)

The study concludes that there is a division of power in the modern corporation. Besides the president and board chairman, the executive vice-president and finance chairman may be endowed with important powers. The vice-presidents are often in the position of being able to outvote the chief executives. The chief executive takes over a well-organised concern. He must persuade those under him to work together effectively, must hold the organisation together and will be considered successful if it makes moderate profits. The growth of government control has curbed the more questionable forms of financial manipulation, and given the big corporation some of the attributes of a public organisation, with obligations to the employee and the customer. It has obligations to the nation and to the community in which it operates. (pp. 141–3.)

Another book that merits attention is Robert Aaron Gordon, *Business Leadership in the Large Corporation*, 1945, 1961 and then, with a new preface, Berkeley and Los Angeles: University of California Press, 1966. Similar ground is covered to that described above, and, after an analysis of the size and growth of the 200 largest corporations in the United States, case studies are presented 'of the manner in which the composite function of business leadership is exercised in come of the largest American corporations'. 'Since a good deal of reliance had to be placed on published material the closely held corporation largely defied analysis.' Adequate information was found for 65 of the giant companies. (pp. 60–1.) Gordon concludes, *inter alia*:

> The primary responsibility for business leadership in the large corporation has devolved upon a group of men who are professional managers. Their position is not achieved through ownership. They are salaried experts, trained by education and experience in the field

of management. Though only salaried managers, they find themselves responsible for making the decisions which affect not merely the dividends their stock-holders receive but also the prices consumers pay, the wages their workers earn, and the level of output and employment in their own firms and in the economy as a whole. (p. 318.)

Roy Lewis and Rosemary Stewart in *The Boss: The Life and Times of the British Business Man* (London: Phoenix House, revised ed. 1961) examine their subject not by way of interview or questionnaire, but by assembling a great deal of published evidence and reach interesting conclusions.

'Soundness' in most British firms today is as highly-prized an attribute as it is in America although generally it will be termed 'reliability'. In many British, as in many American firms, moreover, there is a distrust of the man, however able, who has means of his own. There is a preference for knowing that a man has only the salary appropriate to his grade; his whole 'capital' is his standing with the firm itself. Independence, even in small measure, is not liked, even if the man has the good manners in no way to obtrude his advantages. (p. 88.)

They add a salutary warning about attributing too esoteric a psyche to the tycoon: 'Notwithstanding all the motives which may be ascribed to business men, the love of money remains extremely potent'. (p. 226.) In 1967 Rosemary Stewart published a study based on the diaries that she persuaded 160 managers to keep, over a period of four weeks, and that gave detailed records of how they spent their time. (*Managers and their Jobs*, London: Macmillan, 1967; Pan Books, 1970.)

Cyril Sofer, in *Men in Mid-Career: A Study of British Managers and Technical Specialists* (Cambridge University Press, 1970) presents a review of the literature on management roles and psychology, and then the results of extended interviews with 81 managers in 2 industrial companies. He describes how the organisation interacts with the needs and aspirations of its managerial employees:

The person enters the organization predisposed to accept its influence, to be pervaded by its values, to intertwine his fate with it, to make its concerns his own, to identify himself with it and it with himself. He enters after prolonged exposure to a social system in which he has developed psychological needs to support himself and a family, to perform useful services for others, to occupy an accepted position as a worthwhile member of a community carrying out necessary activities, to occupy himself, to organize his time, to interact with others, to express and differentiate himself as a person with distinctive attributes, to learn and to find significance and meaning in his acts. He feels a need to have an impact on his environment, to struggle toward and reach difficult objectives, and to be recognized as successful.... the work organization is for many adult males today their main social arena, their main portion of social reality, their own sector or cross-section of the social world. It is a model of the world for them both in the sense that they tend to see the nature of the social world as an expanded version of the work organization and in the sense that in their perception of it they will impose on it their own inner versions of what the world of people is like. (pp. 342–3.)

Roger Priouret has produced a book revealing of the views and preoccupations of business leaders in continental Europe: *Les Managers Européens* (Paris: Denoël, 1970). Priouret presents verbatim reports of interviews with sixteen European tycoons, and from these one can get some insight into the nature of their jobs. For example, Professor Bernhard Timm expounds the grand strategy of BASF (previously Badische Anilin) of which he is president. BASF is the third-largest chemical concern in Germany. Timm is asked what his strategy has been since he became director of the company in 1965:

> The strategy has been to develop BASF to a size such that it can survive world competition and be above that level at which an enterprise is in danger of collapsing. That, we say, is the basic objective.
>
> The second strategic theme is to develop the traditional forms of our activity, those where we have experience, competence and positive advantages over our competitors. These areas do not all have the same level of development. We say that the growth of plastic materials is much greater than that of fertiliser. We say, too, that the growth of dyes depends less on the volume than on the quality, because the expansion of textiles is limited.
>
> Third objective: we ought to devote a more and more important effort to research so as to be amongst the most advanced enterprises. Such research is enormously costly. Sometimes, it is negative.

Professor Timm is plainly worried about this question of research,

The Profit-seekers

and explains that they have the intention and the will to find other partners to enable them to make full use of their research efforts. Priouret taxes him with the fact that BASF has a relatively modest place in highly sophisticated chemistry. Professor Timm agrees. They were trying to get back into more sophisticated chemistry, but had never had proper laboratories nor theoretical and applied research centres in that field, though they had always produced primary materials for pharmaceutical laboratories. They had, however, discovered a new process for making vitamin A. (*Les Managers Européens*, pp. 97–9.)

Giovanni Agnelli shows that Fiat, too, is seeking collaborators. The head of Westinghouse's foreign department had revealed to them his grand project. To find a tenable position in Europe Westinghouse would need a turnover of not less than five milliard francs (which would have been a little under a billion dollars). They therefore elaborated a project in which they would have a half-share, with the other half owned by Jeumont-Schneider and its associate Merlin-Gérin (French), Ateliers de Construction Electrique de Charleroi (Belgian), Cenemessa (Spanish) and Marelli (a wholly owned Fiat subsidiary). 'For me, it's very simple. The Europeans ought to constitute their group and give Westinghouse the share it asked. If they did not, the Americans would do it on their own. It is not that they are more capable than us. It is just that they are used to vast strategic operations on a continental scale.' (Priouret, pp. 172–3.)

These, you will note, are the questions that occupy the minds of the directors of great companies. Are they preoccupied with the minutiae of marginal costs and prices? No. Do they behave differently if they are owners or paid managers? No. The Giovanni Agnelli, mentioned above, is the grandson of that Giovanni Agnelli whose portrait hangs in the Fiat Museum in Turin, showing the group of founders of the company when the act was signed constituting the Fabrica Italiana di Automobili Torino. These men, if they are to succeed, have to be in love with their products, and in a special relationship with the materials in which they work. In this there is a curious similarity between them and those primitive peoples who feel a bond with their totem-animals. The relationship has a mystical element. Of course, as Lewis and Stewart noted, money is important but, in part at least, as John P. Marquand has observed, because it is a way of keeping the score.

6.2.4 Organisation theory

I have listed a few of the books dealing with managers. There are many more, but not so many as there are books dealing with organisations, for this is a field in which research has been most prolific in the last thirty years. The fascination of organisations is well founded, for they are the equivalent, in the modern industrial State, of the clans, tribes and extended familes that have played so essential a role in human survival.

People are always, everywhere, throwing in their lot with other people in order to achieve some goal or other: business, religious, recreational, political, educational, charitable, criminal. The aims of these organisations are to get something, provide something or change something; some succeed, some fail; some expire almost before they have begun; some flourish and go on and on. They have one feature in common: that by their very existence they have in some degree modified the situation out of which they arose. In some circumstances the aim of the organisation becomes its own survival and extension rather than that for which it was originally established.

In *The Modern Corporation and Private Property* (New York: Macmillan, 1935) Adolf A. Berle and Gardiner C. Means argued:

> Corporations have ceased to be merely legal devices through which the private business transactions of individuals may be carried on. Though still much used for this purpose, the corporate form has acquired a larger significance. The corporation has, in fact, become both a method of property tenure and a means of organizing economic life. Grown to tremendous proportions, there may be said to have evolved a 'corporate system' – as there was once a feudal system – which has attracted to itself a combination of attributes and powers, and has attained a degree of prominence entitling it to be dealt with as a major social institution.   (p. 1.)

Frankenstein made his monster and the Sorcerer's apprentice conjured up the Devil for limited ends, but the Monster and the Devil turned out to have other ideas. I do not mean to infer that business corporations are monstrous or devilish, but that they have, indeed, taken over the world and are pursuing ends of their own that may not exactly conform with the ends of humanity.

That characteristic in terms of which organisations become interested in their own survival as an end in itself is known as 'bureaucracy': the power or rule of the administrator. This term was originally reserved for governments, so that John Stuart Mill in his *Principles of Political Economy* (first published in 1848) warns against 'the inexpediency of concentrating in a dominant bureaucracy, all the skill and experience in the management of large interests, and all the power of organized action, existing in the community'. (bk V, chap. XL, sec. 11.)

Funnily enough, Max Weber, well known for his writings on bureaucracy, ascribes to it a benign role, arising from 'the demand for the greatest possible acceleration in the despatch of official business, combined with precision, clarity and continuity' which are requirements of a modern capitalist economy. 'Large modern capitalist enterprises are themselves in most cases unrivalled models of strict bureaucratic organisation. Their commercial relationships are completely dependent on increasing precision, reliability and, above all, speed of operation.' (W. G. Runciman, ed., *Max Weber Selections in Translation*, London: Cambridge University Press, 1978, p. 350.)

Berle and Means, too, match the corporation against the State, but in a different sense. 'The rise of the modern corporation has brought a concentration of economic power which can compete on equal terms with the modern state – economic power versus political power, each strong in its own field. The state seeks in some aspects to regulate the corporation, while the corporation, steadily becoming more powerful, makes every effort to avoid such regulation. Where its own interests are concerned it even attempts to dominate the state.' (*The Modern Corporation*, p. 357.)

A concentration of economic power.... The power is, of course, exercised by the management. But the management – the board of directors, heads of divisions and great departments – includes, as Galbraith has argued,

> only a small proportion of those who, as participants, contribute information to group decisions. This latter group is very large: it extends from the most senior officials of the corporation to where it meets, at the outer perimeter, the white and blue collar workers whose function is to conform more or less mechanically to instruction or routine. It embraces all who bring specialized knowledge, talent or experience to group decision-making. This, not the management, is the guiding intelligence – the brain – of the enterprise.

This guiding intelligence Galbraith has named the 'Technostructure'. (John Kenneth Galbraith, *The New Industrial State*, London: Hamish Hamilton, 1967, p. 71.)

I have said enough to justify the designation of human-behaviour-within-organisations as a special field of study. Anyone exploring this field will find the usual difficulties in determining the status of the material: does it arise from experience, empirical research, practice or intellectual fancy? As Chester I. Barnard wrote: 'Knowledge of a science of organization and administration can never be a substitute for specific experience in a specific organization.' This was in his foreword to a pioneering study in organisation theory: Herbert A. Simon, *Administrative Behavior*, first published in 1945. In what follows I refer to the third edition, New York: Free Press, 1976. Barnard also warns, 'the generality achieved implies that the conclusions are highly abstract'.

The major part of Simon's book is dedicated to an exposition of how organisations ought to be studied and the invention of an appropriate terminology. It is a mélange of how organisations *ought* to operate and how they *do* operate.

'*Administrative Behavior* analyzes organizations in terms of the decision-making behavior of their participants, but it is precisely the organizational *system* surrounding this behavior that gives it its special character. The roles of organization members are shaped by their goal identifications, and goal identifications, in turn, are a product of location in the organization.' (p. xxxv.)

He explains that he does not make much use of the term 'role theory', though a person's role specifies some of the premises that underlie his decisions (pp. xxxvi–xxxvii). Behaviour, especially within administrative organisations, is purposive – oriented towards goals or objectives, and is made up of a hierarchy of decisions, each step consisting of an implementation of the goals set forth in the preceding step. But note that all decision is a matter of compromise, with objectives never perfectly achieved.

Administrative organisation is characterised by specialisation: horizontal when it consists of a division of work, vertical when relating to the flow of decisions (pp. 4–11). But across these divisions there stands the phenomenon of identification, or organisational loyalty. This enables the administrator to narrow his focus to the limited organisational aims to which he subscribes. But the same identification may result in interdepartmental rivalries in which the aims of the organisation as a whole are submerged (pp. 12–14). Unity of command is necessary to prevent the currency of contradictory commands, and the principle of authority where a subordinate is guided by someone else's decision, irrespective of his own judgement as to the merits of the decision. (p. 22.)

Simon returns on a number of occasions to the limits of rationality. Real behaviour consists of many disconnected elements. Within each segment rationality may prevail, but the segments fit together in an imperfectly rational way. This 'bounded rationality arises partly from incompleteness of knowledge, partly from incompatibility of aims' (pp. 80–1). There are at least two elements that organisations have in common: some equilibrating mechanism or mechanisms, and the criterion of efficiency as the basis of administrative choice (p. 121). Later, he mentions a third that is of some importance and concurs with Galbraith's view: almost no decision made in an organisation is the task of a single individual (p. 221).

You will, perhaps, have noticed the didactic nature of Simon's ideas: he is instructing us as to how we should think about administration. His role is that of sociologist/psychologist thinking about administrators, and giving us the benefit of his thought. He offers a framework for analysis and a vocabulary for description, and this is very much how, in his conclusion, he summarises what he has done.

Of course, a great deal of theorising in universities is done on this basis. Students are drilled to reach conclusions on inadequate, hastily assembled evidence, their critical faculties thus tranquillised. It was in this spirit that marginalism was elaborated in economics, including the proposition that entrepreneurs maximised profits. I am not sure that Simon understood that, in economic theory, profit maximisation means something special: that, in conditions of diminishing returns, a firm will make its maximum profit at that point of production where marginal cost equals marginal revenue, and where the marginal revenue product of each input equals its price. Since any entrepreneur who devoted his time to calculating these things would have no time to do anything else and would soon go insolvent, the theorem has limited practical importance.

It is understandable, then, that non-economists should misunderstand profit maximisation to mean simply 'make as much profit as possible'. But whereas in economics the principle has a precise meaning (in principle if not in practice), in its vulgar version its precision is lost. 'As possible' implies constraints: the entrepreneur must not kill himself in the process nor terrorize his workers or sacrifice his wife and children nor threaten his customers. It is to obviate the absurdities of the vulgar version that Simon substitutes 'satisficing' for 'maximizing'. The manager need not be a maximalist, that is, 'person who holds out for the maximum of his demands & rejects compromises (esp. as variety of Russian socialist)' (*Pocket Oxford Dictionary*, 1967 ed.). He will not agonise too long over his decisions, but simply seek a course of action that is 'good enough'. (H. A. Simon, *Models of Man*, New York:

Wiley, 1957, p. 246, and D. W. Taylor, 'Decision Making and Problem Solving', in Lawrence A. Welsch and Richard M. Cyert, *Management Decision Making*, Harmondsworth: Penguin Books, 1970, p. 37.)

At the end of *Administrative Behavior* Simon asks, 'What are the next steps that research must take?', and answers, 'First, it must develop adequate case studies of existing administrative situations. It will do well to initiate these on a small scale – dealing in minute detail with organizational units of moderate size. Only in this way can superficiality be avoided.'

Joan Woodward is another sociologist who played an important part in the development of organisation theory. *Industrial Organization: Theory and Practice* (Oxford University Press, 1965) was a study of 100 firms in south Essex. An interim report, for the Department of Scientific and Industrial Research, *Management and Technology*, appeared in 1958 (HMSO). In this she asserted the importance of 'socio-technical systems' in determining the organisational requirements of firms. If it is to catch the academic imagination, a model must be simplistic, and this quality Joan Woodward achieved by specifying three sorts of technology: Group I was small-batch and unit-production; group II large-batch and mass-production; group III continuous-flow or process-production. 'The case studies confirmed that variations in organizational requirements between firms are nearly always linked with differences in their techniques of production.... Thus it was possible to trace a "cause and effect" relationship between a system of production and its associated organizational pattern and, as a result to predict what the organizational requirements of a firm are likely to be, given its production system.' (op. cit. p. 37.)

This is undoubtedly true, but you would not be able to get very far in your organisational design if all you knew was that the method of production was to be small-batch, large-batch or continuous-flow. Of greater interest than these tendencies to regularity was what the inquiries revealed of the adventitious nature of industrial organisation. There were eight firms whose specialists (in contrast to line-managers) were so restricted that there seemed little point in employing them; 'their advice was never taken, the sevices they rendered were trivial, and their control was meaningless' (Woodward, *Industrial Organization: Theory and Practice*, p. 19).

Tracing the history of specialist departments provided the research workers with an interesting insight into the way in which organization grows. In many firms it was almost impossible to find out why a particular department had become established at a particular time. Only a minority of organizational changes seem to have resulted from dissatisfaction with the existing organizational structure. In the firms studied such changes seemed to have come about as a consequence of either a change in top management or an increase in the organization consciousness of the chief executive....

But most of the organizational changes were not so deliberately planned. They had come about almost spontaneously; as the result of a crisis, to accommodate individuals, or in response to a management fashion. Several inspection departments could be traced back to a specific problem relating to the maintaining of quality standards....

In all the firms studied, organization had to some extent been modified to accommodate individuals. 'Empire builders' had distorted organizational patterns in their searches for higher status. Bright young men for whom the existing organization had provided inadequate opportunities had been given newly created posts with potentially wider scope. In a number of firms sinecures had been found for misfits who had been unable to hold down their jobs but who, for one reason or another, could be neither discharged nor demoted.... These new departments persisted long after the people in charge of them had died, retired or moved on. In some cases they had succeeded in making their new departments indispensable, in others the vacancies created when they left their posts became weapons in the hands of factory politicians. More often, however, the posts were filled simply because they had become an accepted part of the structure and the reason for their inception had been forgotten. (Woodward, pp. 21–2.)

I have mentioned the vast output of writers on organisation, administration and management, quite beyond the capacity of anyone interested in them as ancillary to something else. For this reason reviews of the field are useful – such, for instance, as that by W. H. Starbuck, 'Organizational Growth and Development' in the book by the same name edited by him and published by Penguin Books, Harmondsworth, 1971. His article is a reprint from the *Handbook of Organizations* (Rand McNally, 1965). If we can determine why and how organisations grow and develop we shall also learn why and how they exist in the first place.

Organisations are committed to achieving goals by stable structures for the allocation of tasks, roles and responsibilities. (Starbuck, p. 13.)

Why should they grow? Not as an end in itself, but as a means of attaining other goals or a side effect of such attainment. Katona suggests as one of these goals the 'self-realization of a business concern' – the urge to follow through tasks once begun. Newman and Logan, in discussions with nineteen executives, identified five reasons that Starbuck sees as forms of self-realisation: desire of customers for complete service; attempts to master technologies; development of new products by research laboratories; the attraction for retail dealers of complete product lines; if firms do not expand, they contract. (p. 15.)

Other researchers found amongst the motives the pursuit of adventure and risk, and the avoidance of boredom, as well as prestige, power and job security. D. R. Roberts (*Executive Compensation*, New York: Free Press, 1959) correlated the pay of the highest executive and the firm's sales volume (rather than its profit). C. E. Griffin (*Enterprise in a Free Society*, Homewood, Ill.: Irwin, 1949) and W. J. Baumol (*Business Behavior, Value and Growth*, New York: Macmillan, 1959) also stressed the objective of sales volume or revenue maximisation (subject to a minimum-profit constraint). Bigness is also associated with stability, survival and power. (pp. 16–32.)

Starbuck presents this summary of research on loyalty:

> [Organizations] set up indoctrination programs for new employees; they publish organizational newspapers which stress the accomplishments of the organization and of individual members; they withhold responsibility from new members and reward seniority with promotions and special awards; they require members to learn organizational songs and creeds; they make intra-organizational statuses central to their inducement schemes; they put uniforms on members to distinguish them from non-members; they change members' geographic assignments so that extra-organizational loyalties are disrupted; they adopt paternalistic policies which provide for members' health, recreation, retirement and death. (p. 49.)

Pages 62 to 83 are devoted to mathematical models of how growth could conceivably take place, unilluminating because unrelated to reality, presupposing a degree of determinism that human institutions lack. It is important for neo-classical economic theory to demonstrate that unit output costs increase with the growth of the firm, for this is necessary if the model is to be determinate. Without it, the biggest firm would swallow up all the others in an exponential implosion. The fact that in the real world this has not happened is irrelevant: the model must somehow prevent it by its own internal logic. Starbuck quotes P. W. S. Andrews's explanation of the issue:

> Economists have found that the application to the real world of the abstract theory of pure competition requires that long-run costs should rise with increased scale. This has made it easy for the supposition to be accepted in economics that long-run costs do, in fact, rise, and, in the absence of any other plausible explanation as to why they should rise, economists have tended to call in increasing managerial inefficiency as a fairly plausible hypothesis which could not easily be refuted. (p.84.)

This is from P. W. S. Andrews, *Manufacturing Business*, London: Macmillan, 1949.

Starbuck's conclusions are somewhat gloomy: 'Most studies of organizational growth and development are typical examples of social science research, and as such, are subject to faults common in social science research.' (p. 125.) There is a tendency to substitute theorising for data collection; to present data without formal analyses; to base formal analyses on naïve assumptions. He echoes H. A. Simon's cry of twenty years before: 'what is needed more than anything else is data – data on goals, data on behavior strategies, data on structural variables, data on patterns of development, data on nearly every aspect of organizational growth and development'.

Now, to discover what progress has been made since 1965, I turn to Part 3 of Raymond E. Miles and Charles C. Snow, *Organizational Strategy, Structure, and Process* (Tokyo: McGraw-Hill Kogakusha, 1978), 'Overview of the Literature'. The development of the theory falls into three phases: 'For the first half of this century, management and organization theorists tended to ignore the environment, or at least hold it constant, as they sought universalistic principles of structure, planning, control, and the like.' (p. 250.) True or false? At least until the 1930s, classical and neo-classical economists had only one model of man which was supposed to be timeless and universal. So, likewise, to those who thought about it it seemed that the world was following a single road to industrialisation, with the United States in the lead and the rest following eagerly behind. Taylor, Henry Ford, the Gilbreths, Fayol and the other proponents of scientific management developed techniques by which workers could be controlled and manipulated to multiply their powers of production, but they were techniques to be applied within the company.

Then in the 1930s, 1940s and 1950s rival views were developed that stressed the effect on the firm of its environment. '...a series of increasingly elaborate contingency models portraying the linkages among environment, technology, structure, and process were developed. Essentially, the contingency approach argues that "it depends", and the recent thrust of conceptualization in the area of organization theory has been toward the identification and description of the major contingency variables upon which organizational behavior depends'. Contingency: in the sense of being contingent (dependent) on circumstances. The power of managers was limited by the circumstances of the firm's environment.

But firms can also operate to change their environment, and studies are cited that show them so engaged.

Of course it is always interesting to catch one's subjects in the act, as it were, doing those things one's hypothesis predicts they will do, or doing something unforeseen that enables one to formulate new hypotheses, but these demonstrations are of limited use for our present purposes. They confirm the judgement of Miles and Snow that, although the literature is growing rapidly, 'It is still in search of theoretical paradigms that can fully portray the complexities and dynamics of the behavior of total organizational systems.' (p. 250.)

Contingency models have emphasised differences rather than similarities in organisational behaviour, and we now enter a 'neocontingency' phase, characterised by attempts at synthesis and elaboration, but, Miles and Snow warn, 'this perspective has not taken a fully definitive shape nor can its adherents be clearly identified' (*Organizational Strategy*, p. 263).

In the circumstances it is understandable that certain students of organisation have turned against the existing theories and expressed a desire to start again. Such a student is Alberto Guerreiro Ramos, who has appropriately named his latest book *The New Science of Organizations* (University of Toronto Press, 1981). The gist of his criticism is that the theory has taken for granted the market-centric aim of organisations. But market-centred theory is applicable only to a special type of activity. 'Attempts to apply its principles to all forms of activity are hindering the actualization of possible new social systems needed to overcome the basic dilemmas of our society' (p. ix). Thus the 'instrumental rationality' of profit-seeking is allowed to obscure the 'substantive rationality' contained in the other, multi-centred, aims of the organisation. Thus he criticises the thought of H. A. Simon as over-optimistic and uncritical. 'It is presented in overly mechanistic terms and implies a loyalty to the organization which leads to – let us be frank – hideous existential outcomes.' (Ramos, p. 96.)

Such outcomes are to be found in the writings of Machiavelli, some of which seem to be disconcertingly appropriate to the activities of businesses that subordinate morality to the pursuit of profit. Machiavelli was concerned not with truth, but with expediency. 'The prince needs to be instructed about the perspective of the ruler in order to preserve and enhance his assets. He needs to understand the perspective of the "ordinary citizen" in order to deceive him. The prince has to be sensitive to scenic imperatives, i.e., to be virtuous by simulation, and able to induce the citizens to be good through the "wise" exercise of cruelty.' (Ramos, p. 52.)

6.3 BUSINESS IN ACTION

Let us now examine some of the giant companies that dominate advanced capitalist countries as well as much of the rest of the world, and, having done so, try to summarise the lessons of this chapter. Fortunately, these great organisations are so fascinating that there is no shortage of books dealing with them, some in the form of memoirs by those who have governed them, some in that of official histories and some the result of investigative journalism.

6.3.1 Hours and men

'The hour brings forth the man', the saying goes. The man must also be in the right place to demonstrate that he is, indeed, the man. And this having been demonstrated, he may go on to turn history in directions unforeseen at the moment of juxtaposition of time, place and man. Andrew Carnegie, in his *Autobiography* (Boston and New York: Houghton Mifflin, 1920) points to a number of coincidences that gave his life the shape it assumed. He was born in Dunfermline in Scotland in 1835 and, when he was twelve, taken by his parents to live in Pittsburgh where his father worked as a weaver and his mother as a shoemaker. When he was thirteen he got a job as a bobbin boy in a textile factory at $1.20 per week. His big chance came in 1850, when he became a telegraph messenger, for this led him to a position as railway telegraphist, to assistant to the Assistant Secretary of War in charge of the transportation department in the American Civil War and, in 1864, to the establishment of a rail-making concern in Pittsburgh to which each of the partners contributed $1250. From this, the Keystone Bridge Works followed, making iron bridges for the railways, in the technically-advanced material of wrought iron. 'The surest foundation of a manufacturing concern is quality', he remarks. 'After that, and a long way after, comes cost.' (Carnegie, p. 123.)

It is interesting to see the importance of the Scottish connexion in Carnegie's rise. The Scots put opportunities in each other's way and helped each other along. It was, however, a German engineer, Andrew Kloman, who brought in important innovations in their bridge- and rail-making. (p. 130.)

What were the qualities that contributed to Carnegie's business success? He was clearly of high intelligence; he had a genius for identifying and then seizing opportunities; he was a man of high integrity and human sympathy; he was a Scot. 'Speculation is a parasite feeding upon values, creating none', he wrote (p. 154), and 'There is no labour so cheap as the dearest in the mechanical field, provided it is free, contented, zealous and reaping reward as it renders service. And here America leads.' (Ibid. p. 227.)

His steel company features in labour history for the bloodshed that ended the Homestead strike of 1892. Carnegie was in Scotland when the strike broke out and immediately wired that he would take the next ship for America. His partners asked him to stay where he was on the grounds that they would be better able to settle the dispute without him. (Ibid. p. 228.) They called in the Pinkerton men to guard the property, and then the Governor of Pennsylvania moved in with troops.

Carnegie afterwards claimed innocence and ignorance of the ensuing events, but in labour histories the story is told somewhat differently. H. C. Frick, who had made his fortune in the coke busines, was a tough Carnegie manager who was intent on achieving a reduction in the guaranteed wage. After failure to agree with the Amalgamated Association of Iron and Steel Workers of America, an ultimatum was issued by the company saying that the minimum rate would be reduced anyway. Frick announced that the issue was 'whether the Carnegie Company or the Amalgamated Association shall have absolute control of our plant and business at Homestead'. (Philip Taft, *Organized Labor in American History*, New York: Harper & Row, 1964, p. 140.)

At the end of June 1892 the workers decided to strike from 2 July. Carnegie wrote to Frick: 'Of course, you will be asked to confer, and I know you will decline all conferences as you have taken your stand and have nothing more to say.' He also suggested that the opportunity should be taken of eliminating over-manning. (Carnegie, pp. 140-1.)

Three hundred Pinkerton men were sent by boat along the Ohio River, but were met by a crowd of workers. Shots were exchanged and two strikers and two Pinkerton men were killed. On 10 July, Governor Robert E. Pattison sent in 7000 troops, and the strikers were removed from the plant. Five days later the furnaces were relit and the mills manned by non-union labour. In mid-November the men voted to return. The Homestead plant operated without a union agreement for the next forty-five years. (Carnegie, pp. 144-5.)

Carnegie was well satisfied in his own judgement, a satisfaction generally justified, but sometimes leading to conclusions that, with hindsight, seem curiously naive. After the strike, wages were tied to the selling price of iron and steel, a system also followed in Britain. He says of this, 'Of all my service rendered to labour the introduction of the sliding scale is the chief. It is the solution of the capital and labour problem, because it really makes them partners – alike in prosperity and adversity.' (Carnegie p. 247.) And on Kaiser William, whom he met a few years before the First World War: 'He is not only an Emperor, but something much higher – a man anxious to improve existing conditions, untiring in his efforts to promote temperance, prevent duelling, and, I believe, to secure International Peace.' (Carnegie, p. 370.)

When Carnegie was 65 he sold the Carnegie Steel Corporation to J. Pierpont Morgan, and devoted the rest of his life to philanthropy. He loved libraries. His father and some of his friends had pooled their books to form a library in Dunfermline when Andrew was a child; at the time when he was a telegraph messenger in Pittsburgh Colonel James Anderson had established there a free library for working boys, of which Carnegie was a devoted member. So it was that the establishment of libraries formed so important a part of his philanthropic enterprises. He established 2811 free public libraries, of which 1946 were in the United States and 660 in the United Kingdom. Their total cost was a little over $50 million. (See Joseph Frazer Wall, *Andrew Carnegie*, New York: Oxford University Press, 1970, p. 828.)

John Davison Rockefeller (1839–1937), a great admirer of Carnegie's ideas, followed a similar mode. When he was 16 he began work as assistant book-keeper to a firm of commission agents in Cleveland. At age 20 he went into partnership in establishing his own agency; four years later he was in the oil business. By 1880 Standard Oil, the company he and his associates had founded, was the largest and richest in the world. By 1913 the Rockefeller fortune totalled $900 million. (Allan Nevins, *John D. Rockefeller*. A one-volume abridgement by William Greenleaf, New York: Charles Scribner's Sons, 1959, p. 279.)

He was a devout Baptist and, like Carnegie, proud of the straightness of his business dealings, in contrast to some of the millionaires of the day. 'Jay Gould and "Jim" Fisk watered and manipulated the stock of the Erie [railway] shamelessly. The builders of the Central Pacific capitalized that road at $139,000,000, although federal investigators reported that $58,000,000 would have been a generous valuation.... The American Tobacco Company, between 1890 and 1904 capitalized its good will alone in $110,000,000 of stock.' Stock-watering is a technique whereby the promotors of a company market shares in excess of its real worth.

Rockefeller was even more systematic than Carnegie in his benefactions. Carnegie had written: 'The day is not far distant when the man who dies leaving behind him millions of available wealth, which was free for him to administer during life, will pass away unwept, unhonoured and unsung.' The Rockefeller Foundation was created in 1909 and incorporated in 1913 by an act of the New York State Legislature. Rockefeller founded the University of Chicago and, by the time of his death in 1937, had given to the Foundation a total of $182 851 481. (See Arthur Bernon Tourtellot, ed., and others, *Toward the Well-Being of Mankind: Fifty Years of the Rockefeller Foundation*, New York: Doubleday, 1964, pp. 7–8.)

There are many ladders by means of which one may climb up to the realms of gold, and many ways of falling down again. Carnegie and Rockefeller started at the bottom and worked their way up; J. Paul Getty had a rich father whose footsteps he could follow, thereby getting much further in the same direction. He was born in Minneapolis in 1892 and died in Guildford, Surrey, in England in 1976. I turn to his autobiography, *As I See It* (London: W. H. Allen, 1976) in search of insight into his career. He explains that he had lived in almost total anonymity until October 1957 when *Fortune* carried an article naming him as the richest American. He argues that this is a calculation impossible to make. Much of his wealth consisted of shares in industrial concerns, and shares are constantly fluctuating in market price. If you try to market a large block of shares, that alone will affect their price on the stock exchange to an unpredictable extent.

Since much of his wealth was in oil, it fluctuated with oil prices. In 1903 Oklahoma crude was worth $1.03 a barrel at the well-head. Two years later it was down to 52 cents. In 1915 it was down to 40 cents, but in 1920 up to $3.50. In the early 1930s when a flood of oil was coming from the East Texas fields, the price fell to as little as 10 cents a barrel. As I write this, in March 1983, the price of oil is again disturbed with prices, depending on price and quality, drifting down from $35 to $30. A barrel contains 42 US gallons. (Getty, pp. 7-8.)

But though Getty's wealth could not be measured, there was a great deal of it. The co-existence of very rich and very poor people he attributes to Nature's tendency to be randomly and inexplicably disproportionate. He confesses to no pangs of conscience because he happened to be so much richer than other people. 'The Lord may have been disproportionate, but this is how He – or Nature, if you prefer – operates.' (p. 12.)

Getty's father was a Minneapolis attorney whose net wealth in 1903 exceeded $250 000. In that year a client's business took him to Bartlesville, Indian Territory, that was later to become the State of Oklahoma. Having finished his legal business, he bought an oil and gas lease, on which 42 out of 43 drillings struck oil.

In 1909, when Paul was not yet 16, he got his father's permission to spend his summer vacation working on the family oilfield, his father's condition that he work as a roustabout: 'an oilfield labourer whose job it was to perform the heaviest (and usually the dirtiest) work on a drilling site'. Over the next few summers he worked his way up to the job of 'toolie', in charge of sharpening drilling-bits. Then he went to Oxford and did a degree in politics and economics, after which, on his father's suggestion and with his father's support, he went looking for oil-wells on his own. At the end of a year he bought a half-interest in a lease on land on which oil was struck. By mid-1916 he had accumulated a million dollars and retired. He put himself down for the US Air Service but since he was never called up, was able to spend his time in dissipation. By 1919, having grown tired of idleness, he returned to the oil business.

After having been conned by a drilling contractor, he acted as his own drilling superintendent. 'I spent most of my time in the field, working alongside my crews on the drilling sites. Around-the-clock stints were commonplace – and, on one occasion, during a crucial state in drilling operations, I worked straight through for 74 hours.' (p. 35.) A working boss enjoyed a great advantage. 'When a "Boss" knew his way around a rig (and, when necessary, would perform any task from riding the hook during latching up operations to sharpening dulled bits) oilfield workers accepted him as a full member of their exclusive fraternity.' (pp. 36-7.)

In 1930 Getty's father died, leaving an estate valued at $15¼ million. His mother and the executors of his father's will advised drastic retrenchment as a means of riding out the depression: Getty, by contrast, set out on an energetic campaign of vertical integration. His father's and his own companies were engaged in oil exploration and production, selling their crude to refineries: he now aimed at acquiring a company or companies with refineries and retail outlets. He began buying stock in the Tide Water Associated Oil Company, ignorant of the fact that it was owned by Standard Oil of New Jersey. The process by which he got control of Tide Water was complicated and spread over twenty years. It involved the take-over of various other companies, including Spartan Aircraft of which, at the request of the Navy Department, Getty took personal charge in 1942. 'The first step was to sweep out incompetents, replace them with qualified personnel and tighten up operations even while implementing an expansion programme. Soon streams of vitally needed components and sub-assemblies manufactured to rigid specifications were flowing to ... prime contractors. Factory space was increased sevenfold. The number of employees – originally in the hundreds – increased to over 5,500.' (pp. 47–8.)

In 1948–9 Getty beat the seven great oil companies (the Seven Sisters) to a stake in Saudi Arabia, with a down-payment of $9¼ million and an agreement to pay the Saudis what appeared to be extravagant royalties. It was four years before crude oil was produced and the venture proved successful. In 1980 Getty Oil came 68th in the list of leading American companies.

What do we learn of Paul Getty's character and personality? He was married and divorced five times and had five sons. His fifth wife said, 'Paul was a good husband and father, but his first love was business. When there was a new business venture, he couldn't resist.' (p. 100.) He remarked of his own attitude: 'I did not divorce any of my wives. ... A marriage contract to me is as binding as any in business, and I have always believed in sticking to an agreement. It was always my wives who invoked the escape-clauses.' (p. 101.) He quotes one of his cousins, June Hamilton, who was a close friend of the Roosevelts. He asked her how she found FDR as a person – was he easy to get along with?

> 'He's the easiest man in the world to get along with – as long as you do exactly what he wants,' she replied, pausing and giving me a dry look before adding, 'that's one thing you and he have in common.' (pp. 35–6.)

The Profit-seekers

What was Paul Getty's reward for all his hard work and determination? As noted, his marriages did not last, for it was his business that he was wedded to. He was not beautiful – his photographs show a somewhat foxy look – but his wealth gave him entry to the circles of the rich, famous and beautiful in which he moved. At Oxford he made friends with Edward, Prince of Wales, a friendship ended only by Edward's death. In the 1920s and 1930s oilmen and film people fraternised in their California houses. Getty entertained them at his beachhouse at Malibu, and was entertained. Rudolf Valentino, Clara Bow, Dorothy Gish, Igor Stravinsky, Arthur Rubinstein, Charlie Chaplin, Joan Barry, Paulette Goddard and many other talented and beautiful Hollywood people were his friends. As an index of the infantilism of that world of fantasy, I cite what Getty and his friends regarded as an uproarious joke:

> Barging in on people at unexpected – better still, impossible – hours was a form of practical joke that had wide currency in Hollywood during the 1920s and 1930s. Around three or four a.m., the guests at a Hollywood party would suddenly decide to descend on some other member of the movie colony who they knew was at home and fast asleep. All would pile into their automobiles, drive to the victim's house and ring the doorbell until someone – servant or master – answered. Then the entire mob would troop into the house....
> There were many popular variations on the basic barge-in theme. One of the most frequently used involved hiring an entire band – preferably a brass one.   (pp. 189–90.)

'The glories of our blood and state', James Shirley wrote, 'are shadows, not substantial things; There is no armour against fate; Death lays his icy hand on kings....' So the triumphs of Getty's life were counter-balanced by tragedies and disappointments, some of them caused by his great wealth and his preoccupation with running his business. He looked back on an era of deteriorating moral standards and eruptions of crime, and regarded the future pessimistically. Anthony Sampson described him as he was in 1975:

> Today, at the age of eighty-two, Getty remains a monument to individualism, as he looks back with melancholy detachment on his sixty years in the industry. He lives alone in the great Elizabethan mansion of Sutton Place, surrounded by parkland on the edge of suburban London, and protected by extravagant defences. A heavy double gate on the main road guards the estate, with electronic

controls, followed by a traffic light. Guard dogs roam across the park, and inside the walled garden is a cage full of lions. Inside, the dark house seems lifeless, except for the security guards in the passages. (Anthony Sampson, *The Seven Sisters*, London: Hodder & Stoughton, 1975, p. 140.)

His great monument, besides the Getty Oil Corporation, is the museum he established at Malibu, where he and his eldest son are buried. The law-suits and tax disputes were settled only in 1982. The 4 000 000 Getty oil-shares left to the museum are now worth more than $1000 million.

Jean Paul Getty started well up the ladder, and so did Howard Robard Hughes. His father, also named Howard, had graduated in law at Harvard, but, until he was in his 40s, was a wheeler-dealer on the Texas oil-fields. Then he invented an oil drill capable of cutting through the rock shale of south-west Texas and established a tool company that made and leased his drills.

Within a few years of each other, first his mother, and then his father, died. At the age of 18 Howard was the owner of three-quarters of the stock of the Hughes Tool Company. He got a court order declaring him a major and, as company accountant appointed Noah Dietrich, who had answered the newspaper advertisement for the post. Hughes then got married to a long-time friend and left Houston for Hollywood.

Getty was tough, solid and reliable. Hughes was mercurial, unpredictable and utterly unreliable. His wife, sorely neglected, soon divorced him. With immense energy Hughes threw himself into the production of *Hell's Angels*, a film about fliers in the First World War. By the time it was completed, as a silent film, the talkies had arrived. Hughes made it over again, this time with sound, at a cost totalling nearly $4 million, far more than had ever been spent on a film before. It was an enormous success, earning $8 million. (See John Keats, *Howard Hughes*, London: MacGibbon & Kee; New York, Random House, 1966, parts i and ii.) He then produced three films that were flops, and then *Scarface*, another great success. After that he left films to startle the world by his record-breaking flights.

I can recall seeing *Hell's Angels* when I was a boy of 12 or 13. I was entranced. John Keats gives a sample of the dialogue. Boy: 'What do you think of my new uniform?' Girl: 'Oh, it's ripping!' Boy (nervously): 'Where?' I have the impression that audiences were very easily amused in those days. I have only the haziest memories of *Scarface* and

The Front Page. They both made considerable contributions to Hughes's fortune.

Hughes established the Hughes Aircraft Company and made his spectacular trans-continental and trans-world flights. But he would become absorbed in some enterprise, work at it night and day, and neglect everything else. In 1938 the Army Air Corps wanted a new interceptor fighter that the men at Hughes Aircraft thought they could make, but they were unable to get a response from Hughes. Two of the key men, Palmer and Rockefeller, decided to leave.

> Rockefeller first tried to telephone Hughes, but could not reach him. He left word. There was no answer. He wrote a letter of resignation and mailed it to Hughes. No reply. He sent a telegram, giving Hughes three weeks' notice. No acknowledgement. At the end of the third week Rockefeller took a new job. A week after that Hughes visited the Burbank plant and discovered Rockefeller was missing.
>
> He phoned Rockefeller at home to say he needed him, full of plans for the future. Rockefeller explained it was too late – he had already begun his new job. Hughes asked one favour – that he would go and see Hughes's lawyer. But when Rockefeller did so, the lawyer expressed surprise, for he had had no instructions from Hughes.

In the years that followed, Hughes bought Trans-World Airlines, produced another film – *The Outlaw,* planned a giant aircraft to carry American troops. The latter was to have a wing-span of 340 feet, be 220 feet long and have a tail 100 feet high. The Hughes Tool Company and Hughes Aircraft produced vast quantities of aircraft parts and ammunition, but despite government contracts worth $60 million its aircraft (a photographic reconnaissance aircraft and the giant troop-carrier) flew only after the war had ended. The reconnaissance plane crashed, with Hughes at the controls, on its test flight, almost killing him; the other, again with him flying it, flew a mile at 70 feet and was then put back in its hangar and there preserved under lock and key.

Hughes lost millions by buying RKO and then devoting just enough time to it to prevent his directors making saleable films. He lost more millions in TWA. By contrast, one of his executives at Hughes Aircraft pressed him to let the company expand into electronics. Having made up his mind, Hughes lavished money on his projects, collected the best brains money could buy and aimed at perfection. Hughes Aircraft flourished. TWA was taken out of his control, though he remained majority shareholder, and became highly profitable; he also disposed of RKO at a profit.

But his behaviour was becoming more and more eccentric. He had no office; what business he did was done by telephone. He had no fixed address; merely hideouts, protected by guards who denied any connexion with him. When he was 52, he secretly married Jean Peters, who also disappeared into obscurity. But he was like Carnegie, Rockefeller and Getty in his desire to divest himself of a fortune for non-commercial purposes: he established the Howard Hughes Medical Institute in Miami and gave them the Hughes Aircraft Company.

By 1956 he had gone into seclusion, watched over by his Mormon guard whose duty it was to keep him free of visitors and germs. In 1971 he was alleged to be in Nassau. When Clifford Irving published his fake biography it was very difficult to establish whether it was true or false. A controversy ensued as to whether Hughes was alive or dead. In 1976 he left Acapulco on a flight for Houston, Texas. This much was established, for when the flight reached Houston he was dead.

We have been examining the careers of men who have had immense power because of their immense wealth. They were the absolute rulers of their companies, because they owned a majority of the shares – as long, that is, as they remained independent of the banks. They are a fascinating phenomenon of the capitalist age, as astounding as the emperors, tyrants and chiefs of ancient times.

6.3.2 Corporate power

More characteristic of the modern system of production, distribution and ownership are the great bureaucracies, the initiative of whose chief executive is limited by the technostructures through which he must work. We must watch them in action if we want to gain understanding of our economic system. One difficulty, of course, is that they are so different from one another: different in products and methods and in the styles in which they conduct their business. Fortunately, there is no shortage of literature on the subject, though none of the multitude of books and papers is as illuminating as is the experience of working for one of them.

Let us put ourselves in Anthony Sampson's hands and examine the secret history of ITT. (Anthony Sampson, *The Sovereign State*, London: Hodder & Stoughton, 1973.)

Big corporations sometimes establish subsidiary companies to make new products or enter new markets, sometimes they will buy out a

The Profit-seekers

smaller company that is already operating successfully in the chosen field. These latter have generally been established by someone with a bright idea and the funds and ability to exploit it. Such a person was Sosthenes Behn, who had risen to the rank of colonel in the US Signal Corps in the First World War and who, after the war, established the International Telephone and Telegraph Company, so named to make it sound like the giant American Telephone and Telegraph Company. Before the war he and his brother had operated as sugar brokers in Puerto Rico and had acquired a small telephone business in settlement of a bad debt. In 1923 ITT won the contract to operate the telephone system in Spain; in 1925 it acquired the international holdings of Western Electric, including a large British company renamed Standard Telephone and Cables. Along with this went a secret cartel agreement with Western Electric in the United States and its holding company, AT & T, in terms of which they would not compete with ITT abroad nor ITT with them in the United States.

In 1930 Behn established companies in Germany and extended cartel agreements to Europe and Latin America. In 1933 Behn and his German representative were received by Hitler, and influential Nazis were appointed to the boards of Behn's German companies. Throughout the Second World War ITT was able to keep its empire more or less intact. In 1944 Behn appeared in Paris as a communications expert advising the American Army. (Sampson, *The Sovereign State*, p. 39.)

Surprisingly ITT in 1967 obtained $27 million from the US Government for war damage inflicted on its German factories, including the Focke-Wulf aircraft plants, by Allied bombers. (Ibid. p. 44.)

Colonel Behn retired from ITT in 1956, at the age of 74. He died the following year. Harold Sydney Geneen, an executive vice-president of Raytheon, was appointed to fill Behn's place. ITT was already fairly diversified, with a spread of activities and interests, but Geneen set out almost immediately to transform it into a conglomerate: a company difficult to identify with any particular industry. For this purpose he invoked the help of Lazards, the merchant bankers. Felix Rohatyn, of that firm, was in due course appointed to the board of directors of ITT. Sampson comments: 'Lazards were able to find companies for Geneen, to assess them and bargain toughly with them; and on their side, they profited too. Between 1966 and 1969 Lazards received fees from ITT amounting to $3.9 million, of which merger fees comprised $2.1 million'. (Ibid. p. 78.)

The first big acquisition was the Avis car-hire company.

After Avis, companies came to Geneen thick and fast, not only through Lazards, but also through a special new ITT acquisitions department. The mid-'sixties were a boom time; there was a merger-mania sweeping through America, and Geneen was on the crest of the wave. The ITT shares were pushing up, encouraged by the expectations of Geneen's management, which made it easier to acquire companies, whose shareholders were paid – nearly always – in ITT stock. Geneen was prepared to buy anything, whatever it made, provided it was growing fast and profitably. He did not want to have contested bids, which would attract hostile publicity; and partly to avoid this, he was prepared to pay well above the market price for the shares. (Ibid. p. 78.)

Why pay above the market price for the shares, you may ask? Why not just buy shares quietly through nominees until you own a majority, then step in at the next annual shareholders' meeting and replace the sitting directors with your own? The first reason is that rules now apply in most countries requiring a company out to take over another to declare its intention quite early in the process; the second is that the presence of buyers on the market ready to take whatever is offered is itself likely to push up the share price, for shares in a company offered for sale generally constitute a small proportion of the total. One must be able to attract not only the speculators, but also the institutions – pensions funds and insurance companies who have bought the shares for the income they will generate rather than to make a fast buck.

But more important, one must try to pre-empt an attempt by the directors to fight back. If their company is acquired by another they are likely to lose their jobs, a matter not only of money but of vocation, or at any rate a great deal of their power and initiative. But if the price offered is well above that ruling on the stock exchange it will be very difficult to dissuade the shareholders from selling. Another way of avoiding an expensive struggle is to bribe the directors by offers of golden-handshakes or contracts with enhanced salaries after the merger. Generally both devices are applied.

In the first five years of Geneen's rule ITT had acquired Avis, Bramwell Business College, the Nancy Taylor Secretarial Finishing School of Chicago, APCOA (a car-park company), Cleveland Motels, Transportation Displays, as well as insurance companies, mutual funds, pump companies, lamp-makers, publishers, builders, chemical manufacturers and Continental Baking – the biggest bakery company in the United States. (Ibid. pp. 78–80.) Sheraton Hotels were swallowed without difficulty, but American Broadcasting Companies escaped. (Ibid. pp. 81–90.) In 1968 mergers followed with the Canteen Corporation (the leading company in automated food-vending) and the Grinnell Corporation that made 87 per cent of the alarms for American fire stations.

Then, at the end of 1968, Geneen announced what was to be the biggest merger in American history, with the Hartford Fire Company, whose assets totalled nearly two billion dollars. (Ibid. pp. 135–6.)

It was at this stage that the Anti-Trust Act was invoked, under the direction of Richard McLaren. He fought vigorously and deftly against ITT's plans to acquire Canteen and Hartford. There was every indication that he would be successful, and then, abruptly, in June 1971, he announced a settlement. ITT would divest itself of Avis, Canteen, Levitt Houses and part of Grinnell, and would undertake in future not to acquire without special approval any company in the United States with assets of $100 million or more, but they would be permitted to keep Hartford Insurance. (Ibid. p. 156.)

> And the Hartford, as Geneen and Rohatyn had predicted, proved to be a gold-mine for ITT. Already in 1970 it accounted for a quarter of ITT's earnings – more than the whole ITT telecommunications business – and in the next two years the Hartford earnings showed spectacular increases. ... The acquisition of Hartford, with its huge equity investments, made the ITT balance sheet, with its inheritance of heavy debts, look much more healthy. ...   (Ibid. p. 160.)

Why, asks Sampson, did McLaren so suddenly change his mind? Six months later he left the Anti-Trust division to become a federal judge in Chicago, but the mystery remained until the publication of a curious document in February 1972. This was a secret memorandum purporting to come from one official of ITT to another, also dated June 1971, demonstrating a link between the anti-trust settlement and a guarantee of $400 000 by ITT to the Republican Party towards the cost of holding their convention in San Diego. This brought the Attorney-General, John Mitchell, and President Nixon into the act. Sampson tells the story, and gives an account of the ensuing senatorial inquiries, in chapters 9 and 10 of his book.

At about the same time that ITT was fighting to retain Hartford they were also engaged in the protection of their telephone subsidiary in Chile. Their activities here were revealed by Jack Anderson, the same columnist who had publicised the Hartford–San Diego affair, and, again, the US Senate intervened by setting up a subcommittee to investigate the activities abroad of American corporations. One of the prime-movers now was John McCone, a director of ITT who had previously been director of the CIA. The aim of this exercise was to prevent the election of Salvadore Allende to the presidency of Chile, and, once this had failed, to have him overthrown. ITT continued negotiating with Allende for compensation for the nationalisation of their telephone company, a claim valued at $92 million, but after Jack Anderson had made his allegations, the company was expropriated. Allende was in due course the victim of a military take-over, but ITT's claim against the US Overseas Private Investment Corporation for compensation for the loss of their Chilean company was refused, on the grounds that they had failed to disclose material information and had increased the risk of loss 'by failing to preserve administrative remedies'. (Ibid. p. 244.)

How does a multinational control its empire? Colonel Behn's task had been simplified because the company had been concerned mainly with telecommunications. In one war-time conversation, monitored by the State Department, he tells his Argentinian director, 'Tomorrow is always late', and, 'I tell you what I've always found: that when a vice-president didn't want to see me, that was just the time for me to go.' (Ibid. p. 36.) But Geneen had converted ITT into a conglomerate engaged in wildly disparate lines of business. They had only one important thing in common: they were all different ways of making money.

> Geneen gradually set up the most intricate and rigorous system of financial control that the world has ever seen. Weekly meetings, monthly meetings, annual meetings, were summoned to keep check on the managers; a special room with a great horse-shoe table was constructed, where Geneen could inspect and question the managers and their accounts. The head of each company was required to submit to headquarters a monthly report of such complexity that it required a special department to compile it; five-year plans were prepared, targets set, profits compared. Each detail was analysed and cross-checked, so that Geneen, poring over his books in Park Avenue, could tell exactly which of his products, in any part of the world, was failing to reach expectations. He made it clear that he had to know about everything, to be warned of any likely disaster. He insisted that, 'You can't hide mistakes – even from yourself.' And to all his managers he repeated his ominous warning: 'I don't want any surprises.' (Ibid. p. 68.)

ITT subsidiaries are proud of their independence, but the way to preserve that independence is to show a nicely-rising profits curve. Each department of the subsidiary is monitored at head office. 'As soon as the red flag goes up, the experts will move in and "swarm over him." Or, to use another ITT phrase, "Geneen unleashes the pack"'. (Ibid. p. 119.)

Does the system work? Is this an efficient way to organise the production and distribution of goods and services? Sampson quotes Robert Townsend, who reckons it does not. He was a director of Avis who left soon after ITT had acquired it, and then wrote *Up the Organization* (London: Michael Joseph, 1970) to present his point of view. On monthly reports he wrote, 'It's a joke because it consumes ten pounds of energy to produce each ounce of misunderstanding.' (Ibid. p. 75.)

In 1980 ITT came 21st in *Fortune*'s list of the largest industrial companies in the world (Aug. 1981, p. 205). International Business Machines (IBM) came 11th. IBM began life at about the same time as ITT, although its name was first the Computer Tabulating Recording Company and it only became IBM in 1924. IBM was also dominated by a tyrannical messiah (or messianic tyrant) and only became secularised, as it were, when he retired in the middle-1950s. His name was Thomas John Watson. In due course he was succeeded by his sons, Thomas J. Watson Jr and Arthur Kitteridge Watson (Dick), who proceeded to carve it up into divisions in charge of each of which was a man whose power vied with their own. For the story that follows I rely on William Rodgers, *Think: The Amazing Story of IBM* (London: Panther Books, 1971).

Thomas Watson was born in 1874 in the State of New York. He did a course in book-keeping, worked for a while as book-keeper to a butcher, and then became a salesman. From 1903 to 1914 he worked for National Cash Register.

NCR was owned by John Henry Patterson. Patterson beautified his factories and provided all sorts of facilities for his workers.

When money began to pour in, as it did after a few years, Patterson built more factories in garden settings, with broad drives leading to them and riding paths leading to outlying trails. Executives were persuaded – compelled is the more precise word – to ride horses for their health and well-being, regardless of their skills or inclinations. Some suffered broken bones and bruises until they learned, and one family breadwinner on Patterson's management staff was thrown from his horse and killed. Horseback rides began at dawn; the men were called 'the National Cash Rough Riders' by the populace. But Patterson was in dead earnest about horsemanship, and Watson was not with the company long before he, too, was out on the dawn patrol. When Dayton unveiled a monument to Patterson's memory, it was predictably in the form of a great heroic statue of him on a horse. (Rodgers, p. 41.)

Patterson could not bear the idea of other cash registers competing with his own and, with the help of Watson and other salesmen, proceeded to rid himself of the opposition. Dealers in second-hand machines were put out of business (this was Watson's department), competitors were crippled with legal actions for infringement of patent which, however unjustified they might be, involved the competitor in waste of time and money, while his customers, too, would be threatened by legal action. (Rodgers, pp. 46–7.) The day of retribution came at last – Patterson, Watson and others were charged under the Anti-Trust Act, found guilty of criminal conspiracy in restraint of trade and maintaining a monopoly, and were given the maximum sentences: a year in jail and fines of $5000 each. (Rodgers, p. 66.) But, as sometimes happens in these cases, the sentences were in due course set aside on appeal and a new trial ordered. By that time Watson had left NCR to go to the company that would later become IBM. The retrial never took place.

Watson's career with NCR ended in 1913. He had offended Patterson, who first ostracised and then fired him (ibid. p. 72). The next year Charles R. Flint offered to put him in charge of C-T-R (the Computer Tabulating Recording Company) that he had instituted as the holding company of three subsidiaries making equipment for measuring and recording. One of these was the Tabulating Machine Company, owning the punched-card patents and services of Ilerman Hollerith. Watson began as general manager but, once the anti-trust convictions were set aside, became president, but it was not until 1924, when the other top men had vanished from the scene, that his supremacy became unchallenged. C-T-R, renamed IBM, had become the leader in the punched-card field and Watson concentrated his attention on what he knew best – salesmanship.

Watson established the One Hundred Percent Club under whose banner were held gatherings to which were admitted salesmen who had achieved their full quota of sales. Delegates from IBM plants were also admitted, while salesmen who had not reached their quota were sent on tours of the plants. Rodgers quotes Watson: 'We want each of you gentlemen from the factories to select two or three salesmen whom you have met on their visits to our plants and act as sponsor for them. Write them and ask them what you can do to help them get into the One Hundred Percent Club. Tell them about your visit to the One Hundred Percent Club meeting. Tell them you missed seeing their faces there. ... It is a shame for any man, if he is in good health, to put in twelve months in a territory in our business and not come through with 100 percent of quota. He is not cheating anyone as much as he is cheating himself and his family. ... Let us see if you cannot help them to take a little more interest in doing more for the people who are dear to them – their own families, their wives and children.' (Rodgers, p. 97.)

Watson had sold himself to IBM – of course at a very good price. He began, in 1914, at $25 000 a year, 'more than 1200 shares of stock, and a profit-sharing arrangement which, in time, worked out at five per cent of profits after taxes and dividend payments'. Within twenty years he was getting a thousand dollars a day. (Ibid. p. 78.) All employees were expected to reflect his loyalty and devotion, as well as his style of dress: white shirts, ties, dark suits. They were expected (though not directed) to go regularly to church. Nor was there a specific ban on the appointment of Catholics, Jews, women or blacks. (Ibid. pp. 104–5.) At sales conventions the day began with the Lord's Prayer, though Watson questioned whether it need be said on subsequent days, when there might be substituted for it one of the IBM chaplain's 'good' sales talks. (Ibid. pp. 110–11.) Every office was required to display its THINK sign.

Indeed, IBM was very much like a modern Japanese corporation and may, perhaps, have been the model on which they are patterned? At company conferences and ceremonies, they sang songs from the IBM songbook, including the company anthem, *Ever Onward*, the chorus of which ended

> So let us sing, men! SING, MEN!
> Once or twice then sing again
> For the EVER ONWARD IBM.
>
> (Ibid. p. 130.)

There were interminable banquets at which prizes would be acknowledged by three-minute speeches from those who received them. 'Watson would sometimes choke up at these presentations, his eyes shimmering with tears – even though he had previously inspected the inscription and approved the expenditure for engraving it.' (Rodgers, p. 135.) But humiliation was the punishment for those who misbehaved. Rodgers records:

> At one such banquet the attention span of two or three men far in the back of the ballroom wavered, and they got to talking softly among themselves. Watson stopped speaking and coldly, at length, addressed himself to them, almost as though they were alone in the room.
> 'Now, you men there; I don't know what you're talking about, but you can't be listening. You are employees of this company, being paid to come here and listen and learn what your colleagues, and perhaps even I, have to teach you. I am not concerned whether you respect me or think I can tell you anything or not. I would be more concerned if you insult the speakers I am going to introduce to you. I can't understand how you could allow yourselves to do what you've been doing, even when I'm speaking. To men who follow me, it would be outrageous. I want you to understand that this company is going on forever. Unless you realize this, you do not belong to this company.
> As long as you gabble as you have done here, or if it occurs again, just remember the implications of what I've told you. You do not belong in a company that is a world institution that is going on for ever.' (Ibid. pp. 136–7.)

Watson admired both Franklin D. Roosevelt and Adolf Hitler, though Roosevelt's friendship cooled and Hitler's Order of Merit, that Watson had received in Berlin in 1937, was ultimately returned to the German Government. (Ibid. pp. 138 and 145.)

IBM specialised in a branch of technology in which there was enormous development. They began with the advantage of Hollerith's inventions, developed them and dominated the market because, under Watson's inspiration, to survive as a salesman in IBM you had to be a zealot. After his death (at the age of 82) in 1956, his son Tom succeeded to the presidency and set about a process of modernisation. IBM has survived as one of the most successful and fastest-growing American giants. It has the resources to employ scientists and engineers of first-rate ability. They develop their ideas in various countries about the world as part of a world organisation whose nerve systems are co-ordinated at company headquarters at Armonk, in the State of New York. (See Christopher Tugendhat, *The Multinationals*, Harmondsworth: Penguin Books, 1973, pp. 153–5.)

6.4 INTERPRETATIONS

What sort of animal are we dealing with? Can we make useful generalisations about its characteristics, nature, habits? Is it friendly or dangerous? Does it flourish best in the wild or can it be trapped and tamed? Or must we distinguish not one but many sorts of animal, ranging from lions to rabbits, or even ants to elephants?

Bourgeois economic theory begins and ends with the dictum that firms will equate marginal costs with marginal revenue and thus qualify for the title 'maximiser'. But any entrepreneur who believed this was all he needed to do would soon be eliminated by the Watsons and Geneens whose preoccupation is with selling, and outmanœuvring the opposition. With equal single-mindedness Marxist theory has focused on another facet: business firms are exploiters – that is, concerned with the expropriation of surplus value. He who does not maximise shall perish, proclaim the bourgeois prophets; no, he who does not expropriate shall perish, the Marxists reply. Neither dictum takes us very far along the path of understanding.

If we wish to understand, there is really no alternative to systematic observation of the origin, growth and behaviour of the inhabitants of our field of study. The difficulty is that an essential part of this process consists in separating the relevant from the irrelevant, and the classification of the relevant features so that their importance and interconnexions are revealed, and so that generalisations and simplifications can be made.

One simplifying feature of great importance is the dominance of the business world by giant organisations, the measurement of whose size and growth we dealt with in Section 6.1 of this chapter. There is no problem in identifying a few companies who produce and market the greater part of the production of particular industries: oil, chemicals, metals, soap, whisky. . . .

There are certain characteristics that all businesses share: the fact that they are engaged in purchase and sale, that, if they are to survive, their sales must exceed their purchases; their system of book-keeping; the company acts that give them limited liability and make them, in varying degrees, publicly accountable. We can, again, identify certain roles in all businesses, though in very small businesses some of them are doubled-up: salesmen, accountants, technologists, buyers, and the managers who plan and supervise everyone else.

In Subsection 6.2.3 we examined studies of business leaders. There is much complaint in the modern world about invasions of privacy, yet business leaders are expected to allow their private lives to be invaded by their companies, and their wives, too, are expected to play their allotted roles. They are paid enormous salaries and denied the opportunity of spending them.

In Subsection 6.2.4 we examined some of the attempts to encompass organisations in a theory concerned with human-behaviour-within-groups. We quoted that wonderfully discerning study made by Berle and Means nearly fifty years ago:

> The rise of the modern corporation has brought a concentration of economic power which can compete on equal terms with the modern state.... The state seeks in some aspects to regulate the corporation, while the corporation, steadily becoming more powerful, makes every effort to avoid such regulation. Where its own interests are concerned, it even attempts to dominate the state.

Simon identified, and named, the phenomenon of 'bounded rationality' within an organisation, arising partly from incompleteness of knowledge, partly from incompatibility of aims, for interdepartmental rivalries may submerge the aims of the organisation as a whole (above, p. 79). Joan Woodward goes even further in revealing elements of irrationality in organisation.

But the theories have become less determinate, the regularities less pronounced, as research proceeds, and the calls from Barnard, Simon and Starback for 'data on nearly every aspect of organizational growth and development' are still appropriate.

In Section 6.3 we turned to case studies of businessmen and companies that illustrate the degree of eccentricity in their behaviour. Some of their greatest successes involved the lavish, indeed extravagant, use of resources, or the discovery of a formula for profit-making with which, for long periods, the firm could not go wrong.

Can we, on the basis of all this material, formulate a vision or view or paradigm of 'the business corporation' that will serve as a map or guide for further exploration? How should we conceive the corporate system, that Berle and Means compared with the once-dominant feudal system? Despite the laws by which they are regulated the leaders of the great companies have a great deal of freedom of action. At annual general meetings they generally have enough proxies to be able to outvote any individual shareholders who have turned nasty. A proxy is the written authority that shareholders give to someone to vote on their behalf. The representatives of the institutional shareholders (insurance companies, pension funds, investment trusts, banks) will

The Profit-seekers 105

generally support them out of fraternal feeling. Very rarely do they combine to outvote the board. Even the board of directors is very much in the power of the full-time officers. As Robert Townsend describes it (*Up the Organization*, p. 48):

> While ostensibly the seat of all power and responsibility, directors are usually the friends of the chief executive put there to keep him safely in office. They meet once a month, gaze at the financial window dressing (never at the operating figures by which managers run the business), listen to the chief and his team talk superficially about the state of the operation, ask a couple of dutiful questions, make token suggestions (courteously recorded and subsequently ignored) and adjourn until next month.

A factor that enables businessmen to avoid the searching glances of government inspectors is the international scope of their activities. The possession of subsidiaries in a number of countries greatly expands the capacity of firms to reduce taxation, while under- or over-invoicing enables them to shift funds from country to country despite the existence of regulations for exchange control. Companies used to be prisoners in their own countries; we saw, in the example of ITT, how they can now operate successfully in countries that are at war with each other. It is their transnational scope that some people regard as the most remarkable feature of modern business:

> While U.S. firms still hold a commanding lead in the internationalization of production and the development of the global market, the world corporation is far more than an American challenge. Japan- and West Europe-based global companies have expanded aggressively in such traditional U.S. economic preserves as Brazil. U.S. world production figures illustrate the sharp decline in the American domination of the global market. In 1953 the United States was responsible for 69.8 percent of the world motor-vehicle production; by 1968 the U.S. share of the total was down to 37.9 percent. Twenty years ago the United States produced 75 percent of all television sets in the world; now U.S. companies produce less than 25 percent , and as of 1973 only a few black-and-white sets were still being made in the United States. The same trend exists in many other big industries, including crude steel, plastics, cargo ships, and synthetic rubber. But despite the increasing concern in the United States about 'foreign penetration' of the U.S. economy by

Arab sheiks and Japanese firms, U.S. companies are far in the lead in the race to control the new global economy. (Richard J. Barnet and Ronald E. Müller, *Global Reach: The Power of the Multinational Corporations*, New York: Simon & Schuster, 1974, p. 27.)

And,

The introduction of the global payroll has produced dramatic changes in world labor markets. The essential strategy of the global corporation is based on the international division of labor. Top management continues to be recruited from rich countries; workers increasingly come from low-wage areas. For a world corporation it is an ideal combination. While automation continues to reduce the amount of labor relative to capital used in the manufacturing process, wage differentials are becoming more critical in maintaining competitive profit margins as between the global corporations themselves. Thus, a few years ago only the most labor-intensive industries would go abroad looking for cheap help. Today Fairchild Camera, Texas Instruments, and Motorola have settled in Hong Kong to take advantage of the $1-a-day, seven-day-working-week conditions there. Timex and Bulova make an increasing share of their watches in Taiwan, where they share a union-free labor pool with RCA, Admiral, Zenith, and a large number of other corporatons. Kodak imports its top seller, the 'Instamatic,' from Germany. Polaroid is now the only major camera being manufactured in the United States. European companies are also moving to Southeast Asia. Rollei, having figured out that wages make up 60 percent of the cost of the modern complex camera and that wages are six times higher in Germany than in Singapore, has built a huge factory in that 'heavenly city of the global corporations,' as Singapore's Foreign Minister recently billed his industrious little island. (It is heavenly in large part because the government guarantees freedom from union trouble for a given number of years if the foreign companies will agree to make a minimum dollar investment.) (Ibid. pp. 29-30.)

Richard Eells, another student of big business activities, also explores the consequences of the emergence of this 'new sovereign force on the world stage' (or at least their 'quasi-sovereignty'). (*Global Corporations: The Emerging System of World Economic Power*, New York: The Free Press, 1972 and 1976, p. 241.) Christopher Tugendhat cites 'three potentially explosive aspects' of their power: 'These are the companies' power to allocate markets, their freedom of choice about where to invest, and their ability to move vast sums of money between different countries and currencies.' (*The Multinationals*, Harmondsworth: Penguin Books, 1971, p. 249.)

The vision or view, paradigm or conceptual system that we construct must be one that can digest the bizarreries of business behaviour: for instance, on 25 April 1982 the *Sunday Times Business News* had two stories illustrative of the business world – 'Rowland in talks with Israeli arms company', and 'The Humiliation of Lew Grade'. Tiny (so-called because he is so large) Rowland is a star-member of the cast of international entrepreneurs, his company, Lonrho, 35th amongst UK industrial companies in *The Times*' list. Its profit before tax was £160 000 in 1961 and £119 100 000 in 1980. It is a conglomerate whose subsidiaries operate in agriculture, agricultural equipment, machinery, motors, hotels, publishing, finance and trade. Rowland is one of the few chief executives who has retained close personal bonds with African presidents while maintaining important business interests in South Africa. They are active in Nigeria, Kenya, Zambia, Zimbabwe, Egypt, Sudan. But incursions into Israel will cause trouble with the Kuwaiti-owned Gulf Fisheries, who hold 15 per cent of Lonrho stock. In an interview with *Haaretz*, an Israeli daily paper, Rowland said, 'The Arab boycott is pure nonsense. I know my Arab partners well, especially the Royal family of Kuwait. They are interested in making profits so I don't see any reason why they would oppose my new involvement in Israel.' Is this an illustration of the power of business over ideology, political naïveté or a change in the Near East line-up?

The Associated Communications Corporation, chairman Lord Grade, was one of those companies who, through its television franchise, was given 'a licence to print money' as he cogently put it. They produced the Muppets and *On Golden Pond*, but lost £17½ million on *Raise the Titanic*. When the ageing Grade's entravagance began to worry his fellow-directors, they appointed a managing director, Jack Gill, to head a finance committee to bring things under control. But internal rivalries forced Gill to retire – with a golden handshake of £650 000. Then came a take-over bid from Robert Holmes a'Court, like Rupert Murdoch, a tough Australian who has invaded the British business scene. He made an offer of £36 million for the company, that the directors were accepting when Gerald Ronson of Heron International out-bid him with an offer of £42.5 million. Holmes a'Court raised his bid to match this and, with four directors voting against, the board accepted his new offer. Now poor Grade, who is only 75 and had reckoned to go on running ACC until 2001, has been ousted. He gets 5 per cent of the takings on *Jesus of Nazareth*, but will have no pension from ACC. 'Not that Lew Grade will be a pauper. He will collect near £¼ million for his non-voting and voting shares. But he was a tycoon and lived like one; he spent what came in and was generous to charities. What mattered was the job, not the money.' (Patience Wheatcroft, 'The Humiliation of Lew Grade', London: *The Sunday Times*, 25 Apr. 1982, p. 57.)

Sometimes two companies may agree to merge for their mutual benefit; at other times a predator company will assault a victim. The victim will desperately seek allies and appeal to its shareholders not to desert, but these acts of aggression are pursued with the callousness of an invading tribe, though the uniform is the pin-stripe suit and the venue the stock exchange or boardroom. Why is it done? Sometimes, as in the case of ITT, it is a field-marshal diversifying his forces, making each unit more effective by fitting it into a huge army; sometimes one lot of directors reckon they could do better than another with a company's resources; sometimes asset-stripping is the motive. Sometimes it happens that the value of a company's shares, as shown by their stock-exchange quotation, amounts to less than could be realised if the company was dismembered and its assets sold. In that case its purchase and dismemberment could be effected at a profit.

Thus any company with valuable assets but low earnings is vulnerable to asset-strippers. The British firm of F. W. Woolworth, for instance, has fixed assets the current value of which it assessed at £761 168 000 as at 31 January 1982. Its issued ordinary stock consists of 378 496 000 units of 25p. Their price on the London stock exchange on Thursday, 22 April 1982 was 47p. 378 496 000 × 47p = £177 893 000. From the fixed assets you must deduct the current liabilities (creditors, bank loans and overdrafts, current taxation and proposed final dividend) amounting to £272 830 000. But, again, you may add the stock, valued at £195 million.

Thus you could offer the shareholders two or three times the stockmarket value for their shares, and still clean up handsomely. Of course, you would have to sell off the stock for a good deal less than £195 million in order to get rid of it, and then disposing of the properties would take time and be a bit risky, even though they have prime city-centre sites. I bought shares in Woolworths many years ago, calculating that their assets could only rise in value. Unfortunately, sales and profits failed to keep pace and share prices followed a downward trend. Hence the present predicament. And, after this was written, Woolworths was indeed taken over!

Along with asset stripping goes a stripping of social obligations. Even though the taken-over firm may continue as a going concern the bond of responsibility for long-service employees is broken. Output per employee may be raised by a ruthless pruning of the labour force.

Of course it is much easier to acquire another firm if you can get their board of directors to agree, sell you their shares and recommend the other shareholders to do likewise. Hence the golden-handshakes and offers of highly paid jobs that often accompany these exercises.

A final motive sometimes present in take-overs is an elemental lust for power. Occasionally, when two or more companies are pursuing the same quarry, the price offered is thus bid up to ridiculous levels.

One aspect that we have seen emphasised is the multinationals' ability to avoid control by governments. Taxation, customs duties, import-export regulation, exchange control, health, wage, factory regulations may all be circumvented by a judicious disposition of funds and resources.

The Vestey family provide an interesting case study of how, with perfect propriety, liability for tax may be reduced (see Phillip Knightley's reports in the *Sunday Times*, 5 and 19 October and 2 November 1980). One of their 246 companies is Dewhurst with its 1400 butcher's shops. In 1978 Dewhurst's profits amounted to £2 380 000. On this, they paid £10 in tax. Over the previous five years, on profits of £8 831 216, they had paid £215 in tax. The annual report for 1978 explained, 'There is no liability to UK taxation as the total taxable profit will be relieved by losses in other group companies.'

At the end of the First World War, the Vesteys established a family trust, the trustees of which could lend funds interest-free – which they proceeded to do, to themselves. But could it then be deemed that these loans were their income? The House of Lords, in 1979, answered no. 'To say of a man who may direct that the trust income should be invested in a loan to himself that he has the beneficial enjoyment of that income is a misuse of language ... the words point to an out-and-out disposal of the income for the benefit of some person or persons and are wholly inappropriate to an investment by way of loan.' (*The Sunday Times*, 19 Oct 1980, p. 63.)

In the models of perfect and imperfect competition, morality and man-made law are assumed away. The maximising buyer is proof against malpractices and the maximising seller knows it. This is ensured by natural or God-given law, and so, it was effectively argued, the concern of governments to protect their citizens was misdirected. I shall argue that it is quite true that, for the most part, traders give their customers a fair deal, not because they have no alternative but because they prefer doing so. They enjoy the good opinion of their clients. Organisations generally have enough problems without adding to them by contraventions of the law but, protected by their corporate spirit, they are capable, on occasion, of behaving reprehensibly and for that reason have got to be watched.

Strangely enough, Adam Smith was much concerned with this danger, comparing 'the violence and injustice of the rulers of mankind' with 'the mean rapacity, the monopolizing spirit of merchants and manufacturers'. The tribes of manufacturers, like an overgrown standing army 'have become formidable to the government, and upon many occasions intimidate the legislature'.

> The member of parliament who supports every proposal for strengthening this monopoly, is sure to acquire not only the reputation of understanding trade, but great popularity and influence with an order of men whose numbers and wealth render them of great importance. If he opposes them, on the contrary, and still more if he has authority enough to be able to thwart them, neither the acknowledged probity, nor the highest rank, nor the greatest publick services can protect him from the most infamous abuse and detraction, from personal insults, nor sometimes from real danger, arising from the insolent outrage of furious and disappointed monopolists. (*Wealth of Nations*, bk IV, chap. ii, Glasgow ed., p. 471.)

An article in *Fortune*, 1 December 1980, asks 'How Lawless Are Big Companies?' and replies, 'Of the 1,043 major corporations in the study, 117, or 11 per cent, have been involved in at least one major delinquency in the period covered. Some companies have been multiple offenders. In all, 188 citations are listed covering 163 separate offenses – kickbacks, bribery or illegal political contributions; 11 cases of fraud; and five cases of tax evasion.'

By the nature of things it is only those who are found out who get into the records, but this distinction has been achieved by some of the most solid and respectable companies who, on occasion, are capable of perpetrating the most squalid crimes. Their offences against the environment are well known and have been well publicised. It is only by an immense effort by the environmentalists that the flood of pollution has been reversed. Lakes, rivers, forests and seas have been poisoned and are coming back to life only by painful effort. Worse effects may well be waiting in the wings. The arms race, in which the great corporations are heavily involved, threatens the future of mankind and of the world.

Robert L. Heilbroner, Morton Mintz and others have produced a volume of case studies of shady dealings by companies of standing. (*In the Name of Profit*, New York: Doubleday, 1972.) A number of the contributors were employees who turned state-evidence and have since become investigative journalists. It is interesting to see how errors and miscalculation can lead to deception, and how deception draws people into deeper and deeper trouble.

> Vandivier spoke to Lawson's boss, John Warren, and told him they were perpetrating a fraud. Warren: 'I'll admit it's not right, but it's just one of those things. We're kinda caught in the middle. About all I can tell you is, Do like I'm doing. Make copies of everything and put them in your SYA file.'
> 'What's an "SYA" file?' I asked.
> 'That's a "save your ass" file.'
> (Kermit Vandivier, 'Why should my conscience bother me?' in Heilbroner *et al.*, chap. 1, p. 12.)

The case of the Firestone 500 has been well publicised. So has that of the Ford Pinto (see, particularly, *The Ford Motor Company*, London: Counter Information Services, Anti-Report No. 20, undated). So has the bribery that was a common sales-technique of aircraft and other companies. It is interesting to see that it was United States Government agencies that uncovered the slush-money scandals, while the British Government preferred to pretend that it was a non-British problem. In their outline of their government's views presented in January 1979 to the UN Committee on Illicit Payments, the British delegation stated, 'That corruption is a feature of international trade is genuinely repugnant to the UK Government and UK trading enterprises. The UK will not tolerate corruption in its own territory, and within the limits of its own jurisdiction, will continue to eradicate it.' (See Alex Brummer, 'Bribes begin at Calais', London: *The Guardian*, 26 Feb. 1979.) This is a surprising view in the light of the revelations of the Poulson case in the early 1970s, and of the multitude of cases that have emerged since then.

But it is important to note that bribery and corruption were not invented by business corporations. They are short-cuts to the acquisition of wealth that are resorted to by people in the public as well as the private service, and in socialist and pre-industrial as well as capitalist countries. A series of cases have emerged from the Crown Agents in Britain, who are supposed to be dedicated to the service of the struggling countries of the British Commonwealth. A professional and technical officer in the Property Services Agency of the Department of the Environment in London is sent to prison for six months for demanding gifts in response to government contracts. His defence counsel stated, 'He found himself in an environment where there was almost total lack of moral standards. Once he reached a relatively senior position for a man of his age he found that corruption was rife, and not only at his level but above him.' (*The Times*, 23 Mar. 1982.)

The bourgeoisie achieved wealth and power under the banner of *laissez-faire*. Now it is curious to see it becoming more and more common for them to demand public funds, free or subsidised power and accommodation and remissions of taxation before they agree to invest in a particular town or country, or to persuade them not to close an existing plant. The British Government put up or guaranteed nearly £90 million to persuade John DeLorean to open a car factory in Northern Ireland. It has taken great injections of public funds to keep Chrysler and British Leyland on their feet. In the United States and Europe, cities compete with one another in the facilities offered to persuade industrialists to come their way. But government officials are ill-equipped in law or experience to control the companies into which funds are channelled, and the officials themselves, alas, are sometimes liable to be bought.

6.4.1 Participant observation

'Learning against a background of no experience means that there is no way of assessing the importance or the relevance of what is being taught', said the Duke of Edinburgh, which I thought quite clever of him. (Philip Howard, 'Duke of all trades, master of most', *The Times*, 26 Apr. 1982, p. 6.) It is, indeed, impossible to judge the importance or relevance of what has been said in this chapter about business enterprises unless you have worked for one. In my youth I worked for Siemens Brothers (British) and then for General Electric (American, not British). Later, as an official of the Industrial Council for the Clothing Industry I was able to observe the activities of manufacturers and their workers. Later still, as research worker, I saw things from without instead of from within. Nowadays, in Britain and the United States, most students, particularly graduate students, have had some experience as employees of business or other sorts of organisation, and I have encouraged those whom I supervised to draw on that experience and work it into their thought and writings. It is surprising how difficult it is for them to do so, for the material of their experience often seems foreign to that of the learned books and journals to which they are referred. Thus it is that academic thought avoids confrontation with the real world.

But it is the real world that we must confront. In it, life goes on; people are born, educated, earn their living, pursue their pleasures and die. We are, nearly all of us in advanced capitalist countries, dependent for our everyday existence on multinational corporations. In particular we have become richer than it seemed mankind could ever become because of the economies of mass production. It developed first in the textile industry and then was applied by Henry Ford to engineering, and as a result of that, suddenly, within a few years, ordinary working families could afford carriages. About the same time we were beginning to afford electric light, running water, sewerage, stoves that could be switched on and off. Mass production in great factories was an essential condition for all this.

Again, in day-to-day existence, people deal fairly honestly with each other. In fact a very large part of it consists of routine where standards have been long since established. We talk of built-in obsolescence, but the typewriter that I am now using is 14 years old and still in perfect order. My other typewriter, now used by another member of my family, is 43 years old and still works well. Public criticism has at last persuaded the car manufacturers to produce cars resistant to rust and guaranteed against it. There is abundant evidence that manufacturers generally like producing good products and take some pride in doing so. We should be on our guard, but do not have continually to be so.

Now let us take a view of organisations from within. The element neglected in organisation theory is that of bureaucracy: not the bureaucracy modelled by Weber – a machine performing its tasks with mechanical precision – but a bureaucracy intent on defending itself. Assemble a group of people, give them a task, and they will soon be looking for ways of increasing their own comfort. They will mystify their own functions so that outsiders cannot fully understand what they are doing; they will begin a gradual but persistent attempt to increase their revenue, to create and protect their perquisites and raise their own status in the eyes of those with whom they do business.

Like the hunters and gatherers from whom we draw our heritage, they will generate and maintain a sense of identity with and loyalty to the band. Business corporations, especially in the United States, have a reputation for ruthlessness, and on occasion they act ruthlessly, especially when they are fighting for survival or when there is an internal struggle for power. But for most of the time they are tolerant towards those members of the firm who are worn out before retiring age: they will find them a soft job rather than cast them out. But it is the acts of ruthlessness of which we hear rather than the acts of tolerance, simply because the latter are too usual to be noteworthy.

The jargon of organisation theory suggests to me that the theorists regard organisations as much more purposive than they really are. Simon speaks of goal identification and bounded rationality: bounded in part because of incompleteness of knowledge, in part from incompatibility of aims. I would add a third bound to the rationality of people, not infrequently encountered in organisations: those who are simply confused about what they are supposed to be doing. It is easy, then, to identify their goal: it is to prevent other people from finding out. There are others who, though still employed *de jure*, have *de facto* long since given up work. The higher you rise in a department and the more people you have under your control, the easier it is to do this. The underlings may positively enjoy the extra responsibility placed on their shoulders and the element of freedom that accrues from having a delinquent boss, and it may be years before the latter is found out. If this happens before his date of retirement, he is likely to be disposed of with a golden handshake rather than fired for incompetence.

So we have a great many types to encompass in our typology: great, self-protective bureaucracies; tyrannies with high rewards but ruled by cupidity and fear; millenarian enterprises with zealots obsessed with some brilliant new idea; outfits who make useful things or deliver essential services by highly developed routines. Some of them will be attempting spectacular short-cuts to riches; most of them will be reasonably honest, because they prefer it, and also prefer to make products of which they will be proud, or at least not ashamed.

7 Work and Pay

7.1 THE NATURE OF WORK

The question, 'What is work?' may seem too obvious to merit consideration. There must be very few people who have never done any. But, because it is at the very foundation of economic systems, one of the main (if not the sole) determinant of exchange value, it is worth spending a little time to get it into focus. And, as Yves Simon wrote, 'The daily life of man is composed of things whose meaning is hidden in the mystery of familiarity. Work is one of these.' (*Work, Society, and Culture*, ed. Vukan Kuic, New York: Fordham University Press, 1971, p. 1.)

The etymology of the words used for work gives support to the idea that it is disagreeable and to be avoided. In most European languages and in classical Greek, the word for 'work' is also used for the 'pangs of birth'. The French 'travailler' is derived from tripalium, which was some kind of torture. (Ibid. p. 18.) Labour in birth introduces the idea of pain with a purpose, or productive pain.

It is true that, in his addiction to labour, man is more like the ants and the bees than the other vertebrates. He seems to act under a compulsion to improve upon nature. As Eugen Loebl puts it, to convert natural forces into productive forces, and natural goods into useful goods. (*Humanomics*, New York: Random House, 1976, pp. 21-3.) It is the process by which this is done that we call work. We might define it as, 'those of people's activities that are designed to adapt the environment to meet their wants'.

The labour theory of value states that goods exchange in proportion to the amount of labour necessary to produce them. The subsistence theory of wages, to which it is related, assumed that the working classes worked because they had no alternative. To maintain the supply of labour wages must be sufficient to support a man and wife and enable them to raise a family. Those free of this compulsion would naturally be idle. Jevons, one of the early marginalists, incorporated in his system the notion of work as pain which, in equilibrium, would be just balanced by the pleasure derived from the marginal increment of pay. He defined labour as 'any painful exertion of mind or body undergone partly or wholly with a view to future good'. (W. Stanley Jevons, *The Theory of Political Economy*, London: Macmillan, 1871, chap. V.)

This fitted in neatly with the notion of all economic relationships as consisting of a balance of opposing forces. There was a symmetry of pleasure and pain, in work between labour and wages, in investment between consumption foregone and profit, in consumption between the surrender of money and the enjoyment of goods. The 'marginalists' were so called because they believed this happy state was reached by incremental adjustments – a little more of this or a little less of that, extending or contracting the margin of pain or pleasure.

This is a convenient doctrine for a leisure class, for it teaches that all people would loaf who were under no necessity to work. The industrious cannot claim moral superiority over the idle, for they, too, would be idle if they had the chance.

Yet there is an opposing view of work, for while some avoid it, others, since the beginnings of capitalism, have demanded it as a right, and it came very near to being so inscribed in the laws of the United States by the Employment Act of 1946. It is abundantly clear that, whatever may be said against work, unemployment is regarded as even worse. Dennis Marsden and Euan Duff collected case histories of people unemployed in the 1970s:

> Mr. Haigh said, 'At first it feels marvellous. It's as though you've left the rat race, you're not in it any more and you can look at it and wonder why people bother. You look at them setting off in the morning at 7.30 and coming back at night at half past five, and you think, "Why bother?" The first few days ... [are] like a holiday. ... After a bit you get bored, and by the end of the first week you're bored stiff, and you realize you haven't a place in life.'

Another respondent described his increasing anxiety and the failure of alternative activities:

> You don't realize, not until you've been out for a couple of weeks. It costs money, decorating, and you can't keep it up. Mostly it's just pottering. I get bored stiff ... Sometimes when you're working you wish you had a bit more time to do things, but I'd rather be working now and have no time. Sometimes I get to walking up and down with my hands in my pockets. ... A man *needs* work. If a man hasn't got

work he's half way to being defeated. (Dennis Marsden and Euan Duff, *Workless: Some Unemployed Men and their Families*, Harmondsworth: Penguin Books, 1975, pp. 190-3.)

Of course, the degree of physical hardship has been much reduced compared with the 1930s, with unemployment pay more humanely administered and carrying more than double the purchasing power that it then had, but the psychological effect remains surprisingly similar. For the 1930s Georges Friedmann described it thus:

> Loss of work is often preceded by a period of anxiety, an anxiety which is aggravated when it occurs. The unemployed person shows signs of an emotional instability which increases more or less rapidly and intensely in accordance with his occupational history and the successes or failures he has previously experienced during his working life.... It has been observed generally that after a first period of shock, when the personality resists and remains almost unchanged, there comes a second in which there is a more or less active search for work, the worker's demands constantly decreasing until a paid job of any sort would be accepted. Finally a stage of depression ensues. The loss of the settled framework provided by a job and its daily routine, combined with a decreasing awareness of the passage of time and a kind of apathetic attitude towards it, unite with family complications to produce in the unemployed man a growing inferiority complex as regards the members of his family and particularly his wife and children.

Friedmann emphasises the connexion between work and the family. '... work is also one of the most active ways in which the individual is linked to the family group, forming in many cases its indispensable cement without which both the group and the individual become unbalanced and disintegrate. Loss of work, while constituting a social setback for the unemployed person, also produces after a while a 'toxic condition' requiring complete readaptation.' (Georges Friedmann, *The Anatomy of Work*, London: Heinemann, 1961, pp. 128-9. See, too, Marsden and Duff, *Workless*, chap. 7.)

Perhaps, then, work is not so much a pain to be traded increment by increment for pay, as a human institution necessary to give form and purpose to a person's life? If so, this will have important implications when we come to the consideration of pay.

Certainly work and religion are closely intertwined, though the

Christian and Hebrew Bibles are somewhat ambiguous on the subject. Life in Eden was initially all found and it was as a punishment for curiosity that God decreed, 'In the sweat of thy face shalt thou eat bread'. Likewise as punishment Noah condemned the sons of Ham to be hewers of wood and drawers of water. Jesus hailed the lilies of the field as more glorious than Solomon, though they neither toiled nor span, but Solomon, in his proverbs, did enjoin sluggards to go to the ant, consider his ways and be wise.

But there was no ambiguity in medieval Christian doctrine. Tawney cites the saying *Laborare est orare* – to work is to pray:

> By the Puritan moralist the ancient maxim is repeated with a new and intenser significance. The labour which he idealizes is not simply a requirement imposed by nature, or a punishment for the sin of Adam. It is itself a kind of ascetic discipline, more rigorous than that demanded by any order of mendicants – a discipline imposed by the will of God, and to be undergone, not in solitude, but in the punctual discharge of secular duties. It is not merely an economic means, to be laid aside when physical needs have been satisfied. It is a spiritual end, for in it alone can the soul find health, and it must be continued as an ethical duty long after it has ceased to be a material necessity. (R. H. Tawney, *Religion and the Rise of Capitalism*, Harmondsworth: Penguin Books, 1938, p. 240. The book was first published in 1926.)

In the *Bhagavadgita* the motive to work is explicitly divorced from the thought of profit:

> Therefore, who doeth work rightful to do,
> Not seeking gain from work, that man, O Prince!
> Is Sanyasi and Yogi – both in one
> And he is neither who lights not the flame
> Of sacrifice, nor setteth hand to task.
> Regard as true Renouncer him that makes
> Worship by work ...

And:

> And live in action! Labour! Make thine acts
> Thy piety, casting all self aside,
> Contemning gain and merit ...

(*The Song Celestial*, translated from the Sanskrit by Sir Edwin Arnold, London: Routledge & Kegan Paul, 1972, Book the Sixth, chap. VI, pp. 34 and 13. Arnold dates the poem to the 3rd century A.D., but it is now thought to have been some centuries earlier.)

Marx saw work as fulfilling a vital psychological need. Adam Smith, he remarked, equated *rest* with liberty and happiness.

> It seems to be far from A. Smith's thoughts that the individual, 'in his normal state of health, strength, activity, skill and efficiency', might also require a normal portion of work, and of cessation from rest. It is true that the quantity of labour to be provided seems to be conditioned by external circumstances, by the purpose to be achieved, and the obstacles to its achievement that have to be overcome by labour. But neither does it occur to A. Smith that the overcoming of such obstacles may itself constitute an exercise in liberty, and that these external purposes lose their character of mere natural necessities and are established as purposes which the individual himself fixes. The result is the self-realisation and objectification of the subject, therefore real freedom, whose activity is precisely labour. (David McLellan, *Marx's Grundrisse*, London: Macmillan, 1971, p. 124.)

Mao Tse-tung also regarded work as an integral part of the human personality:

> Above all, Marxists regard man's activity in production as the most fundamental practical activity, the determinant of all his other activities. Man's knowledge depends mainly on his activity in material production, through which he comes gradually to understand the phenomena, the properties and the laws of nature, and the relations between himself and nature; and through his activity in production he also gradually comes to understand, in varying degrees, certain relations that exist between man and man. None of this knowledge can be acquired apart from activity in production. ... This is the primary source from which human knowledge develops. (Mao Tse-tung, *Four Essays on Philosophy*, Peking: Foreign Languages Press, 1966, pp. 1–2.)

This is the answer to Bishop Berkeley and the philosophical idealists who maintained that man could never know the real world, since all he saw of it was his own inner interpretation and projection of the lightwaves that reached him from without. In fact our senses are constantly engaged in exploring ourselves and our surroundings, distinguishing things that threaten us from those that promote our well-being. Our own survival testifies that we have done this well. So, of course, have locusts and shell-fish, though the world they experience is different from our own.

As we go through the day we are constantly testing the accuracy of our interpretations of the world about us, in the only way that matters to us – in so far as we are affected by it. My map of New York City does not look at all like a city. It is in fact a bit of paper. But it tells me that if I take a north-bound train on the 7th Avenue subway from Greenwich Village I will in due course arrive at Columbia University. I do so, and I do. The map did not lie and I have correctly interpreted it. In cultivating, planting, growing, building and making, mankind has for ages been testing the truth of his interpretations. The possession of a job testifies to membership of the human family, the receipt of a paycheck to the fact that your contribution is valued. Conversely, sensory deprivation is one of the quickest ways of breaking down the personality. The victim loses his grip on reality and, in due course, on his political and moral beliefs.

In Freudian terms:

> Stressing the importance of work has a greater effect than any other technique of living in binding the individual more closely to reality; in his work he is at least securely attached to a part of reality, the human community. Work is no less valuable for the opportunity which it, and the human relations connected with it, provide for a very considerable discharge of fundamental libidinal impulses, narcissistic, aggressive and even erotic, than because it is indispensable for subsistence and justifies existence in society. The daily work of earning a livelihood affords especial satisfaction when it has been freely chosen, i.e. when through sublimation it enables use to be made of existing inclinations, of instinctual impulses, hitherto repressed, or more intense than usual for constitutional reasons. (Sigmund Freud, *Civilization and its Discontents*, London: Hogarth Press, p. 34. Quoted in Georges Friedmann, *Anatomy of Work*, p. 126.)

It may seem curious that I am prolonging the discussion of the nature of work, whereas the orthodox texts dismiss it in a few lines. But it seems to me that it is of fundamental importance that we should see the work-function in sharp focus, for it is from work that the substance of economics is derived. If work is a disagreeable or painful intrusion on an ideal state of idleness, then it is something that must be forced on mankind by rewards and punishments. Conflict would then be an unavoidable side-effect between those doing their best to be idle and those trying to make them work.

On the other hand, if the possession of a job is both a right and a privilege, giving the owner identity and social usefulness with the fulfilment of psychological needs, the outlook is altogether different. There follow important implications for employment policy, pay policy and job design. If one begins from the premise that work is inherently painful, then all sorts of painful elements may be tolerated that may, in fact, be susceptible of elimination. On the other hand, certain painful elements may be necessary to the therapeutic action of work: the challenge, strain or stress whose mastery may develop the personality.

Resorting to speculation, I suggest that horror of work may be an acquired characteristic of a leisure class. Certainly in slave societies or those that enforce castes or colour-bars, children of the privileged classes are taught from an early age to regard manual work with distaste. Outside these classes, it is performed as part of the natural order of things, free of the mental agonies of those who believe they have a natural right to avoid it. Animals are by nature programmed to pass through stages of development: helpless and dependent, playful, food-gathering. Here, parents are cast off in favour of a mate. The parental stage is followed by old-age with its return to dependence. The children of the leisure class may be fixated by early pampering so that they never develop the urge or psychological need to work. They can physically survive, oppressed only by the difficulty of devising ways to pass the time. 'Gentlefolks in general have a very awkward rock ahead in life – the rock ahead of their own idleness. Their lives being, for the most part, passed in looking about them for something to do, it is curious to see – especially when their tastes are of what is called the intellectual sort – how often they drift blindfold into some nasty pursuit.' (Wilkie Collins, *The Moonstone*, Harmondsworth: Penguin Books, 1966, p. 84. First published 1868.)

7.2 CLASSIFICATION

We create order out of chaos by ordering phenomena into categories where like is put with like. Initially we divided the world's man- and woman-power by occupations and industries, an occupation being a class consisting of similar jobs, an industry of similar products. Industries are made up of people doing all sorts of jobs; occupations by people doing the same sort of job but in all sorts of industries.

In Chapter 6 we made some reference to employment *status*, in terms of which those gainfully employed are divided into employers, the self-employed (or those working on their own account) and employees. Employees are divided by status into managers and others (that is, those they manage), and, again, into manual- and non-manual workers (synonyms for blue-collar and white-collar, or wage-earners and salary-earners). There are, in addition, but of vanishing importance, unpaid family workers.

The data are also classified in rather more obvious ways: by age, sex, marital status, location, years of full-time education. Manual workers are divided into skilled, semi-skilled and unskilled groups; production or process workers (those engaged on directly making the product of the industry) and maintenance or service workers (whose contribution to the product is indirect). The labour force is divided, too, between the employed and the unemployed.

7.2.1 Sources and uses

I have already mentioned the *Year Book of Labour Statistics*, published in Geneva by the International Labour Office. The United Nations and its agencies have done much to standardise statistics throughout member countries. So have the European Economic Community and the Organisation for Economic Co-operation and Development. In what follows I shall use the OECD's *Labour Force Statistics 1968-1979* (Paris: OECD, 1981) because they present fairly up-to-date and well-standardised data for the advanced capitalist countries.

But of course each of those countries has an elaborate statistical service (from which the international agencies draw their data) to whose publications reference must be made for studies relating to particular countries. Until ten or twenty years ago the most important source was the population census that most countries take every ten years. But with the advance of social services, other sources have been developed, with labour departments making periodic household surveys or requiring employers to submit regular returns. The OECD *Labour Force Statistics* conveniently lists the major publications for each country in which statistics relevant to the labour force may be found. (Ibid. pp. 10-12.)

Manpower analysis can be used to measure the changing contours of status, participation, occupation, industry, employment and unemployment: the changing face of a country as skills change and industries rise and fall. It reveals the continuing subordination of women, and measures their slow and halting progress. The occupational analysis of unemployment and job vacancies shows the extent to which formal and in-plant training are keeping pace with the changing needs of industry.

Employers and self-employed
Pre-industrial societies consist mainly of households engaged in own-account farming, who constitute more than 90 per cent of the work force. A large proportion of the remainder are self-employed traders. As the economy diversifies, the proportion of farmers falls; as its wealth increases, the proportion of traders increases. This is evident in the principal cities of the poor countries, where street traders busy themselves selling to wealthy people immobilised in traffic jams.

Employers become managers as businesses are incorporated; in farming, holdings are consolidated and farmers and labourers leave the land; in retail distribution, supermarkets engulf the corner stores; cafés and hotels give way to the franchise-holders of the big catering chains.

The number of employers and self-employed in Great Britain is estimated to have reached a highpoint of 1 884 000 in 1973, and, by 1979, to have fallen to 1 795 000. (*Employment Gazette*, vol. 90, no. 1, Jan. 1982, pp. 15-16.) But in the United States (see Section 6.1 above) their numbers continued to grow, though much less rapidly than the number of companies. They numbered 7 148 000 in 1969 and 8 233 000 in 1979. (OECD *Labour Force Statistics*, pp. 84-5.) Many move between employee and own-account status, so are hard to enumerate. If they form part of the 'black economy' they do not enter into the official statistics at all.

Participation rates
Age, education, sex, social insurance, wealth, industrial and occupational structure all combine to determine participation rates - that is, the proportion of people in an age-group who offer themselves for employment. Amongst the OECD countries Denmark had the highest participation rate: of the population of working age (aged 15 to 64 years) in 1979, 80.9 per cent were in the labour force (employed or seeking work). Sweden came a close second, with 80.5 per cent. (The Organisation for Economic Co-operation and Development is a sort of rich countries' United Nations. Its members are Canada, the United

States, Japan, Australia, New Zealand, Austria, Belgium, Denmark, Finland, France, Germany, Greece, Iceland, Ireland, Italy, Luxembourg, Netherlands, Norway, Portugal, Spain, Sweden, Switzerland, Turkey and the United Kingdom.) At the other end comes Italy, whose participation rate is only 60.3 per cent. Participation rates for all those aged 15–64, and for males and females, 1969 and 1979, are shown in Table 7.1. Why should there be these wide differences between countries? It has nothing to do with unemployment, for work-seekers are included in the labour force. Observe that the differences in over-all rates are much wider than the differences in the rates for males, that range from 82.3 for Austria to 90.2 for Denmark. The major differences, then, are brought about by the much wider dispersion of female participation rates.

Table 7.1 shows some interesting features. Do you notice how the participation rate has risen in the Scandinavian countries between 1969 and 1979? In Iceland it rose from 67.9 to 73.1 per cent. It rose, too, in the United States, Canada and Portugal. For Portugal we cannot say by how much because there was a break in the coverage between 1969 and 1979. But in the countries lower on the list it hardly

Table 7.1 *Participation rates by sex in 15 OECD countries, 1969 and 1979*

	1969			1979		
	M	F	T	M	F	T
Denmark	91.8	58.0	74.8	90.2	71.6	80.9
Sweden	89.3	57.8	73.7	87.9	72.9	80.5
Norway	88.8	38.1	63.7	87.0	61.7	74.5
United Kingdom	94.7	50.5	72.5	90.0	57.8	73.9
United States	87.6	48.2	67.9	85.6	59.9	72.1
Japan	89.3	55.6	72.1	89.3	54.7	71.8
Finland	83.9	60.1	71.7	77.7	65.7	71.7
Canada	86.2	42.7	64.6	86.4	55.6	71.0
Australia	93.3	44.7	69.5	87.6	50.3	69.3
France	87.7	47.1	67.4	83.2	52.5	68.0
German FR	92.9	48.0	69.4	82.5	49.2	65.7
Austria	85.3	48.9	66.1	82.3	49.6	65.5
New Zealand	92.1	36.1	64.3	85.2	40.4	63.5
Ireland	97.7	34.6	66.5	88.9	35.2	62.5
Italy	87.7	33.6	59.9	82.7	38.8	60.3

Numbers employed or seeking employment as a percentage of those aged 15 to 64.
Source: OECD, *Labour Force Statistics 1968–1979*, Paris, 1981, country tables II.

changed or actually fell. These changes (or failures to change) are the result of two opposing trends: a fall in the participation rate for men, and a rise for women.

In Sweden, of the females aged 15 to 64, nearly three out of four were gainfully employed in 1979. But a smaller proportion of the men in that age span were at work compared with 1969. In 1969 women constituted 37.4 per cent of the labour force; in 1979 45.7 per cent.

Women were flocking in at all ages, but this applied particularly to married women, and still more particularly, to older married women. The pattern seemed to be: get married, stay at work; have children, leave work; children at school, go back to work. At the same time the male participation rate was falling because males were staying longer in full-time education and because they were retiring earlier. In the United States 80.5 per cent of males aged 18 and 19 were at work in 1947, and 89.6 per cent of those aged 55 to 64. In 1977 74.4 per cent of those aged 18 and 19 were at work, and 74.0 per cent of those aged 55 to 64.

The rise in the female participation rate is indicative of a great social change that occurred in some advanced industrial countries after the Second World War, and is no doubt waiting to occur in others. Germany, Austria, New Zealand, Ireland and Italy are somewhat backward in this respect.

During the war masses of women were drawn into the labour force to replace men and increase the production of armaments, but after the war they were rapidly replaced by the returning men or discharged on the closure of munitions plants. In Great Britain in 1951 the female activity rate was 35 per cent, exactly what it had been in 1851. In between it had fallen to 32 per cent in 1901, where it remained in 1911 and 1921, but by 1931 had moved up to 34 per cent. In 1961 it was 36 per cent and, as shown in Table 7.1, by 1969 it had reached 50.5 per cent and, in 1979, it was 57.8 per cent.

Table 7.1 is indicative of cultural changes in countries and of cultural differences between countries. In Muslim countries where, among the orthodox, a woman's face must be kept hidden except within the family, the female participation rate is small; in Italy and Ireland, dominated by Catholic traditionalism, it remains comparatively low. Of course, within each country one would find a wide range of usages and views, from husbands who would refuse to allow their wives to go out to work, to those who absolutely depend on it. These cultural differences are important determinants of the economic state of any country.

7.2.2 Classification by industry

As already mentioned, an occupational classification has regard to what each worker does; an industrial classification, to what he or she contributes to making. Under the former, if you are allocated to agriculture, it means you are employed on the cultivation of plants or animals; under the latter, merely that you work, in no matter what capacity, in a concern producing agricultural products. In the United Kingdom the distinction was made clearly for the first time in the presentation of the findings of the population Census of 1921.

We can get an idea of the industrial architecture of the last century, and its differences from this, by comparing employment in the key industries of Great Britain in 1871 and 1921. This is done in Table 7.2. Mitchell and Deane have reconciled the figures as far as possible, but there remain some differences: the 1871 figures include for each industry those who had retired from it as well as dealers classified, as far as possible, in the raw material in which they dealt.

Table 7.2 *Employment in 9 industrial orders, Great Britain, 1871 and 1921*

	1871 000s	%	1921 000s	%	1921 as % of 1871
Agriculture, horticulture and forestry	1 769	15	1 434	7	81
Mining and quarrying	528	4	1 249	6	237
Chemicals	66	0.6	128	0.7	194
Metals and metal products	915	8	2 300	12	251
Textiles	993	8	1 110	6	122
Domestic offices and personal services	1 908	16	2 216	11	116
Commercial occupations	217	2	1 491	8	687
Professional occupations and their subordinate services	356	3	856	4	240
Public administration	113	1	464	2	411
Other industries	4 887	42	8 106	42	166
Total occupied	11 752	100	19 354	100	165

Source: B. R. Mitchell and Phyllis Deane, *Abstract of British Historical Statistics*, Cambridge University Press, 1962, p. 60.

These statistics give a revealing picture of the societies of their time. In 1871 nearly a third of the labour force was engaged in agriculture or domestic offices and personal services. Textiles employed more people than the metal-making and metal-using industries. But by 1921 employment in the metal industries had gone up 2¼ times, and that in textiles by only 12 per cent. In 1871 textile exports, at £119 million, were nearly three times the value of exports of metals and metal products. In 1921 exports of ships, electrical goods and vehicles had raised the total for metal products and metals to double that of textiles. (See Mitchell and Deane, *Abstract of British Historical Statistics*, p. 305.)

In Table 7.3 we take the story in more detail up to 1981. At one extreme, note how the decline in agricultural employment is accelerated; at the other, how the rise in professional services is maintained. Remember professional services in an industrial classification include all sorts of ancillary and supportive workers as well as the professional people who provide the core of the service: educational services include school janitors, cleaners, administrators; health services include porters and clerks as well as doctors and nurses. To make it still more complicated, remember, too, that an architect working for a firm of building contractors would be included in the building or construction industry and not in architectural services.

In 1921 a fifth of the labour force was employed in three industries: agriculture, mining, textiles. In 1981 employment in those industries was down to 5.7 per cent, just over one-seventeenth. By contrast, finance and professional services accounted for 6.3 per cent of employment in 1921, and 20.9 per cent in 1981. A society that makes its living from farming, mining, spinning and weaving is much less sophisticated than one engaged in banking, insurance and other financial services, teaching, health, the arts, consultancy and other professional services.

While the labour force increased by a third between 1921 and 1981 employment in manufacturing hardly changed, so that the proportion of the labour force so employed fell quite substantially:

	Manufacturing industry	
	Nos 000s	%
1921	6793	36
1981	6802	27

The amount produced by manufacturing industry (as well as mining and quarrying, construction and gas, electricity and water) is measured

Table 7.3 Employment in 23 industrial orders, Great Britain, 1921, 1971 and 1981

	1921 000s	%	1971 000s	%	1981 000s	%
I. Agriculture, etc.	1 372	7.3	635	2.7	644	2.6
II. Mining, etc.	1 305	6.9	391	1.6	363	1.5
III. Ceramics, glass, etc.	214	1.1	306	1.3	242	1.0
IV. Chemicals	215	1.1	518	2.1	469	1.9
V. Metal manufacture	562	3.0	551	2.3	400	1.6
VI. Engineering and shipbuilding	1 203	6.4	2 149	9.0	1 852	7.4
VII. Vehicles	375	2.0	789	3.3	688	2.8
VIII. IX. } Metal goods, n.e.s.	424	2.2	731	3.1	522	2.1
X. Textiles	1 305	6.9	591	2.5	407	1.6
XI. Leather, etc.	87	0.5	53	0.2	37	0.1
XII. Clothing	873	4.6	470	2.0	357	1.4
XIII. Food, drink and tobacco	623	3.3	738	3.1	694	2.8
XIV. Wood	304	1.6	302	1.3	295	1.2
XV. Paper and printing	403	2.1	612	2.6	538	2.2
XVI. Other manufactures	205	1.1	325	1.4	301	1.2
XVII. Building	795	4.2	1 669	7.0	1 861	7.5
XVIII. Gas, electricity and water	179	0.9	362	1.5	341	1.4
XIX. Transport, communication	1 570	8.3	1 564	6.6	1 608	6.5
XX. Distributive trades	2 239	11.9	3 016	12.7	3 183	12.8
XXI. Finance	311	1.6	952	4.0	1 325	5.3
XXII. Public administration and defence	1 007	5.3	1 572	6.6	1 965	7.9
XXIII. Professional services	886	4.7	2 901	12.2	3 877	15.6
XXIV. Miscellaneous services	2 398	12.7	2 357	9.9	2 928	11.8
Total	18 855	100	23 733*	100	24 897	100

*1971 total includes working overseas and inadequately defined.
Includes employers, self-employed, employees and unemployed. The unemployed are allocated to the industry in which they are usually employed or last employed.
Sources: 1921 and 1971, Guy Routh, *Occupation and Pay in Great Britain 1906–79*, p. 42; 1981, employers and self-employed, *Employment Gazette*, vol. 90, no. 1, Jan. 1982, pp. 15 and 16; employees, ibid. vol. 90, no. 4, pp. S8–S10; unemployed, ibid. vol. 89, no. 6, June 1981, pp. S33–S35.

by the index of industrial production. This differs from the national accounts in that it is a measure of physical output: the month-by-month production of bricks, tons of steel, yards of cloth and so on is measured for a sample of establishments and a chain-index calculated.

From this, we can see that, while numbers employed in manufacturing were almost the same in the two years, the quantity of goods produced had multiplied by a factor of more than five. (For the period to 1965 see C. H. Feinstein, *Statistical Tables of National Income, Expenditure and Output of the U.K. 1855–1965*, Cambridge University Press, 1972 and 1976, table 51, pp. 112–13. For more recent years see Index of Industrial Production published, *inter alia*, in Central Statistical Office, *Annual Abstract of Statistics*.)

In the current depression the numbers employed in manufacturing have declined – by a quarter between 1974 and the end of 1981. Output has also fallen (by 16 per cent), but output per person employed has risen by 9.5 per cent. (See *Employment Gazette*, Apr. 1982, p. S17.)

These phenomena are not peculiar to Britian: they are common to the advanced capitalist countries of Europe and the United States, though seen in Britain in a pronounced form.

I have compared industrial distribution in Great Britain at various points in time, and we have thereby been able to observe economic history unfolding itself. Let us now do a brief cross-sectional study of four advanced capitalist countries in mid-1979. This is shown in Table 7.4.

These wealthy capitalist countries have a distinctive industrial profile. If we average the distributions we get:

	%
Agriculture, etc.	7.5
Mining, etc.	0.8
Manufacturing	27.1
Electricity, gas, water	0.9
Construction	8.1
Trade and catering	18.5
Transport and communications	6.1
Finance	6.0
Community, etc., services	25.0
	100.0

Japan and France both show vestiges of their peasant past, with 11.2 and 9 per cent still in agriculture. Italy is still further behind, with 14.8. Germany remains heavily committed to manufacturing industry: 35.1 per cent compared to an average of 27.1. In Japan only 0.6 per cent work in gas, electricity and water, while in France and Germany 0.9

Table 7.4 Employment by industry in 4 countries, mid-1979

ISIC Major Division	USA 000s	%	France 000s	%	German FR 000s	%	Japan 000s	%
All activities	96 945	100	21 127	100	25 041	100	54 790	100
1. Agriculture, etc.	3 455	3.6	1 897	9.0	1 588	6.2	6 130	11.2
2. Mining and quarrying	899	0.9	150	0.7	329	1.3	120	0.2
3. Manufacturing	22 102	22.8	5 515	26.1	8 793	35.1	13 330	24.3
4. Electricity, gas, water	1 101	1.1	182	0.9	220	0.9	330	0.6
5. Construction	6 299	6.5	1 823	8.6	1 891	7.6	5 360	9.8
6. Trade, restaurants and catering	20 769	21.4	3 363	15.9	3 617	14.4	12 280	22.4
7. Transport and communication	5 576	5.8	1 329	6.3	1 493	6.0	3 450	6.4
8. Financial services	7 979	8.2	1 487	7.0	1 369	5.5	1 850	3.4
9. Social and personal services	28 764	29.7	5 381	25.5	5 771	23.0	11 810	21.6
10. Not adequately defined	—	—	—	—	—	—	90	0.2

The International Standard Industrial Classification (ISIC) has ten major divisions, each of which is further subdivided. See United Nations, *Statistical Papers*, series M, no. 4, rev. 2, New York, 1968.

Major Division 1: Agriculture, hunting, forestry and fishing; 6. Wholesale and retail trade, restaurants and hotels; 7. Transport, storage and communication; 8. Financing, insurance, real estate and business services; 9. Community, social and personal services. The data are from the country tables in OECD, *Labour Force Statistics 1968–1979*.

Work and Pay   131

per cent are so employed, and 1.1 per cent in the United States. In 1979 the Japanese used 16.5 per cent more electricity per head of population than the French, and the Germans 15 per cent more than the Japanese. The Americans used more than twice as much as the Japanese. (*Energy Balances of OECD Countries 1976/1982*, Paris: OECD, 1982.) I postpone consideration of the distributive trades until Chapter 8.

There is not much difference in transport and communication, and it is well known that German and, even more, Japanese financial services have lagged behind other affluent countries.

There is a falling proportion of workers engaged in growing things, mining things, making things or building things, though the volume of the resulting products has expanded greatly. Employment in the distributive trades and catering is fairly stable, while a strong increase is shown in financial, community, social and personal services. The governments of the United States and United Kingdom have created much disruption by trying to reverse these trends.

7.2.3 Classification by occupation

A job is what a worker does; an occupation consists of a set of characteristics applying to a collection of similar jobs. Truck-drivers' jobs vary according to the types of truck they drive, their cargo, the distance travelled, and, though the occupation is that of truck driver, we can make as many subdivisions as may be deemed appropriate.

One of the results of the application of science to production has been a great multiplication of occupations. Plato, in his *Republic*, specified the need for farmers, builders, weavers, shoemakers, personal servants, carpenters, smiths, cowherds, shepherds, merchants, shippers, shopkeepers and hired labourers. Socrates commented that no two people are born exactly alike. 'There are innate differences which fit them for different occupations.... So the conclusion is that more things will be produced and the work be more easily and better done, when every man is set free from all other occupations to do, at the right time, the one thing for which he is naturally fitted.' (*The Republic of Plato*, ed. F. M. Cornford, Oxford: Clarendon Press, 1941, pp. 55–7.)

Xenophon, Plato's contemporary in the 5th–4th century B.C., described the advantages of what later came to be called 'the division of labour':

> In large cities – inasmuch as many people have demands to make upon each branch of industry, one trade alone, and very often even

less than a whole trade is enough to support a man: one man, for instance, makes shoes for men, and another for women; and there are places even where one man earns a living by only stitching shoes, another by cutting them out, another by sewing the uppers together, while there is another who performs none of these operations but only assembles the parts. It follows, therefore, as a matter of course, that he who devotes himself to a very highly specialized line of work is bound to do it in the best possible manner. (*Cyropaedia*, trans. Walter Miller, Loeb Classical Library, bk VIII, ch. II. Quoted by Georges Friedman, *The Anatomy of Work*, p. xx, and by Karl Marx, *Capital*, Moscow: Foreign Languages Publishing House, 1961, vol. I, p. 366.)

But the proliferation of occupations did not occur until the advent of capitalism and the breakdown of the feudal system. At the beginning of the eighteenth century Boisguillebert remarked on the speed at which new occupations were appearing: 'In the infancy or innocence of the world, man was rich by the enjoyment of simple needs, procured by the pursuit of only three or four occupations. . . . But today, in some countries contrary dispositions have carried opulence and voluptuousness to excess, and there are more than two hundred occupations, with more invented every day.' (*Dissertation sur la Nature des Richesses, de L'Argent et des Tributs*, about 1707, Eugene Daire, ed., *Économistes-Financièrs du XVIIIe Siecle*, Paris: Chez Guillaumin Libraire, 1843, pp. 403–4.)

Since the days of Boisguillebert occupations have multiplied from 200 to about 3500 – at least, this is the number of separate occupations distinguished by the Department of Employment in their *Classification of Occupations and Directory of Occupational Titles*. (See vol. I, *Introduction, Structure, Index*, and vols 2 and 3, *Occupational Definitions*, London, HMSO, 1972.) The *International Standard Classification of Occupations*, devised by the International Labour Office to encourage international standardisation, distinguishes 1506 occupations (Geneva: ILO, 1969), but even this is far more than it is practical to present in official statistics. The 1970 *Classification of Occupations* compiled by the British Office of Population Censuses and Services uses only 222, with an additional category for 'occupations inadequately described'. 'The basic common factor of all groups is the kind of work done and the nature of the operation performed. But if, by reason of the material worked in, the degree of skill involved, the physical energy required, the environmental conditions, the social and economic status associated with the occupation, or any combination of these factors, unit groups based solely on kind of work done seemed too comprehensive they were further broken down on the basis of these other factors in order to identify what are substantially separate occupations.' (*Classification of Occupations*, p. vi.)

The most complete reports of the occupational distribution of the population are derived, in most countries, from decennial censuses of population, when heads of households have to report on the occupations of members of their households, but, because of the mass of information involved, these reports are seldom issued until four or five years after the date to which they refer. In some countries much more up-to-date information is obtained by household surveys. Of necessity these are based on small samples of the population, and are subject to statistical error. But these samples are useful for the calculation of trends, and can be used to adjust the data of the decennial census to take account of current changes.

In the United States a monthly household survey is conducted by the Bureau of Census. Amongst much else this produces figures for the occupational distribution of the occupied population, presented in the US Department of Labor Bureau of Labor Statistics annual *Handbook of Labor Statistics*. Look, for instance, at table 19, Employed Persons by Detailed Occupation, 1972–7, which appears on pp. 82–4 of the *Handbook* for 1978.

The table shows 195 occupations, some of which are subdivided to give further details of another 93 sub-occupations. Almost every country publishes such tables, though generally only as a by-product of their decennial census of population, and generally not in such detail. These are an economic stocktaking of their human capital: the amount of training and experience from which their populations have benefited. The data are of social and political as well as economic interest, for occupation influences not only productivity and wealth, but also political views, health and expectation of life as well as level of education, sophistication and gullibility.

By making comparisons over a series of years or between two years, one can also see how the quality of the labour force is changing. For instance, between 1972 and 1977 the civilian labour force in the United States grew by 10.8 per cent. To maintain its size as a proportion of the labour force an occupational group would have to grow by 10.8 per cent too. Those that grew more were of rising importance; those that grew less of falling importance. Some occupations (but not many) fell not only in proportion, but also in absolute number. Others, by contrast, greatly increased their numbers, suggesting that they were of growing importance. Those showing the greatest growth and fastest decline are shown in Table 7.5.

Table 7.5 *Occupations of greatest growth or decline in the USA, 1972–7*

Occupation	Nos. in 1977 as % of those in 1972
Psychologists	184
Computer systems analysts	174
Warehouse laborers	157
Economists	156
Computer and peripheral equipment operators	154
Biological scientists	153
Lawyers and judges	144
Real estate agents and brokers	144
Bank tellers	142
Mine operatives	141
Taxicab drivers and chauffeurs	101
Sales clerks, retail trade (shop assistants)	99
Typists	99
Compositors and typesetters	98
Stock and bond sales agents	97
Farmworkers	90
Hucksters and peddlers	86
Garbage collectors	86
Sales representatives, manufacturing industries	84
Private household workers	81
Longshore workers and stevedores	81
Delivery and route workers	58

Source: US Department of Labor, *Handbook of Labor Statistics*, 1978, table 19, pp. 82–4.

These movements are connected with the great technical, social and economic changes of the age, and you will find them duplicated in all industrially advanced capitalist countries. They may be made more comprehensible by grouping the 195 occupations into socio-economic groups. These are shown in Tables 7.6 and 7.7, the first of which concentrates the data into four classes, the second presenting ten subdivisions of these four classes.

Table 7.6 *The civilian labour force in four classes, USA, 1972 and 1977*

	Nos. in thousands				
	1972		1977		1977 as
	Nos.	%	Nos.	%	% of 1972
White-collar	39 091	47.8	45 187	49.9	115.6
Blue-collar	28 576	35.0	30 211	33.4	105.7
Service	10 966	13.4	12 392	13.7	113.0
Farm	3 069	3.8	2 756	3.0	89.8
All	81 702	100	90 546	100	110.8

Source: as Table 7.5.

White-collar and blue-collar workers are more generally distinguished in Britain as non-manual workers and manual workers, or sometimes salary-earners and wage-earners. Farm workers include farmers and farm managers as well as farm labourers. The service workers are a bit more difficult to define. Their jobs can be quite strenuous, but may also require training, skill and experience. The best way of knowing who they are is to read the list. In 1977 they included:

	Thousands
Housekeepers, child-care workers, cleaners and others in private households	1158
Cleaning service workers, other than private household	2363
Food service (catering) workers	4095
Nursing aides, dental assistants and other health workers	1747
Hairdressers and others in personal service	1705
Police and others in protective services	1324

Of course shop assistants (sales clerks in the United States) who serve their customers, bus drivers and conductors who serve their passengers, performers who serve their audiences, postmen who deliver your letters and telephonists who answer your calls are all service workers, too, but are arbitrarily allocated to other groups. This is not very logical but, as long as we know what we are doing and all do the same thing, no harm is done and it can be quite convenient.

Tables 7.6 and 7.7 show how the occupational contours are changing. The proportion of blue-collar and farmworkers falls while white-collar and service workers increase. Skilled manual workers (craft and

Table 7.7 *The civilian labour force in 10 occupational groups, USA, 1972 and 1977*

	1972 Nos.	1972 %	Nos. in thousands 1977 Nos.	1977 %	1977 as % of 1972
White-collar					
Professional and technical	11 459	14.0	13 692	15.1	119.5
Managers and administrators	8 031	9.8	9 662	10.7	120.3
Sales workers	5 354	6.6	5 728	6.3	107.0
Clerical and kindred workers	14 247	17.4	16 106	17.8	113.0
Blue-collar					
Craft and kindred workers	10 810	13.2	11 881	13.1	109.9
Operatives, except transport	10 340	12.7	10 354	11.4	100.1
Transport equipment operatives	3 209	3.9	3 476	3.8	108.3
Non-farm laborers	4 217	5.2	4 500	5.0	106.7
Service workers	10 966	13.4	12 392	13.7	113.0
Farmworkers	3 069	3.8	2 756	3.0	89.8
All	81 702	100	90 547	100	110.8

Source: as Table 7.5.

Table 7.8 *Percentage of occupied population in occupational groups, USA (1910 and 1970) and GB (1911 and 1971)*

	1910/11 US	1910/11 GB	1970/71 US	1970/71 GB
Professional and semi-professional	4.4	4.1	14.2	10.6
Proprietors, managers, officials	23.0	10.4	12.7	12.3
of whom farmers	16.5	1.6	2.2	0.9
Clerical and kindred	5.2	7.3	17.4	15.7
Sales	5.0	5.7	6.2	9.0
Skilled workers and foremen	11.7	13.9	12.9	15.5
Service	6.8	10.4	12.4	11.8
Farm laborers	14.5	6.5	1.7	1.1
Semi-skilled and unskilled, not elsewhere classified	29.4	41.7	22.4	24.0

Source: Guy Routh, *Occupation and Pay in Great Britain 1906–79*, p. 11.

kindred) are barely keeping level with the rise of the labour force; semi-skilled manual workers (operatives) and unskilled workers (labourers) are falling behind.

I have said that these trends are in evidence in all advanced capitalist countries. Table 7.8 makes a comparison of the United States and Great Britain for the years 1910 or 1911 and 1970 or 1971.

Rural populations have given strong support to traditional values: now their influence has been greatly eroded. On the other hand, militant trade unions have drawn their strength from blue-collar workers, who constitute a declining proportion of the labour force. The most highly educated occupations are those that are growing fastest. Will this strengthen liberal-democratic or elitist-conservative forces? At time of writing this remains an open question.

7.3 JOB DESIGN AND ASSESSMENT

7.3.1 Work study; time-and-motion study

'The habit of sauntering and of indolent careless application, which is naturally, or rather necessarily acquired by every country workman who is obliged to change his work and his tools every half hour, and to apply his hand in twenty different ways almost every day of his life; renders him always slothful and lazy, and incapable of any vigorous application even on the most pressing occasions.' (Adam Smith, *The Wealth of Nations*, Glasgow ed., p. 19.)

One thing revealed by a comparison of modern industrial with peasant societies is their contrasting view of work. In the first, work is clearly demarcated from social and domestic life; in the second, it is part of domestic and social life. This was a change brought about by factory production, when workers were herded together in squalid surroundings and there retained from early morning till late at night. In the one, there is no hurry; in the other, time is of the essence.

As soon as attention is drawn to the need to increase output, possibilities for doing so are revealed.

One method is by mechanisation: the replacement of human effort by other sorts of power, and of human skill and dexterity by machines. Another method is to examine the production process with given capital equipment with a view to eliminating idle time and wasted effort. When a process has to be repeated a hundred times a day, a minute saved by a better arrangement adds up to the saving of a hundred minutes per worker per day.

The pioneers in this field were F. W. Taylor, *The Principles of Scientific Management*, New York: Harper & Row, 1911, and Frank and Lillian Gilbreth, *Motion Study*, New York: Van Nostrand, 1911. From their work 'scientific management' and 'industrial engineering' have been developed until today the division of labour has been carried to the extent of distinguishing those who *study* work from those who do it, to the great benefit of the productivity of the latter. Many handbooks have been written to explain the method. Of particular merit is C. R. Wynne-Roberts and E. J. Riches, *Introduction to Work Study*, Geneva: International Labour Office, 1957. A revised edition prepared by R. L. Mitchell was published in 1974.

Work-study techniques may be applied to any task, from writing an exam or essay to the manufacture of goods. It is used in the design of office systems as well as transport or trade. They apply the principle that the effectiveness of work can be increased by devoting more time to preparation and less to execution. This was the system elaborated by Aleksei Stakhanov in the Soviet Union in the 1930s. It required the worker to plan his task before he began it: all the necessary tools had to be at hand and the parts and materials ready in proper order to avoid delay. Workers who increased their output in this way were hailed as Stakhanovites. It is, in fact, peculiarly difficult to persuade workers to do this – they prefer to get straight on to the job, feeling that preparation is a waste of time. Hence the appearance of work-study departments with industrial engineers to do it for them.

In the 1920s and 1930s this evoked great hostility from the workers whose work was being studied, since they associated it with the speed-up of conveyor belts and the reduction of piece-rates. This applied particularly to time-and-motion study, since this required close observation of a worker's movements by people with stop-watches, so that every gesture was recorded and timed. This is reminiscent of the objection of people in pre-capitalist societies to having their photos taken (except at their own request). He who has had his work recorded has surrendered some of his secrets to the recorder. This is a serious matter, since every group of workers has secret ways of alleviating the tedium and exertion of their work. They also like to determine their own work-rhythm rather than having it determined for them.

Nowadays it is usual to draw union representatives into work-study exercises, and to give workers a predetermined share in the gains arising from it. If there is a restrictive practice in the way of the introduction of more efficient method, it may have to be 'bought out' by the employer, if the workers concerned are willing to sell it. British Rail are currently trying to persuade their train drivers to substitute a 7- to 9-hour day for an 8-hour day so as to make more effective use of their time, and offered a 6 per cent increase as part of the deal. The drivers, however, have refused to relax their 8-hour day and say that they want the 6 per cent anyway.

Work study is a fascinating subject, a knowledge of which you may wish to develop. At the moment there are particular aspects of it that I want to emphasise: that is, the indeterminacy of the amount of output that may result from a given period of work. Also, that a rise in output may very often go along with a reduction of effort. The difficulty of measuring the real value of capital is well known, for the value of capital is determined by the value of what it produces, and this fluctuates. The quantity of any given product comes from the application of labour and equipment. Work study reveals considerable variations in output between different plants in different countries, different plants in the same country and the same plant at different times. It is unlikely that any state of equilibrium would arise in these circumstances; the only pervasive feature is that of change.

7.3.2 Job evaluation

We have so far in this chapter dealt with the nature of work, different ways of classifying workers and what can be read from these differences. We come now to the difficult question of what it is that determines what different sorts of workers are paid. Let us begin with job evaluation, for here we can see how, within an organisation, relative rates are determined for different sorts of work.

In pre-capitalist societies price and pay are fixed by tradition: the status of the farmer, potter, carpenter and blacksmith is well known and his pay and status accord with each other. The religious teachers of the Middle Ages taught that this accorded with the will of God and that disputes and queries relating to price and pay should be settled by reference to the Church. Richard Cantillon, writing in the 1730s, offered a secular explanation:

> The Arts and Crafts which are accompanied by risks and dangers like those of Founders, Mariners, Silver miners, etc. ought to be paid in proportion to the risks. When over and above the dangers skill is needed they ought to be paid still more, e.g. Pilots, Divers, Engineers, etc. When Capacity and trustworthiness are needed the labour is paid still more highly, as in the case of Jewellers, Book-

keepers, Cashiers and others. (*Essai sur la Nature du Commerce en Général*, London: Frank Cass, for the Royal Economic Society, 1959, p. 21.)

Adam Smith identified five factors that occasion differences in rates of pay:

First, The wages of labour vary with the ease or hardship, the cleanliness or dirtiness, the honourableness or dishonourableness of the employment.
Secondly, the wages of labour vary with the easiness and cheapness, or the difficulty and expence of learning the business.
Thirdly, The wages of labour in different occupations vary with the constancy or inconstancy of employment.
Fourthly, The wages of labour vary according to the small or great trust which must be reposed in the workmen.
Fifthly, the wages of labour in different employments vary according to the probability or improbability of success in them. (*Wealth of Nations*, Glasgow ed., pp. 117–22.)

Thus, according to Adam Smith, the highest-paid jobs should be those that are strenuous, dirty, dishonourable, hard and expensive to learn, insecure, responsible and uncertain of success. One could then say that the requirements both of justice and demand-and-supply were being served. It is considerations such as this that systems of job evaluation purport to take into account. The system introduced in 1947 by Lever Brothers at Port Sunlight also took five factors into account:

(1) *Mental Requirements*, which includes standard of education required, memory, initiative, team-work etc.
(2) *Physical Requirements*, including concentration and duration of physical effort, and any specific physical characteristics required by the job.
(3) *Skill and Experience*, of which an important aspect is learning time; previous experience, complexity of the job and any special aptitudes are also considered.
(4) *Responsibility*, for material, equipment, for safety of other people and for maintenance of records.
(5) *Conditions of Work*, which includes unpleasant surroundings and hazards. (Leaflet, undated, *Job Evaluation at Lever Brothers, Port Sunlight.*)

Work and Pay

Be warned: job evaluation does not present a formula for an absolute calculation of what a job is worth; it enables one to rank jobs in order of value and suggests how much a particular job is worth compared with others. Lever Brothers began with seven key jobs each of which was ranked under each of the five headings, for each of which it was allocated points. A chargehand sheet-metal worker ended up with 135 points, a turner with 126, a motor driver 113 and so on. Points were converted into money by making the Soap and Candle Trade Basic Rate = 100. Eventually, 3000 different jobs were described, studied and evaluated with reference to the seven key jobs.

These are analytical systems of evaluation. Factors are selected important to the performance of work in the organisation concerned. These will vary considerably as between, for instance, an office, a supermarket or a factory. They will vary between factories according to the materials used and the products made. The more homogeneous the group of workers, the easier the process of comparison.

Again, because evaluations are relative and not absolute, the system has to be such as to accord with what those to whom it applies deem to be right and proper. A foreman or manager must not get less than those they supervise, however pleasant the jobs of the former or disagreeable those of the latter. This result can be achieved by weighting the factors. Each factor can, for instance, be marked out of ten for each job, and a total calculated by multiplying the points for each factor by a predetermined factor. If you were allocating points to the departmental manager and the departmental unskilled labourer the results might be something like this:

	Manager	*Labourer*
Mental requirements	8	0
Physical requirements	0	8
Skill and experience	8	0
Responsibility	8	0
Conditions of work	0	8
Total	25	16

The unweighted total suggests that the labourer ought to be paid two-thirds the rate of the departmental manager, which (according to accepted usages) is ridiculous. But this is easily corrected by giving discriminatory weights to each factor, say, in the order shown above, 14, 5, 13, 12, 6. Multiply the points for each factor by its weight and add them together. The manager then gets 312 points and the labourer

88, giving the former 3¼ times the pay of the latter, much nearer to what custom dictates.

Of the non-analytical methods the simplest consists of allocating jobs to a limited number of grades, each of which has a range of pay linked to the years of experience of the worker concerned. Five grades is generally adequate to distinguish the blue-collar jobs of an establishment, and the same number for the office jobs.

Another method that gives satisfactory results is that of paired comparisons. Each job is compared with every other job in the establishment. It is given 0 if it is less important than the other, 1 if it is of equal importance and 2 if it is more important. So that justice may be seen to be done it is advisable to have the comparisons done by representatives of the manual workers, clerical workers, technicians and managers. This also reduces to insignificance the effect of idiosyncratic answers that might rank the general manager below the dishwasher. The resulting scores enable one to rank the jobs in accordance with the consensus of importance or to simply allocate jobs into a given number of grades according to what is considered to be their importance.

There are many books that explain the techniques of job evaluation. The shortest is Advisory, Conciliation and Arbitration Service Guide No. 1, *Job Evaluation*, London: ACAS, undated. See also, International Labour Office, *Job Evaluation*, Geneva: 1960. (New edition forthcoming.)

7.3.3 Payment by results

From the earliest days of the industrial revolution, payment in textile factories was calculated by piecework, so that the earnings of the worker varied according to the number of yards of thread or cloth produced. Coal-miners, too, were paid according to the amount of coal produced. The system was applied, too, in the mass-production industries that developed early in the twentieth century. Where production was by teams of workers whose individual product could not be identified, the incentive was less strong, for the individual effort of each worker would be shared by the whole team. But in batch-production involving machining or assembly it was possible to identify the products of each worker and individual incentive systems could be applied.

It was in preparation for the introduction of incentive systems that work study and time-and-motion study became of particular importance. Before piecework systems were applied it was important to ensure that the system of work was already efficient and that workers were working as fast as could reasonably be expected. If this were not done those workers who were able to discover better methods would earn high bonuses, thereby exciting the jealousy of those who were not so lucky. It is differences in capability and effort that payment-by-results (PBR) systems are supposed to reward, not lucky breaks.

When systems of PBR are first introduced they sometimes encounter a curious difficulty: workers in a department usually establish for themselves a permissible rate of work. Those who exceed the accepted rate find themselves in trouble with their fellow workers. The incentives offered in the piecework system have to be strong enough to break down these norms. In one case with which I was concerned, the norms had been calculated on the basis of average output for the preceding year. Workers were then offered payment pro rata for additional output. The employer waited expectantly for a rise in output, but none came. He then offered double rates for output above the norm. Differences then appeared between the fast and the slow workers. Some were incapable of working faster; a few were able to double their output.

In another case study in my collection, the employer said to his workers: 'I know you could work faster if you wanted to. I offer you a deal: we will agree on the week's output for each of you. When you have finished it, you can go home.' Again, the differences in speed of output appeared. Some workers were able to go home for the week on Thursday, while those who could work no faster fumed with frustration. After some weeks the employer called the workers together again. 'It appears', he said, 'that some of you have been cheating me. You have been holding back production instead of doing your best. From now on, we will go back to the old system, but with the higher output from those who have shown themselves capable of it.'

In the 1920s and 1930s there were many cases of this sort where employers, having established the capacity for higher output, resorted to rate-cutting. In more recent years the roles were reversed: workers exerted a constant pressure on rates, edging them higher and higher. This applied particularly to batch production in the engineering industry, when new norms had to be established when products were changed. As Richard Hyman describes it: 'Often, rate-setting became a battle between the operator or his steward and the rate-fixer: a battle in which first-line management is willing to make concessions rather than risk a stoppage by a small group which could disrupt production schedules over a whole section.' (*Industrial Relations – A Marxist*

Introduction, London: Macmillan, 1975, pp. 114–15. See also, W. A. Brown, *Piecework Bargaining*, London: Heinemann, 1973.)

The result of these difficulties has been a disenchantment with piecework systems by both managers and workers. It is unusual now for payment-by-results to amount to more than an insignificant part of the pay packet.

7.3.4 Merit rating

Job evaluation is concerned with the characteristics of the job, not the individual differences of the workers who perform it. Workers are required to perform their job satisfactorily: if they do not, they are transferred or fired. But other workers may do the job exceptionally well, better, as it were, than required by the call of duty. Do they not then deserve a special reward? This is what merit-rating schemes have been designed to provide.

Once or twice a year the worker's supervisor must complete an assessment form, rating the worker for those qualities that distinguish a good worker from a satisfactory one. Is he or she a clock-watcher, or keeps good time and readily stays on to finish a task? Reliability: is much supervision necessary or can he or she be relied upon implicitly to perform tasks conscientiously? Is interest displayed in the work or can the worker not be bothered? Is the worker helpful and co-operative, cheerfully lending a hand when it is needed – or surly, ill-tempered and egotistical?

The supervisor considers the specified factors and then allocates the individual to one of (generally) five categories ranging from very good to bad. The worker will then receive the appropriate merit payment until the next assessment falls due. Merit rates are generally quite modest, but the receipt of the payment does convey to the worker that efforts are being recognised.

But there is an additional, even more important, function that merit rating can perform, when the worker himself is required to sit in on the assessment. He is then led to see himself as others see him, sometimes a painful but salutary process. It warns the worker if his job is in danger, and is a useful aid in deciding questions of promotion.

7.4 PAY

Man doth not live by bread alone, but his pay, all the same is an important facet of his work. Delivered week by week or month by

Work and Pay

month, it is an acknowledgement that he is worthy of his hire, that his services are of value to his employers, and that society at large is prepared to buy, or otherwise pay for, the goods or services that are the end-products of his own and other people's labour.

We have noted the wide range of occupations in which the labour force is distributed, and the great multitude of jobs in which those occupations are pursued. Work, as we have seen, can be studied, planned and improved, and it can be performed well, indifferently or ill. As products move down the production line, from farm or mine by road, rail, sea or air, into the factories and out of them again and into the shops, they carry with them accumulating costs. If these costs are recouped, all is well; if they are not, danger signals flow back, warning that procedures or products must be changed.

But long before this final reckoning the workers must be paid. If the venture is a failure they may lose their jobs, but until this happens the contract of labour must be adhered to, and part of that contract stipulates the rate of pay attached to the job in question, the required hours of work, paid holidays and other conditions of employment. Hours and holidays are fairly well standardised; not so rates of pay. These vary according to sex, age, occupation, industry, place, as well as for no apparent reason. There is no insurmountable difficulty in ennumerating the labour force and marshalling it according to the criteria suggested in the first part of this chapter; but their rates of pay are as numerous and various as the stars of the heavens.

7.4.1 Structure and dispersion

'The price of labour', wrote Adam Smith, 'cannot be ascertained very accurately anywhere, different prices being often paid at the same place and for the same sort of labour, not only according to the different abilities of the workmen, but according to the easiness or hardness of the masters.' (*Wealth of Nations*, Glasgow ed., p. 95.) Nowadays, government and business agencies and research workers collect and publish great quantities of data on the subject, one effect of which is to confirm Adam Smith's finding.

Let us begin our consideration of pay structure by looking at an arrangement that makes the whole thing look rather sensible and orderly: median pay by occupation. If you rank rates of pay by order of magnitude, the median is the one in the middle. The numbers in Table 7.9 are for males and females aged 25 to 64 who worked for 50 to 52 weeks in the United States in 1969. In the decennial population censuses in the United States respondents are asked to state their occupations and the income derived therefrom in the preceding year. The information is unlikely to be very precise, but when large numbers of people are concerned, those that overstate are likely to be balanced by those that understate. There is no particular reason to expect a systematic bias in either direction.

So here is the data arrayed in satisfying order. Those at the bottom of

Table 7.9 *Pay structure by occupation in the USA in 1969, men and women aged 25 to 64*

Nos. 000s			Median income $ per year	
M	F		M	F
5 918	1 843	Elementary education 0–8 years	6 828	3 801
2 279	384	College 5 years or more	14 201	8 877
4 729	1 562	Professional, technical and kindred	12 237	7 172
		Of whom:		
408	—	Accountants	11 969	—
166	—	Clergymen	6 671	—
1 036	—	Engineers	13 699	—
200	—	Lawyers and judges	20 139	—
149	16	Life and physical scientists	13 018	9 051
46	—	Dentists	22 682	—
174	—	Physicians	25 000	—
—	433	Registered nurses, dietitians and therapists		6 775
69	10	Social scientists	14 327	9 253
43	—	Airplane pilots	18 446	—
63	—	Editors and reporters	12 210	—
4 292	665	Managers and administrators, except farm	12 101	6 246
2 183	784	Sales workers	10 093	3 809
2 254	4 514	Clerical and kindred	8 536	5 366
6 885	278	Craftsmen and kindred	9 034	5 370
3 837	1 890	Operatives, except transport	7 863	4 432
1 779	35	Transport equipment operatives	7 955	4 898
1 354	108	Laborers, except farm	6 646	4 170
978	—	Farmers and farm managers	5 561	—
310	19	Farm laborers (wage workers)	4 037	2 594
2 024	1 695	Service workers, except private household	6 857	3 666
13	367	Private household workers	3 549	1 792

Source: US Department of Commerce, Bureau of Census Subject Reports, *1970 Census of Population, Earnings by Occupation and Education*, Washington: 1973.

the educational ladder, with only elementary schooling, got less than half of those at the top with five years or more at college. Of course these are just indicators of a complex of circumstances: those with only elementary education will be largely confined to the least-skilled jobs, are likely to be of lower intelligence, to be present disproportionately in the south. Those with five years or more of college education would be in professional, technical and kindred occupations.

You will notice that women suffer from two disadvantages; there are very few of them in the higher professions and, in general, they get between one-half or two-thirds as much as men. But let us put aside for the moment the question of discrimination against women, and consider male and female incomes relative to themselves.

Amongst the men the three highest-paid professions are physicians, dentists and lawyers. At the bottom come private household workers: butlers, chauffeurs, cleaners, gardeners, cooks.... But their position is complicated by the fact that they are often lodged and fed. Indeed, these jobs are unpopular not because those in them do not make a good living in comparison with other service workers, but because of the curtailment of independence that they involve. Let us take 'laborers, except farm' as the base and show the incomes of the major groups relative to theirs, and do the same for the women:

	M	F
Professional, technical and kindred	184	172
Managers and administrators, except farm	182	150
Sales workers	152	91
Craftsmen and kindred	136	129
Clerical and kindred	128	128
Transport equipment operatives	120	117
Operatives, except transport	118	106
Service workers, except private household	103	88
Laborers, except farm	100	100

What do you make of these income structures? We refer to the ratios of pay between different occupations as differentials. If these differentials applied to a particular organisation, would you regard them as equitable, the sort of thing one might expect after an exercise in work-study and job evaluation? The professionals (engineers, scientists, draughtsmen, technicians) get about the same as the managers and administrators; the salesmen get 83 per cent of the managers and 12 per cent more than the craftsmen; the clerks get 94 per cent of the craftsmen.

What purpose is served by these differentials? Entry to a profession requires additional years of education and much learning which, as Solomon remarked, is a weariness of the flesh. Management requires less formal education, but the assumption of responsibility and the need to wheedle work out of intractable underlings. If everyone were paid the same, would the supply of managers and professionals come to an end and the whole labour force opt to become unskilled labourers, so that a rapid reversion to the old system would be necessitated? Against this argument are the facts that professional work is much more interesting than labouring and that there is much satisfaction to be had from the exercise of power and responsibility.

The differentials for women display some curious features. There were 11 956 000 who had worked between 50 and 52 weeks in 1969, compared with 30 640 000 men. Of those in the labour force (in or seeking work) 63 per cent of men had worked for a full year, but only 41 per cent of women. Service and sales workers, in particular, come and go and may pull down the pay of those in permanent jobs. There are other curiosities that require further analysis:

	Women's pay as % of men's
	%
Professional, etc.	58.6
Managers, etc.	51.8
Clerical, etc.	62.8
Sales	37.7
Service	53.0
Operatives	56.3

Within each group one finds that most of the senior jobs are performed by men, most of the junior by women. This is an important form of discrimination. But even when the same job is done, ways are often found of paying women less, so that the aims of equal pay legislation are circumvented. An ingenious case was reported in *The Times* (of London) of 1 April 1976:

> An industrial tribunal in Birmingham yesterday rejected a claim by two sisters for equal pay although it ruled that the physical work done by them, packing rifles and moving packing cases in loads of up to one hundredweight, was similar to the work done by three men alongside them. But Mr P. Trevor Gray, the tribunal chairman, said that the men also did clerical work. It meant their jobs were not the same in terms of the Equal Pay Act.

Mrs Yvonne Wilson, aged 27 ... and Mrs Sandra Vace, aged 32 ... said later that they would consider an appeal.

Mrs Wilson said if that did not succeed then the Equal Pay Act was a confidence trick. 'If this was the other way about and we were doing the clerical work, they would say the men should have more money because they were doing the harder work. They have been allowed extra money because they are doing a softer job, a bit of clerking. The physical work we do is harder than theirs, and we do some clerical work as well. If a girl clerk were to come to these tribunals tomorrow and claim her work was more important than a labourer getting twice her wage, she would lose.'

Henry Phelps Brown has portrayed national differences in differentials between occupational classes. 'The unskilled workers in West Germany and Norway ... were paid 60 or 70 per cent more, relatively to the rough average we have taken for their countries, than those in France and Italy. At the other end of the scale the relative pay of the higher administrative group in France was double that in West Germany; that of the two top grades in Italy exceeded that in Norway by nearly 70 per cent, and that in West Germany by 120 per cent. Evidently the West German and Norwegian structures and also that of the United States are much more compact than those of France and Italy.' (*The Inequality of Pay*, London: Oxford University Press, 1977, pp. 32-3.)

One should always be suspicious of the comparison of great aggregates or averages, because there are likely to be significant differences in their composition. But these differences have been eliminated in a study by J. P. Daubigny and J. J. Silvestre, quoted by Phelps Brown. They took seven pairs of industrial firms, one French and one German in each pair, similar in size, product, technique and environment, and compared the pay of higher managers with that of administrative, technical and clerical grades, and manual workers. The differentials in France were considerably and consistently higher than in Germany. Phelps Brown comments: 'The economist is not surprised to find one factor of production costing more relatively to another in country A than in country B. He expects that country A will arrange its production so that it uses less of the relatively dear factor together with each unit of the cheap one .... But in fact it was the other way about. In six of the seven pairs the ratio of non-manual to manual employees was substantially higher in the French firm.' (Ibid. p. 33.)

The Royal Commission on the Distribution of Income and Wealth, established by the British Government in 1974, produced eight reports between then and its demise in 1979. Amongst many other aspects of income and wealth they compared managerial salaries in various countries. Salaries were graded at seven levels, adjusted for price levels and taxation. In Australia in 1975 they were 39 per cent higher than in the United Kingdom at lower levels and about the same at higher levels. In France they were 36 per cent at lower levels, rising to more than double at the penultimate level. In Germany they were consistently higher by between 33 and 38 per cent, in Canada by between 94 and 70 per cent, in the United States by between 72 and 79 per cent, with 93 per cent at the top.

It is clear that very different differentials are tolerated in different countries. One would have thought that the influence of the multinational corporations would be sufficient to equalise managerial pay, at least at the higher levels, but this is far from being the case.

Pay varies by sex, occupation and between countries; it also varies between industries and between towns and regions in a single country. It varies for similar jobs in different industries and places and, most baffling of all, it varies between different individuals engaged on identical jobs in the same industry and place. The result is a dispersion of earnings for specified jobs that exceeds the differentials between jobs at different levels of skill. For instance, the differential at the median between maintenance fitters (non-electrical) and general managers in the engineering industry in Britain in April 1978 was 55 per cent. That is, with maintenance fitters' median = 100, general managers' median was 155. This is the same as the differential given by Phelps Brown for skilled and semi-skilled manual workers, on the one hand, and higher administrators on the other in the United States in 1958 (Phelps Brown, p. 32). So far so good. But at the same time, general managers' pay at the highest decile is 408 per cent of that at the lowest decile. (Whereas the median is the mid-point of a dispersion ranked by magnitude, the lowest decile is one-tenth of the way up and the highest decile nine-tenths of the way up.) There is a considerable overlap between the general managers and even repetitive assemblers:

	Q10	Q90
	£ per week	
General managers	76.00	310.00
Repetitive assemblers	55.00	104.90

Thus it is only when the statistics have been manipulated into medians or averages that they give the appearance of equity and order. In reality a considerable proportion of the unskilled, semi-skilled or skilled manual workers are getting more than a considerable proportion of managers and professional workers. (See Guy Routh, *Occupation and Pay in Great Britain 1906-79*, pp. 212-13.)

The US Bureau of Census Subject Report, *Earnings by Occupation and Education*, cited in Table 7.9 above, also gives occupational income by ranges and age-groups. Again the tables display a wide dispersion within each occupation and age-group. There were (in the tables for 1969) 241 340 electrical and electronic engineers aged 35-54 years. They are thus likely to be men of maturity and experience, in the prime of their careers.

> 13 206 earned less than $10 000
> 56 565 earned $10 000 to $14 999
> 96 207 earned $15 000 or more

A useful (because easily understood) measure of dispersion is the semi-interquartile range expressed as a percentage of the median. The lower quartile comes one-quarter up the income range – in this case the earnings of the engineer at the 25th percentile. The upper quartile is the income of the man at the 75th percentile, when the earnings are ranked by order of magnitude. We estimate these values to be as follows:

	$
LQ or Q1	11 200
Median or Q2	13 908
HQ or Q3	16 882

The inter-quartile range is then $5682, half of which is $2841 which is 20.4 per cent of the median. Thus half the engineers had $13 908 ± 20.4 per cent and half of them were more than 20.4 per cent above or below the median.

The earnings of manual workers were also widely dispersed. In the case of electricians

> 31 425 earned less than $6,000
> 132 005 earned $6000 to $9,999
> 131 809 earned $10 000 to $14 999
> 33 009 earned $15 000 or more.

The median income was $10 026 and the semi-interquartile range was 32.9 per cent of the median, relatively considerably greater than in the case of the professional engineers.

I need not weary you with further statistics: suffice it to say that for white-collar workers in the United States dispersion has been consistently wide; for the blue-collar occupations it narrowed in the Second World War, so that it was substantially less in 1949 than in 1939. By 1959 it was a bit wider and by 1969 had returned to the level of 1939.

Besides the sorts of difference I have mentioned there are fluctuations in earnings over time: between men and women, adults and juveniles, between adult age-groups, between regions, occupations and industries. These can be seen and measured in the data that appear in official publications or in the various books to which reference has been made. The reports of the (British) Royal Commission on the Distribution of Income and Wealth merit study, especially their final report (October 1979).

7.4.2 Theories of pay

When faced with incomprehensible phenomena the human mind gives forth hypotheses, the most plausible, convenient or expedient of which are dressed up into a theory, after which tranquillity may be restored, 'this chaos of jarring and discordant appearances' brought to order, 'this tumult of the imagination' allayed. This is how Adam Smith described the process in his essay on astronomy. (See R. H. Campbell and A. S. Campbell and A. S. Skinner, *Adam Smith*, London: Croom Helm, 1982, p. 84.)

The most widely held theory at the time of Adam Smith was that the price of all the different sorts of labour, like that of everything else that was bought and sold, was determined by the interaction of supply and demand. You will find this theory repeated in every economics textbook right down to the present day. This, it is claimed, determines the movement of labour from occupation to occupation, industry to industry, place to place, so that pay and production are always in process of being maximised. From the 1870s it has been generally claimed that this process takes place by marginal adjustments. Like the ether of medieval times, or phlogiston, it is invisible to the naked eye but known to be there.

Strangely enough Adam Smith, in his lectures and his writings, faithfully taught the theory of the market, interspersed with observations suggesting it did not really work. Different rates of profit could not be relied upon to allocate capital, because tradesmen were frequently unsure of their own rates of profit, let alone other people's.

(*Wealth of Nations*, p. 105.) People remained immobile in the face of considerable differences in pay, because 'a man is of all sorts of luggage the most difficult to be transported'. (*Adam Smith*, p. 93.) The dispersion of rates of pay for the same sort of work was observable in his time as in ours: 'The price of labour ... cannot be ascertained very accurately any where, different prices being often paid at the same place and for the same sort of labour, not only according to the different abilities of the workmen, but according to the easiness or hardness of the masters'. (Ibid. p. 95.)

Other theorists were much more extravagant in their claims. Leon Walras (1834–1910) claimed to have established an important truth 'in the face of the denials of socialists': 'that under certain conditions and within certain limits the mechanism of free competition is a self-driven and self-regulating mechanism not only for transforming services into products but also for turning savings into capital goods proper ... Free competition in exchange and production results in maximum utility from services and products ...' (*Elements of Pure Economics*, first published 1874. Translation by William Jaffé, London: Allen & Unwin, 1954, pp. 305–6.) Alfred Marshall (1842–1924) claimed that, 'despite restrictive combinations and other influences', 'the fluidity of labour is sufficient to make it true that the wages of labour of the same industrial grade or rank tend to equality in different occupations throughout the same western country'. (*Principles of Economics*, first published 1890. London: Macmillan, 1961, p. 539.) And John Bates Clark (1847–1938): 'As real as gravitation is the force that draws the actual pay of men *toward* a standard that is set by the final productivity law. This law is universal and permanent: everywhere it will outlive the local and changeful influences that modify its operation. We are to get what we produce – such is the dominant rule of life; and what we are able to produce by means of labor, is determined by what a final unit of mere labor can add to the product that can be created without its aid. *Final productivity governs wages.*' (*The Distribution of Wealth*, first published 1899. New York: Kelley & Millman, 1956, p. 180.)

One of the deductions of the theory was that anyone who really wanted to sell his products or his labour could do so if he were prepared to accept a low enough price. Thus, if workers were unemployed, it was because they were asking too much. This was the theme of the presidential address to the Royal Economic Society in 1932 (*Economic Journal*, vol. XLII, 1932), while Keynes, in the *General Theory*, 1936, argued that unemployment could be *involuntary*.

After the Second World War criticism mounted against the orthodox creed: R. A. Lester, 'Shortcomings of Marginal Analysis for Wage-employment Problems', *American Economic Review*, 1946, vol. 36, pp. 63-82; Clark Kerr entered the field in 1947, with 'Economic Analysis and the Study of Industrial Relations', reprinted in *Labor Markets and Wages Determination*, Berkeley: University of California Press, 1977. An important distinction between the two sides was that the critics took the trouble to observe the real world, gather data and study them, while the orthodox theorists deduced their conclusions from assumptions or principles arrived at *a priori*. The monastic sages had argued that man is sinful so that rules had to be made and enforced to ensure that social justice was done; the Physiocrats and, after them, Archbishop Whately and Stanley Jevons argued that it was by holy miracle that people in civilised society were enabled to pursue their own selfish ends and yet achieve the general good. (See Routh, *The Origin of Economic Ideas*, pp. 215-16.) If you are *certain* that this process is taking place, then it is both tempting and easy to rationalise events that seem to contravene your expectations. Marshall reasoned that if some workers were getting less than others for doing similar work it must be because they enjoyed hidden benefits that equalised the *net advantages* of the various groups. Or, if not that, it must be because the higher-paid workers were more efficient and enjoyed an *efficiency wage*. Thus, he argued, Cliffe Leslie had naïvely laid stress on local variations of wages as illustrating the ineffectiveness of competition for employment. 'For it is found that local variations of weekly wages and of efficiency generally correspond: and thus the facts tend to prove the effectiveness of competition, so far as they bear on the question at all.' (*Principles of Economics*, p. 548.)

Some theorists, Walras being the supreme example, displayed blissful indifference to the realities of the world. Economics should compose itself from abstract and ideal-type concepts, and only then return to reality, not for testing but to apply its principles. (*Elements of Pure Economics*, p. 71.)

Nowadays, however, the world is generally permitted to intrude in the form of statistics. Sometimes, perhaps even usually, this is mock empiricism, with the statistics subjected to econometric torture until they admit to effects of which they are innocent. The Phillips Curve is an example of this process. (See Routh, *Occupation and Pay in Great Britain 1906-79*, pp. 208-10.) The theorists use statistical series with Walrasian indifference to how they were compiled and what they really mean. As Wassily Leontief remarked: 'The same well-known sets of figures are used again and again in all possible combinations to pit different theoretical models against each other in formal statistical combat.' (Presidential address to the American Economic Association, December 1970. 'Theoretical Assumptions and Nonobserved Facts', *American Economic Review*, vol. LXI, no. 1, Mar. 1971.)

It is, however, of the greatest importance to pay respect to the relevant statistics and to test one's own and other people's theories against them. But they are much more useful for refuting theories than for confirming them. If we see that two statistical series are not correlated, then we may conclude that there is not a causal connexion between them; if they are correlated, there are generally various and conflicting explanations – x may be determining y or y may be determining x, or they may both be dependent variables of some quite different cause or set of causes.

If the statistics do suggest a chain of causation, one must always enter the field to find, interrogate and observe the decision-makers. Then, and only then, can we hope to understand what is going on.

Lester and Clark Kerr did enter the field, as researchers, or observers and participants. W. B. Reddaway, in Britain, did not enter the field in this sense, but his examination of wage and employment statistics did illustrate that wage differentials were not a necessary instrument for the allocation of labour: a conclusion of great importance for policy purposes. ('Wage Flexibility and the Distribution of Labour', *Lloyds Bank Review*, vol. 54, Oct. 1959, pp. 32–48. Reprinted in B. J. McCormick and E. Owen Smith, *The Labour Market*, Harmondsworth: Penguin Books, 1968.) His hypothesis: 'Changes in the demand for labour in the various industries and occupations operate to secure a redistribution of the labour force mainly through direct changes in the "job opportunities" made available by employers, and the vigour (or lack thereof) with which the employers seek to recruit workers.' (*The Labour Market*, p. 182.) The non-operation of the orthodox theory is best illustrated within the food, drink and tobacco industrial order. The data covered the years 1951–6, when some of the constituent industries expanded considerably while others contracted, for example employment in chocolate and sugar confectionary expanded by 39 per cent, while that in tobacco contracted by 9 per cent.

> The earnings-increases were all much the same, except that tobacco showed a significantly *higher* one than any other industry in the order. There is clearly some force which produced the big changes in the distribution of labour, and there seems no reason to look beyond

the 'obvious' one, which we have christened job opportunities. Nobody need *regret* the fact that substantial changes in the distribution of labour can be secured in response to changing demands without the need for 'corresponding' changes in the wage-pattern, which would be hard to secure. (*The Labour Market*, p. 197.)

This is very much the same conclusion that was reached by a working party of distinguished economists appointed by the OECD. The group, that included Professors P. de Wolff (the Netherlands) E. H. Phelps Brown (United Kingdom) and Lloyd Ulman (United States), collected and studied a great mass of statistics, drawn from many countries. They reported in 1965.

The most important finding of the Expert Group's report is that in the labour markets and periods studied, large short-term changes in relative earnings do not seem to have been necessary to bring about substantial changes in the pattern of employment. It is true that in a number of countries there has been a tendency, when industries are studied in fairly aggregative groupings, for wages to rise faster in branches which were increasing their share of the labour force. But the experts feel that this should not generally be interpreted as a causal relationship, and their study, in particular their examination of the process of job changing in Chapters IV and V, clarifies the way in which expanding industries have in fact generally been able to increase numbers as required through the attractive force of new job vacancies opening up within the framework of the existing wage structure. (*Wages and Labour Mobility*, Paris: OECD, 1965, p. 9.)

The findings of Reddaway and the de Wolff Committee were reinforced and extended by a study by Richard Wragg and James Robertson of the (British) Department of Employment Unit for Manpower Studies who correlated trends in employment, productivity, output, labour costs and prices in 82 manufacturing industries (1954–73) and 22 retail distributive trades (1950–71). The findings demonstrate that there was no connexion between growth in earnings per operative and the growth or decline in employment in the industry concerned, nor with changes in output per worker. 'Over the long run, earnings increases between industries moved in parallel and were not determined by differential rates of growth in labour productivity.' (*Department of Employment Gazette*, vol. 84, no. 8, Aug. 1976, pp. 851 ff.)

Work and Pay

It is clear that the reality of pay-determination contradicts the imaginings of traditional economics. If the textbooks continue to repeat them it is from perversity or intellectual inertia. There is no excuse for doing so.

Custom and practice
So what are the determining factors? After five years' study at the National Institute of Economic and Social Research in London I concluded that the most important determinants were defence of and respect for status. I constructed tables for average income by occupational class for the period 1906 to 1960 that demonstrated the persistence of occupational differentials and relativities for long periods, interspersed with short, sharp changes.

Richard A. Lester came to similar conclusions for the United States:

> In examining the statistics of hourly earnings for an industry over a long period, one is struck by (a) the persistence of a pattern of occupational differentials and (b) a tendency during certain periods (especially wars) for the percentage difference between unskilled and skilled rates to narrow (although the cents-per-hour continue to increase). During such inflationary periods the whole wage structure tends to be compressed.   (*Economics of Labor*, New York; Macmillan, 2nd ed., 1964, p. 303.)

It is as if labour markets were fitted with stabilisers that enabled them to ride through the waves of economic change. Adam Smith remarked, 'in many places the money price of labour remains uniformly the same sometimes for half a century together' (*Wealth of Nations*, p. 92) and Phelps Brown and Sheila V. Hopkins note the stability of building wage rates, and the differential between craftsmen and labourers, in their seven-century study: 'In all, there seems to have been no change, of the sustained kind we record, in about 500 years out of 690. It is unlikely that supply and demand remained exactly balanced at the ruling price; rather it must have been that their movements were not wide enough to overcome the inertia of convention. ...' ('Seven Centuries of Building Wages', *Economica*, vol. 22, no. 87, Aug. 1955, pp. 201-2.)

Certainly, labour markets are well supplied with inertia. Clark Kerr refers to the 'hard core of the employed', attached to their jobs or areas as in a marriage contract, vaguely conscious of the job market, but not actively in it, sufficiently satisfied with their jobs or fearful of the uncertainties of change. (*Labour Markets and Wage Determination*, pp. 5 and 41.) This is remarkably similar to the conclusions reached after interviews with 1017 households in Brighton, Sussex, in 1971. Of these, 442 had moved into Brighton or moved back to Brighton after having moved away, or at least one of the partners had done that during his or her adult life. Only 140 had at some time moved for reasons connected with their jobs, and, having moved, most relapsed into immobility. Of the non-movers, 453 were ignorant of and indifferent to job opportunities and pay in other towns, and displayed a certain surprise that the interviewer should expect them to bother themselves with such considerations. To anyone addicted to travel and change it was surprising to find that so large a section of the population found positive satisfaction in being left where they were, untroubled by anxiety that they might be doing better somewhere else.

There is thus a strong conservative element in employment contracts. As Barbara Wootton put it, 'Change – always, everywhere – requires justification: the strength of conservatism is that it is held to justify itself.' (*The Social Foundations of Wage Policy*, London: Allen & Unwin, 1954, p. 162; second ed. 1962.) Almost everyone, from trade unions to an individual asking for a rise, asks for the restoration of pay relative to that of some other group or person, and of real income to what it was at the time of the last increase.

7.4.3 The decision-makers

In economics, as in other spheres, if you want to understand the process of change or of the prevention-of-change, you must begin by identifying the decision-makers. For pay the most important decisions are taken by process of collective bargaining. In the United States this is done between unions and companies or plants, negotiations for a whole industry being the exception. (See Walter Galenson and Robert S. Smith, 'The United States', in John T. Dunlop and Walter Galenson (eds), *Labor in the Twentieth Century*, New York: Academic Press, 1978, p. 44.) In Sweden it is done nationally, with separate agreements for manual and white-collar workers, supplemented by agreements by industry. In Germany it is done by industry. In Britain, until the 1950s, the most important mode was by industry, since when company bargaining has grown in importance, sometimes surpassing the industrial agreements in effect. (On these national practices, see Dunlop and Galenson, *Labor in the Twentieth Century*. There are chapters on the United States, Great Britain, the Federal Republic of Germany, France and Japan.)

The union representatives generally get as much out of the employers as they can. How much this is depends on politics and psychology, as well as on business conditions. Sometimes the union leaders exercise a restraining influence on their members – they are professional negotiators and both they and the representatives of management went to stay in business. At other times it is the members who do the restraining and decline, when consulted, to vote for a strike. But almost always a strike or a lockout is resorted to with great reluctance: it is a costly business for both sides and rarely brings immediate gains to either. But Richard Hyman argues: 'In no way does this mean that their action is futile: *only* because trade unionists are from time to time willing to prove their readiness to endure the costs of militancy can they sustain a position of power in their negotiations with the employer. A union would lose all credibility if it never took a firm stand. For similar reasons employers are often willing to bear considerable strike losses....' (*Industrial Relations: A Marxist Introduction*, London: Macmillan, 1975, pp. 190–1.)

Of course trade unions do a great deal more than contrive to get higher pay for their members: they give individual members protection against arbitrary action or inaction by their employers and offer legal, medical and other forms of service. They have been major influences in the shaping of legislation and election to government of people sympathetic to the workers' cause, and they have educated generations of workers to an understanding of their societies.

Trade unions are also organisations subject to the internal forces discussed in Chapter 6: particularly in their own survival and the job security of their officials. Directors of a company must apply a strategy that will keep their shareholders quiet and ward off predators; union officials must contrive to keep their members under control and prevent poaching or even take-over by other unions. But just as businessmen are typically inclined to conservatism, so union officials are inclined to socialism or, in the United States, to liberalism. A career in the trade union movement generally begins with some years as unpaid official, an activity thankless, boring and sometimes damaging of one's own promotion, and thus requires a strong sense of sympathy with one's fellow workers.

Shareholders judge performance by the size of dividends; workers by the pay increases their union is able to exact. In inflationary times the restoration of purchasing power may account for a high proportion of negotiated increases. A second line of argument will concern what other groups of workers have been able to achieve. There is today a complex communications network that communicates pay data from firm to firm and union to union: government departments, international organisations, trade union research departments, employers' associations and management consultants devote much effort to this process.

In the United States, where company agreements are the mode, 'pattern bargaining' is a familiar phenomenon. In any round of negotiations the union chooses first that company with which it is most likely to succeed; having set the pattern, it brings pressure on other companies to conform. In the United Kingdom industry-wide bargaining set the pace until the 1950s; changes in climate would be engineered by a union or confederation that obtained an exceptionally high increase; other unions would follow suit and whole industries be brought into line. A run on the banks or panic buying has been paralleled in recent years by a 'run on the pay bill' where managers have been unable to resist demands for increases that in past times would have been unaskable because unthinkable. Inflationary pay rises take on the nature of epidemics, spreading from industry to industry and nation to nation.

Aubrey Jones was a businessman, a Conservative Member of Parliament for a Birmingham (Warwickshire or West Midlands) constituency, Minister first of Fuel and Power, then of Supply, who resigned from Parliament to become Chairman of the National Board for Prices and Incomes. Here he received an intensive education in the processes of pay and price determination. In 1973, after the Board had been dissolved, he wrote down the lessons he had learnt. (*The New Inflation: The Politics of Prices and Incomes*, Harmondsworth: Penguin Books, 1973). After having summarised the doctrine on this matter of orthodox economics (he had got a First in economics at the LSE) he goes on:

> An inherited body of thought retains a powerful hold over the minds of men long after the moment of utterance, and the thinking briefly summarized above still does. It is, however, at odds with what we observe in contemporary society, because it would be more realistic to say that the present-day phenomenon is one of 'wage leadership'. In other words a 'leading' sector grants wage increases which set the pace for other sectors to follow. Let us suppose that this leading sector is the one in which the growth in productivity is fastest; then if similar wage increases follow in the sectors in which productivity is growing more slowly, wages in these will be rising faster than productivity, and prices will accordingly need to be raised

if the rate of profit is to remain unchanged. Thus the leading sector could be an important force in the inflationary process, particularly if it is a fast-growing sector. . . .

The initiating causes can indeed be manifold. A more 'militant' union leader might have come to power and, anxious to appear different from his predecessor, might have sought and obtained a large settlement which is widely broadcast. Whatever the initiating cause, the increase then becomes a signal, a 'social' standard for others to follow. The rationale often given for this following movement is economic, the market establishing a competitive rate; the inspiration behind it is social and political: each feels entitled to the increase which others, particularly those near him, are seen to be getting.   (*The New Inflation*, pp. 19 and 21.)

It is interesting to observe that, to workers, this does not seem to be a process of wage-inflation. In discussions with shop stewards who came to the University of Sussex on day release I was unable to persuade them to accept even part responsibility for the fall in the value of money that is such a conspicuous feature of our time. To them it was all they could do to keep abreast of prices and obtain those small improvements in living standards that mean so much in family life. Aubrey Jones remarks on a similar attitude on the part of management:

> I suspect . . . that the deeper reason for the wage–price connection is that there is an imitativeness of behaviour which operates in the field of prices just as much as it does in the field of wages. The Board's experience with prices suggests that there is an attitude which causes prices to rise wherever wages rise, even in the face of circumstances which make the onward passage of prices difficult. The attitude of management is the mirror image of the attitude of labour. Just as labour presses for higher wages when prices rise, so managements raise prices when wages rise. Just as there is wage leadership . . . so also is there price leadership. . . . To most managements the new inflation means, not rising prices, but rising labour costs.   (*The New Inflation*, p. 27.)

So the parties work towards an outcome that is acceptable to each other, to their teams of managers and workers. If they get too little or give too much this time, then there is always next time when they may seek to put things right.

At national level the amount to be claimed may be determined by political pressures at the union's annual conference, or the conference may specify 'a substantial amount' that may be put into a range of the possible by the union's research department, or left to the intuition of the union's chief executive. At the local level there are a number of ill-defined influences at work. On the management side the matter is also an exercise in the art of the possible. These influences were investigated in a research programme at the University of Sussex conducted by Geoffrey Walker, a brief report on which I have given in *Occupation and Pay in Great Britain 1906–79* (pp. 210–11). Walker suggests one phenomenon that might serve to carry messages as through a nervous system:

> Transcending all the above questions of size and timing of claims was one circumstance in which the rank and file had very clear views of magnitude, size and immediate necessity for a claim, and this circumstance arose where a cherished relativity with a well-known immediate and clearly perceived comparator was changed. This situation, it cannot be emphasised too strongly, was the one which exercised the imagination and determination of all trade union members at all levels, and indeed it might be said that the rank and file level was that which perceived most keenly such a change.

Internal labour markets
In sum we may say that there is a large casual element in pay determination (casual = due to chance, undesigned, random). Market forces, tending to equality of pay between similar jobs, skills and efforts, are so feeble as to be difficult to catch in the act. This is demonstrated particularly by the wide dispersion of rates of pay between workers in a specified occupation that is likely to be wider than the differentials that distinguish higher and lower occupations in linked groups or industries. This is demonstrated by Christopher Saunders and David Marsden for occupational classes in manufacturing industry in six Common Market countries – though there are also quite wide variations between countries both in dispersion within occupational groups and in differentials between occupational groups (see Royal Commission on the Distribution of Income and Wealth, Background Paper No. 8, *A Six-Country Comparison of the Distribution of Industrial Earnings in the 1970s*, London: HMSO, 1979). There are also wide differences between countries in the amount of overall variance in pay accounted for by occupational class, industry, age,

region, establishment size and length of service (ibid. table 11, p. 47). In Great Britain nearly half the variance for men's earnings is left unexplained when the effect of these elements has been exhausted; in the German Federal Republic a little more than half (ibid. p. 50). In Belgium, Italy and the Netherlands, however, the unexplained residue is much smaller.

The indeterminacy (by standards of morality or economics) of the labour market is transformed at the level of the organisation into something much nearer the vision of equity and common sense entertained by Cantillon and (in his Chapter 10) by Adam Smith. This has led a number of researchers to identify the *internal labour market* as the appropriate venue in which to look for determinants. As Clark Kerr has said, 'The internal market reacts to what is considered to be "right"; the external market to what is "necessary".' (*Labor Markets and Wage Determination*, pp. 8–9.) Other works that identify and explore this phenomenon are Derek Robinson (ed.), *Local Labour Markets and Wage Structures* (London: Gower Press, 1970); D. I. MacKay and others, *Labour Markets under Different Employment Conditions* (London: Allen & Unwin, 1971) and Peter B. Doeringer and Michael J. Piore, *Internal Labor Markets and Manpower Analysis* (Lexington: D. C. Heath, 1971). Certainly it is within organisations that job evaluation is practised and some sort of justice is attempted to be done. Particularly in the public sector, relativities and differentials are adhered to based on education, rank and grade, distinctions whose preservation is jealously watched over by the employees to whom they apply.

But even here, be it noted, the justice that is done is of a cursory nature. In almost any department at which you care to look you will find workers in the same job at the same rate of pay who do very different amounts of work. It is a tribute to human ingenuity that some people, especially those in positions of responsibility, can enter a permanent state of suspended animation and yet preserve a façade of activity for their own superiors. And even within the same plant earnings may vary widely between workers doing the same job, a phenomenon investigated by H. M. Douty ('Sources of Occupational Wage and Salary Rate Dispersion within Labor Markets', *Industrial and Labor Relations Review*, Oct. 1961) and Kenneth Mayhew ('Earnings Dispersion in Local Labour Markets: Implications for Search Behaviour', *Oxford Bulletin of Economics and Statistics*, vol. 39, no. 2, May 1977).

8 Consumers and Distributors

8.1 PERFECT COMPETITION?

Firms, with their workers, their organisation and command of material resources, create the goods with which the shops are filled, and disseminate the purchasing power by which those goods may be bought. So now we see the worker, with his or her household, turned consumer, confronted by the shopkeeper who constitutes the frontline of the productive process.

It used to be thought (and is maintained to this very day in the standard textbooks) that utility would be maximised, effort minimised and the use of resources optimised by consumers and producers being left to go their own sweet way. Such would be the perfection of the resulting system that no other could conceivably improve on it, especially if it sought to interfere with the rights of private property then in operation. The great economists sought to prove and justify this in most ingenious ways, thereby allaying the envy of the mob and expunging from the conscience of the rich any sense of guilt. Whether they succeeded in the first or were necessary for the second it is difficult to say. In the small print of such expositions was always the proviso, 'Given the existing distribution of property'.

'Nature has placed mankind under the governance of two sovereign masters, *pain* and *pleasure*.' From this fundamental law Jeremy Bentham deduced the absolute selfishness of all. If you did 'good' it was purely so that you would get back something even better for yourself. And, happily, of all passions, 'That is the most given to calculation, from the excesses of which, by reason of its strength, constancy, and universality, society has most to apprehend: I mean that which corresponds to the motive of pecuniary interest.' (W. Stark, *Jeremy Bentham's Economic Writings*, London: Allen & Unwin, 1954, vol. III, p. 434.)

Thus people will deftly manage their own affairs, buying a little more of this and a little less of that, as prices change, so that the marginal utility derived from the last dime, penny or centime spent on each of all their purchases is equalised. If there is perfect competition between producers and ditto between buyers, then the good things described in the previous paragraph will result. Prices will respond to changes in supply and demand so that no one is left feeling he would have liked to have bought or sold more or less at the going price.

What would be the consequences of perfect competition? Imagine General Motors, Ford and Chrysler, Renault, Fiat, Toyota and the other giants being split into hundreds of competing firms, each car fashioned by hand-made tools out of steel bought in from the friendly neighbourhood iron works. (Remember, each firm has to be too small to make a perceptible difference to aggregate supply or price.) Consumer durables, if they could be made at all, would be so expensive as to be beyond the reach of all except very rich people. The second result is that the manufacturers would immediately begin combining to escape from the intolerable situation in which they had been placed. We would rapidly return to the position in which monopolies commissions, food and drug acts, offices of fair trading, consumer associations and fraud squads were again indispensable.

To proclaim that supply and demand determine price does not promote our understanding: what we have to seek is what governs supply and demand in each case. (I paraphrase from J. E. Cairnes, *Some Leading Principles of Political Economy Newly Expounded*, London: Macmillan, 1874, pp. 151–2.) Or as Kenneth Boulding remarked (of demand and supply), 'In whatever sense they are used, they are not ultimate determinants of anything, but they are convenient channels through which we can classify and describe the effects of the multitude of determinants of the system of economic magnitudes.' ('A Liquidity Preference Theory of Market Prices', *Economica*, vol. IX, 1944. Reprinted in American Economic Association, *Readings in Price Theory*, London: Allen & Unwin, 1953, p. 311.) Thus we must forgo the temptation to sit comfortably in our studies contemplating the perfections of perfect competition and, with whatever reluctant glances it may entail, set out into the world to see what we can see, strenuous and difficult though such a course will be.

8.2 HOUSEHOLD EXPENDITURE

Government statistical offices, as part of their estimation of national income and expenditure, calculate the total amount spent by households. It is a most laborious job, necessitating the collection of data on hundreds of items of consumption. Table 8.1 is derived from these calculations for the United States for the years 1929, 1933 and 1979. I choose 1979 because this is the latest year for which I have statistics, and 1929 because it allows a comparison of the changes that have taken place over half a century. Real consumption per head of population increased by a factor of about 2.3 in this period. I have put in 1933 because this was the very depth of the depression of that era, when real consumption per head had fallen by about 25 per cent compared with 1929.

Table 8.1 *Percentage distribution of consumer expenditure in the USA, 1929, 1933 and 1979*

	1929	1933	1979
		Percentages	
Food and beverages	24.7	24.8	20.0
Tobacco	2.1	2.7	1.3
Clothing and related products	12.3	10.3	7.1
Jewelry and watches	0.7	0.4	0.7
Laundering and cleaning in establishments	1.2	1.0	—
Personal care	1.4	1.4	1.3
Housing	14.2	16.7	16.0
Household furniture, equipment and supplies	5.8	4.7	6.6
Gas	0.7	1.1	1.1
Electricity	0.8	1.4	2.1
Water, other fuel and ice	2.4	3.1	—
Telephone and telegraph	0.7	0.9	1.7
Domestic service	3.2	2.8	0.5
Other household operations	—	—	2.5
Medical care	4.5	5.1	9.7
Personal business	6.4	6.3	5.4
User-operated transport	7.5	6.5	13.3
Other transport	2.1	2.1	0.8
Recreation	5.5	4.7	6.7
Private education and research	0.8	1.0	1.6
Religious and welfare activities	1.5	1.9	1.3
Foreign travel and remittances	1.0	0.8	0.3
Total	100	100	100

Sources: *Historical Statistics of the United States Colonial Times to 1957*, Washington: Bureau of Census, 1960, p. 178. *Statistical Abstract for the United States 1980*, p. 442.

Money expenditure had fallen in 1933 by more than 41 per cent, real expenditure by less because of the fall of prices. For every $100 spent about $25 still go on food and beverages, but less on clothing, jewelry and watches. The proportion spent on 'user-operated transport' has also been reduced, ditto recreation and foreign travel. By 1979, as I have mentioned, households are spending more than double what they did in 1929 in real terms. Now only $20 in every hundred go on food, the proportion on tobacco has been almost halved (but this no doubt for health reasons) and the proportion spent on clothing greatly reduced. Gas, electricity and telephones have increased, but domestic service, as in all developed countries, is a shadow of its former self. The proportion spent on own transport has nearly doubled compared with 1929, while public transport has suffered a great decline. How strange that foreign travel should be so far reduced – from a dollar in a hundred in 1929 to 30 cents in 1979.

Alfred Marshall introduced the term 'elasticity' to describe what happens to purchases when the price of something changes. If for a fall in price consumption goes up more than proportionately and vice versa for a rise we say that demand is relatively price-elastic; if less than proportionately, relatively price-inelastic. We talk, too, of income elasticity; in Table 8.1 food and tobacco appear as income-inelastic, while cars and recreation appear as relatively income-elastic.

Of course, these are changes that have taken place over time. Habits change; new products appear and others fade away. Real incomes rise (which means that money incomes have risen faster than prices), but *relative* prices also change. For instance in the United States between 1935 and 1977, the price of all items on the consumer price index rose on average by a factor of 4.4. But the factors by which the prices of individual groups rose were as follows:

Food	5.3
Housing	3.8
Apparel	3.8
Transportation	4.2
Medical care	5.6
Personal care	4.6
Reading and recreation	3.8
Household durables	2.9

(US Department of Labor, *Handbook of Labor Statistics 1978*, table 117, pp. 398–9.)

The poorer a country is the higher the proportion of expenditure that must be spent on food; as the country becomes richer this proportion will fall. We may see the same effect in cross-sectional studies: if households are divided according to incomes the poorer households will be seen to spend a higher proportion of their outgoings on food. It is an obvious enough point, but what magnitudes are involved? Most governments conduct annual surveys of the expenditure of a sample of households, from which the results may be read.

For example, in the Netherlands in 1978, households whose income was less than 25 500 florins spent 23.9 per cent of their expenditure on food; those in the range 25 500 to 33 000 florins spent 22.0 per cent, and those at 33 000 florins and over, 20.1 per cent. This was despite the fact that the first group averaged 2.2 people per household, the second 3.2 and the third 3.6. (*The Statistical Yearbook of the Netherlands 1981*, of which an English version is published, The Hague 1982, p. 336.)

8.3 THE APPETITES OF MEN ... AND OF WOMEN

Following the example of the *Wealth of Nations*, every economic textbook was required to include a paean to parsimony. Capital was that part of income that was saved and utilised for the employment of productive hands – that is, for the production of goods that, in due term, could be sold at a profit. 'What is annually saved is as regularly consumed as what is annually spent, and nearly in the same time too; but it is consumed by a different set of people.' (*Wealth of Nations*, pp. 337–8.) 'Parsimony, by increasing the fund which is destined for the maintenance of productive hands, tends to increase the number of those hands whose labour adds to the value of the subject upon which it is bestowed.' (Ibid. p. 337.)

Malthus argued, with some force, that if everyone were to limit his consumption to bare subsistence, there would be no market for the flood of products that the resulting increase of capital would occasion (*The Principles of Political Economy*, 2nd ed., London: William Pickering, 1836. Reprinted by the International Economic Circle, Tokyo, and the London School of Economics, 1936, pp. 416–18). So, instead of employing productive hands for whose product there will be no market, employ unproductive ones: menial servants, statesmen, soldiers, judges and lawyers, physicians, surgeons and clergy. (Ibid.

p. 407.) As we should say today, make up in the public sector for the deficiencies of the private.

In the *General Theory*, Keynes quotes at some length from Malthus and an earlier advocate of extravagance, Bernard de Mandeville, the author of the *Fable of the Bees* (*General Theory*, pp. 359–64). But these writers had been anticipated by Sir Dudley North, co-inventor with John Locke of the theory of demand and supply. It was, perhaps, from his long years growing rich as a merchant in the trade with Turkey that he had observed:

> The main spur to Trade, or rather to Industry and Ingenuity, is the exorbitant Appetites of Men, which they will take pains to gratifie, and so be disposed to work, when nothing else will incline them to it; for did Men content themselves with bare Necessaries, we should be a poor World.
>
> The Glutton works hard to purchase Delicacies, wherewith to gorge himself; The Gamester, for Money to venture at Play; the Miser, to hoard; and so others. Now in their pursuit of these Appetites, other Men less exorbitant, are benefitted; and tho' it may be thought few profit by the Miser, yet it will be found otherwise, if we consider, that besides the humour of every Generation, to dissipate what another had collected, there is benefit from the very person of a covetous Man; for if he labours with his own hands, his Labour is very beneficial to them who imploy him; if he doth not work, but profit by the Work of others, then those he sets on work have benefit by their being employed....
>
> The meaner sort seeing their Fellows become rich, and great, are spurr'd up to imitate their Industry. A Tradesman sees his Neighbour keep a Coach, presently all his Endeavour is at work to do the like, and many times is beggered by it; however the extraordinary Application he made, to support his Vanity, was beneficial to the Publick, tho' not enough to answer his false Measures as to himself. (*Discourses upon Trade*, 1691. Reprinted in J. R. McCulloch, ed., *Early English Tracts on Commerce*, London: The Political Economy Club, 1856, and Cambridge University Press, 1954, pp. 14–15.)

These intimations of human psychology were not followed up, however, for they were out of character with the *laissez-faire* model of man. Economic Man was prudent and canny, demanding value for his money, while the fate of spendthrifts was their own destruction.

8.3.1 The theory of the leisure class

It was a peculiarity of Economic Man that he enjoyed earning and was willing to subject himself to the pain of labour in order to do so, but he did not enjoy owning and had to be bribed (by the payment of interest) to endure the pain of abstinence. This was convenient for mathematical models, but gave little insight into human motivations. It was Thorstein Veblen, a very unconventional American economist, who drew attention to the importance of the possession of wealth and the curious methods devised for its enjoyment.

> It is of course not to be overlooked that in a community where nearly all goods are private property the necessity of earning a livelihood is a powerful and ever-present incentive for the poorer members of the community. The need of subsistence and of an increase of physical comfort may for a time be the dominant motive of acquisition for those classes who are habitually employed at manual labor, whose subsistence is on a precarious footing, who possess little and ordinarily accumulate little; but it will appear in the course of the discussion that even in the case of these impecunious classes the predominance of the motive of physical want is not so decided as has sometimes been assumed. On the other hand, so far as regards those members and classes of the community who are chiefly concerned in the accumulation of wealth, the incentive of subsistence or of physical comfort never plays a considerable part.... The dominant incentive was from the outset the invidious distinction attaching to wealth, and, save temporarily and by exception, no other motive has usurped the primacy at any later stage of the development. (Thorstein Veblen, *The Theory of the Leisure Class*, first published 1899. New York: Mentor Books, 1953, pp. 35-6.)

To obtrude an observation of my own: the difference between the poorest peasants and urban-dwellers of Africa and the wealthier people of that continent is not the inadequacy of the diet or even the clothing of the former. Inquiries conducted at the University of Dar es Salaam showed that the distinction lay in the extraordinary austerity of the peasants' household possessions, which matched that of the poorest urban workers. By contrast, a working-class household in an industrialised country will have a vast accumulation of furniture, household equipment, ornaments, pictures and toys. It is only the poorest classes of Africa and Asia and, perhaps, Latin America, who obey the Christian precept: 'Lay not up for yourselves treasures upon earth, where moth and rust doth corrupt, and where thieves break through and steal.' (Matthew vi. 19.) Our investigations suggested that they were able to accommodate themselves to their lot by a singular freedom from acquisitiveness. It was not *resignation*, as the affluent describe this state of mind, but something positive: a freedom from envy possessed by those who expect nothing.

Economic man is self-centred but Veblen's people are concerned with each other, seeking one another's good opinion, as were Adam Smith's people in the *Theory of Moral Sentiments*. Adam Smith regarded them as endowed 'not only with a desire of being approved of, but with a desire of being what ought to be approved of; or of being what he himself approves of in other men'. (R. H. Campbell and A. S. Skinner, *Adam Smith*, London: Croom Helm, 1982, p. 105.) But Veblen's people seek admiration not by virtue, but by a show of wealth. This he describes as 'conspicuous consumption', a term now taken into the vocabulary of sociology.

In previous epochs reputation depended on success in hunting or battle. Later property became the measure. 'When accumulated goods have in this way once become the accepted badge of efficiency, the possession of wealth presently assumes the character of an independent and definitive basis of esteem.' (Veblen, *Theory of the Leisure Class*, p. 37.)

> The exigencies of the modern industrial system frequently place individuals and households in juxtaposition between whom there is little contact in any other sense than that of juxtaposition. One's neighbors, mechanically speaking, often are socially not one's neighbours, or even acquaintances; and still their transient good opinion has a high degree of utility. The only practicable means of impressing one's pecuniary ability on these unsympathetic observers of one's everyday life is an unremitting demonstration of ability to pay. In the modern community there is also a more frequent attendance at large gatherings of people to whom one's everyday life is unknown.... In order to impress these transient observers, and to retain one's self-complacency under their observation, the signature of one's pecuniary strength should be written in characters which he who runs may read. (Veblen, *Theory of the Leisure Class*, pp. 71–2.)

Both Cantillon and Adam Smith had remarked on the different

standards of living that workers in different countries had accustomed themselves to. This affected the operation of the subsistence theory of wages, in that custom dictated the income at which a man and woman regarded it as proper to get married. Bastiat (1801–50) had observed that the standard of living was flexible upward but intractable downward (the ratchet effect), and Veblen described a similar phenomenon:

> Many items of customary expenditure prove on analysis to be almost purely wasteful, and they are therefore honorific only, but after they have once been incorporated into the scale of decent consumption, and so have become an integral part of one's scheme of life, it is quite as hard to give up these as it is to give up many items that conduce directly to one's physical comfort, or even that may be necessary to life and health. That is to say, the conspicuously wasteful honorific expenditure that confers spiritual well-being may become more indispensable than much of that expenditure which ministers to the 'lower' wants of physical well-being or sustenance only. It is notoriously just as difficult to recede from a 'high' standard of living as it is to lower a standard which is already relatively low; although in the former case the difficulty is a moral one, while in the latter it may involve a material deduction from the physical comforts of life.
>
> But while retrogression is difficult, a fresh advance in conspicuous expenditure is relatively easy; indeed, it takes place almost as a matter of course. In the rare cases where it occurs, a failure to increase one's visible consumption when the means for an increase are at hand is felt in popular apprehension to call for explanation, and unworthy motives of miserliness are imputed to those who fall short in this respect. (Veblen, *Theory of the Leisure Class*, pp. 80–1.)

So it is that a standard of living is a matter of habit; to recede from such a standard requires the breaking of a habit. 'The relative facility with which an advance in the standard is made means that the life process is a process of unfolding activity and that it will readily unfold in a new direction whenever and wherever the resistance to self-expression decreases.' (Ibid. pp. 82–3.) People cling to various categories of consumption with varying degrees of tenacity: most tenacious, that compromising the subsistence minimum. But there is also extreme reluctance to abandon habitual forms of conspicuous consumption. In forming these habits *emulation* is a pervading trait of human nature. Veblen describes the propensities of emulation as 'alert and deep-reaching'. (p. 85.) As an economic motive it is second only to the instinct of self-preservation.

Expense makes an important contribution to prestige, to the extent that costliness masquerades as beauty (p. 95): expensive flowers are deemed more beautiful than cheaper ones. Refinements that serve no purpose may contribute to a canon of reputable futility. For this, Veblen gives dogs a high rating. 'He is the filthiest of the domestic animals in his person and the nastiest in his habits. For this he makes up in a servile, fawning attitude towards his master, and a readiness to inflict damage and discomfort on all else. The dog, then, commends himself to our favor by affording play to our propensity for mastery, and as he is also an item of expense, and commonly serves no industrial purpose, he holds a well-assured place in men's regard as a thing of good repute.' (p. 103.) What is simple and unadorned may be both efficient and aesthetically pleasing, in which case 'the canons of beauty must be circumvented by some contrivance which will give evidence of a reputably wasteful expenditure . . .' (p. 109.) In the superior status of handmade over machine-made goods we indulge 'the exaltation of the defective'. (p. 115.) Our dress gives an indication of our pecuniary standing to all observers at first glance. 'It is also true that admitted expenditure for display is more obviously present, and is, perhaps, more universally practiced in the matter of dress than in any other line of consumption.' Display and a respectable appearance are more important than the protection of the person. The conscious motive is the need to conform, and thus 'avoid the mortification that comes of unfavourable notice and comment . . . but besides that, the requirement of expensiveness is so ingrained into our habits . . . that any other than expensive apparel is instinctively odious to us. Without reflection or analysis, we feel that what is inexpensive is unworthy.' (p. 119.) New fashions, then, are required to come up to the 'accepted standard of expensiveness'. (p. 123.)

We have followed Veblen through the first half of his book; in the second half he continues his consideration of human behaviour, but not in matters relating to consumption. I give only one more quotation and that from the penultimate page of his book. I have sometimes wondered why we make such a fuss about spelling, when until the eighteenth century you were allowed to spell any way you liked, provided the word was easily recognisable. Veblen offers an explanation:

A breach of the proprieties in spelling is extremely annoying and will discredit any writer in the eyes of all persons who are possessed of a developed sense of the true and beautiful. English orthography satisfies all the requirements of the canons of reputability under the law of conspicuous waste. It is archaic, cumbrous, and ineffective; its acquisition consumes much time and effort; failure to acquire it is easy of detection. Therefore it is the first and readiest test of reputability in learning, and conformity to its ritual is indispensable to a blameless scholastic life.   (p. 257.)

We all of us live in colonies of consumers, so have plenty of opportunity of seeing the function of consumption in operation. How far do Veblen's observations conform with your own? It seems to me that emulation is an important factor whose presence explains the rapidity with which new fashions spread: I write in a period in which video has been discovered by the British, who, in this respect, are second only to the Japanese. Am I missing out on something important by not having the necessary equipment in my home? I recall the similar period when it was television that was spreading rapidly. Children at school whose house did not possess a set were regarded first as unfortunate, later as objects of curiosity. In due course the introduction of colour television followed a similar course.

Car-ownership is even more conspicuous. In my street there are a Rolls–Royce and several Mercedes, Volvos and BMWs as well as a number of cars of British make, all fairly new. There is also my ancient Alfa-Romeo, suffering from rust and other ravages of age. I hope the neighbours regard me as eccentric rather than of low status.

There are some streets where all the houses have beautifully kept gardens that are a pleasure to behold. Are the householders competing with one another, their prestige at stake?

The importance of expense would also be a possible explanation for a curious phenomenon that can be observed in the smart shopping area of any important city: the scale of prices for women's dresses is not continuous between the cheap and the very expensive, whilst the quality is. You can get any number of dresses of good quality and design up to $200; and then at some stage, prices will leap to $1000 or above. It is true that amongst these fabulously priced raiments will be the labels of the great couturiers, but none of them will contain the material or the workmanship to justify their price. Do they attract simply because they are so expensive, as Veblen would suggest?

For men following non-manual occupations established usage and respectability play important roles. Even in tropical Africa, suits, waistcoats, collars and ties are worn by businessmen and officials, despite the considerable discomfort that they entail.

We may judge, then, that there is a lot of truth in what Veblen said. But *how* true is (or was) it? To what proportion of the population would his canons apply? And with what force? His methodology makes these questions impossible to answer. In his Preface he explains: 'Partly for reasons of convenience, and partly because there is less chance of misapprehending the sense of phenomena that are familiar to all men, the data employed to illustrate or enforce the argument have by preference been drawn from everyday life, by direct observation or through common notoriety, rather than from more recondite sources at a farther remove. It is hoped that no one will find his sense of literary or scientific fitness offended by this recourse to homely facts, or by what may at times appear to be a callous freedom in handling vulgar phenomena or phenomena whose intimate place in men's life has sometimes shielded them from the impact of economic discussion.' Of course, it is far better to make your hypotheses out of material that you have observed in the real world than to try to do it by process of logical deduction from assumptions that are themselves absurd. But that leaves Veblen's propositions with the status of brilliant hypotheses. Before they can be accepted as legitimate theories confirmation has to be sought in much more systematic investigations.

8.3.2 The affluent society

Fifty-nine years elapsed between the publication of Veblen's *Theory of the Leisure Class* and Galbraith's *Affluent Society*. (John Kenneth Galbraith, *The Affluent Society*, London: Hamish Hamilton, 1958. My references are to the Penguin ed., 1962.) It cannot be said that in this period conventional theory had advanced – indeed, it had used immunising stratagems to save itself from extinction. In their first flush converts to marginal utility had held out hopes of being able to measure it, as Edgeworth suggested in atoms of pleasure. But was there not a danger that this doctrine would be used as an argument for the redistribution of wealth, just as the labour theory had been? No, said Edgeworth, for pleasure would be maximised and distributive justice done when more was given to those most able to enjoy it – that is, the most evolved sections of society. 'Aristocratical privilege' consisted of 'the privilege of man above brute, of civilised above savage, of birth, of talent, and of the male sex.' (Francis Ysidro Edgeworth, *Mathematical Psychics*, London: Kegan Paul, 1881,

p. 77.) This argument was not found to be very convincing, so the orthodox creed retreated from cardinal to ordinal utility: more would always be preferred to less, but it was impossible to say by how much. Indifference curves measured the trade-off between one good or group of goods and another, and a higher indifference curve, signifying more of both, was always preferable to a lower, for it signified a higher contour on what Pareto christened 'the hill of pleasure'. But no one could say that if the millionaire came down a bit so that the beggar could move up, the sum-total of happiness would be increased or diminished. Later, Samuelson relieved the subject of all such painful comparisons by asserting that, since no one knows what utility is, it would be better to drop the idea and talk instead about 'revealed preference'. If people were observed to prefer more to less that was enough. There was no need to try to find out why. (On this evolution of economic thought see Galbraith, *Affluent Society*, pp. 127-30.)

And yet in this period profound changes had come about. In 1900 trade unionism in the United States was still limited to a few craft unions; nearly two-fifths of the occupied population were employed on farms; only one in seven were in white-collar jobs. By the middle of the twentieth century powerful unions and social security had considerably improved the position of American workers, while real national income per head had doubled. With general consumption so much increased it was no longer so easy to consume conspicuously. This leads Galbraith to identify the New Class into which the Leisure Class has been absorbed. It is not very clearly defined, but seems to be a sort of middle class that has spread its boundaries to embrace much of the proletariat and bourgeoisie. Two sorts of poverty remain: case poverty, where a household or individual is deprived because of family circumstances – sometimes because of drink or drugs, sometimes mental or physical incapacitation – and insular poverty, where a whole region or district has been by-passed by the flow of progress.

Veblen's conspicuous consumption depended on the prestige derived from expenditure on the useless, the ostentatious, the extravagant, but in the Affluent Society this ceases to be conspicuous. A man who is hungry does not need to be told so, but a household encumbered with possessions have to be persuaded that there are still more things that they want – the vestigal Puritan ethos must be 'overwhelmed by the massive power of modern merchandising'. Their ability to keep up with the flow of production depends more and more on their ability and willingness to incur debt (Galbraith, *Affluent Society*, pp. 166-7). This process of persuasion, in which 'needs' are generated by those whose business it is to sell, Galbraith names the Dependence Effect. The aim is diverted from supplying needs to creating them. The concern for goods no longer arises out of spontaneous consumer need, but grows out of the process of production:

> If production is to increase, the wants must be effectively contrived. In the absence of the contrivance the increase would not occur. This is not true of all goods, but that it is true for a substantial part is sufficient. It means that since the demand for this part would not exist, were it not contrived, its utility or urgency, ex-contrivance, is zero.... Clearly the attitudes and values which make production the central achievement of our society have some exceptionally twisted roots.   (Ibid. p. 137.)

Are Veblen's and Galbraith's views complementary or contradictory? The range of goods competing for the consumer's cash has been transformed. In quantity and variety consumers are better off than they were when Veblen wrote. Do they today get the same satisfaction from *displaying* their acquisitions or is the emphasis now on usefulness? Perhaps the social ethos is changing before our very eyes? – the awareness of ecology, the desire to preserve and develop instead of destroy natural resources, the demand for smaller cars, for natural foods....

Galbraith developed his ideas in the *New Industrial State* (London: Hamish Hamilton, 1967) and they do indeed seem to be complementary to and extensive of those of Veblen. He has been emphasising the need for planning entailed by the vast resources that the great corporations employ. They cannot leave their fortunes to the vagaries of the market: they must create and control their markets:

> As so often, change in the industrial system has made possible what change requires. The need to control consumer behavior is a requirement of planning. Planning, in turn, is made necessary by extensive use of advanced technology and capital and by the related scale and complexity of organization. These produce goods efficiently; the result is a very large volume of production. As a further consequence, goods that are related only to elementary physical sensation – that merely prevent hunger, protect against cold, provide shelter, suppress pain – have come to comprise a small and diminishing part of all production. Most goods serve needs that are discovered to the individual not by the palpable discomfort that

accompanies deprivation, but by some psychic response to their possession. They give him a sense of personal achievement, accord him a feeling of equality with his neighbours, divert his mind from thought, serve sexual aspiration, promise social acceptability, enhance his subjective feeling of health, well-being or orderly peristalsis, contribute by conventional canons to personal beauty, or are otherwise psychologically rewarding.

Thus it comes about that, as the industrial system develops to the point where it has need for planning and the mangement of the consumer that this requires, it is also serving wants which are psychological in origin and hence admirably subject to management by appeal to the psyche. (Galbraith, *Affluent Society*, p. 201.)

8.3.3 The psychology of consumer behaviour

Neither Veblen nor Galbraith give evidence that they have systematically researched the matters upon which they pronounce. They have observed, questioned and taken counsel, and then interpreted their findings, but we must evaluate their findings as hypotheses rather than theories. George Katona, on the other hand, has combined theorising with carefully designed research into consumer behaviour. It is significant that it was to a chair of economics and psychology that he was appointed by the University of Michigan in 1948, and there organised the Survey Research Center to determine what consumers were likely to do, and what made them pursue or change their spending and saving habits. His work has been ignored by orthodox economists, but has made its impact on social psychology and sociology. His most important book, as not infrequently happens, was also his first – *Psychological Analysis of Economic Behavior*, New York: McGraw-Hill, 1951.

You may have noticed that economic terminology is as often designed to hide as to reveal: perfect competition, if it had ever existed, would have been hellish; indifference curves are concerned with agonies of choice, revealed preference is what we imagine would be revealed if we ever got round to observing it; exploitation (as defined by Pigou) is the difference between marginal product and average product; Pareto optimum is when the poor cannot be made richer without making the rich poorer. So too with the model of *rational* economic man – he who, like Alberic in Wagner's *Ring*, has renounced love in favour of gold.

In the 1950s, after it had been established that economic forecasts were devoid of predictive power, the disappointed predictors petulantly complained that it was because people were irrational. In fact, the reason was quite the opposite: sheep are irrational and their behaviour is quite easy to predict; it is because people reason, learn by experience and can take evasive action that it is difficult to foretell what they will do.

Katona divided expenditure by consumers into three major types: habitual, contractual and discretionary. Much human behaviour is ordered by habit and thereby results in considerable economy of mental and physical effort. Habit is formed only when a course of action has been learnt and/or experimentally discovered to serve a specified purpose.

> Suppose my telephone rings; I lift the receiver with my left hand and say, 'Hello.' Should we then argue that I made several choices, for instance, that I decided not to lift the receiver with my right hand and not to say 'Mr. Katona speaking'? According to our use of the terms decision and choice, my action was habitual and did not involve 'taking consequences into consideration'. (George Katona, 'Rational Behavior and Economic Behavior', in Harold H. Kassarjian and Thomas S. Robertson, eds, *Perspectives in Consumer Behavior*, Glenview: Scott, Foresman, 1968, p. 11.)

Habits guide much of our working and social lives, the use of our leisure time, washing, dressing, going to bed and getting up. It might be that we should be the better if we spent more time questioning what we do and how we do it; as it is, we do so only in times of crisis, and otherwise continue for months or years doing what habit tells us is safe, convenient and satisfying to do. This is one of the factors that makes human activity unresponsive to price changes. When relative prices change, economic man is supposed to adapt his spending so that he buys more of what has become cheaper and less of what has become dearer. His habits make him price-resistant. He and his children would be outraged if they came home in the evening to be served pasta with their fish because the price of potatoes had risen or the price of macaroni come down. Foods take on a special savour because people are used to them. So consumption patterns assume a durable form.

Katona distinguishes, too, contractual expenditure. If one is committed to buying a house, a substantial amount of one's expenditure may be fixed for many years ahead. The same applies, for varying periods of time, to hire-purchase, life insurance and taxation.

The third category is discretionary expenditure, that we may or may not undertake, depending on the circumstances. This applies particularly to household effects and consumer durables. There is considerable latitude about when, or even if, these purchases should be made. If decisions to buy, postpone or not to buy were a stochastic process, with each household acting in isolation from every other, decisions to postpone would be likely to be offset by decisions to advance, so that demand would be fairly steady. But from the very birth of capitalism, as we have seen, this has not been so: there have, instead, been epidemics of buying or not-buying, saving or spending, whose characteristic has been the alternation of booms and slumps.

I have already quoted the passage from Boisguillebert describing how 'opulence and voluptuousness' had resulted in the multiplication of different sorts of occupations. He goes on to describe the phenomenon that, two and a half centuries later, Katona was to christen 'discretionary expenditure', that had to be handled with caution, 'otherwise, it happens that that which has been instituted to allow the enjoyment of the surplus, only acts, when the measures have been misconceived, to deprive of necessities, throwing a country in an instant from opulence to the last degree of misery'. (See the *Origin of Economic Ideas*, p. 59.)

It must be plain that one cannot say *a priori* what it is that determines discretionary expenditure. Keynes, for convenience' sake, assumed a constant consumption function, but of course consumption fluctuates and this, together with fluctuations in industrial investment, occasion the instability of the economy. To gain understanding of these processes one must follow the standard pattern of empirical research: ask, observe, study, analyse, interpret. This is precisely what the Survey Research Center at the University of Michigan has been doing for the past thirty years, though it is rare for an economics textbook to refer to their findings. You may find some of these conveniently summarised in George Katona, *The Mass Consumption Society* (New York: McGraw-Hill, 1964). Chapter 23 deals with spending on automobiles. 'The variety of the good things of life which Americans aspired to possess was much larger in the early 1960s than in the late 1940s. The automobile became just one among several greatly desired objects, yet one which was necessary in order to accomplish other desired goals.' (Katona, p. 256.) I have remarked on the curious freedom from envy of the peasants of Tanzania; it is interesting to note the discovery by the Survey Research Center of a positive relation between wealth and unfulfilled desires. Respondents were asked 'Now about your wishes, are there any special expenditures you would really *like* to make, or anything you would like to spend money on?' A negative answer was returned by 43 per cent of the income group under $3000, 33 per cent of those $3000–4999 and between 23 and 25 per cent of those in income groups of $5000 and above.

In the 1960s the list of items for discretionary purchase had lengthened:

> In addition to the valued possessions of ten or twelve years earlier, a summer cottage, a motorboat, numerous hobby and sporting goods, power tools, and additions or repairs to the home were each mentioned by a sizable proportion of respondents. Very substantial was the increase in the frequency with which travel was mentioned – vacation trips as well as trips to visit distant parts of the United States and foreign countries. Educational needs both for children and adults were likewise often referred to in discussion of unsatisfied wants.   (Katona, pp. 256–7.)

It is interesting to notice the substantial numbers of consumers in favour of smaller cars, and against annual model changes. 'The higher the income, the more frequent was the notion that changing the appearance of cars every year served no useful purpose and was wasteful.' (Ibid. p. 259.)

Others chapters deal with the complex matter of home-ownership and leisure-time activities.

Part Five of the book deals with saving. The textbook treatment of this has been particularly unsatisfactory because of the need felt by orthodox economists to pretend that saving is associated with agonies of self-restraint as the savers are confronted by all the things it would be nice to buy. It was this that was supposed to make the lot of the rentier just as disagreeable as that of the worker.

The findings of investigations do not confirm this view. 'Saving in order to earn additional income in the form of interest or dividends and saving in order to bequeath money to one's heirs represent purposes that are conspicuous by their absence in the discussion of the average consumer.' (Ibid. p. 176.) The major purposes are for emergencies, for retirement, for children and family needs and for a variety of other purposes – to buy a house, business, or durable goods or to pay for vacations.

> The accumulation of savings for the purposes mentioned constitutes a highly valued goal. The American people do not speak of saving as a negative act – as refraining or abstaining from using

money. Savings are associated with important values and are seen as a goal for which it is worthwhile to strive. Not saving is regretted and sometimes considered morally wrong. (Ibid. p. 177.)

People are not indifferent to the interest or dividends they receive, but since this is not their principal aim they do not stop saving when the rate of inflation is higher than the rate of interest – that is, when the rate of interest is negative. This is in flat contradiction to the assumptions of the orthodox model. In contradiction, too, is that people do not regard saving as the opposite of spending, for the acquirement of a financial asset is regarded as desirable in much the same way as that of a durable good. The equation, much used in the Keynesian model, income = saving + spending is misleading when related to the behaviour of those who earn the income and do the saving and spending. Their alternatives are more diverse and may be elaborated: discretionary spending; other spending; discretionary saving; contractual and other saving. Changes in the deployment of income over these four categories may have important implications for the economy. (Ibid. p. 179).

Consumer behaviour becomes easier to predict because consumers form part of nations, classes and groups under common influences, trying to interpret information that they share in common – from the media and at their work-places – and who behave according to common patterns. While movements in income, prices and taxation determine ability to buy, *willingness* to buy, determined by motives, attitudes and expectations, may change independently. (Ibid. pp. 300–1.) In general, uncertainty and insecurity have the same effect in restraining expenditure as a belief in a deterioration of economic conditions.

Because of the length of time for which investigations have been made it is now possible to observe changes of mood, particularly marked in the 1970s as compared with the previous two decades. In the earlier periods Americans were asking 'Is the business cycle obsolete?', while in the 1970s they wondered when the next recession would occur. There was evident a loss of faith in the purchasing power of currency and a fatalistic acceptance of price rises, a scepticism in the powers of government to correct social evils and, following charges of bribery and corruption, a cynicism about the honesty of big business. (Ibid. pp. 300–8, and George Katona and Burkhard Strumpel, *A New Economic Era*, New York: Elsevier, 1978, chap. 4.)

Much talent has been devoted to the study of consumer behaviour in recent years, but the subject has been unsympathetically received by orthodox economists. However, it has found a home in the business schools, particularly in connexion with marketing. 'A general theoretical perspective now taken in marketing is that of the behavioural sciences – psychology, sociology, and anthropology. In this context the consumer is viewed as a psychological entity, acting within a social and sociological environment.' (Harold H. Kassarjian and Thomas S. Robertson, eds., *Perspectives in Consumer Behavior*, Glenview: Scott, Foresman, 1968, p. 3.) See, too, A. S. C. Ehrenberg and F. G. Pyatt, *Consumer Behaviour*, Harmondsworth, Penguin Books, 1971.

Gestalt psychology, and in particular the theories of Kurt Lewin, have been of great appeal. The *Gestalt*, or *pattern*, of behaviour is readily identifiable. Details of expenditure fluctuate, but important, enduring changes involve a redesign of the whole pattern and thus do not lend themselves to marginal analysis. Different patterns are discernible between countries and cultures, regions and classes, males and females, age-groups. Important shifts take place over time. For a theoretical frame, electro-magnetic field theory has been borrowed from physics. (See Harold H. Kassarjian, 'Field Theory in Consumer Behavior', in Scott Ward and Thomas S. Robertson, eds, *Consumer Behavior: Theoretical Sources*, Englewood Cliffs: Prentice-Hall, 1973.)

Empirical research into consumer behaviour has made so much progress that there is really no excuse for those economists who continue to peddle the old theories, as if everything worth knowing about consumption can be deduced from the model of economic man. Fortunately the subject lends itself very readily to research by students, who can conduct their own inquiries into expectations, intentions and consumption patterns. They are much better able to evaluate empirical findings when they have themselves participated in the research.

8.4 SHOPKEEPERS

What has been made so hopefully is now put on display, collected by the distributive trades, wholesale and retail, from every quarter of the globe. Of course, most things have been well-tried and constitute a flow rather than a stock: food, clothing, hardware and software are in regular demand, and the shopkeeper can fairly well estimate how much will be sold on any day or in any week. But in order to maintain and, if possible, increase his trade, he must try to attract, hold and satisfy his customers. Manufacturers or wholesalers persuade him to buy and he, in turn, must persuade the public. They work in the ebbs and flows of the tide of business, swept into insolvency or carried through to success. I write at a time when this process is seen at its most cruel, with to-let signs appearing on what were the premises of attractive and useful shops, some large ones that originated in a previous era, some small, the culmination of their owners' dreams of independence.

Although merchants and traders are of ancient origin, while factories, or the factory system, is comparatively new, retailing lagged far behind manufacturing in its process of modernisation. Until the middle of the nineteenth century, trade was limited by the low standard of living of the labourers, hand workers, outworkers and the new factory workers. 'The living conditions characteristic of these classes, a poor and monotonous diet, shoddy or home-made clothing with a life prolonged by endless darning and mending, and a few sticks of home-made furniture along with the basic pots and pans, did not offer great scope to the retail trades.' (James B. Jefferys, *Retail Trading in Britain 1850-1950*, Cambridge University Press, 1954, p. 3.) It was not until 1875 that a transformation began in the distributive trades comparable to the industrial revolution.

Dorothy Davis points to a process of simplification, in which the work of the shop assistant was deskilled, with many of their most difficult tasks taken over by the manufacturers, while at the same time the organisation of the retail trade became more complicated. (*A History of Shopping*, London: Routledge & Kegan Paul, 1966, p. 277.) But a further change began, that we shall examine in the next section, one of whose manifestations was the end of retail price maintenance whereby the manufacturer dictated the price and conditions of sale, and could cut off the supply of retailers who objected.

The department stores set this new change in motion, with a style and power that ultimately imparted itself to the chain stores and supermarkets that now serve the consumers of affluent industrial states. Bon Marché was established in Paris in 1852; Bloomingdale in New York in 1872; Harrods in London in 1849. (John William Ferry, *A History of the Department Store*, New York: Macmillan, 1960, pp. 2, 36, *212*.)

8.4.1 Dimensions of distribution

Farmers and manufacturers have traditionally regarded the distributive trades with suspicion. As Patrick McAnally remarks: 'For many, if not most, people retail shopping is the main sort of "business" in which they engage. There is a strong tendency, and one that is important, for them to approach it with the idea that retailers as business men are "out to do them" and sometimes this is true.' (*The Economics of the Distributive Trades*, London: Allen & Unwin, 1971, p. 26.) The author is the head of the Research Department of the John Lewis Partnership, a large retailing corporation partly owned by its employees.) It has been to cut out the 'middle-men', or at least reduce their power, that farmers' co-operatives have been set up in most countries of the world and that consumer co-operatives have become important.

Certainly the distributive trades employ a high proportion of the labour force: $18\frac{1}{4}$ million in the United States in 1978, out of a total of 90 million, or one in five of the occupied population. In 1919 it was one in six. About one in five were sales workers – that is, directly engaged in selling. In the United States in 1979, value added in the distributive trades accounted for 14.7 per cent of the national income, so that labour costs per person employed were rather low: 20.5 per cent of the workers received 14.7 per cent of the income.

Manufacturers or growers deliver their products to the distributive trade who, with a theatrical flourish, present them for collection by the consumers, with a cast in the United States of one person so engaged for each twelve members of the population. People as customers appear to be lavishly served, especially when you consider that each person employed in agriculture can feed sixty-four members of the population.

The OECD in their *Labour Force Statistics 1968–1979* include those employed in restaurants and hotels with employment in wholesale and retail trade. This raises the figure for the United States (1978) from 18.5 to 20.3 million. Table 8.2 shows the proportion of the labour force so employed in the OECD countries in 1979.

One might have expected that the more affluent a country the more workers would be required to sell its products. Turkey is by far the poorest of these countries and, true enough, only one worker in 23 is employed in distribution and catering. Portugal is the second poorest and is second from the bottom in Table 8.2, despite its thriving tourist trade. Japan and the United States are at the top, but why should the affluent Scandinavians conduct their trade so economically?

In most of these countries there has been an upward trend in numbers employed in the last ten years, but since the middle-1970s in the Nordic countries (except Norway) and in Germany, the trend has been downward. One would have expected the economies of scale and

Table 8.2 *Proportion of those in civil employment in wholesale and retail trade, restaurants and hotels OECD countries, 1979*

	%
Japan	22.4
United States	21.4
Australia	20.3
Spain	19.6
Switzerland	19.5
Belgium	18.7
Italy	18.6
Netherlands	18.2
Canada	17.4
United Kingdom	17.4
Austria	17.0
Norway	16.9
Ireland	16.5
France	15.9
German Federal Republic	14.4
Finland	14.4
Sweden	13.8
Denmark	13.5
Iceland	13.5
Portugal	11.7
Turkey	4.4

Source: *Labour Force Statistics 1968–1979* (Paris: OECD).

computerised stock-keeping, ordering and sales registering to have had a much more marked effect on the work force, more than offsetting the rise in sales, but the changes now taking place in the industry are very complex, with the growth of hypermarkets at the one end and of specialist shops and boutiques at the other. (See John A. Dawson, *Commercial Distribution in Europe*, London: Croom Helm, 1982, chaps 2 and 3.) There are, in addition, cultural changes of great importance. The British, from experience of rationing and queueing in and after the Second World War, have grown accustomed to wait, while in the United States customers expect, and get, prompt service.

We may get an idea of the range of outlets, size, employment per shop, turnover and selling margins by examining the results of the (British) retail inquiry for 1979. (Business Statistics Office, *Business Monitor 1979 Retailing*, London: HMSO.)

Table 8.3 *Retail trade in the UK, 1979*

No. of firms	No. of outlets	Total outlets	Persons per outlet	Turnover per outlet £000	Gross margins %
235 174	All	351 187	6.9	148	28.0
207 530	1	207 530	4.3	79	26.5
26 394	2–9	69 465	5.2	106	29.0
950	10–49	18 816	12.4	264	30.5
149	50–99	10 438	16.2	416	27.6
84	100–199	11 739	15.4	340	30.1
48	200–499	15 566	17.3	420	31.0
13	500–999	8 390	22.5	571	22.6
7	1000 and over	9 243	15.1	387	30.2

Source: Business Statistics Office, *Business Monitor 1979 Retailing.*

One is first impressed that there are seven giants (or octopuses?) with a thousand or more branches each, and then that there are still so many single-shop firms who account for nearly 32 per cent of the turnover. The big chains, with a hundred or more shops each, account for only 36.3 of the turnover. Notice the variations in the gross margins – the difference between buying price and selling price as a percentage of selling price. Businesses with only one shop work to the lowest margins. Does that mean that their prices will be lower? No, for they generally have to pay higher prices to their suppliers. In part the differences are made up by the product-mix of each range: margins vary inversely with *rate* of turnover and are lower, for instance, on groceries than on furniture.

8.4.2 The shopkeepers' role

How do the distributive trades fit in with the rest of the economy? The roles of the other sectors are unambiguous enough: fishermen, farmers, miners, foresters, who set the raw materials on their way; manufacturers who convert them into consumable products; workers (self-employed or employees) whose brawn and brains do the work; the transporters who, like Milton's messengers, course o'er land and water without rest; and then the inhabitants of the earth who depend on the daily flow of products for their survival and edification. The interests of all these groups are fairly clear; not so the retailers who appear to have dual dependence – on the manufacturers who supply them and on the customers who support them.

You may have noticed that the textbooks of economics have little or nothing to say about the distributive trades, despite their great economic and social importance. In them are put on display the hundreds of thousands of consumer goods, collected from all over the world. It is the shops that give cities their character and their magnetic power, with all the inhabitants of the earth moving through them to buy or admire. Surely they merit a chapter? The difficulty is that even the smallest shop deals in so many goods that marginal costs cannot be identified, nor can limits to output be ascribed to diminishing returns. Of course, these limitations pertain to manufacture too, but there at least one can postulate a one-product factory, whereas this would be a contradiction of the whole idea of retailing.

Patrick McAnally elaborates these aspects:

> For reasons of this sort top management controls things by prescribing a rate of mark-up and correcting it if necessary by manipulating mark-downs and those expenses which are not completely fixed. The rate of mark-up is controlled not so much by the immediate relationship it is thought to have with sales as by what seems to be needed to maintain the firm's posture on the price parameter.
>
> This leads to a rather rigid attitude towards rate of mark-up and gross profit – a state of affairs described as follows by Alfred Marshall: 'there is in each trade and every branch of each trade a more or less definite rate of profits on the turnover which is regarded as a "fair" or normal rate ... such traditions are the outcome of much experience tending to show that, if that rate is charged, a proper allowance will be made for all the costs (supplementary as well as prime) incurred for that particular purpose, and in addition the normal rate of profits per annum in that class of business will be afforded. If they charge a price which gives much less than this rate of profit on the turnover, they can hardly prosper; and if they charge much more they are in danger of losing their custom, since others can afford to undersell them.'
>
> Accordingly when additions to cost, whether in the form of taxation or otherwise occur, the retailer's inclination, if competition permits, is to pass them on, preserving his percentage rate of gross profit.... In any case the retailer's battle with costs is so constant and strenuous that it is very difficult for him to absorb increases. They tend to affect all retailers at the same time, and in so far as the situation is non-revolutionary most raise their rates of mark-up

simultaneously. (*The Economics of the Distributive Trades*, London: Allen & Unwin 1971, pp. 55–6.)

Prime costs are those directly occasioned by a product – the materials, labour and power that would be saved if it were not made. Supplementary costs are the indirect costs that would have to be met whether the product is made or not – rent, interest, obsolescence of fixed capital, staff salaries, that add up to make 'overheads'. McAnally refers to non-revolutionary effects as those that arise in the ordinary course of business in which businessmen respect the accepted procedures of their trade. These are distinguished from the revolutionary effects of a change of mode, when supermarkets invade the territory of corner-shops or hypermarkets or discount houses the territory of supermarkets. These present their threat by applying rates of mark-up with which the older institutions cannot compete.

The dress-buyer of British Home Stores explained the system of mark-up thus: if there was likely to be a keen demand for the dress, with rapid turnover of stock, the mark-up would be below average; if demand were unlikely to be brisk the mark-up would be raised: the greater the demand the lower the price, the reverse of the prediction of orthodox economics.

The selling price of each article consists of the price paid by the retailer plus his mark-up. Considerations that determine the rate of mark-up include the length of time within which the goods are likely to be sold, the sort of premises from which they are sold and the

Table 8.4 *Gross margin as percentage of purchase price in divisions of the retail trade, GB, 1980*

	%
Total retail trade	36.4
Food retailers	25.5
Drink, confectionery and tobacco	17.1
Clothing, footwear and leather goods	61.2
Household goods*	44.2
Chemists	31.5
Booksellers, stationers and newsagents	54.4
Jewellers	78.1
Florists, nurserymen and seedsmen	58.9

* Including carpets, furniture, electrical and musical goods, hardware and do-it-yourself equipment.
Source: Department of Industry and Trade, *British Business*.

labour-costs of selling them. The British Department of Industry and Trade in their retailing inquiry for 1980 gives a breakdown for various sections of the retail trade of gross margins as a percentage of total turnover, exclusive of value-added tax. (See Department of Industry and Trade, *British Business*, 11 June 1982, p. 278.) In Table 8.4 I have converted this into gross margin as a percentage of purchases: the percentage, that is, that the retailer adds to purchase price to calculate selling price.

Jewellers lead all the rest, but then they have to keep expensive jewellery and watches for quite a long time before selling them. But whatever the reason, retailing plainly adds very substantially to the cost of the things we buy.

8.4.3 Shops and customers

Fifty years ago customers were served by shop assistants, or sales clerks as they are called in the United States. Even in Woolworths, each customer required personal attention, and each assistant was also a cashier who operated her own till. Grocers were people who had acquired great skill in their trade. They stood in their aprons or white coats, advising and chatting while they worked. They would grind and blend coffee, blend tea, pat butter into pounds, weigh and package sugar and other materials. Nowadays, of course, almost everything is pre-packed, labelled and priced, and only in the specialist shops does the old system still apply.

Despite the loss of human contact, people seem to prefer the supermarkets, where they will usually exchange no word with an assistant until they reach the check-out. Why do they prefer it that way? Because they can operate at their own speed (except at the check-out). If they are in a hurry, then they can hurry; if they are not, they can take their time. They can read the labels, make the complicated calculations to discover whether the price per ounce or per kilo is less on the small sizes than on the large (which it sometimes is). Shopping can be made a family occasion with various members participating. In the fruit and vegetable section they may now choose and packet their own oranges or tomatoes and other articles instead of helplessly watching an assistant bundling the good in with the not-so-good. I add an unproved (and perhaps unprovable) hypothesis: that self-service satisfies an atavistic streak that takes the shopper right back to the era of the hunter-gatherer. You will perhaps know how satisfying it is to go mushroom or wild strawberry or blackberry gathering, and the excitement of the fisherman when he is hauling in a fish. In all these cases the satisfaction seems quite disproportionate to the achievement. From where can it arise if not the vestiges of a memory lost in the mists of time? The same would perhaps explain the fever with which shoppers attend the periodic sales in Harrods or Macys and other great stores, where excitement is heightened by an element of physical danger.

The best of the department stores have traditionally sought to give the shopper the impression that she (or he) is being left to move around undisturbed, though an assistant will mysteriously be there if she sees she is needed. The shopper must be given the impression that she is in a sumptuously equipped palace, lulled by a sense of luxury to buy things that ordinarily she would not. By this means, too, the pain and the panic is alleviated from buying something expensive, however justified the purchase may be.

The great department stores, with their restaurants and rest-rooms, have found it hard to survive and many of them have disappeared, but the departmental chain-stores or multiples have taken over some of their functions and continue to flourish. Store decor as well as merchandise has been centrally designed, so that the loyal customer immediately feels at home in whatever city or suburb she may enter the store. Lighting, colour, display of merchandise is done with a characteristic appearance of grace and order, so that one may enjoy an aesthetic pleasure on entering the shop. So these shops attract and soothe, and engender in the customers a sense of trust, calm and security, so that they become more susceptible to the lure of the merchandise and the discreet persuasiveness of the salespeople.

Please do not think I am being unduly cynical about the motives of those who manage the department stores. There is, it is true, much to be sceptical about in the pretensions of business men who are engaged in getting very rich, but I believe that a significant part of the expenditure of the big stores is made because the chief executives are intensely proud of what they are doing. Some very rich people establish art galleries for the same reason. So the great shops of the great cities constitute one of the wonders (or at least delights) of the world, whether you visit them to buy or simply to admire. Such a place is Eatons in Toronto where one can spend a day enjoying its gardens, water-spouts and perspectives, secure from the Toronto weather.

Retailers are well versed in techniques for persuading customers to buy. In the first place the customer must be lured into the shop. It helps to have a well-known name and a reputation for quality, reasonable prices and honesty. It helps, too, to have won a reputation as 'the best place to buy' something or other, and not to be out of stock when the customer arrives. Once customers have become attached to a certain shop, some degree of price-indifference may set in: they may not care if they pay a little more for some things. The convenience of not having to bother gives compensation. This applies particularly to that extensive class of goods where quality is both important and difficult to measure with a fine degree of precision.

There are some curious psychological characteristics of shoppers, some of which are no doubt a nuisance to the shopkeeper, some of which play into his hands. Customers are prone to make a fuss if they think they have been overcharged, even by quite a small amount. Some stores disarm them by advertising that they are 'never knowingly undersold'; if purchasers find they could have got an identical product more cheaply somewhere else and can establish the fact, they will be repaid the difference. Secure in this knowledge they may not bother. The other very usual procedure is for customers to judge quality by price rather than price by quality. It is assumed that that which is more expensive must *ipso facto* be better, at least when the goods are on sale in the same shop. An official of the Union of Shop, Distributive and Allied Workers has informed me that it is possible to set two lots of the same article side by side with different price tags, and customers will first examine the cheaper and then buy the more expensive. Parker Pen got into difficulty in Britain during the regime of the National Board of Prices and Incomes when they were not permitted to increase the price of their standard pen. This was priced at £14, when Watermans brought out a new model and proceeded to over-cut Parker by charging £16. Overcut? Yes, because 70 per cent or more of these pens are bought for presents or presentations, and the buyers preferred giving the more expensive item.

In affluent societies consumers have become more sophisticated over the years as they get more practice in buying, though along with this has gone the price-indifference that enables different shops to charge different prices for the same goods – even branded goods whose quality is standardised. Shops of horror still exist, where one is almost dragged in off the street and where the shop assistant, under the eagle eye of the manager, tries to bully the customer into making a purchase. One hopes that such places will languish and die.

Of course dishonest practices are not performed only by shopkeepers: shops are every year plundered of great quantitites of goods, whose total value by the very nature of things it is impossible to calculate. The big retailers play down the value for fear that its magnitude may encourage other people to try their hand. Others, no doubt, exaggerate it because it enables them to write off imaginary losses against income tax. When theft is a problem for university libraries, patronised by the elite of our societies, who can wonder that it afflicts variety stores! Sometimes it is the work of kleptomaniacs, acting under psychological compulsion, sometimes of organised gangs, sometimes ordinary people acting under impulse. Sometimes visitors from poor countries, where controls are much stricter, find themselves overwhelmed by the lavish displays and laxer supervision of shops in the rich countries, and help themselves. Firms counter this with more and more sophisticated security devices: concealed scanners or devices locked on to their garments that raise an alarm if they are taken through the doors.

8.4.4 Shopkeepers and manufacturers

Fifty years ago, before the process of amalgamation and expansion of the retail trade had got under way, the big manufacturers were in a dominating position. It was their trade marks that were known to the public and that they looked for when buying shirts, dresses, suits, shoes, hats, breakfast foods, cans and confectionery, tea and so on. Manufacturers could dictate their terms to the retailers: selling-price as well as buying-price and length of credit.

But just as the States of Europe in the Middle Ages suffered from waves of invaders, more virile and war-like than the established powers, so has the peace of the retail trade been disturbed from time to time by innovators. Sometimes price-wars would break out between existing firms bringing, to paraphrase the Communist Manifesto, the reconstitution of the trade at large or the common ruin of the contending parties. So the five- and ten-cent stores and the penny-bazaars hit the established traders of the 1920s and 1930s. The rise of F. W. Woolworth and of Marks & Spencer demonstrated the price-cutting power of high turnover, and also the effectiveness of chain-store organisation, to achieve this end.

By March 1930 Marks & Spencer had 131 stores, of which nearly three-quarters had been built or extended during the previous five years. Between 1931 and 1935 they built or rebuilt 129 more. Their policy

> was based on a belief that the chain-store method of retailing, which did for distribution what large-scale production has done for manufacture, could effect large economies in its cost. Moreover, because

of the very large turnover involved, and the very large orders which it enabled the distributor to place, it could provide the basis for a new relationship between the retailer and the manufacturer which would lead to further economies. ... This was in fact the principle which, after 1926, Marks and Spencer applied to both its store development and its merchandising policy ... which was above all responsible for its success in the inter-war years. (Goronwy Rees, *St Michael: A History of Marks & Spencer*, London: Weidenfeld & Nicolson, 1969, pp. 80–1.)

Now there are six companies whose main activity is retailing amongst the top fifty in the United Kingdom; five amongst the top fifty in West Germany, thirteen in France, four in the United States. But surprisingly, single-unit shops continue to account for a considerable volume of trade. Like family farms they have certain advantages: those concerned work harder and more devotedly than the employees of corporations, and communication is easier: you just shout across the shop. But they have also developed what Galbraith calls 'countervailing power': co-operative buying agencies, in which they join together to get the discounts that go along with big orders. Sometimes they are taken under the wing of wholesalers who have warehouse space and trade under a common name. Another aid was the establishment of Cash and Carry traders. They can undercut the traditional wholesalers because the retailer provides his own transport, does his own loading and pays cash at the check-out. The biggest of these have chains of depots. (See Frank Livesey, *The Distributive Trades*, London: Heinemann, 1979, pp. 107–12.)

The upshot of all this is an immense increase in the power of the retailers *vis-à-vis* their suppliers. Manufacturers have more and more to work to the specifications and designs of the retailers. This is exemplified in Marks & Spencer, who established a Merchandise Development Department in 1936 that had a major effect on the progress of textiles in the United Kingdom, and a Food Development Department in 1948, which proceeded to perform the same task for food.

Technical services comprise today over 200 scientists, technologists and supporting staff. The number of staff with scientific, technological or engineering qualifications, including textile and food technology, chemistry, production engineering or chemical engineering, exceeds 100. . . .

They keep in close contact with the technologists employed by the company's suppliers, with trade research associations and with national research institutes and stimulate suppliers to make full use of available scientific and technological 'know-how' in overcoming production difficulties and in furthering development work. (Goronwy Rees, *St Michael*, p. 174.)

The result is a close liaison between the decision-makers: the customer whose purchases or failures-to-purchase express her sentiments; the stores who convey the results to head office; the manufacturers who, fortnight by fortnight (these are the modules in which Marks & Spencer work), will know how much to ship across for distribution to the stores.

The manufacturer is saved the cost of a team of commercial travellers (or 'reps' as they are now called) who used to do their rounds soliciting orders, and he is kept abreast of technical developments and changes in taste. His fabrics may be bought with the advantages of bulk-buying. Even for his margins, he will turn to the Marks & Spencer margin book. He will estimate his costs, and quote the selling price that will produce the accepted margin. It is his own business if he now improves his efficiency, reduces his costs and is able to increase his profit. There may be other manufacturers producing the same goods, and this will give a basis for comparison of price and quality. Against the advantages of these arrangements is the sacrifice of independence in which the manufacturer is placed, and the painful consequences that would follow if the arrangement broke down.

Marks & Spencer sell their merchandise under the 'St Michael' label – a guarantee that it conforms with their standards. The 'own-brand' style is of course widely followed in the grocery trade: the product is made by the big manufacturers, and perhaps sold in the same style of bottle, jar or tin that they employ, but carries the supermarket's name. It generally sells for a few pence less. Is it really the same quality? *Which?* tried out different brands of instant coffee on a panel of five expert coffee-tasters and 225 of their readers. 'A large proportion of the instant coffees were rated by the experts as being of similar quality – both supermarket own-brands and widely-advertised brands. However, the few instant coffees that the experts rated as being of better quality than the others were all higher-priced widely-advertised brands; among those rated as being of lower quality, all but one were own-brands.' As for the 225 readers: they disagreed with one another about which coffees tasted better than the others. Own-brand instant coffees cost around 10 to 30 pence less for a 100-gram jar. (*Which?*, June 1980, pp. 326–8.)

The increased power of the supermarkets put an end to retail price maintenance. Before that, manufacturers could cut off supplies if retailers sold their products below the marked price. RPM protected the retailers' margins and, more important, protected those of the manufacturers. Its disappearance, as a result of legislation or legal battles, has meant that the customer pays less and that lower prices have been forced on the manufacturers.

Other manifestations of the retailers' power has been their ability to make manufacturers pay for a mention of their brands in the retailers' advertisements, and to pay the retailer for special displays of their products in the store. A final device of dubious ethical value is for the retailer to return to the manufacturer periodically and demand special discounts from him with retrospective effect. In 1978 some details of this practice were revealed in a Canadian case: the supermarket chain had a special department whose job it was to visit the manufacturers demanding rebates. The stores could apply their margins to the suppliers' original price, so could not be accused of profiteering; the rebates would enter the company's flow of profits *ex post*, via a special account.

Who gets the benefit of the retailers' augmented power? Prior to this they acted as commission agents of the manufacturers, who administered their products and their prices according to their own convenience, within the tolerances of competition and what the consumer had been trained or could be persuaded to buy. Now distribution is more economically performed and pressure has been exerted on the manufacturers to cut their margins and reduce their costs. In these respects the retailers are acting as agents of their customers. The rebellion against retail price maintenance is an illustration of the process. Their power is used, too, to raise and enforce standards of quality.

The profits of the big corporations in distribution in the United States are modest, compared both with manufacturers in the United States and distributers in the United Kingdom:

	Net income after tax as % of capital employed, 1979
Sears Roebuck	4.6
Safeway	7.1
K Mart	9.3
Woolworth	8.5

This does not mean that they are voluntarily sacrificing profits for the welfare of their customers. They have to try to keep up their dividends if not for love of the shareholders at least to avoid the horrors of a takeover by a predator. It also does not mean that their top managers are not receiving the lavish remuneration to which top managers believe themselves to be entitled. But one may, none the less, conclude that people, in their role of customers, are being served as well as the limitations of the position permit.

One may compare the profit-seekers with the co-operatives whose shareholders are their customers. Between 1961 and 1978 their share of retail trade in Britain declined from 10.9 to 6.8 per cent. (J. A. N. Bamfield, 'The Changing Face of British Retailing', *National Westminster Bank Quarterly Review*, May 1980, p. 34.) However commendable their aims, the purchasing public was drifting away to the new commercial chains. It is only after a great effort at reorganisation and modernisation that the trend has been reversed.

Later, I shall have something to say about Migros, 55 in *The Times* list of the 500 leading European companies, whose shops span Switzerland and whose founder gave the company as a present to its customers. Under their direction it continues to expand, while they manage it with imagination and a sense of moral purpose.

8.5 THE ART OF PERSUASION

In the orthodox economic script only money talks. Purchasers buy shrewdly, slaves neither to sentiment nor habit, guided only by their indefatigable quest for value for money. In the world as we know it this is too much like hard work. Custom and habit relieve us of many of the agonies of choice that would otherwise constrict our waking hours and disturb our sleep. When serious problems require solution – what sort of car to buy, whether to get a deep-freeze, who to insure what with and for how much, where to go for our holiday – we discuss it with our friends, read the papers, take professional advice. People do not as a rule buy recklessly, and they try to avoid the disagreeable regrets that follow money ill-spent. But a great many of the apparent choices with which we are confronted today are not really choices at all: the shelves of the supermarkets are stacked with identical products under different names, or if they are not identical the differences are not such as to be discernible in the results that they have been bought to produce. This is problem number one that the advertising agencies are employed to solve. They have to persuade the consumer that out of identical products at the same price one is superior to all the rest. Problem number two is a bit more difficult: the consumer must be persuaded that of a range of identical products, they must select one that costs more than the others, or that of a range of products at the same price, the consumer must select one that is inferior. Problem three is to create in the consumer a want for something that up till now has been unwanted. Of course, there are many reasons for not wanting things: one is that you may be unaware of their existence; another that, though you knew of their existence, you had not thought that they were meant for you; a third that you have up till now looked upon them with distaste or at least apathy.

In some cases all that is necessary is to tell the consumer about the availability of something, and he will take the necessary steps to buy it. But in the majority of cases, he or she must be persuaded to buy something that he would otherwise not have done, or to buy it sooner than he had intended. In the small-ads columns you put down what you have to sell and hope that it will catch the eye of someone who wants to buy one. Your advertising is informative or descriptive. But where persuasion is required, the consumer must somehow be conditioned to buy your product in preference to the other options. The process of conditioning was discovered by Ivan Petrovich Pavlov, a Russian physiologist (1849–1936) who won the Nobel prize for medicine in 1904. Dogs, when hungry, will salivate on the appearance of food. He rang a bell at the same time that food was presented, and before long had the dogs salivating at the sound of the bell, whether food was present or not. Within limits, the louder the bell, the greater the salivation. This he referred to as a conditioned reflex.

It is a process of this sort that persuasive advertising attempts to emulate. For cigarettes – masculinity. Here is a splendid Formula I racing car; the slogan – Black Power; the merchandise – John Player Special King Size. Rothmans say simply 'World Leader'. Beneath a hemisphere is a coat of arms with lions, a crown and a golden R on a red background, and under that again is a well-manicured hand protruding from a cuff with four golden rings – the Captain himself? In the hand is, of course, a packet of Rothmans. Here is Marlboro – cowboys and horses in a setting of the great out-doors. And in the same copy of *Time* that I am looking at, Camel follow the same theme. A country man contrives to look both tough and poetic. He sits in the firelight, behind him his tent and hurricane-lamp. He cups his hand round a flame to light his Camel Filter. None tastes better, we are told.

Surely these advertisements will cancel each other out? We will think of manliness whichever brand we see. But manliness, strength, leadership, the outdoor life – these all stand in contrast with the highly unpleasant ailments that we now know cigarettes promote. So perhaps the tobacco companies are not so much interested in taking away each other's share of the market as in trying to ensure that that market contracts no more?

But of course, you can analyse advertisements for yourself. What is it they are seeking to condition you to associate with their product? Manliness, femininity, sex, luxury, elegance? Nostalgia for an aristocratic past? We are in the cellars of a château; cobwebs, bottles and bins, silver candlesticks in which candles glow. The caption: THE NEW 1982 BMW COUPE. EVEN RARER THAN A 1929 CHÂTEAU LAFITE. There are indeed three bottles lying in the Lafite 1929 bin, and only one BMW Coupé which has somehow found its way into the cellar and glows elegantly in the candlelight. We are now conditioned, when we see a BMW, to think of *class*.

Brides, filmstars, countesses, okay, you may say, but what of nasty smells? It is true that sometimes the attempt is made into terrifying us into buying something. This is so particularly in Canada, where cleanliness is held in high esteem. The horror of our kitchens or ourselves smelling! But here to wake us from the nightmare is some hygienic product to which it is hoped we shall henceforth fly like a child to its mother.

Advertising accounted for 3.7 per cent of personal consumption expenditure in the United States in 1960. Personal consumption expenditure in real terms (constant prices) about doubled between 1960 and 1979, but advertising almost held its own, at 3.4 per cent: $49 720 million. In 1979 it was allocated as follows:

	%
Newspapers	29.2
Magazines	5.9
Farm publications	0.2
Television	20.5
Radio	6.8
Direct mail	13.4
Business papers	3.2
Outdoor	1.1
Miscellaneous	19.7
	100.0

In view of the complaints they make about the inroads of television it is interesting to see that, between 1965 and 1979, newspapers maintained their position: 29.0 per cent in 1965, and 29.2 per cent in 1979.

Television advanced its share, but only from 16.5 to 20.5 per cent, at the expense of magazines and direct mail, who each lost two percentage points.

How effective is advertising in influencing our buying, perhaps turning us into people we would otherwise not have been and, uninfluenced, might not have wished to be? Martin Mayer studied advertising agencies and reported his findings in *Madison Avenue U.S.A.* (London: Bodley Head, 1958). Some agencies have grown to enormous size and operate throughout the capitalist and Third World. Like the big corporations we looked at in Chapter 6, they vary one from another in what they can do and what they will do. Stanley Resor, then chairman of the board of J. Walter Thompson, would not take on products of which he did not approve, and this included whiskey, rum and other hard liquor.

Sometimes the agency will pin a slogan to the product. The slogan by association acts as a mnemonic (aid to memory) and the brand-name will spring to mind at the appropriate moment. 'Don't be vague, ask for Haig' adds a rhyme for good measure, with an added feeling that if you just ask for whisky, or even Scotch, you will be thought to be suffering from vagueness. White Horse, too, is anxious to imprint its brand-name on your mind, with its picture of its emblem incongruously placed in an elegant restaurant or banquet and the slogan 'You can take a White Horse anywhere'. There is something rakish in selecting White Horse instead of red or white wine with your dinner. Lever Brothers' Vim came to fame with the simple slogan 'Won't wash clothes', and Ivory soap 'it floats'. But a number of things have to come together to make a product a success. Martin Mayer quotes a Ford sales manager: 'I don't like to talk about advertising alone. We like to say advertising does this and that, but it doesn't – unless it's supported by sales promotion, public relations and solid sales effort. Right after the war, the ad people thought they were responsible for all those sales, the promotion people the same, the selling people thought they did it. Then competition set in, the ads didn't go, the promotion didn't work, the salesmen couldn't sell. Everybody stopped waving his own flag.' (Mayer, *Madison Avenue U.S.A.*, p. 109.)

At the beginning of the *Waste Makers* (New York: David McKay, 1960) Vance Packard quotes Dorothy Sayers, 'A society in which consumption has to be artificially stimulated in order to keep production going is a society founded on trash and waste, and such a society is a house built upon sand.' He argues that this is precisely the role of the advertising industry. In *The People Shapers* (London: Macdonald & Jane's, 1978) Packard focuses on the manipulation of people, by psychological or physiological means. Many advertisements are designed to modify life-style and attitudes. 'They seek to make people more hedonistic, more narcissistic, more status-conscious, more prone to live against the future. The goal is to create more insatiable consumers. And this is starting to be seen as functional in highly technological societies.'

The massiveness of the behavior-molding effort of advertising can be seen in the viewing of television commercials. By the time young people in the United States are eighteen they have seen and heard about eighteen hundred hours of commercial messages on TV. If you divide that up into thirty-five-hour workweeks you find that they have spent a full year of time listening just to commercials. Adding in radio commercials would take them well into a second year of time.   (Packard, *People shapers*, pp. 128-9.)

Since the Second World War immense experimental and research effort has been put into the study of human conditioning. One learns with horror of the technique used by political police to dismantle the personality and extract information from their victims. Hitler and the Nazis were experts at evoking mob responses. On the other hand, people are capable of developing resistance, political and commercial. In affluent societies, where people are bombarded with suggestions, claims and counter-claims, they acquire a protective coating of cynicism. At the conscious level they are capable of reasoning quite toughly. It may well be that the people whom the advertising agents are most skilled at influencing are the advertisers themselves. It is their ego, after all, that is boosted when they see their products and sometimes themselves on television or in the newspapers or magazines.

Clearly, advertising is a phenomenon of considerable importance in capitalist societies, the source of finance of the mass-media (with the notable exception of the BBC). It is surprising that the orthodox textbooks can hardly spare it a mention.

8.6 CONSUMER PROTECTION: BEWARE THE UNSEEN HAND!

Before the nineteenth century it went without saying that consumers needed protection from the wolves of commerce. Not just anyone could manufacture and market a product; it required a licence in which method and quality would be prescribed and that would guarantee the public against spurious claims. The publicists of the new age could not wait to get rid of these impediments to enterprise. Any restriction on choice was bad, and if Economic Man wished to purchase faulty goods he should be at perfect liberty to do so.

Adam Smith asserted that every individual preferred the support of domestic to that of foreign industry (in relation, that is, to the investment of his capital) and, for his own gain, directed that industry so as to produce the greatest value. He thus added to the wealth of society, being 'led by an invisible hand to promote an end which was no part of his intention'. (*The Wealth of Nations*, bk IV, chap. ii, p. 456.) But he also warned, 'People of the same trade seldom meet together, even for merriment and diversion, but the conversation ends in a conspiracy against the public, or in some contrivance to raise prices.' (Ibid. bk I, chap. x, p. 145.) Fortunately for the survival of mankind, people who have to co-exist in a village or street or town do not as a rule try to enrich themselves by swindling each other. But sometimes they do, and we must beware the invisible hand that attempts to pick our pocket or, by its quickness, deceive the eye.

'People of the same trade' – take, for example, the motor trade. Here the manufacturers of the famous marques are in a conspiracy against the *British* public, therein aiding and abetting British Leyland and other firms who manufacture in Britain. By tacit or overt agreement they charge hundreds or thousands of pounds more for cars bought in Britain than in Continental Europe. British buyers could thus save great expense by ordering a right-hand drive car from a Continental dealer, going to Belgium to fetch it and paying duty and value-added tax on their return to Britain:

	British list price £	Euro-price inc. car tax and 15% VAT £	Saving £
Ford Escort XR 3 1597 c.c.	5 750	5 067	683
Fiesta XR 2 1598 c.c.	5 150	4 275	875
Austin Mini Metro 1300S	4 575	3 535	1 040
Jaguar XJ13 5345 c.c.	18 209	16 000	2 209
Renault R9 GTS 1397 c.c.	5 378	3 802	1 576
Mercedes 280 CE 2746 c.c.	14 830	9 500	5 330
Volkswagon Golf GL Cabriolet 1457 c.c.	6 937	5 302	1 635

Source: the (London) *Sunday Times*, 4 Apr. 1982, p. 13. They note: Euro car prices fluctuate and should be taken only as an approximate guide.

The rules of the European Economic Community prohibit price discrimination. The *Sunday Times* comments: 'Unfortunately, motor manufacturers and dealers throughout Europe, wedded to the idea of rigidly controlled national markets, all with their own elaborate price structures, have done their best to thwart the aims of the treaty.' The Consumer's Association had issued a booklet explaining to British car-buyers how they could save sums of this order by buying a car from a Continental dealer. Of course, in the United Kingdom we drive on the left, and on the Continent on the right, so an order had to be made for a car with the steering-wheel on the right. But after a few weeks delay this could be collected, the documents completed and the car driven back to Britain. The *Sunday Times* continues: 'Since our articles last year, most main dealers in Belgium and Germany have been told by manufacturers not to accept such orders – or, if they do, to quote British customers ridiculous delivery times and to insist on a 25 per cent deposit.' The (British) Consumers' Association maintained that this was in breach of the Treaty of Rome and the rules of the Common Market and, through the Bureau Européen des Unions de Consommateurs, complained to the EEC Commission. Ford had put out a memo to their German dealers instructing them to refuse orders for right-hand drive cars from British customers; the Commission ordered them to withdraw the memo and resume sales. Ford objected, but, in October 1982, their objection was overruled by the European Court, who directed them to restore the *status quo*. (*Which?*, Nov. 1982, p. 607.)

This illustrates a curious feature of competition: sometimes it 'breaks out' into a price war, and at others, even in the highly competitive motor trade, the competitors achieve a state of mutual accommodation, their pocket-picking hands happily at work.

In the past twenty or thirty years there has been a great advance in consumer protection, both aided and provoked by advances in the way consumers, through their organisations, have learnt to protect themselves. Consumers' associations have been established in most advanced capitalist countries, new laws passed or strengthened, and statutory bodies set up to enforce them.

The associations modelled themselves on the Consumers' Union, founded in 1936 in the United States and chartered under the Not-For-Profit Corporation Law of the State of New York. 'The purposes of Consumers Union are to provide consumers with information and counsel on consumer goods and services, to give information on all matters relating to the expenditure of the family income, and to initiate and to cooperate with individual and group efforts seeking to create and maintain decent living standards.' (Repeated on the second page of *Consumer Reports*.) While manufacturers know a great deal about the technical aspects of their products, purchasers have had to test them by using them and discovered their defects when it was too late. Of course, information was carried on the grape-vine, but this is not much help when new products are constantly appearing. So consumers' unions, with laboratory testing and centralised collection of information, were able to play an important part in improving the relative positions of buyers.

In Britain the Consumers' Association, and its magazine *Which?*, were launched in 1957.

> The very first issue of *Which?* was based on principles already established by Consumers Union of the US. The organization must be financially independent. The first issue was made possible by a loan from CU and a charitable trust, but from then it was to derive its funds from the sale of its magazine to subscribers (it has never been available on bookstalls) and other forms of information. The goods it reported on were bought anonymously in shops. The tests were carried out by independent laboratories and scientists. The reports in the first issue compared the performance and safety of electric kettles and the price and eating characteristics of cake mixes. In succeeding years the methodology of testing was to become more complex and the range of subjects much wider, but the broad principles remained the same. (Daphne Grose, 'Consumers' Association and *Which?*', in Jeremy Mitchell (ed.), *Marketing and the Consumer Movement*, Maidenhead: McGraw-Hill, 1978.

On the United States see J. S. Haskins, *The Consumer Movement*, New York: Franklin Watts, 1975.)

The International Organization of Consumers' Unions (IOCU) was established in 1960 and by 1978 had 101 member organisations in forty-five countries. A European federation, Bureau Européen des Unions de Consommateurs (BEUC) followed in 1962. This comprises twelve consumers' unions in the countries of the EEC, its function 'to represent and defend consumer interests to the Common Market institutions, especially to the Commission'. (See Mitchell, *Marketing and the Consumer Movement*, pp. 272 and 274.)

The consumer associations have had an impressive record of solid achievement. They have compelled manufacturers to exercise greater care in product-design, and in their claims for their goods and their pricing policies, but they have been put to practical use mainly by well-to-do middle-class households. In fact it takes quite a high level of literacy and application to apply their finding to actual purchases of electric kettles, cosmetics, stockings or whatever the item may be. Of more widespread effect has been their influence on governments in the creation of a network of laws for the protection of consumers, but I postpone a consideration of these until Chapter 10.

These organisations did most estimable work, but it was Ralph Nader who, with the help of General Motors, converted consumerism into a messianic movement. Nader's book, *Unsafe at Any Speed*, was published by Grossman Publishers, New York, in 1965. His theme was that the 'death, injury, and the most inestimable sorrow' that resulted from road accidents was the fault of defects in cars, not in drivers. The book did not occasion much stir, partly because it was very little reviewed. Grossman recounts that a reviewer for *Life* magazine told him, 'I wouldn't touch this book with a ten-foot pole.' A Houston newspaperman reacted similarly. 'With all our automobile advertising? You must be crazy'. (Charles McCarry, *Citizen Nader*, New York: Saturday Review Press, 1972, p. 8.)

So things might have continued if General Motors had not had Nader tailed. The agency told its investigators, 'Our job is to check his life and current activities to determine what makes him tick, such as his real interest in safety, his supporters, if any, his politics, his marital status, his friends, his women, his boys, and so forth, drinking, dope, jobs – in fact all facets of his life'. (McCarry, p. 13.) These revelations made the headlines and drew a press release from GM, acknowledging that they had authorised a routine investigation 'to determine if Ralph Nader was acting on behalf of litigants or attorneys in Corvair design cases pending against General Motors'. (Ibid. p. 21.) The matter was brought to a splendid climax by the appearance before a Senate Subcommittee, including Abraham Ribicoff and Robert F. Kennedy, of James M. Roche, the President of General Motors.

Since then Nader and his Public Citizens have carried their campaigns into a multitude of areas. With the $280 000 damages received from General Motors, the Public Interest Research Group was established. They have established a Congress Watch, Health Research Group, Critical Mass (emergency planning for radiological accidents), Tax Reform Research Group and Litigation Group (for handling cases on behalf of 'consumers, workers, and interested citizens'). (*The Public Citizen*, issue eleven, Winter 1980, p. 5.) In Chapter 10 we shall consider the role of governments in consumer protection.

If we are to gauge rightly the economies of modern capitalist societies, we must take account of the changes that have taken place in the distributive trades and in the awareness and organisation of consumers. At various times in the last hundred years or so, governments have reached decisions that 'something must be done about the workers', and legislation has resulted to enable them to organise and to protect their organisations. In the past ten years the decision has been that 'something must be done about consumers', and much legislation has followed. Newspapers, television and radio programmes have become bolder in their investigative reporting, but even so, the abuses inflicted on consumers seem endless. (See, for instance, 'Life Insurance Selling Methods', in *Which?*, Jan. 1983, pp. 10–14.) But the consumers' associations and the mass media are doing good work in educating them. What has been done, and what remains to do, illustrate how inadequate economic man as consumer would have been in the face of 'perfect competition'.

9 Money and Banking

9.1 NOTES, COINS, SHELLS AND OXEN

Children in affluent societies are taught the uses of money from a very early age. Once a week, on pocket-money day, they get their cents or centimes, pennies or pfennigs, or whatever the unit of currency may be, and they very soon learn that these coins, not much good for eating or playing with, can be exchanged for a variety of desirable things.

Possession of money gives you the right of spending it at your own convenience. Of course, a great deal of expenditure must be made as a matter of necessity or duty: rent, food, fuel, transport must be paid for when payment is due. As we remarked in Chapter 8, a very high proportion of expenditure is concerned with people's daily needs for food, clothing, shelter and locomotion. Like cattle in a field or caterpillars on a leaf, we are preoccupied with day-to-day existence.

It is for discretionary expenditure that money really comes into its own, for with it one can exercise one's right to spend, on what to spend, or not to spend, and, if to save, to save in a great variety of ways. Here we realise money's full magic. Fortune smiles on him or her who has a surplus after unavoidable expenses have been met. As Mr Micawber so truly said, 'Annual income twenty pounds, annual expenditure nineteen nineteen six, result happiness. Annual income twenty pounds, annual expenditure twenty pounds ought and six, result misery.'

In pre-monetary societies you can live a lifetime without the use of money, though governments may compel you to produce a little of it every year to pay your taxes, and you may stand in need of it for school-fees or hospital expenses for your children; but in capitalist societies, where the cash nexus reigns, it is your pass to society and, without it, you are shut out: no bus will carry you, no café feed you, no bar quench your thirst.

Money, in appropriate quantities, frees one from the constraints of time and place: we may buy in a moment what has taken many man hours to make and, within a day, transfer ourselves to the other side of the earth. Power, of course, can be used for good or evil. 'Love of money', said Paul, 'Is the root of all evil', and many sages echo him. 'Money is social blood, but alienated, spilt blood', wrote Moses Hess, and his friend Marx elaborated this: 'Money is the alienated essence of man's work and existence – this essence dominates him and he worships it. Politics is in principle superior to the power of money but in practice it has become its bondsman.' (See Julius Carlebach, *Karl Marx and the Radical Critique of Judaism*, London: Routledge & Kegan Paul, 1978, p. 122.)

In the textbooks money is defined by its uses: a medium of exchange, a store of wealth and a unit of account. Of course, businesses keep their accounts in money units of the country in which they operate. People carry round in their heads a notion of what a unit of money is worth, measuring it in terms of the sort of things they spend it on or the amount of work they have to do to get it, but these things vary from place to place and from time to time. The value of money is measured in terms of goods, and the value of goods in terms of money. In times of stable prices and stable money, people form and retain very precise ideas of just wages and just prices; in times of inflation or rapid changes in relative prices, these ideas get out of focus and it becomes easy for sharp operators to profit at other people's expense.

Loss of faith in the currency has a baneful effect on social affairs; faith in the currency is part cause, part effect of that state of confidence that is a necessary part of prosperity. I stress the word 'faith', for faith is a state of mind. Faith in your ability to perform a task must be carefully built up and established as a necessary preliminary to success. Faith in the currency, too, is established by a process of learning: you confirm that sellers are willing to accept units of the currency in exchange for their goods. They know, in turn, that at such time as they wish to obtain goods or services they will be rendered in exchange for their money.

In subsistence societies services and goods within the commune, village or manor were provided by obligation from one class or caste to another, as they still are in some parts of the world even today. Trade between villages, districts and countries was a very specialised business, and I imagine that it was as traders got to know each other that sale on credit began. Cowry shells became a medium of exchange across tropical Africa from east to west. They were used, too, in the countries of the Pacific, where they were prized for their ornamental value. It may be that they were first used as a method of counting.

The adoption of a standard of value goes back at least as far as the adoption of a common means of payment, and the two have always been closely linked together. The Homeric Greeks reckoned values in oxen. The golden armour of Glaucus was said to be worth a hundred oxen, and the gold tassels on the cloak of the goddess Athene, a hundred oxen each. At the funeral games of Patroclus, the winner of a wrestling match received 'a big three-legged cauldron, worth twelve oxen by Achaean reckoning', while the loser was consoled with 'a woman thoroughly trained in domestic work', valued at four oxen. (E. Victor Morgan, *A History of Money*, Harmondsworth: Penguin Books, 1965, p. 34)

Oxen are still important over much of Africa as a store of value and a medium of exchange. Amongst pastoral peoples, a man's wealth is reckoned by the number of cattle in his herds, and gifts, bride-price, fines and tribute are all paid in cattle. In the city-states and empires, gold, silver and copper were used and the custom arose of minting coins as a guarantee of their fineness, weight and value. 'The earliest coins were probably made by merchants, but the function of coinage was soon taken over by governments, and between the eighth and sixth centuries B.C. the various States and cities of the Aegean and Asia Minor each came to issue coins bearing their own emblem – the lion's head of Lydia, the turtle of Aegina, the winged horse of Corinth, and the owl of Athens.' (Ibid. p. 13)

When paper money was issued it was in the form of a contract to exchange it for a specified quantity of gold or silver when presented to the specified authority. Failing this, it was thought, people would refuse to accept it. This idea was in more recent times proved to be erroneous: people were quite willing to accept the bits of printed paper, provided they believed everyone else would too. A subsequent development dispensed even with the notes. All you had to do was to write an instruction (called a cheque) to your bank to pay a specified sum to a specified person or firm. A single piece of paper could then perform the function of a dozen or more notes. In this case, however, there were certain precautions that the person accepting payment would take to satisfy himself that the cheque would be honoured.

The possession of a banknote entails an obligation by society to exchange it for goods or services at such time as its owner shall determine. The ownership of a credit entry in a bank account is a still more abstract expression of the same obligation. How these obligations are obtained we shall go into below when we consider banking.

9.2 THE VALUE OF MONEY

One of the disturbing features of money is its inability to maintain its value. One acquires it in return for goods and services, and the payment seems appropriate for the quantity and quality of what one provides, but by the time the money comes to be spent, its value may have changed. Of course, most people earn their money in one week or month and spend it the next, so that the value of their money has hardly had a chance to change, but if the money happens to be saved for a year or more the changes may be quite disturbing of the relative positions of those who own goods and those who own money. If prices are falling, the money-owners will be placed at an advantage; if they are rising, then those who own goods will be better off.

The 'value of money' is measured by the quantity of goods and services for which a unit of it may be exchanged. The Consumer Price Index is a weighted average of the movement of prices of goods and services entering into household expenditure. The inverse measures changes in the purchasing power of the dollar (or other money unit) in terms of household consumption. There are seasonal and annual fluctuations, but long periods when the secular (long-term) trend has been upward or downwards:

	Prices	*Value of $*
1800–1850	Halved	Doubled
1850–1864	+88%	−47%
1864–1895	−47%	+88%
1895–1901	No change	No change
1901–1920	+140%	−58%
1920–1933	−35%	+55%
1933–1981	+627%	−86%

In three of the seven periods the dollar rose substantially in value; in four it fell. But the falls were more substantial than the rises. Over the whole span, 1800 to 1981, prices rose by a factor of $5\frac{1}{4}$, so that the dollar of 1981 could buy no more than 18 cents of 1800.

For England one may trace these trends over several centuries (see John Burnett, *A History of the Cost of Living*, Harmondsworth: Penguin Books, 1969, p. 328).

Money and Banking

	Prices	Value of £
1320–1500	Fell	Rose
1500–1650	Rose	Fell
1650–1760	Steady	Steady
1760–1813	+192%	−66%
1813–1851	Halved	Doubled
1851–1873	+50%	−33%
1873–1896	−34%	+52%
1896–1909	+12%	−10%
1909–1920	+171%	−63%
1920–1933	−44%	+80%
1933–1981	+1733%	−95%

Sources: *A History of the Cost of Living*, p. 199; Guy Routh, *Occupation and Pay in Great Britain 1906–79*, pp. 134–5; *Employment Gazette*, Dec. 1982, p. 562.

The overall result: between 1760 and 1981 prices rose by a factor of 31 and the value of the pound of 1981 had fallen to 3¼ pence in 1760 values.

For the past half-century prices have followed an upward trend, so that most people alive today have never known a period in which they did anything else, and have come to think that this is a built-in feature of the modern world. Can it be that we shall ever again experience a sustained period of falling prices? We shall return to this question in the last section of this chapter.

9.3 BANKS

The money system in affluent capitalist countries is today operated not by governments but by banks. In earlier times the most important providers of money were the governments or central banks that printed it. Now the main work is done not by the exchange of notes and coins, but by entries in the banks' account books.

In principle the banks perform a simple function. They are recording angels of the monetary scene. Nowadays most salaries and wages are paid by cheque or by direct credit from the employer into the employees' bank accounts. The Inter-Bank Research Organisation reports that only one in a hundred workers in the United States are paid in cash, and in Canada and West Germany, 5 per cent. 85 per cent of

Dutch workers receive monthly cashless pay. In France, all workers are paid monthly and only a quarter in cash. In the United Kingdom, by contrast, 54 per cent still received their pay in cash in 1979, though the proportion has fallen from 75 per cent in 1969 and 59 per cent in 1976. (Department of Employment, *Employment Gazette*, vol. 89, no. 10, Oct. 1981, p. 428.)

This process has had many repercussions: unemployment amongst pay clerks and pay-roll snatchers, and a general move into the cashless age. It would not have been possible without the computer revolution. It has entrenched the banks as controllers, or at least conductors, of our financial affairs. How do they operate? Payments are made and received by credit and debit entries in the bank accounts of the parties concerned. On pay day, if payment is by direct debit and credit, employers' accounts are debited with the amounts owing to each employee as shown on the payroll, and the account of each employee is credited by the appropriate amount. If payment is by cheque, the employer's computer will produce a cheque for each employee, who will pay it in to his bank account. His account will be credited. If the employee and employer use the same branch of the same bank the employer's account will be debited by the same amount. If they use different banks the cheque will be sent to a clearing house where the participant banks will strike a balance from all the debits and credits so that the final amounts to be transferred from bank to bank are generally quite small.

All this is obvious enough, as is also the fact that banks make most of their profits by lending money. They invite you to lend them money by paying it into a deposit account (or time deposit), withdrawal from which requires notice of a week or whatever time may be specified. The longer the notice required, the higher the interest paid. The banks then lend this money at a higher rate of interest, acting, as it were, as commission agents.

In Chapter 5 we considered the problem caused by the discretion that receivers of income possess of spending immediately or at some future time – or not at all. The banks, by getting deposits from people with unspent funds and lending them to others who wish to spend now what they will earn only later, provide shock-absorbers for what would otherwise be a very bumpy ride. It was this inequality between decisions to save and decisions to invest that was the central point of Keynes's *General Theory*.

But in fact the true magic of banking consists of going even further than that: they can lend the savings of those who wish to spend less than they receive, but they can also create credits out of thin air. The banker can create purchasing-power (or bank money) by giving a customer a loan or simply giving him permission to overdraw his current account. But must the banker not have spare cash in order to be able to do this? No, for only a small proportion of transactions are done in cash. Now the borrower will use the credit to pay his creditors. The creditors will deposit the resulting cheques in their bank accounts. If they are at the same bank, the result will have been two book entries, a debit balanced by a credit. It is true, some of the additional credit may be needed in cash, but only a small proportion. Even if the creditor has his account at a different bank there will be no difficulty if all banks are expanding credit at about the same pace.

Of course, it would be a great calamity if a bank, or even the local branch of a bank, were to run short of cash. People have awful memories of banks that failed; an entirely healthy bank might be reduced to this state by a run caused by unfounded rumours. Thus it is that banks will carefully cultivate their liquidity by having available a safe proportion of cash, supported by an additional proportion of investments that can be converted into cash with the minimum of delay – money lent at call (that is, instantly repayable) and government stocks. Table 9.1 demonstrates this in respect of a year-end balance-sheet.

Now we must note an important constraint on a bank manager's discretion to create bank money, lack of recognition of which would not allow him to continue as a bank manager for very long. His advances are permissible only if he is sure they will be repaid. Thus bank managers, when asked for loans of more than minor extent, are prone to ask for security. You may have to pledge the deeds of your house or shares or government securities or have the advance guaranteed by some person of adequate wealth and good repute. The bank manager does not want your house: he wants you to repay the loan, and the danger of losing your house will no doubt induce you to do so.

What you have done when you have taken a loan or exercised an overdraft is to mortgage your future. 'I am sure of getting this money in the future', you say, 'But I want to spend it now. When I get it, it will be sufficient for me to repay you and pay interest for the duration of the debt.' In fact, most bank loans are used not for purposes of consumption, but to tide merchants or farmers over the interval between the purchase of goods or sowing of crops and the receipt of funds from

Table 9.1 *Barclays Bank plc, consolidated balance-sheet, 31 December 1981*

Liabilities:	£m	Assets:	£m
Deposits and customers' current accounts	42 834	Cash and short-term funds	7 470
Other accounts	2 569	Items in course of collection	651
Current taxation	3	Investments	1 773
Deferred taxation	161	Advances and other accounts	35 613
Proposed dividends	33	Equipment leased to customers	2 054
	45 600		47 561
Long-term borrowings of overseas subsidiary companies	321		
	45 921		
Capital resources:			
Loan capital	432		
Minority interests in equity of subsidiary companies	132	Investments in associated companies and other trade investments	267
Stockholders' funds:			
Issued share capital	284		
Reserves	1 983	Property and equipment	924
	48 752		48 752

Source: Barclays Bank plc, *Report and Accounts 1981*, pp. 56–7.

their sale. There are a multitude of ways in which business men can employ funds now that will bring in a return later on, and that give bank managers secure ways of employing their resources.

The result is that although the banks can create funds out of air, the air in due course becomes a solid accretion of wealth, resources will have been mobilised, products made or transported to where they can be sold, and from the proceeds the bank repaid with interest. If the advance has been for purposes of consumption the effect is negative: he who has borrowed that he may consume now must curb his consumption in future that he may repay.

A venture that fails, a loan that becomes a bad debt, is a calamity for the bank manager concerned. Of course it may happen occasionally – if it did not, it would be a sign that the bank was being over-cautious and therefore missing remunerative business. The ironic thing is that the more urgent it becomes to inject credit into the system in the trough of the business cycle, the greater the risk in lending money, though the constraint is not so much the banks' caution as the unwillingness of businessmen or private individuals to mortgage their future. This is one of the paradoxes by which capitalist systems are marred.

Paul Ferris describes the spread to Europe of American methods:

> American lending techniques are being practised in a dozen European centres, accelerating the move away from the old notion that lending and borrowing were solemn rituals enacted in whispers between the banker and his client. Industry is increasingly anxious to borrow money for a few years at a time, and the Americans are skilled at arranging these medium-term loans, which they enclose in largely foolproof agreements between bank and borrower. The company gets the money after its future has been examined with a microscope. The bank will inspect the industry in general and the management of the particular company; it will want detailed financial projections, and these have to be fulfilled if the agreement is to continue. In the United States, this type of rigidly defined term-lending has already replaced much bond-market borrowing because companies find it simpler and cheaper; now the Americans are doing it in Europe, mainly with American subsidiaries but occasionally with local companies. Some companies have been refused because they won't be tied by a formal loan agreement. 'I guess they feel it's a question of their integrity,' said a Chicago banker, adding charitably that European managements must find it disturbing to have their affairs so rigorously examined....
>
> Americans are obsessed with the need to acquire information so that decisions can be arrived at on the basis of full evidence. (Paul Ferris, *Men and Money: Financial Europe Today*, Harmondsworth: Penguin Books, 1970, pp. 231–3.)

Alexander Ross describes the contrast between Canadian and US bankers in this respect. In Canada the entrepreneur's request for finance 'is met with incomprehension or, at the very best, a cautious display of interest that's followed, weeks later, by a short letter saying no thanks'. He cites the case of Bennett and Cutt, producers of a mini-computer to correct data before it is fed into the big computer. Having met with no success in their search for funds in Toronto, they flew off to New York for an interview with First National City Bank. Bennett described the result:

It's nine o'clock in the morning, okay? I thought we were going to have to make the usual educational pitch, the way you have to do with the Canadian banks – you know, explain the basics, all that. So we go in there, and one guy introduces himself as Joe Boakes who's in charge of the bank's computer section – *in charge* of the computer section, okay? And there are five other guys in the room, and I'm introduced around. This is Joe Smith, he's in charge of data entry products for our computer division. And here's so-and-so, who's interested in peripheral areas. All specialists. *Five* of them!

So the head guy pulls out this file and says, 'Okay. Consolidated Computer. Here's what we have on you.' And, my God, they have this 30-page updated report on our company, where we stood in the industry, the strides we were making in the US, where our marketing offices were, how our product compared to the competition's. It was fantastic.

Then they got into the questions.... Why do you use a fixed-head storage device when your competitor uses a moving-head device? What's the memory cycle time? And then they got into other areas – our marketing strategy, our pricing strategy, how the product works – I mean, they knew our company. Not because they'd been expecting us to ask them for a loan, but because they'd made it their business to know the industry.

It was one of the toughest financial meetings I've ever had, and one of the most enjoyable. Geez, here were financial men who actually knew what they were talking about! As bankers, they took the attitude that, hey, we hope you need *lots* of money. They wanted to lend it to us, because that was their business. I can't describe how good I felt after that meeting.   (Alexander Ross, *The Risk Takers*, Toronto: Maclean-Hunter, 1975, p. 21.)

On my first visit to the United States, in 1962, I was impressed by the manifest eagerness of the New York banks to persuade people to borrow money. In London I had had difficulty in persuading my bank to lend me a hundred pounds, and here, all about the Columbia campus, I saw advertisements appealing to students to allow various banks to finance them through their studies. The student was being asked to mortgage his future, but as a qualified man or woman, he would be a sound investment.

In less affluent times banks used to draw an important part of their income by charging customers for their services. They keep a record of your payments in and out, with a list of their origin or destination, and for this you pay bank charges. Now, on certain conditions, banks provide these services free. Here is a leaflet from the (British) Midland Bank that explains: 'If you keep at least £100 in your current account right through a quarterly charging period the following services will be completely free during that period.' They list payments into and drawings from your account, and regular payments made at your request by Standing Order and Direct Debit. But if your balance falls below £100 at any time during a service charging period automated debits (AutoBank, cash card and direct debits) will be charged at 15 pence per item and other debits at 20 pence per item. No charge is made for credits. If the account becomes overdrawn interest is charged.

In 1959 the Radcliffe Committee explained: 'English bankers have... traditionally regarded, and continue to regard, themselves as properly engaged in financing working capital, particularly of the 'seed-time to harvest' kind, 'bridging transactions', and (within cautious limits) the temporary financing of fixed capital development pending the raising of long-term finance through other channels. Thus the lending banker does not directly promote the purchase of real resources, but stands ready to help with temporary finance....' (Committee on the Working of the Monetary System *Report*, London: HMSO, 1959, p. 46.)

Since then, however, British banks have overcome some of their inhibitions and boldly expanded their search for borrowers. Partly this has been brought about by the inflow of vast sums of oil money for recycling that has compelled them to relax their prejudice against lending long. Until very recently they had kept out of the housing market, where the average length of loan is about twenty years, and in which mortgage debt outstanding amounted to £52 thousand million in 1980. Now they have invaded this market with great success, offering the borrower loan-raising procedures less vexatious than the building societies. They have also joined the scramble to lend money to the underdeveloped countries. The long-term external debt of the non-oil underdeveloped countries (UDCs) has risen from $97 thousand million in 1973 to $425 thousand million in 1981, of which 49.6 per cent was owed to private creditors in the former year and 57.7 per cent in the latter. (See David T. Llewellyn, 'Avoiding an International Banking Crisis', *National Westminster Bank Quarterly Review*, Aug. 1982, p. 32.)

Every country, even the smallest, has a central bank that plays the dual role of banker to the government and banker to the bankers. The functions of the Bank of England, similar to those of other central banks, are described as follows:

> Principally, the Bank acts as adviser to the government on economic and financial matters and executes monetary policy on behalf of the Government; it manages the government's borrowing operations and maintains the country's foreign exchange reserves; it has a statutory responsibility for supervising the banking sector, and an accepted responsibility for watching over the good order of the financial system as a whole; it acts as banker to the government, and to other banks, including other central banks; and it is responsible for the note issue. (Committee to Review the Functioning of Financial Institutions, Chairman, the Rt Hon. Sir Harold Wilson, *Report*, London: HMSO, 1980, Appendix 4, p. 521.)

The Bank of England has considerable authority in the fixing of interest rates. The rates applied by the commercial banks move in sympathy with the Bank of England's minimum lending rate, partly for technical reasons, but mainly in obedience to custom.

The Wilson Report describes the work of the Bank of England in Appendix 4 of its Report, and summarises the activities of nineteen other central banks in Appendix 8. See, too, the admirably clear exposition in the Report of the Radcliffe Committee, chaps V and IX, and Bank for International Settlements, *Eight European Central Banks* (London: Allen & Unwin, 1963).

9.4 OTHER FINANCIAL INSTITUTIONS

In the olden days people lived a hand-to-mouth existence, spending almost as quickly as they earned, so that there was limited scope for financial institutions. Nowadays, in the rich countries, about a fifth of gross domestic product (GDP) is saved (on average in the years 1973–7, savings constituted 17 per cent in the United Kingdom, just over 17 per cent in the United States, and nearly 33 per cent in Japan). (Central Statistical Office, *Financial Statistics: Explanatory Handbook* London: HMSO, 1980, p. 35.) These vast sums must be recorded, lent or otherwise invested, dividends or interest paid and received, insurance policies serviced and so on.

The largest operators in this field are pension funds and insurance companies. In the United Kingdom in 1978 they collected £8500 million, about three-quarters of which went into public sector or company securities. Their net purchase of securities in that year amounted to £6000 million. The growth of pension schemes is one of the striking phenomena of our time: three million people belonged to them in Britain in 1936, ten million in 1953 and 11¼ million in 1975. Their assets in 1978 amounted to £31 000 million, while those of life insurance companies amounted to £38 000 million (there is some double counting here, for about one-third of this came from pension funds). In the same year investing institutions (insurance companies, pension funds, investment and unit trusts) owned 47 per cent of UK company ordinary shares by market value; 72 per cent of preference shares and 42 per cent of their loan capital. (See the Wilson Committee *Report*, p. 73.) 'Over the period between 1957 and 1975 the proportion of ordinary shares beneficially owned by persons fell from 66 to 38 per cent; it is estimated to have fallen further to 32 per cent by the end of 1978.' (Ibid. p. 499.)

Most private shareholders own only a few shares in any company. They may attend the annual general meeting and make a nuisance of themselves for an hour or two, but that is all. By contrast the fund managers are people of enormous power, with more power in important respects than Ministers of Finance; but perhaps I should say *potential*, for they use their power with great discretion. Though they can unseat the boards of directors of the companies whose shares they hold, they rarely do so, on the principle that though they (the fund managers) are expert in fund management, the company directors are expert in whatever it is their company is engaged in doing. There is, too, a strong sense of fellowship between the people involved: they live and have their being in realms of business and finance from which the mass of humanity is excluded.

There is something curiously old-fashioned about this element of the economic system, as well as an element of science-fiction that gives glimpses of the future. There are old-fashioned money-lenders as described by Dickens in *Nicholas Nickleby*, who own their own money and lend it to desperate people at ridiculous rates of interest, and there are the credit-card companies whose business gets into such a tangle that it will never be straightened out. At those levels finance has been taken over by microchips and there are always people who are ready to match their wits against the system. Sometimes they succeed; sometimes they get found out and we are given a view of their crime; sometimes they do not, but how often and for how much, by the nature of the case, we shall never know. But studying the case-histories of those who did publicly come to grief is an excellent way of getting insight into the system, from the bottom, as it were, up. I shall remind you of some of these cases by and by.

So suspicious are Americans about the natures and vices of banks that banks in the United States are not allowed to spread beyond their home State. They may invade every other country in the world, but, at home, are limited to California or New York State or Iowa or whatever the case may be. The farming crisis of the 1920s, the stock market crash of 1929, followed by the great depression of the early 1930s, resulted in the failure of thousands of banks, a process stemmed only when the newly elected Roosevelt administration compulsorily suspended banking operations while the position was sorted out. But what US banks are not allowed to do between States, they, and the banks of the rest of the world, are permitted to do between countries – that is, effectively escape the jurisdiction of any single government. It is not possible, in some important respects, for the British Government to control what the branch of a British bank is up to in France or Italy, and virtually impossible for the tax or financial inspectors of any other government to know what is going on in the tax havens – Liechtenstein, Luxembourg, the Bahamas, the Cayman Islands, amongst others – through which funds can be passed with little cost to their owners. I learn from Simon Winchester (*Sunday Times*, 2 Jan. 1983, p. 13) that every day of the year at least $2 billion flow into the Cayman Islands. There are 17 000 islanders, but 420 banks, 300 insurance companies and 15 000 registered corporate offices. So strict are the secrecy laws that it is an offence even to make inquiries.

A private company is registered as such, thereby affording limited liability for its owners, – only the company can be sued for its debts, though those who operate it may be prosecuted for criminal acts perpetrated in the course of their business. If the private company flourishes it may 'go public' – register as such and offer its shares for sale to the public. Permission may then be sought to have its shares bought and sold on the relevant stock exchange. George J. W. Goodman, writing under the name Adam Smith in inverted commas, explains how it is done, with examples, in *Supermoney*, London: Michael Joseph, 1973, pp. 20 f.

Stock exchanges play an important role in money markets, though whether for good or evil is a matter of dispute. Superficially, they appear to be a perfect example of perfect competition, so it is surprising to find very little said about them in textbooks on economics. Henry Clay devoted half a page to them in his *Economics for the General Reader* (London: Macmillan, 1920, p. 113):

The Stock Exchange is a market for the shares of companies that exist; it facilitates the transference, not of capital from one industry to another, but of shares of existing businesses from one owner to another. Indirectly, however, it is the means of guiding new capital into the industries in which it is most needed; if railway stock rises in value on the Stock Exchange, people with disposable capital are inclined to put it into new railways; if cycle shares have fallen more than shares in other industries, investors are warned not to put any more capital into the cycle industry.

Marshall has even less to say, and says it with caution. Referring to dealers on the stock exchange or the produce markets, he concludes: 'The good and evil effects of the action of speculators such as these are however very complex....' (*Principles of Economics*, p. 293.) He is less evasive in a footnote on p. 432, where he remarks: 'It has been well observed that a speculator, who, without manipulating prices by false intelligence or otherwise, anticipates the future correctly; and who makes his gains by shrewd purchases and sales on the Stock Exchange or in Produce Markets, generally renders a public service by pushing forward production where it is wanted, and repressing it where it is not....'

Marshall rightly described the effects of speculators as very complex. Keynes was able to pronounce on the question with authority and insight from participant observation:

> In 1921 he became Chairman of the National Mutual Insurance Company. He was a director of the Independent Investment Company for a time and later of the Provincial Insurance Company. His touch was golden. In Robinson's words, 'about his flair for investment there can be no doubt. The prosperity of the National Mutual, of his College, of the Royal Economic Society, of his own finances, all bear ample witness'. (Robert Lekachman, *The Age of Keynes: A Biographical Study*, Harmondsworth: Penguin Books, 1967, p. 45.)

Keynes's views of the stock market are to be found in the inspired chapter 12 of his *General Theory of Employment*, which, having been read for pleasure, deserves careful study. It is called 'The State of Long-Term Expectation', and shows that this has a very uncertain relation with what will actually happen, and that, on the stock exchange, it has little relevance to the welfare of the community. If we wish to know what stocks are going to rise we have to divine the judgement of other speculators on what the judgement of other speculators will be.

> If the reader interjects that there must surely be large profits to be gained from the other players in the long run by a skilled individual who, unpertubed by the prevailing pastime, continues to purchase investments on the best genuine long-term expectations he can frame, he must be answered, first of all, that there are, indeed, such serious-minded individuals and that it makes a vast difference to an investment market whether or not they predominate in their influence over the game-players. But we must also add that there are several factors which jeopardise the predominance of such individuals in modern investment markets. Investment based on genuine long-term expectations is so difficult to-day as to be scarcely practicable. He who attempts it must surely lead much more laborious days and run greater risks than he who tries to guess better than the crowd how the crowd will behave; and, given equal intelligence, he may make more disastrous mistakes. There is no clear evidence from experience that the investment policy which is socially advantageous coincides with that which is most profitable. It needs *more* intelligence to defeat the forces of time and our ignorance of the future than to beat the gun. Moreover, life is not long enough; – human nature desires quick results, there is a peculiar zest in making money quickly, and remoter gains are discounted by the average man at a very high rate. The game of professional investment is intolerably boring and over-exacting to anyone who is entirely exempt from the gambling instinct; whilst he who has it must pay to this propensity the appropriate toll. . . . Finally it is the long-term investor, he who most promotes the public interest, who will in practice come in for most criticism, wherever investment funds are managed by committees or boards or banks. For it is in the essence of his behaviour that he should be eccentric, unconventional and rash in the eyes of average opinion. (Keynes, *General Theory*, pp. 156–7.)

So if stock exchanges are the nerve-centres of capitalist societies, they are of dubious social benefit. They do not have the effect 'of guiding new capital into the industries in which it most needed' nor out of those where it is not. Clive W. J. Granger and Oskar Morgenstern found little correlation between the movements of stock prices and the future, or even the past, performance of the corporations concerned.

(*Predictability of Stock Market Prices*, Indianapolis: Lexington Books, 1970.)

Stock exchanges are strong in ritual, their bursts of frenzy reminiscent of hypnotic dances of the !Kung San mentioned in Chapter 2. The London exchange was one of the last British institutions to admit women. Paul Ferris described it thus:

> It's a masculine place, often hearty and facetious; telegraphic addresses of stockbrokers include Fiddle, Oddness, Overmodest and Contrive. Women may not be members – a poll in 1967 turned down a proposal that would have admitted them to membership as long as they didn't set foot on the trading floor during business hours. The floor of the Stock Exchange is still sacred ground, a place where a man can swear a little or play the fool with his friends. (A Milan stockbroker said he had been told by an English colleague that if a broker carried a newspaper under his arm for long enough in the London Stock Exchange, some joker would be sure to set fire to the end of it. 'That couldn't happen in Milan,' he said severely, 'and if it did, the person would be suspended for a fortnight.') Sons and nephews still slide into family firms; some brokers still exist on a shoestring, managing a few portfolios and mouldering away with a certain elegance. But mergers between Stock Exchange firms are creating fewer and larger units, especially among stockjobbers – the English brand of specialists, who trade as wholesalers in securities, for their own account, and so need greater resources.   (Paul Ferris, *Men and Money: Financial Europe Today*, Harmondsworth: Penguin Books, 1970, pp. 152–3.)

By definition it is impossible to allow for the unexpected, so forecasters and speculators proceed on the assumption that from what we know about today, we can predict tomorrow. Stock exchanges thus become curiously set in their rituals. The price of government stock when the rate of interest is 17 per cent is fixed as if it were always going to be 17 per cent; if it falls to $8\frac{1}{4}$ per cent the market price of government stock will be almost doubled (depending on the date of maturity). Look at the stock exchange report in the *Financial Times* or the *Wall Street Journal* and you will see that the prices of government stocks vary according to the interest which is paid at specified rates on the face-value of the stock. When the banks change their interest rates the market price of the stocks will change accordingly. For example, in November 1980 I bought Treasury 14 per cent stock that matures in

1996 and paid £90 for each £100 certificate. The Treasury will go on paying £14 interest on each certificate until 1996, when they will repay the owner £100. So on each £90 that I paid I get 15¼ per cent interest. Why? Because banks, building societies and other borrowers of money were offering 15¼ per cent (or something in that vicinity) when I bought my stock. Then interest rates began falling, and the market price of the Treasury stock began rising until it reached £127.75. Anyone buying them at that price would get nearly 11 per cent on his money, something like he could have got by investing his money elsewhere. There are other considerations: you must pay your stockbroker commission when you buy and sell on the stock exchange, whereas putting your money into a Post Office savings account, bank or building society deposit account, is costless.

If you follow the Dow Jones or Financial Times or any other share price index you will see that it fluctuates for the most absurd and irrelevant reasons, having little relevance to the profitability of the companies upon whose shares the indexes are based. This is the crowd trying to decide what the crowd is going to do and acting accordingly. For an illuminating exposition of crowd behaviour in this context, see George Goodman's ('Adam Smith') *The Money Game*, London: Pan Books, 1970, chap. 4, 'Is the Market Really a Crowd?'.

Keynes in his chapter 12 (mentioned above) was inspired to break out of his own model when he came to expose the operations of the stock market, and so was Samuelson in the Appendix ('Stock Market Fluctuations') to chapter 4 of his *Economics*. I am looking at the sixth edition, New York: McGraw-Hill, 1964, pp. 74–6, which I commend to you as a concise explanation of stock-exchange operations.

Millions of people have joined together for purposes of insurance, security in old age, house-buying. At first sight one might think that these immense efforts, built on co-operation rather than competition, would carry with them immense extensions of industrial democracy. This does not, however, appear to have been the effect. As already noted, the boards of directors of these wealth-managing institutions, and the fund managers who place their investments, are themselves part of a powerful business coterie that works very closely with the tribe of top managers who run our service and manufacturing industries.

Counter Information Services, in their report on insurance companies and pension funds, found that their 'massive concentration of economic power is held in the hands of a small tightly knit group – a self perpetuating oligarchy subject to no social or democratic control'. 'The wealth thus aggregated into giant accumulations is in the hands of a few large and growing concerns whose boards are drawn from the same small circle which dominates the boardrooms of industrial and financial power. And, as elsewhere, the trend is to growing concentration, not only within the industry, but across its frontiers, to spawn new financial conglomerates.'

Directors of insurance companies must be eminently respectable to maintain the confidence of those whose lives they insure and whose premiums they invest. The report presents a vignette of the directors of 13 insurance companies. Of the 129 directors who were listed in *Who's Who*, '106 went to public school, 42 of them to Eton. Rugby, Winchester, Harrow and Marlborough were the other most popular schools. Of the 87 university graduates in the total, 70 went to Oxford or Cambridge. Nearly all the directors listed are members of exclusive London clubs, with Boodle's the most popular.... Also noticeable is the high number of directors with backgrounds in the armed forces, government, the civil service and the diplomatic corps, which taken together were the most common background of the directors quoted.' (Counter Information Services, *Your Money and Your Life: Insurance Companies and Pension Funds*, Anti-Report Number 7, undated but about 1974, p. 5.)

I have mentioned ritual and convention as being important elements in the operation of financial institutions. Devotees of perfect competition will reject this as implausible: how could rational people, engaged in maximisation of their fortunes, indulge in metaphysics? Yet you will note great differences in behaviour between financiers in different countries, as well as in their personal behavioural patterns. In Italy and France major banks were nationalised, in Italy in the 1930s to rescue them from collapse, in France after they had compromised themselves by collaboration with the Nazis in the Second World War. In Italy they brought with them large industrial institutions in which they had had controlling interests and which have since flourished and grown to enormous size. You will see these differences well depicted in Paul Ferris, *Men and Money: Financial Europe Today*, Harmondsworth: Penguin Books, 1970, chap. 4, 'Inside the Six'. Goodman comments:

> Anyway, irrationality and mystery and magic are no strangers to us in the money markets. That was one of the points of *The Money Game*, to show that while the language of the game was built on rationality and precision, the Game itself was played by behavior, and with all sorts of totems and taboos that would do credit to any tribe in New Guinea with an anthropologist in residence. (*Supermoney*, p. 288.)

9.5 LIGHTS THAT FAILED

As already noted, strange activities take place in the world of finance that writers of textbooks curiously omit, perhaps because they do not fit comfortably in their models. Most bank clerks, insurance agents and even stockbrokers are undoubtedly models of probity and can be relied upon not to short-change or otherwise swindle you. It is those with the grand designs who require the closest scrutiny, perhaps because it is there that the prizes, opportunities and thus temptations reach their maximum. Some of the great calamities are the result of the chief actors being carried away by forces of their own creation that they can no longer control. But whatever the motivations there is much to be learnt in these events about the world we live in, and I describe now a few of the more revealing.

9.5.1 Investors Overseas Services

Everyone who read the financial pages in the 1960s will be familiar with the name of Bernard Cornfeld and his mutual fund, Investors Overseas Services. When the IOS crashed in 1970 it controlled funds totalling $2400 million, drawn from a million investors. The story is told in Charles Raw, Bruce Page and Godfrey Hodgson, *Do you sincerely want to be Rich? Bernard Cornfeld and IOS: An International Swindle* (London: André Deutsch, 1971).

Bernie was born in Istanbul in 1927, the son of a Romanian actor, impresario and film producer, and was brought up in Brooklyn, New York City. He spent two years on a ship as assistant purser, campaigned for Norman Thomas (Socialist Party) for President in 1948, graduated in psychology from Brooklyn College, went on to Columbia University School of Social Work, and sold mutual funds. His statements are full of populist ideas about bringing capitalism to the poor. In 1955 he went to Paris and established Investors Overseas Services, selling for the rapidly growing (New York) Dreyfus Fund to Americans in Europe. The salesmen were well rewarded: investors agreed to make monthly payments on a contractual programme, but the salesmen drew their commission on the total programme. By 1962 IOS was bringing in 31 per cent of all the Dreyfus Fund's new money.

IOS recruited salesmen through a standing advertisement in the Paris *Herald-Tribune* that offered American men and women over $10 000 a year for sales ability, a willingness to work hard, and a sense of humour. One of the salesmen described the Cornfeld of those days, and his methods:

Physically, he was completely unprepossessing.... His clothes were baggy – there was never a suit off the peg which could fit Bernie. But then he started to speak. His voice is very soft, and reassuring. His smile is very engaging.

I didn't at all like the idea of selling mutual funds. And he didn't seem to sell the idea very hard. But by the time I left the flat, I had agreed to give it a try.

There was nothing elaborate about the operation.... The firm's chief and almost only asset was a Chrysler Imperial convertible.... It was the headquarters of the firm, really... Each weekend Bernie would load it up with salesmen and sales material, and drive out to Orleans. Sometimes, we would sleep over Saturday night in the car before starting in again on Sunday. (Raw *et al.*, p. 60.)

In 1958 the French authorities began to make things difficult, so the entourage moved to Geneva. Eleven years later, in September 1969, IOS had fifty-five principal subsidiaries controlling hundreds of companies around the world, nine banks with deposits of nearly $100 million, ten mutual funds with $2000 million in investors' accounts, a real estate company with properties valued at $100 million. In that month IOS went public, offering eleven million shares at $10. The shares were underwritten by 122 banks, including Banque Rothschild, Drexel Harriman Riply Inc., Guinness Mahon, and Hill Samuel.

Cornfeld had promised his salesmen that they would become millionaires – and a number of them did (ibid. pp. 320–2). He himself had a Rolls, a custom-built Lincoln, a Cadillac and a Sting-Ray; a villa in Geneva on the edge of the lake, a château in Haute-Savoie, another in Switzerland, and houses or apartments in Paris, London and New York. He described himself as a 'sexual anarchist', but married a model some years after IOS had gone bust. One woman in his orbit described him as 'a man who never had any idea of where to settle down – or where to go to; the kind of man who loved every woman he saw, but could not love any one in particular; a man whose elaborate explanations were likely to mystify.... When he appeared to confess everything, he revealed nothing; when he gave, it was only to take away'. (Raw, *et al.*, p. 196.) *Business Week* labelled him 'King of Europe's Cash', *Time*, 'part Peter Pan, part Midas'. *The Times* described the IOS Fund of Funds as 'the phenomenon of phenomena'.

What was the magic formula? Unit trusts (mutual funds) collect money by retail and invest it by wholesale. The investors get units of a mixture of shares, and the management gets a profit by charging a percentage for their services. Their superiority over a bank deposit account depends not on the dividends earned on the shares, but on their capital appreciation.

The fund uses its depositors' payments (1) to pay their management charges and (2) to buy shares in other companies, including other funds. A close-ended fund is made up of a fixed quantity of specified shares; in an open-ended fund, the managers shift investments around according to expediency. When the depositor withdraws his savings he is paid according to the current market price of the shares that make up the fund, minus management charges.

Part 1 of the magic formula was that after 1942, and in the 1950s and 1960s, stock prices (with a few brief interruptions) moved strongly upward; the capital appreciation was beautiful to behold. A thousand dollars spread over Standard & Poor's list of stocks in the United States in 1950 would have been worth $5250 in 1969 (in constant consumer dollars of 1950, £3465). You will find indexes of share prices in International Monetary Fund, *International Financial Statistics*.

Part 2: salesmanship! Our studies of corporations have revealed selling as a high art in the United States, and salesmen leading great business ventures. It was to this that Cornfeld applied his genius. Europe at that time had been invaded by two American armies: the one of soldiers and officials, rich by European standards, the other of students and adventurers, poor but talented. Why not use the talent to persuade the rich where to put their wealth?

The applicants from the *Herald-Tribune* advertisements were put through an intensive course. They practised 'firm handshakes' and 'sincere smiles' and were taught how to win their prospect's confidence. Sit beside him rather than across the table; talk about 'if something happens to you' rather than 'when you die'.

> The art of supplementary dialogue was probably raised to its highest point by . . . a flaxen-haired Australian with a visionary and innocent eye, who specialized in selling IOS programmes linked to life insurance. He recommended goosing the prospects with this kind of phrase: 'Let's lean over your executor's shoulder for a moment. How long is it before your widow is working?' Or, he suggested, a salesman could tell the prospect, 'about the letter you once saw which said, "I don't want you to think my husband didn't love his family. It's just that he didn't plan to die at this time" '.

Cornfeld would ask the prospective salesmen, 'Do you sincerely want to be rich?' If they did he would make them millionaires.

Part 3 of the formula was the trustfulness of the customers. It was explained to them that they could expect $10 000 turned into $54 000 within ten years. Or if they wanted to pay $100 a month for ten years, they could expect a pay-out of $34 000. This must have seemed an attractive proposition to a well-paid American whose prospects, on his ultimate return to the United States, were somewhat uncertain. It was one of the advantages of entrusting their savings to skilled investors. But, of course, there was no guarantee that this would be the result – if the market turned downward the IOS could not be held responsible.

It was not peculiar to the IOS that a customer on a ten-year programme who withdrew after a year or two might find he had made a *loss*, for out of the first year's payments the fund would help itself to salesman's commission and its own management charges. On a programme requiring a downpayment of $50 followed by $25 a month for ten years, of the first year's payment of £325, the salesman would get $120 and the IOS $40. An administrative service fee raised total charges over the life of the programme to 12 per cent. The Investment Company Act in the United States prescribes a maximum of 9 per cent.

Clients were reassured by the impressive institutions involved. 'Few people realized that none of the eminent international concerns whose names appeared on the sales literature bore any responsibility to check up on the securities bought. . . .' (Raw, *et al.*, p. 88.)

When IOS went public in September 1969 its shares rose from $10 (at which they had been offered) to $14. Many of its salesmen borrowed all they could get to buy them, believing Cornfeld's estimate that the price would rise to $25 or even $50. At the gathering of salesmen in Geneva in August of that year Cornfeld had hailed them not as salesmen, but as 'missionaries, philanthropists, even statesmen'. (Raw, *et al.*, p. 118.) But by then the division between fantasy and reality had disappeared; IOS salesmen had been hunted from country after country, in the United States because of its breaches of the codes of the Securities and Exchange Commission, from Latin America, Asia and Africa because it was acting as an agency for the illegal export of funds.

One of the trio of men at the top of IOS spent over $20 million of IOS money, buying back its own shares in a desperate attempt to maintain their market price, but in the early months of 1970 stock markets throughout the capitalist world slumped and the effort was hopeless. 'A point can be reached at the height of speculative booms when transactions become so complicated that they baffle the very minds which devised them, so that men, and companies, end up swindling themselves. That point had now been reached: IOS was now supporting itself into a state of collapse.' (Raw, *et al.*, p. 381.)

Cornfeld and his directors were compelled to resign. Unfortunately for the people who had entrusted their savings to the IOS funds, the company was 'rescued' by Robert Vesco, who was later charged with defrauding IOS of $225 million when he disappeared somewhere in the Caribbean. In 1973 Cornfeld was arrested by the Swiss authorities and held for eleven months while they investigated charges of fraud. In 1974 he was released on bail of five million Swiss francs. When he came to court in 1979 the charge was one of fraud for persuading IOS employees to buy IOS shares at $10, while he himself made $7.8 million by secretly selling his own shares. But at the trial the witnesses one by one withdrew their allegations. 'In a way, the fact that not a single witness would testify against Cornfeld, and indeed took time out to say kind words about him, is a tribute to the respect for a man whose financial and social career is virtually without parallel in modern times.' (Kevin Page, in *The Times*, 16 Oct. 1979.)

9.5.2 Conspiracy to defraud

The Securities and Exchange Commission has the duty of overseeing the activities of public companies in the United States. As a government agency their role will be considered in the ensuing chapter. At this point it will be useful to consider one of the multitude of cases that they send to court each year. In June 1979 Erickson and Wilson appealed to the US Court of Appeals against their criminal conviction as chairman of the board of a bank and vice-president of the same bank. 'Defendants were convicted of causing false entries to be made in the records of the bank of which they were officers and of causing false and misleading financial statements to be filed by an affiliated bank holding company, in violation of the False Banking Entry Act and the Securities Exchange Act of 1934, and of conspiring to do the same.' (Commerce Clearing House, *Federal Securities Law Reports*, 7 May 1979, pp. 95, 737).

Their grounds of appeal included 'instances of prosecutorial misconduct' including the prosecutor's remark in his opening address: 'Now many people have a concept of white collar crime as somehow being different from a crime of violence. In many respects and in this case in particular, a white collar crime is more insidious than a street crime.'

The case arose because Wilson had sold federal securities short, in the belief that the market would continue to fall. When you sell short you enter into a contract to deliver stock (that you do not then possess) at a specified future date. You are gambling that, by the date of delivery, their market price will have fallen so you will be able to buy them at less than the contractual price; the buyer is gambling that the reverse will have happened. In this case Wilson was wrong and the bank stood to lose $800 000.

Instead of buying the securities for delivery, and thereby clocking up the loss immediately, Wilson caused the bank to borrow them from its own portfolio. Later, identical securities were purchased to replace those that had been borrowed. But how to avoid writing down the portfolio securities to their new market value? This was to be achieved by 'negotiated overtrades' in terms of which the bank sold 'replacement securities' at inflated prices, agreeing at the same time to buy back from the purchaser other securities at equally inflated prices.

The auditors advised that the transaction was complete when the bank had delivered the securities taken from its portfolio, and that the loss of $800 000 would have to be shown in the books at that date. Wilson objected, arguing that 'what he had done was common practice in the industry, and that he would obtain letters from other banks to support his position'. But he failed to obtain such letters. About this time a new firm of auditors replaced the old. They ruled that the full loss resulting from the sale of the 'replacement securities' had to be recognised, by writing down the value of the securities acquired to their true market value.

One gets some insight into the tension that must have been built up during these manœuvres. Gillis, the internal auditor, had discovered the losses and the attempts to cover them up during his audit of Wilson's department. He refused to sign a letter to the external auditors stating that 'no facts have been discovered since the statement date which would make the financial statements for the year materially inaccurate or misleading'. Erickson called him up on the telephone and said, 'If you don't sign that goddamned letter, you're through.' Erickson also said, 'You're saying that I'm aware of these transactions which is an attempt to defraud the stockholders, and that I'm going to lose my investment, and that I'm probably going to jail.' (p. 95, 748.)

The major charges were confirmed by the Appeal Court.

It is interesting to see that the two lots of (external) auditors took a different view as to the rights and wrongs of the transactions and of the way in which they were recorded. Accounts can be manipulated in such a way as to lead to very different interpretations by those who do not have direct knowledge of the events that they are supposed to reflect. This is particularly true of banks, who deal in merchandise whose value changes from time to time, sometimes from hour to hour, in unpredictable ways.

Many white-collar crimes result from the misappropriation of funds; but others from attempts to cover up errors arising from misjudgement or negligence.

9.5.3 Tiger Balm

Tiger Balm is an ointment celebrated for its powers to soothe and cure. It is manufactured by Haw Par, whose benevolent founder presented public gardens to Singapore. The firm prospered and grew into Haw Par Brothers International, in which many of the thrifty citizens of that city-state invested their savings. Meanwhile, on the other side of the world, Jim Slater had left school at the age of 16 to become a book-keeper. In the fifth year of his working life he joined Cooper Brothers, a firm of auditors and accountants of international repute. The next ten years of his life were spent in industry. He became commercial manager of Leyland, manufacturers of high-grade commercial vehicles, then deputy to the sales director. In the early 1960s he began advising clients on matters of investment, and cultivated his own wealth so that it grew from £2000 to £50 000. In 1964 Slater, Walker Securities was established. Six years later his partner, Peter Walker, was to become a Minister in the Conservative Government.

The *modus operandi* was to study the Extel cards, which show, for each company, the assets and earnings. If a company's assets exceed its market valuation (share price on the stock market multiplied by the number of shares) it might be worth going after it. You and your friends begin buying its shares; at the strategic moment you make a take-over bid, oust the directors, buy up the remainder of the shares, sell off the company's assets and pocket the difference between what you have paid for it and what you get for them.

The escapade need not always end in asset-stripping; if, responding to your covert share-buying the shares rise substantially, you can simply off-load your shares on the market and make your profit that way. Or you may, indeed, continue the business as a going concern and make a go of it. This happened to some of the Slater, Walker acquisitions so that, by the latter part of 1969, they had a turnover of £38 million.

Peter Walker resigned when he joined the Conservative Cabinet, but the group continued to flourish. Slater, Walker Securities became a merchant bank, Slater, Walker Ltd. Acquisitions were made in North America, Europe, Australia and the Far East – including the ill-fated Tiger Balm. Money was borrowed to speed the process. Then, in a variation of the IOS story, the magic was no more. The 1974 accounts revealed the first fall in profits, from £13.1 million to $8.7 million, *before* taking into account extraordinary losses of £33.6 million, mostly due to selling shares of subsidiaries and associate companies. 'Basically, the Slater story is one of a dynamic man's speculative enthusiasm. History is studded with financial promoters carried away by their own ingenuity in times of boom, only to fall when the game changes. Mr Slater had a longer innings than most.' (*The Economist*, 1 Nov. 1975, pp. 72–4.)

One may learn much about the ways of the business world by observing what ensued. The Bank of England decided (no doubt after consultation with the government) that the company must not be allowed to collapse (and thereby injure the reputation of British businessmen throughout the world) and produced an initial amount of £40 million on stringent conditions, to prevent this happening. The Finance Minister of Singapore alleged that a private company, Spydar Securities, had been registered in Hong Kong to execute share deals for the benefit of the directors of Haw Par and at the expense of Haw Par's shareholders. The process was simple: Haw Par sold Spydar Securities shares at below their market price, and Spydar sold them *at* their market price, the profit being distributed to the six Slater, Walker directors as an incentive.

The Board of Trade might have appointed inspectors to investigate, under the Companies Act, but did not do so. Instead, an investigation was undertaken by two firms of chartered accountants, who reported ten months later, in September 1976. The 1975 accounts, published at the same time, showed group losses of £42 million. The accountants noted various irregularities: Section 54 of the Companies Act prohibits companies from lending money to buy their own shares, but Slater, Walker Ltd had provided funds for four related companies to do this, though, the Report noted, there was no evidence that Slater or any other director had benefited from the transactions. Substantial amounts had been lent to directors: at the end of October 1975 £585 000 had been lent, including £228 000 for housing mortgages. House mortgages to other members of staff totalled £623 000. It was also noted that some £¼ million had been advanced to a retiring managing director, after it had already been decided he would leave the group. This was to enable him to buy shares in another company that he would then develop, and so be able to give better security for what he owed Slater, Walker for previous advances. The company's shares now stood at 9p, down from a peak in 1972 of 309p.

Also in September 1976 the Singapore Government issued sommonses against Jim Slater and his four other directors, and applied for their extradition. In January 1977 the extradition application was considered in London by the Chief Metropolitan Magistrate. The ruling: that Slater had no case to answer. There was no evidence that he was a director of Haw Par and, though the Prosecution claimed he aided and abetted others, he had not been charged with that, but only as a principal. Richard Tarling, the Chairman of Haw Par, did have a case to answer, however, and extradition was granted. His appeal was dismissed and, in November 1979, the Singapore High Court sentenced him to six months' imprisonment.

In response to civil litigation Slater, Walker repaid £1 100 000 to Haw Par.

In London, in February 1977, Jim Slater was cleared of fifteen charges of breach of Section 54 of the Companies Act of 1948. This prohibits companies from buying their own shares or helping others to do so. There is an exception: banks *are* allowed to lend money for the purchase of their own shares, provided this is done *in the ordinary course of business.* If a customer borrows money from a bank he may or may not tell the bank what he wants it for. But even if he tells the bank he wants it for the purpose of buying shares in the bank this does not debar them from lending it to him. In the case in point Slater had lent over £4 million to Bion Securities for the purpose of buying shares in the parent company, Slater, Walker Securities. The defence argued that this was in the ordinary course of business; the magistrates agreed. It is interesting to note that in France, Germany and the United States companies are allowed to buy their own shares, but in the United States their action must be disclosed to the shareholders.

9.6 INFLATION

Money has the disadvantage, for a measuring-rod, of stretching or contracting over time so that what was measured by one of its units this year differs from the year before and will differ from the year after. In periods of deflation, the command of money over goods increases, while that of goods over money declines, and in periods of inflation, of course, the reverse. To inflate, the *Shorter Oxford Dictionary* explains, means to blow out or distend with wind or air. This is what happens to our money in inflationary times: it is distended with wind or air.

There are various ways of measuring inflation, giving different answers to its extent, because we are gauging the value of money in terms of a heterogeneous collection of goods and services whose prices move differently over time:

> A consumer price index or retail price index measure price movements as they affect the average household budget.
> A wholesale price index measures price movements as they affect production costs.
> Import or export price indexes measure price changes in a country's imports or exports.

Inflation was supposed to be associated with rising economic activity, including rising employment, investment and production; deflation, with its fall in prices, brought rising unemployment, gloom and economic contraction. The disconcerting feature of the inflation of the 1970s and 1980s is its accompaniment of rising unemployment and falling output – gloom and misery instead of hyperactivity.

The gloom, misery and rising unemployment have been induced, or at least exacerbated, by government policies in some OECD countries, convinced by the monetarists that inflation was worse than unemployment and that the one could be cured by the other. It is unfortunate, particularly for the unemployed, that the two appear to have achieved a state of mutual accommodation. There are, unfortunately, few unemployed monetarists. The term 'stagflation' is used to describe the co-existence of stagnation and inflation.

Is inflation indeed the symptom of an illness greatly to be feared? We look with horror at its outbreaks in some Latin American countries and in Israel, but these attacks have been much more severe than any experienced by OECD countries in modern times:

Consumer Price Indexes, 1980
1975 = 100

Average for OECD countries	158
Argentina	21 555
Brazil	703
Chile	1 512
Israel	1 097

Does it really matter that between 1981 and 1982 inflation in the United States was running at between 5 and 8 per cent per year? Or in the United Kingdom, 6 to 11 per cent, Canada 10 to 11 per cent, France 10 to 14 per cent, Germany 5 to 6 per cent? To some people, including those in the governments of the United States, Britain and Germany, it does, and hence their efforts to contain it.

It is perfectly true that inflation is generally unpopular. Price rises cause little stabs of pain every time one does a round of the supermarket. Bus fares, season tickets, telephone charges, petrol prices, reach heights that seem scandalous. Even house-buyers whose income is rising faster than their loan repayments are confronted by rising local taxes and interest rates that postpone the day of final repayment. While increases in pay and indexed pensions are pleasant to those who receive them it is then painful to be robbed of their fruits by price rises.

Inflation warps the pattern of economic relations, favouring debtors who repay their loans in devalued money, and this is held to be justification for rates of interest high enough to exceed the rate of inflation. But if you add the current uncertainties of business to high rates of interest, the range of enterprises is greatly reduced whose return is likely to exceed that on government bonds. Inflation, by its nature, favours those who own things as against those who own money, for by definition it is characterised by rising prices. But in its mode of stagflation the ownership of industrial companies ceases to be a sound protection against the fall in the value of money because of the uncertainty of profits.

In some respects similar arguments may be used against deflation, that warps the economic framework by favouring owners of money as against owners of things. There are certain social forces, however, that apply brakes to deflation that are not operative in the case of inflation: the ratchet effect prevents the fall of wages and salaries. Profits fall, employment falls, but the real income of those who keep their jobs actually rises. Over the long periods in history in which falling prices have prevailed, the fall is due to a fall in costs caused by technical advances, including improvements in transport that bring savings through the expansion of world trade. The changes are beneficial rather than harmful. As long as money incomes are not reduced the benefits will be disseminated throughout society.

But, to my mind, the principal evil of inflation is that it is disruptive of the moral element in economic activity. The effect of the just wage and just price is to give stability to economic relations. Justice and equity distribute wealth according to merit. Of course there is a powerful element of tradition in what is held to be meritorious. As Barbara Wootton remarked, 'Change – always, everywhere – requires justification: the strength of conservatism is that it is held to justify itself.' (*The Social Foundations of Wage Policy*, London: Allen & Unwin, 1962.) But attrition is preferable to the struggle and disruption caused by rapid inflation. There are alternatives to this process: for instance, the status of manual workers was raised by the spread of education; that of women by legislation and social movements.

In periods of inflation the order of relative prices is disrupted and it becomes difficult for purchasers to know when they are being conned. Occasionally suppliers are met with organised resistance, such as occurred with regard to meat prices in various countries in the early 1970s, but as a rule there is little that the buyer can do. In the face of rising prices people struggle instead for compensatory increases in income. This disrupts the order of relative incomes, so that there develops a competitive struggle for higher pay, in which trade union strength is mobilised for winning advances that time continues remorselessly to erode, so that they must be won and won again in an irregular but unending struggle. Instead of mobilisation for social changes of lasting value the trade unions compete against each other, while their employers use their ingenuity to exact increases in prices to match those imposed by other employers.

Please note that in the last two paragraphs I am presenting my interpretations of complex phenomena whose appearance changes according to one's viewpoint. As we shall see later, in conducting their affairs workers believe themselves to be reacting to price increases and employers believe themselves to be reacting to unavoidable cost increases.

9.6.1 In search of explanations

Economists have been unable to produce any explanation for inflation so well supported by evidence as to eliminate the rival explanations. Some emphasise the power of excess demand to bid up the prices of goods, which leads to employers bidding up the price of labour. But what is the origin of the excess demand? It arises from an increase in the quantity of money (not only, or even principally, cash, but also bank deposits and other forms of bank money). The quantity theory of money was rehabilitated by the Chicago School (economists at the University of Chicago) in the 1950s. (Milton Friedman, ed., *Studies in the Quantity Theory of Money*, Chicago University Press, 1956.) Friedman argued: 'There is perhaps no other empirical relation in economics that has been observed to recur so uniformly under so wide a variety of circumstances as the relation between substantial changes over short periods in the stock of money and in prices; the one is invariably linked with the other and is in the same direction; this uniformity is, I suspect, of the same order as many of the uniformities that form the basis of the physical sciences. There is an extraordinary empirical stability and regularity to such magnitudes as income velocity that cannot but impress anyone who works extensively with monetary data.' (Ibid. p. 21.)

The arithmetic of the quantity theory was set out by Sir William Petty in the seventeenth century. How much money is necessary to 'drive the Trade of a Nation', he asked? He estimated the total annual expenses of England to be £40 million (what we now call the national income). The amount of money necessary to meet these expenses depended on the 'revolutions and circulations' entailed. If payments were made weekly, as was the case with poorer artisans and labourers, then one-fiftysecond of 40 million pounds would be sufficient. But other payments were made quarterly, so that in general there would be 'a mixed circle between One week and 13 ...'. (See Routh, *The Origin of Economic Ideas*, p. 43.)

This was taken up by subsequent theorists, who suggested that the price of any commodity would be determined by the amount of money chasing it. The overall relationship would be expressed in the equation

$$MV = PQ.$$

Money times velocity equals price times quantity. Is this an important clue to the working of the economic system? No, it is a tautology. If you multiply the price of everything sold (in a specified period) by the quantity of the relevant items, the answer has to equal the quantity of money times the number of times each piece of money was used. For the quantity of money to achieve any operational significance one had to maintain that its velocity of circulation was invariate for practical purposes, and this is what Friedman did. Then, given the quantity of goods to be sold, the price level is determined by the quantity of money.

While the monetarists emphasised 'demand pull', institutionalists emphasised 'cost push', arguing that firms, trade unions and, in general, employers and employees, were able to use their discretion to push up the costs and prices of their products. This led the Deputy-

Governor of the Bank of England to remark that cost push and demand pull were two wings of the same bird, a thought that merits consideration.

The same idea had been presented by Paul Einzig in 1923 in the thesis for his degree at the University of Paris (*Le mouvement des prix en France depuis 1914*). The reviewer in the (London) *Economist* gave the idea qualified approval. 'No further interest was taken in it, however, and it faded into oblivion.' (Paul Einzig, *Inflation*, London: Chatto & Windus, 1952, p. 16.) This leads him to define inflation as 'an expansionary trend of purchasing power that tends to cause, or to be the effect of, an increase of the price level'. (Ibid. p. 17.)

The term 'inflation', according to the *Shorter Oxford English Dictionary*, was first applied in a monetary setting in 1864, to the issue of inconvertible paper money. But, as with the common cold, there are a multitude of different viruses that may cause the condition. Einzig distinguishes twelve:

1. Currency inflation.
2. Credit inflation.
3. Purchasing power inflation.
4. Budgetary inflation.
5. Price inflation through taxation.
6. Inflation through over-investment.
7. Inflation through under-production.
8. Inflation through dis-saving.
9. Inflation through devaluation.
10. Imported inflation.
11. Commodity price inflation.
12. Price inflation through restrictions on foreign trade. (Ibid. pp. 24-5.)

In 1961 the OECD published a Report by a committee of six economists (Swedish, British, Swiss, Dutch and two Americans), *The Problem of Rising Prices*. Their general report is followed by country studies devoted to the role of demand and to wage determination. They note the considerable contrasts between the rate of inflation in different countries between 1953 and 1960, and the considerable differences between different groups of goods and services.

In Spain rents rose little, food rose much; in Greece, rents much, food little; in France, too, rents almost doubled, while clothing rose by only 18 per cent. In the United States, where the consumer price index rose only 9 per cent, fuel and light rose by 12 per cent and household and durable goods actually fell by 4 per cent. (Ibid. p. 99.)

Plainly there was no overriding influence at work. The Committee examined four possible causes: excess demand, excessive negotiated wage increases, monopolist pricing and 'special' price increases. The special price increases related particularly to rent and other price controls and to indirect taxation. A third of the price rise in Sweden from 1953 to the third quarter of 1960 was due to indirect tax increases. In a number of countries rent controls, initiated early in the war, had been removed in the 1950s, as had controls on food prices.

The two major determinants were, the Committee concluded, excess demand and excessive negotiated wage increases, though Professor Richard Kahn (Cambridge) warns that he 'does not believe that the concept of "excess demand" provides a satisfactory method of analysing the processes of inflation'. (Ibid. p. 33.) It is interesting to note that they identified very limited periods of excess demand in most of the OECD countries – 'not significant' or one or two years, though it is described as 'prolonged' in Iceland, Spain and Turkey. (Ibid. p. 35.)

9.6.2 Inflation in one country

Now, since I have available the relevant statistics, let us closely examine the course of inflation in one country: the United Kingdom. The OECD consultants took their study to 1960. After that, inflation in Britain fluctuated about an ascending trend:

Index of Retail Prices in the United Kingdom

Percentage increase on previous year

1963	2.0	1966	3.9	1969	5.4
1964	3.3	1967	2.5	1970	6.4
1965	4.8	1968	4.7	1971	9.4

Source: *British Labour Statistics Year Book 1974*, table 56, p. 128.

The average rise between 1961 and 1970 was 4.1 per cent per year. After the jump to 9.4 per cent between 1970 and 1971, it fell back to 7 per cent between 1971 and 1972, and 9 per cent, 1973 on 1972. After that it took off in the most alarming fashion:

Percentage increase on previous year

1974	16	1977	16	1980	18
1975	24	1978	8	1981	12
1976	16¼	1979	13	1982	9

Source: *Employment Gazette*, table 6.4, Dec. 1982, p. S58.

Let us examine the price movements in these nine years in an attempt to identify their causes. Between 1953 and 1959 the consumer price index in the United Kingdom registered an increase of 20 per cent; between 1973 and 1979 the rise was 150 per cent, so compared with the OECD consultants we shall be viewing inflationary processes on a scale multiplied by 7½.

What was it that set the process off between 1973 and 1974, causing prices in 1974 to average 16 per cent more than in 1973? There was a large element of *imported inflation* in the change. The food group (composed of a representative collection of foods, weighted together) had risen by 18 per cent. Of these, items mainly imported for direct consumption (not manufactured) rose by 20.4 per cent, while those home-produced for direct consumption *fell* by ¼ per cent.

Price Indexes 1974, with 1973 = 100

Rises above average	
All food	118.0
Bread, flour, cereals	122.1
Fish	126.3
Butter, margarine, fat	125.0
Sugar, preserves, confectionery	132.3
Electricity	121.7
Books, newspapers	123.7
Soaps, detergents	126.4
Less than average	
Milk, cheese, eggs	99.4
Tea, coffee, cocoa, soft drinks	112.3
Meat and bacon	112.4
Alcoholic drink	110.9
Housing	111.8
Coal and coke	111.6
Gas	104.8
Durable household goods	114.9
Services	112.25

The (in retrospect) moderate price increases of the early 1970s began accelerating in 1973:

	%
January–July 1973	+ 4.9
July 1973–January 1974	+ 7.3
January–July 1974	+ 9.7

Was this due to only one cause, as some of the theorists ask us to believe? Excess money supply, perhaps, or pay increases in excess of increases in output? No. There was an astonishing variety of factors at work.

Food
A large part of the world grain surplus was absorbed by the Russians in 1972. They imported 18 million tons from the United States, while China doubled its imports to 6 million tons. In 1973 world wheat prices rose 42 per cent, to £88 per ton. Bread, flour, cereals were, of course, directly affected. Meat prices had risen by 30 per cent in 1973, and milk, cheese and eggs 14 per cent. (*Three Phase Trick: A Handbook on Inflation and Phase Three*, Anti-Report Number Six, London: Counter Information Services, undated, pp. 18–19.)

Exchange rates
Fixed parities for international currency exchange were generally abandoned about this time. The United States devalued the dollar against gold in 1971, and suspended gold payments. In January 1973 the British Government gave up its attempt to maintain a fixed exchange rate for the pound; Japan and Italy followed suit in February, and in March the other European Common Market countries established their 'joint float', in terms of which their currencies were supposed to float together. The pound floated downwards and that in itself raised the sterling price of imports. (*Three Phase Trick*, p. 29). Against the EEC unit of account it lost nearly 5 per cent in 1972 and another 14.5 per cent in 1973.

Commodities
The dollar had ruled the world since the end of the Second World War. It was as stable as gold and a good deal easier to carry around. It had been used lavishly for the reconstruction of Europe and Japan, as well as to promote military and political adventures at frightful expense. By 1971 the stability of the dollar was under question. There were $65

billion in foreign debts and only $10 billion worth of gold in Fort Knox to back them up with. Paul E. Erdman described the problem:

> The president's advisors came up with what appeared to be a clever solution. The United States simply announced that the dollar was no longer convertible into gold. As simple as that. Payment was just stopped on all those IOUs which the United States had been issuing to the world in the form of dollar bills for many years past....
> A few months later the finance ministers of the eleven most powerful nations in the world met in Washington. ... But as so often before, the wise men of the world played midwife to a mouse. European governments and Japan agreed to revalue their currencies by a few percentage points if the United States devalued the dollar a few percentage points by raising the price of gold from $45 to $48 an ounce....
> But there was an extremely serious flaw in the entire Washington settlement, which the US President termed the greatest monetary agreement in the history of the world. It solved nothing. The dollar remained greatly overvalued. Convertibility of the dollar into gold was not restored.... The fact remained that there were still 65 billion unwanted dollars floating around the world, with more going out all the time, which anybody in his right mind would have exchanged for US gold with the speed of light at the price of $48 an ounce. For the free market price of gold was moving inexorably toward $100 an ounce, and well beyond. (Paul E. Erdman, *The Billion Dollar Sure Thing*, New York: Pocket Books, 1973, pp. 8-9.)

The price would ultimately reach $850 an ounce (at the beginning of 1980), but gold was only one out of many possible stores of value. Japanese financiers moved their massive reserves into commodities. Their example was followed by speculators in other countries, not least the United States. There were now three factors at work, pushing up commodity prices: the business boom of 1970-3, the food shortages mentioned above, the flight from the dollar into commodities (in other words, the activity of the speculators themselves). Bulk carriers moved round the world, the owners of their cargoes watching themselves growing rich. The changes in commodity prices are shown in Table 9.2.

Between 1974 and 1975 there was a downturn that would have distressed those speculators who did not get out in time. The unweighted average of imported commodities fell by 11.5 per cent. But by

Table 9.2 *Price indices of UK imports, 1970 = 100*

	1971	1972	1973	1974
Hides and skins	108	169	202	174
Aluminium	100	92	96	128
Copper	75	73	123	149
Lead	82	95	138	200
Zinc (London Metal Exchange)	103	123	282	429
Palm oil	108	88	159	320
Phosphate rock	100	105	127	361
Cotton, raw	113	117	204	229
Jute	103	107	104	128
Silk, raw	93	106	194	158
Sisal	114	143	312	677
Wool, raw	93	152	316	242
Hardwood	107	123	198	243

Source: CSO, *Annual Abstract of Statistics 1979*, table 18.5, p. 468.

1976 the rise had been resumed, so that 1977 was 32 per cent up on 1974.

Later on we shall consider the terms of trade between the rich and poor countries (the changes in the relative prices of those of their products that they sell one another). Now I mention merely that by December 1982, with 1975 = 100, the British Retail Price Index stood at 242.6. Saudi light crude oil was 317.2 ($34 a barrel), while the simple average for other commodities was 154. The index for items manufactured in the United Kingdom entering into the Retail Price Index was 222. Compared with 1975 the commodities could have bought 69 per cent of British manufacturers. Only tin and coffee had improved on their 1975 position.

Oil

The Organization of Petroleum Exporting Countries (OPEC) was established in 1959 and began skirmishing with the oil companies. Weakened by their own disunity they achieved little. Then the position was transformed by three circumstances: a shortage of oil resulting from the boom in the rich countries, the rising price of their exports that was reducing the real price of oil, and, in October 1973, the invasion by Egypt and Syria of Israeli-occupied territory. In negotiation with the oil companies OPEC demanded an increase to $6 a barrel, a doubling of the price. The companies offered 15, then 25 per cent. (A barrel = 42 US gallons = 35 Imperial gallons = 159 litres.)

The talks broke down, but meanwhile the Arabs had agreed to use oil 'as a weapon of war'. Supplies to the United States and the Netherlands were cut off because of those countries' undue friendliness with Israel. Buyers, fearing interruptions in supply, began bidding up the price. On 1 November 1973 OPEC posted a price of $5.18 and on 1 January 1974, $11.65. (See *The Oil Fix: An Investigation into the Control and Costs of Energy*, Anti-Report Number Eight, London: CIS, undated, but 1974, and Anthony Sampson, *The Seven Sisters*, London: Hodder & Stoughton, 1975, chaps 8 and 9.)

After that the price of Arab light crude stayed at about that level until 1977 when it averaged $12.40; 1978, $12.70; 1979, $17.26; 1980, $28.67; 1981, $32.50; 1982, $34.00.

The United Kingdom reduced the volume of its petroleum imports, but between 1973 and 1974 their costs almost tripled:

	£ million	% change
1973	1687	44
1974	4550	170
1975	4175	−8
1976	5535	32
1977	5089	−8

Source: *Annual Abstract*, p. 317.

The difference in oil costs between 1973 and 1974 represented an increase of 3.45 per cent in total final expenditure. Gross domestic product (GDP) at constant factor cost fell by 1.8 per cent between 1973 and 1974, and 1.9 per cent between 1974 and 1975. Is 3.45 per cent much or little? Of course, it occasioned an enormous fuss and a near-panic as the rationing of petrol came under discussion, but it was less than some year-to-year increases in real GDP that had occurred within the preceding decade. It was disruptive, of course, because the effects were not evenly spread but were concentrated in heating, power, transport and petrochemicals.

Rates of interest
The balance of payments on current account had been in credit from 1969 to 1972. The difference in value between goods imported and goods exported is the *visible balance*. In the United Kingdom, there is generally a debit visible balance that is more than offset by a credit *invisible balance*: insurance, transport, travel, financial services, interest, profit and dividends paid by people or institutions overseas in excess of what British people or institutions pay them.

There was a credit balance even on visibles in 1971, but in 1973 and subsequent years, Britain went heavily into the red:

            Debit balances on current account
                       £ million
            1973   999
            1974   3591
            1975   1855
            1976   1137

Source: *Annual Abstract*, table 13.2, p. 331.

Of course, speculators in such circumstances add to a currency's difficulties by running away, or rather, by withdrawing their funds and converting them into other currencies that are less likely to be devalued. They have to be bribed not to do so by offering them higher interest rates. The Bank of England sets the tune with the minimum lending rate at which it will lend funds to the money market; the commercial banks follow.

Although there had been a credit balance on current account in 1972 (£135 million), there had been an outward flow of investment funds of £468 million (*Annual Abstract*, table 13.11, p. 337) and, to offset this, minimum lending rate was raised from 6 per cent to 7½ per cent. By 9 December 1972 it was up to 9 per cent. It was then allowed to fall slightly, but in November 1973 was raised to 13 per cent. After minor fluctuations, it was fixed at 15 per cent in October 1976. (*Annual Abstract*, table 17.13, p. 429.)

This had the effect of luring funds into the country and discouraging them from leaving, but, like many government measures, it also had adverse effects: it raised the amount of interest payable on the national debt, and it raised production costs for all those operating on borrowed money, thus contributing to inflation. On funds owned by foreigners, interest payments served to increase the deficit on foreign account.

Profits

Unemployment in Great Britain fell from 4.0 per cent of the economically active population in January 1972, to 2.1 per cent in December 1973, a sign that business was improving. It then began a gentle rise until, in August 1977 it reached 6.3 per cent. The years 1973 and 1976 were good for insurance, banking, rent and interest. In both those years they rose more than consumer prices and employee income.

Money and Banking

	% increase on previous year				
	1973	1974	1975	1976	1977
Net trading profits and surpluses of manufacturing corporations	8	−9	23	39	18
Rent and interest	44	25	7	23	7
Insurance, banking, finance and business services	41	−6	16	49	19

Source: Central Statistical Office, *National Income and Expenditure 1967–7*, pp. 49 and p. 9, and 1981, p. 44.)

Labour costs

The Conservative Government, under Edward Heath, worked indefatigably at maintaining a prices and incomes policy. On 28 February 1974 they were defeated by the Labour Party, who continued the effort to enforce restraint.

	% increase on previous year				
	1973	1974	1975	1976	1977
Employees income, total	15	21	29	14	10
Average weekly earnings	13	14	30	19	9¼
Consumer price index	9	16	24	16¼	16

(Total employee income, *National Income and Expenditure*, table 1.3, p. 7. Average weekly earnings, adult men and women, from the New Earnings Surveys, April each year.)

Money supply

Lastly let us look at the stock of money, M_3, that includes notes and coins in circulation with the public as well as sight and time deposits. Sight deposits are current banking accounts, from which drawings may be made without prior notice; for time deposits notice is required.

	% increase on previous year						
	1971	1972	1973	1974	1975	1976	1977
M_3	13.0	27.7	27.5	12.0	7.6	11.2	9.8

Source: *Annual Abstract*, table 17.12, p. 428.

Summary and conclusion (?)

Let us now put these bits of information together to see if the perpetrators of inflation will reveal themselves. Table 9.3 presents the variables introduced in Subsection 9.6.2. The first line shows the extent of inflation as measured by the retail price index. The rate of inflation had declined slightly in 1971-2. Between January 1972 and January 1973 the rise was 7.7 per cent; from November to November of those years, 10.6 per cent. January 1973 to January 1974, 11.9 per cent; December to December, 19.1.

Table 9.3 *Summary of changes, UK*

% increases on previous year, 1972-7	1973	1974	1975	1976	1977
Retail price index	9	16	24	16¼	16
Commodities	63	21	-12	36	9
Oil (Arab light)	0	228	0	0	6
Cost of oil imports	44	170	-8	32	-8
Profits: manufacturing	8	-9	23	39	18
Profits: financial services	41	-6	16	49	19
Rent and interest	44	25	7	23	7
Employee income, total	15	21	29	14	10
Employee income, average, Apr-Apr	13	14	30	19	9¼
Money supply (M_3)	27¼	12	8	11	10

Sources: retail price index: *British Labour Statistics Year Book 1974*, table 56, p. 128; *Employment Gazette*, table 6.4, Dec 1982, p. S58; commodities: CSO, *Annual Abstract of Statistics 1979*, table 18.5, p. 468; oil: information provided by British Petroleum; cost of oil imports: *Annual Abstract of Statistics 1979*, p. 317; profits, rent and interest: CSO, *National Income and Expenditure 1967-77*, pp. 49 and 9, and *1981* p. 44; employee income - total, CSO, *National Income and Expenditure 1967-77*, p. 7; employee income - average: Department of Employment, *New Earnings Surveys*, April each year; money supply: *Annual Abstract of Statistics 1979*, p. 428.

How is Table 9.3 to be interpreted? Commodities are clearly leading the way, with oil, banking profits, rent and interest giving support. In 1974 inflation is still being imported, with the rise in commodity prices still in advance of the retail price average, but oil now dominating the scene. Total employee income is swollen by increases in the number employed, but employee average earnings were a bit ahead of the rise in retail prices, with 1974 ahead of 1973 by 17.5 per cent (*British Labour Statistics Year Book 1974*, table 49, p. 121). The coal-miners, whose strike in January 1974 had occasioned the resignation of Mr Heath's Conservative Government, went back to work with an increase of 30 per cent, and by December 1974, their earnings were up 54 per cent on those of December 1973, an increase matched only by transport workers. The coal-miners could claim that the competitive position of their product had been suddenly improved by the rise in the price of oil.

Now how to explain the accelerated rise in retail prices in 1975, coinciding with a fall in commodity prices and what must have been considerable economies in the import of oil? (It was only in 1976 that North Sea oil began to arrive in substantial quantities. Oil imports in 1975 were reduced by 19 per cent.) Profits had made a rebound, the cost of coal, gas and electricity to manufacturing industry had risen by 34 per cent, and average employee earnings for 1975 were 26.5 per cent above those for 1974. All these elements must have played a part, mitigated by the fall of commodity prices. In 1976 commodity prices and profits in manufacturing, financial services, rent and interest moved strongly ahead, while the rise in employee income, total and average, was moderated to 15.6 per cent above 1975.

Let us now consider the money supply. I have quoted Milton Friedman on the link between the stock of money and prices, whose uniformity, he suggested, was of the same order as those that formed the basis of the physical sciences. There is little sign of this uniformity in Table 9.3. The rate of increase of the money supply goes down and inflation goes up. To postulate a lag of one or even two years between changes in the money supply and changes in prices, as some monetarists have done, does not help.

It would be unnecessarily boring to pursue the analysis further at this point. It would be useful, however, to look for some parallels with the great German inflation. I have quoted Paul Einzig on twelve possibly different types of inflation. Expansion of money supply may indeed be caused by other types of inflation rather than cause it. Of Germany in 1923 he writes:

> Indeed, during the more advanced phases of inflation the rise in prices and in monetary requirements advanced so much faster than the expansion of the note issue that there was from time to time an acute scarcity of currency even though the printing press was working to capacity to produce the required quantities of notes of astronomic denominations. At that stage the expansion of currency could not be the cause of the spectacular rise in prices, since it lagged far behind that rise instead of preceding it. (*Inflation*, p. 13.)

The conclusion that I am suggesting is that there is no formula with which to explain the advent and course of inflation. It is a process of great complexity resulting from the actions of millions of decision-makers in many countries. One may argue that it was mistaken of the British trade unions to set out to maintain the real incomes of their members in the face of substantial elements of imported inflation. But if they had not, would not even higher profits have accrued to businesses, landlords and rentiers? In the event, people in the United Kingdom collectively avoided a fall in living standards by running into debt, that is by making up the deficit on current account by raising interest rates to attract funds. After 1976 North Sea oil revenue came as a bonanza to achieve the same objectives, an example of the inability of sensible people, in a system of atomised decision, to take sensible collective action.

Once the inflationary process has begun it is subject to positive feedback. We may trace the chain of causation: the flight from the dollar, the commodity boom, the Arab–Israeli War and the OPEC reaction, rise of interest rates, pay explosion, profits explosion.... 'Common sense tells us that an advanced inflationary vicious spiral, in which prices, monetary requirements, cost-of-living, wages, cost of production, etc., were chasing each other incessantly, was in operation in Germany in 1923, and that Britain experienced the early stages of an inflationary vicious spiral in 1950–51, in spite of the relative scarcity of money in both instances.' (Einzig, *Inflation*, p. 15.)

It is important to consider that there may be no solution to this problem under our present institutions, except to engage in the destruction of that which we desire to protect.

10 Government

10.1 VADERE SICUT VULT

'Let it go as it will', said William Petty. 'Laissez-nous faire', said the merchants of Lyons, and the thought that no government is the best government has lived on in the minds of some economists to the present day. It is at that point that the anarchists of the right meet those of the left. In fact the French Physiocrats, although most clamorous in support of the unmitigated sway of natural law, were insistent on the defence of the rights of private property, the owners of which must be defended from the owners of none.

Adam Smith identified the three duties of 'the sovereign or commonwealth' to be defence, justice and public works. 'The art of war, ... as it is certainly the noblest of all arts, so in the progress of improvement it necessarily becomes one of the most complicated among them.' (*The Wealth of Nations*, bk V, chap. 1, Glasgow ed.; p. 697.) Its development shifted the balance of power from the poor and barbarous to the rich and opulent. 'The invention of fire-arms, an invention which at first sight appears to be so pernicious, is certainly favourable both to the permanency and to the extension of civilization.' (Ibid. p. 708.)

Where there is no property, civil government is not necessary, but 'The affluence of the rich excites the indignation of the poor, who are often both driven by want, and prompted by envy, to invade his possessions. It is only under the shelter of the civil magistrate that the owner of that valuable property, which is acquired by the labour of many years, or perhaps many successive generations, can sleep a single night in security.' (Ibid. p. 710.) But the liberty of every individual, 'the sense which he has of his own security', depends on the separation of judicial from executive power. 'The judge should not be liable to be removed from his office according to the caprice of that power. The regular payment of his salary should not depend upon the good-will, or even upon the good economy of that power.' (Ibid. p. 723.)

It was obvious that the services of defence and justice could be undertaken only by the State. But 'publick Works and publick Institutions'? Those should be undertaken by the State which, though 'in the highest degree advantageous to a great society, are, however, of such a nature, that the profit could never repay the expence to any individual or small number of individuals...'. (Ibid. p. 723.)

Adam Smith finds one more area in which public expenditure is justified. The division of labour has condemned the worker to spend the whole of his working life in performing a few simple operations, in which he ceases to exert his understanding. 'He naturally loses, therefore, the habit of such exertion, and generally becomes as stupid and ignorant as it is possible for a human creature to become.' (Ibid. p. 782.) People of rank and fortune are better left to pay for their own education, but the children of the common people must earn their subsistence as soon as they are able to work. Reading, writing and accounting, however, can be acquired at a very early period of life. 'For a very small expence the publick can facilitate, can encourage, and can even impose upon almost the whole body of the people, the necessity of acquiring those most essential parts of education.' (Ibid. pp. 784–5.)

Thus legitimate categories of government expenditure were easily listed. But how were the required funds to be raised? The arbitrary nature of taxation, the injustice and brutality with which it was raised, occasioned a vast output of texts. As we have noted, the rights to the proceeds of different taxes were sold to the highest bidder, who then 'farmed' the tax, endeavouring to extract more than he had paid for it. The more extravagant the monarch the more costly his wars, the more ruthless were the methods of raising revenue. Nepotism and corruption dominated the public service; in France, positions could be sold by those who occupied them; in the British army, commissions were bought and sold; not until 1870 was entry to the British civil service made conditional on competitive examination.

Of course the countries we are talking about were sparsely populated, and most of the population consisted of voteless and illiterate subsistence farmers and labourers. In the middle of the eighteenth century France had a population in the neighbourhood of 21 million, European Russia 28 million. Great Britain had 7 400 000, the Netherlands 1 600 000, Spain just over 8 million, Sweden just under 1. In the modern world they would be regarded as very small countries. (B. R. Mitchell, ed., *The Fontana Economic History of Europe*, vol. 4, *Statistical Appendix 1700–1914*, 1971, pp. 14–15.) In the United States the Census of 1790 showed a population of just under 4 million, of whom only 5 per cent lived in towns.

By the middle of the nineteenth century, with the growth of towns and industries, these countries were spending 4 or 5 per cent of GNP on government consumption; by the turn of the century in Germany and the United Kingdom this had risen to over 7 per cent. (Mitchell, p. 79.)

The nadir of public responsibility was reached in Europe in the first half of the nineteenth century. In Britain workers were prohibited from combining to seek higher pay or oppose reductions in pay by the Combination Acts of 1799 and 1800. The Act of the latter year was guided through Parliament by Wilberforce of Anti-Slavery fame, because combinations of workers were an infringement of the rights of employers. But the Acts were repealed in 1824, and, as the century unfolded, a bitter but successful war was carried on for reform. In 1802 the first Factory Act was passed, to regulate Health and Morals of Apprentices: really pauper children who were hired out to cotton mills. At least it recognised the principle that conditions of work were not to be left to 'the free play of the market'. So legislation was drafted, fought for and pushed through Parliament by people who, like Ralph Nader, were obsessed by the need for social reform: Robert Owen, William Cobbett, Francis Place, Lord Shaftesbury, Samuel Plimsoll, were amongst those who, by their fixity of purpose and unyielding obstinacy, helped on the progress of the world.

10.2 THE PUBLIC PURPOSE

'The statesman, who should attempt to direct private people in what manner they ought to employ their capitals, would not only load himself with a most unnecessary attention, but assume an authority which could safely be trusted, not only to no single person, but to no council or senate whatever, and which would nowhere be so dangerous as in the hands of a man who had folly and presumption enough to fancy himself fit to exercise it.' (*The Wealth of Nations*, bk IV, chap. ii, Glasgow ed., p. 456.) Alas, the pursuit of the private interest failed to promote the public interest to the extent that Adam Smith and his predecessors had hoped. Gradually, against much opposition, the right of employers to do what they liked was curtailed by a combination of trade union organisation and legislation.

Factories Acts were passed raising the age at which children might be employed, limiting hours of work and providing for health and safety. Laws were passed permitting workers to organise and their organisations to own property and safeguard funds. Their unions were protected against prosecution for acts that would not be illegal if performed by individuals (they were freed, that is, from actions for conspiracy).

Workmen's Compensation laws were passed in country after country, providing for the insurance of workers against accidents suffered in the course of their work. In the twentieth century minimum wage laws became general, making it illegal to employ workers (generally in specified industries or occupations) at less than a stated wage. Laws were passed for conciliation and the settlement of industrial disputes by negotiation or arbitration. Labour Departments were established to enforce these laws, providing factory and wage inspectors for this purpose.

In earlier centuries most countries had had some arrangement for aiding the destitute, through parish councils, the church or charitable foundations. In Bismarck's Germany, in the latter part of the nineteenth century, there was established the first modern system of social security, providing income for those unable to work because of old age, illness or unemployment. It was Ferdinand Lassalle, Marx's disciple, who argued that the working class should not overthrow the State, but convert it into an instrument for their own advancement:

> the Bourgeoisie conceive the moral object of the State to consist solely and exclusively in the protection of the personal freedom and the property of the individual. This ... represents to itself the State from a point of view of a policeman, whose whole function consists in preventing robbery and burglary.

On the contrary, he argued, the object of the State was to enable individuals to attain objects and reach such a state of existence that they could never have reached as individuals; to enable them to acquire education, power and freedom otherwise wholly unattainable. (Ferdinand Lassalle, 'The Working Class Program', in Albert Fried and Ronald Sanders, *A Documentary History of Socialist Thought*, Edinburgh University Press, 1964, pp. 386–7.)

Lassalle sent Bismarck a copy of his *Programme* with the message: 'Herewith I send your Excellency the constitution of my realm, for which you will perhaps envy me.' They had some discussions of his ideas and, though Lasalle was sentenced to imprisonment for high treason, he seems to have impressed Bismarck sufficiently for the Chancellor to implement a scheme of social security that became a model for the rest of the world. (See Edmund Wilson, *To the Finland*

Station, p. 250.) When Churchill (then Liberal Chancellor) engaged Beveridge in 1910 to establish a social scheme for the United Kingdom, it was to Germany he sent him to find out how it should be done.

The invention of fire-arms, mentioned by Adam Smith, began a process that has since then got out of hand, and has developed into Eisenhower's military-industrial complex that makes it very difficult in the United States to tell where government ends and private enterprise begins. 'No sharp line separates government from the private firm; the line becomes very indistinct and even imaginary. Each organization is important to the other; members are intermingled in daily work; each organization comes to accept the other's goals; each adapts the goals of the other to its own. Each organization, accordingly, is an extension of the other. The large aerospace contractor is related to the Air Force by ties that, however different superficially, are in their substance the same as those that relate the Air Force to the United States government. Shared goals are the decisive link in each case.' (John Kenneth Galbraith, *The New Industrial State*, p. 314.)

So military expenditure accounts for resources and a share of national wealth that Adam Smith would have found inconceivable. As inconceivable, perhaps, would have been the fact that this is matched, in a modern State, by the resources devoted to health and educational services. These are not services foisted on unwilling publics by officious governments: rather the reverse – they come from public demand so strong as to be irresistible. Resistance to the extension of national or state health services in the United States has come not from the public but from medical people in private practice and the owners of private hospitals.

Urbanisation and the growth of conurbations has required the creation and maintenance of a complex of services: sewerage, water, roads, refuse disposal, traffic control, policing, public transport, airports. Libraries, sports grounds, art galleries, theatres, parks, orchestras, are all thought worthy of public expenditure.

As time goes by, the homes of people in the affluent countries become replete with consumer durables. With thought turning more and more to preservation, desires are sated as household space is used up, and while demand falls production methods become more and more efficient. Declining birth-rates, at the same time, cause a fall in the number of newly established households, and employment in manufacturing industries declines.

There is much anxiety about these prospects. Where, it is asked, will the jobs come from? Must we not reconcile ourselves to a permanent and growing army of unemployed? Only if you believe that public consumption is not legitimate. And as the policies of the American and British Governments continue to demonstrate their failure, fewer and fewer people will surely believe that the trends of the last half-century can or should be reversed?

There is no visible limit to the resources of capital and labour that may usefully be applied to education, health, culture, urban beautification and renewal. It is to these purposes that the OECD countries should be putting their 26 million unemployed, and to which, in due time, they may transfer the resources at present allocated to defence.

Table 10.1 shows the trend in public expenditure in selected coun-

Table 10.1 *Public consumption and social protection, various countries*

(i) *Public consumption 1970 and 1978*

	% of GDP	
	1970	1978
Germany, FR	15.8	13.8
France	12.1	15.1
Italy	12.8	16.4
Netherlands	16.1	18.3
Belgium	14.0	17.6
Luxembourg	10.8	15.5
UK	18.3	20.3
Norway	17.5	18.5
Denmark	18.8	24.3
Sweden	21.2	28.9
USA	20.9	18.9

(ii) *Social protection 1970 and 1980*

	% of GDP	
	1970	1980
Germany, FR	21.4	28.3
France	19.2	25.8
Italy	18.4	22.8
Netherlands	20.8	30.7
UK	15.9	21.4
Ireland	13.2	22.0
Denmark	19.6	28.0
All EEC	19.0	25.9

Sources: *Basic Statistics of the Community*, Brussels, annual: *Social Protection Statistical Bulletin*, Luxembourg: Eurostat, 1, 1982.

tries, as a proportion of GDP, and the proportion of GDP spent on social protection – that is, payments to households from public or other agencies for pensions, sick and unemployment pay and allowances. It is mainly unemployment relief that has caused the costs of social protection to rise so that it swallows up a quarter of GDP. One of the major causes of the rise in unemployment was the successful attempt to reduce the proportion of public expenditure in some countries: one of the great paradoxes of the world of today.

In the model of perfect competition the consumer reigns. The whole scheme of production is designed to meet his wishes, and these are conveyed to producers by market signals – the quantities the consumer is prepared to buy and the prices he is prepared to pay. Some thought was given to the consumer's powers of judgement – what if his anticipations of utility were disappointed? – but on the whole it was considered an unwarranted interference to query his choice. So his sovereignty was deemed to be exercised in his 'revealed preference': what he chose and what he truly wanted were assumed to coincide.

Governments have, in fact, since governments began, concerned themselves with weights and measures, the maintenance of the coinage and the prevention of the adulteration of merchandise. The Romans laid the foundation for modern mercantile law. But it is only in recent years that the consumers' needs for protection have been recognised and that steps have been taken to redress the balance between consumer and producer. This need should have been plain enough: the producer is technically expert in his product; he knows how it is made and what it is made from, and how much it costs to make it. Consumers are ignorant of these things and their attention is not focused on one commodity, but dispersed amongst hundreds.

In Chapter 8 we considered the consumer associations that consumers have established to protect themselves from manufacturers and suppliers anxious to relieve them of their wealth. But, however wary the buyer may be, the world remains a dangerous place, replete with traders eager to grow rich and not too scrupulous about how they do it. Urged by the consumer associations and popular need, governments have brought the force of law to the task of consumer protection and have established agencies to enforce it. It is interesting to note that it is in the United States, haven of free enterprise, that the roughest treatment is meted out to offending firms. Federal enforcement agencies are well supplied with statutory powers to demand information, issue directives and, if necessary, enforce them by judicial process.

There have been great changes in the last ten or twenty years with consumers acquiring countervailing power (to use Galbraith's phrase) and much publicity on radio, television and in the press for consumer complaints. The law of libel has changed and the courts become much more liberal in their interpretation of what is legitimate comment for the public good, so that it is merely, perhaps, that wrongs committed against consumers, that previously we should never have heard about, are now made public? But, again, with the growth of affluence consumers buy more of an extended range of goods that have themselves become more complex, electronically or chemically, or, with the density of traffic on the roads, more dangerous.

One such danger was described in the BBC programme, *Panorama*, on Monday, 17 January 1983. An anti-arithritic drug with lethal capabilities was allowed to be marketed in Britain for two years before its licence was suspended and the drug withdrawn. Tom Mangold commented:

> Arthritis is mankind's most prevalent disease, and consequently it is big business. Because its cause is unknown, it remains incurable. However, the inflammation and pain of the condition can be relieved through anti-arthritic pills, and the majority of arthritis victims will inevitably graduate to these sophisticated painkillers. Worldwide, the market in these pills is inestimable. In Britain alone, it's worth about £100 million a year. A popular anti-arthritic can make its manufacturers a fortune, with the result that most major drug companies have gone into the business. There are aspects of the world of rheumatology that resemble the headier days of the Yukon. The stakes are similar. Consequently, in Britain, there are now at least 23 similar, competing anti-arthritis pills. (*The Listener*, 20 Jan. 1983, p. 2.)

One disturbing element is the lavish entertainment that the giant drug companies offer to medical practitioners, and that the latter accept, for the promotion of drugs. Trips to Venice, week-ends in Paris.... Mangold asks, 'Why do most major pharmaceutical companies spend as much (or more) in the promotion and marketing of drugs as they do in discovering and producing them?'

There have been significant advances, but the build-up of countervailing power is a game that two can play. So the great corporations that dominate our economic life have gained in power and subtlety, and skill at slipping out of the hands of governments as they spread their activities across the world. Senator Warren G. Magnuson wrote in 1971:

Since I first came to Congress in 1936, I have seen the national concern over consumer protection greatly accelerate. In 1938, we extended the jurisdiction of the Federal Trade Commission to empower it specifically to prevent consumer deception. That same year we passed the Food, Drug and Cosmetic Act.... In 1953, we passed the Flammable Fabrics Act, outlawing explosively flammable fabrics used in wearing apparel. Soon afterward came legislation requiring that refrigerator doors be designed to be opened from the inside, preventing children's entrapment. With the Kefauver-Harris Drug Amendments, we had in 1962 significant reforms in the labelling of prescription drugs and the testing of new drugs. About that same time Senator Paul Douglas introduced the first consumer credit reform law, calling for 'truth in lending', a disclosure of finance rates in percentages....

Then there were the landmark laws setting minimum safety standards for tires and automobiles which we passed in 1966. Later the Fair Packaging and Labelling Act, the Child Protection Act, the Gas Pipeline Safety Act, the Toy Safety Act, and the unprecedented ban on broadcast cigarette advertising, all of which bear the imprint of our Committee.   (Warren G. Magnuson and Jean Carper, *The Dark Side of the Market Place*, Englewood Cliffs, N.J.: Prentice-Hall, 1972, pp 2–3.)

The Federal Trade Commission was established in 1914 to oversee inter-State competition and operates a 'Maintaining Competition Mission' whose primary aim is 'to relieve anticompetitive pressures and restrictions on the prices and supply of goods and services to consumers', and a 'Consumer Protection Mission' concerned with the prevention of 'possible unfair or deceptive practices that inhibit the flow of useful product information to consumers or that unnecessarily support prices at artificially high levels'. (Federal Trade Commission, *Annual Report, 1977*, pp. 3 and 15.) They administer numerous statutes concerned with consumer credit, debt collection, advertising aimed at children, reliability of products and professional services.

The Food and Drug Administration is part of the Federal Public Health Service and administers a number of laws to protect the public against injurious substances that they are invited to buy without warning of their dangers.

The Federal Food, Drug and Cosmetic Act is the basic food and drug law of the United States. With numerous amendments it is the most extensive law of its kind in the world. Many of the States in the United States have laws similar to the Federal law, and some have provisions to add automatically any new Federal requirements.

The law is intended to assure the consumer that foods are pure and wholesome, safe to eat, and produced under sanitary conditions; that drugs and devices are safe and effective for their intended uses; that cosmetics are safe and made from appropriate ingredients; and that all labeling and packaging is truthful, informative, and not deceptive. Another law, the Fair Packaging and Labeling Act, affects the contents and placement of information required on the package. (*Requirements of Laws and Regulations Enforced by the US Food and Drug Administration*, Rockville: US Department of Health, Education, and Welfare, 1979, p. 1.)

In Britain the Department of Prices and Consumer Protection was established by the Labour Government in 1974. The Trade Descriptions Act dates from 1968 and the Fair Trading Act from 1973. The Office of Fair Trading was set up in terms of the latter Act, it functions similar to those of the Federal Trade Commission in the United States. (On laws and institutions in Britain see Peter Smith and Dennis Swann, *Protecting the Consumer, an Economic and Legal Analysis*, Oxford: Martin Robertson, 1979, and Jeremy Mitchell, ed., *Marketing and the Consumer Movement*, Maidenhead: McGraw-Hill, 1978.)

The European Economic Community officially adopted a consumer programme in 1972, and in 1973 set up its Environment and Consumer Protection Service and Consultative Committee of Consumer Representatives. The Commission, with its independence of political affiliation, has shown a good deal of enterprise in promoting worthy measures and encouraging a levelling-up of member governments. It is making it more difficult for suppliers to operate discriminatory price policies, such as that concerning car prices that we noted in Chapter 8. In its new programme for 1981–6, 'It will continue – and develop more extensively – scientific investigation into some of the price differences which persist within the Common Market.' (Commission of the European Communities, *New programme for consumers*, European File 13/81, p. 3.) See, too, Dennis Swann, *Competition and Consumer Protection* (Harmondsworth: Penguin Books, 1979) chap. 8.

10.3 THE ENVIRONMENT

Sixty years ago, when transnational corporations were still young, the Webbs remarked on how, under capitalism, 'it is impossible to create an interest in production that is not also an interest in decay and destruction'.

Nor is it man and man's environment alone that the profit-maker destroys: it is not only the older civilisations that he contaminates. In pursuit of the limitless natural wealth of new and slightly peopled lands the profit-maker proceeds with his destructive process from continent to continent. Natural resources are abundant and cheap: in many places they are costless. Hence fur-bearing and food animals are killed, in season and out of season, to the point of extermination of the species; primeval forests are levelled to the ground; natural pastures are denuded; virgin soils are defertilised; coal and metals, oils and gases – all reserves of potential power – are wasted and exhausted; the rivers are dried up, and the very climate is impaired. . . .   (Sidney and Beatrice Webb, *The Decay of Capitalist Civilisation*, London: Allen & Unwin, 1923, p. 86.)

This is another area of 'free competition' in which governments, belatedly, have been compelled to intervene. Intervention has come very late, after much, some irreparable, damage has been done. It was not until the passage of the Town and Country Planning Act of 1944 that local authorities in the United Kingdom were adequately equipped to control land use, nor until the 1960s that the Clean Air Act put an end to the pea-soup fogs from which London suffered, nor until a few years ago that fish returned to the lower reaches of the Thames. Before that, if anyone fell into the Thames, he or she died of poison, not from drowning.

In the United States anti-pollution functions of the federal government were centralised in the Environmental Protection Agency in 1970. The task of the Agency is to set standards for clean air and water, which the States and local authorities then have the responsibility of enforcing. The State produces an Implementation Plan for the achievement of these goals, and the EPA reviews the plan to make sure it meets the requirements of Federal law and EPA regulations. (The US Environmental Protection Agency, *Legislation, Programs and Organization*, Washington: Office of Resources Management, 1979.)

Car emissions have been rigorously controlled in the United States, and lead-free petrol made compulsory. In Europe the authorities have been more timid, but the European Economic Community has been gathering strength since it adopted its environmental policy in 1973.

'Community action in the environmental area is very extensive. It covers all natural resources (natural environment, energy, raw materials) which are harmed or over-exploited by economic and social development. . . . Work in progress revolves around two principal axes: the battle against pollution and nuisances and, increasingly, the improvement of the management of the countryside, of the environment and of resources. The means employed range from scientific study and research to the adoption of directives which oblige Member States to draw up their own laws or regulations to ensure respect for Community provisions (some sixty European directives have already been approved and numerous nothers are at the discussion stage).   (Commission of the European Communities, *The European Community and Environmental Protection*, European File 2/81, p. 3.)

10.4 PROTECTING INVESTORS FROM BUSINESSES, AND BUSINESSES FROM EACH OTHER

In the four preceding chapters we have seen something of government intervention in industrial relations, business organisations, consumer affairs and banking. Nowadays all wealthy capitalist nations have legal codes for business behaviour and institutions to enforce them. Fraud squads go after the smaller fry, and departments of trade and industry after the larger.

In the United States these functions are the responsibility of the Securities and Exchange Commission. In the 1920s it seemed that perfect competition had established its happy sway and that an era had arrived of affluence without end. Those who had participated in this happy process were utterly unprepared for the crash of 1929. The Securities Act of 1933 (a 'truth in securities' law), the Securities Exchanges Act of 1934, with the Securities and Exchange Commission (SEC) that it established, were supposed to ensure that investors were protected from misfortunes of this sort.

Companies wishing to offer their securities for sale to the public must register with the SEC and produce a prospectus. The SEC will require to know the terms of the issue, the kind of business in which the company is engaged, and to have copies of the balance-sheet and profit and loss accounts, usually for the last five years. Of course approval by the SEC does not imply a recommendation of the company – it means merely that the necessary requirements have been met. The company must submit quarterly and annual reports, and proxy statements when there is an election of a new board of directors.

If the Commission finds information to have been misleading, inaccurate or incomplete it may prevent or suspend the sale of securities and, if the matter cannot be resolved by correspondence, call a hearing at which evidence will be presented.

This examination process naturally contributes to the general reliability of the registration disclosures – but it does not give positive assurance of the accuracy of the facts reported. Even if such a verification of the facts were possible, the task, if not actually prohibitive, would involve such a tremendous undertaking (both in time and money) as to seriously impede the financing of business ventures through the public sale of securities. (*The Work of the Securities and Exchange Commission*, Mar. 1978, p. 4.)

Stock exchanges, brokers and dealers must also register with the Commission. The rules of exchanges require the approval of the Commission, and must provide for the expulsion, suspension and other disciplining of members 'for conduct inconsistent with just and equitable principles of trade'. (Ibid. p. 7.)

Inquiries and complaints of investors and the general public provide one of the primary sources of leads for detection of law violations in securities transactions. Another is the surprise inspections by Regional Offices of the books and records of brokers and dealers to determine whether their business practices conform to the prescribed rules. Still another is the conduct of inquiries into market fluctuations in particular stocks which appear not to be the result of known developments affecting the issuing company or of general market trends. (Ibid. p. 9.)

When I visited the SEC in 1980 it was receiving documents at the rate of 52 000 a year. These are examined on a random basis except where a specific complaint has been made concerning a specified issue. If the law has been broken the Commission may apply to the appropriate District Court for an injunction restraining the continuance of the objectionable practice, or the matter may be referred to the Department of Justice with a recommendation for criminal prosecution, or it may suspend or revoke the registration of those concerned.

In Britain financial companies are regulated by the Prevention of Fraud (Investments) Act 1958. Like the Companies Acts this is enforced and administered by the Department of Trade. Dealers in securities must be licensed. If they refuse or propose to revoke a licence, the matter may, if the applicant or holder so elect, be referred to a tribunal of inquiry. There is a maximum penalty of seven years for fraudulently inducing or attempting to induce, anyone to invest money.

There is provision for stock exchanges, and associations of dealers in securities to manage their own affairs and to be exempt from the provisions of the Act, provided the Department of Trade makes an order to this effect.

More generally, the Companies Act of 1948 made provision for the investigation of a company's affairs on application of not less than two hundred shareholders or members holding not less than 10 per cent of the issued shares. The applicants must satisfy the Department of Trade that an inquiry is warranted, and the Department *may* then appoint an inspector to investigate. The Department may itself initiate an investigation if it appears that the affairs of the company have been conducted by fraud, misfeasance or other misconduct towards its members, or if the members have not been given all the information with respect to the company's affairs that they might reasonably expect. (Sections 164–5.) (See Keith Walmsley, ed., *Butterworth's Company Law Handbook*, 2nd ed., London: Butterworth, 1980. Also L. C. B. Gower, *Principles of Modern Company Law, Supplement to the Fourth Edition*, London: Stevens & Sons, 1981.)

Except in the tax havens company law in Europe follows similar basic principles (see P. Meinhardt, *Company Law in Europe*, Farnborough: Gower, 1981, or S. N. Frommel and J. H. Thompson, *Company Law in Europe*, London: Kluwer–Harrap, 1975.)

10.5 THE MANAGEMENT OF ECONOMIES

After the First World War governments rapidly divested themselves of their powers of economic control; the financial crises of 1929 that spread from Europe to the United States, and the depression of the 1930s proved that there had been excessive optimism in the capacity of market forces to manage themselves. The years of the Second World War were marked by declarations that the horrors of the 1930s would never be allowed to happen again. Governments committed themselves to policies of full employment, social security and general education that would inaugurate a new social order to compete against the (at that time much advertised) socialist order of the Soviet Union.

It will, I trust, perplex future generations who read the history of our times to see the helplessness displayed by our governments in the face of unused resources. It was not that masses of people were deprived of their needs because we lacked the resources to supply them; they were deprived of them because we had a superabundance of resources and did not know how to distribute them.

Between 1924 and 1929 a Committee on Industry and Trade was engaged on studying the problems confronting British industry. At the end of their term, having taken the advice of 240 witnesses, read masses of memoranda, held 136 plenary meetings and innumerable meetings in subcommittees, there was nothing that they were able to tell the government to do other than to continue to promote freer international trade. They were, they complained, faced by a dilemma, 'for industrial health can only be restored by the aid of fresh capital, and fresh capital can only be attracted by the restoration of healthy conditions. What is the way out of this vicious circle?' The first steps must come from the industries themselves. They must 'take the first measures towards their own regeneration, provided that they are thoroughly convinced that such measures are essential and unavoidable, and that they must be taken by themselves without reliance on any outside authority'. Don't do anything unless you feel you absolutely have to, they seemed to be saying. And, in particular, do not expect the government to do anything to help. (*Final Report of the Committee on Industry and Trade*. Cmd 3282, HMSO, 1929, p. 299.)

In 1931, as the world sank into depression, Ramsay MacDonald, the Labour Prime Minister, formed a 'national government'. Their response to the depression was to devalue the currency, abandon free trade and institute a general reduction in pay, including a reduction of 10 per cent in unemployment benefit and the institution of a means test. The unemployment fund was in the form of *insurance* and was derived from contributions from workers and their employers, despite which payments were reduced if any member of the family was working. The government was helpless: between a fifth and a quarter of the labour force was unemployed, hungry and hopeless, and there were great gluts of unsaleable agricultural produce. What should they do? Answer: cut unemployment benefit and destroy the surpluses.

In the United States in November 1932 Roosevelt defeated Hoover overwhelmingly in the election for President. Yet, ironically, Roosevelt wooed the electorate with promises of drastic economy and a balanced budget, necessary for the maintenance of a sound currency. (John Major, *The New Deal*, London: Longmans, 1968, p. 52.) It is probable that while not many people knew what 'drastic economy' portended, balanced budget and sound currency sounded reassuring enough. To his more general statements he managed to impart a more populist ring, without really committing himself to anything. For instance, those who controlled the great financial and industrial combinations had undertaken to be 'not business men but princes of property. I am not prepared to say that the system which produces them is wrong. I am very clear that they must fearlessly and competently assume the responsibility which goes with power. . . .' (Ibid. pp. 55-6.) Is he threatening or flattering the princes of property? Indeed, it was Hoover who presented Roosevelt as threatening a profound change in American life, a radical departure from the foundations of 150 years. The election 'means deciding the direction our nation will take over a century to come'. (Ibid. p. 59.) It may well have been on Hoover's say-so that Roosevelt was elected.

The policy actually implemented was a hotch-potch of disparate acts: abolition was abolished, the dollar devalued, agricultural production drastically reduced and agricultural prices raised, inflation encouraged to raise prices and so encourage businessmen, union organisation promoted to raise wages to counteract the rise in prices. . . . At the same time, creative forces were unleashed for the employment of actors, musicians and artists and in the establishment of the Tennessee Valley Authority. There was, it is true, a relapse in 1938, but by then the probability of another world war suggested the need for rearmament to offset the peace movements of the 1920s and earlier 1930s, and problems of depression and unemployment were soon to be replaced by problems of a different kind.

In Germany, with the advent of the Nazis, a policy of autarky (self-sufficiency) was pursued, with essential imports secured by way of barter, and the economy was put on a war footing. Trade unions were banned and workers' leaders disposed of so that wage-inflation was prevented. In France, by contrast, the Popular Front Government, with its mixture of different brands of socialist and communist political parties, instituted the 40-hour week, while workers practised sit-down strikes to raise pay, and set off an inflationary spiral.

Governments came out of the Second World War full of good intentions. All sorts of things were never to be allowed to happen again. Health services, education and social security were greatly improved, and the maintenance of full employment accepted as a primary economic aim. In the United States the right to a job was almost incorporated in the Employment Act of 1946; in Britain there was much discussion about just how full full-employment ought to be.

In Beveridge's report of 1944 (*Full Employment in a Free Society*, Woking: Allen & Unwin, 1944, 2nd ed., 1960) he suggested 3 per cent of the total labour force as likely to be idle at any time. In the second edition he recalls: 'Maynard Keynes, when he saw this figure, wrote to me that there was no harm in aiming at 3 per cent, but that he would be surprised if we got so low in practice.' (2nd ed., p. 1.)

Governments now had the will, it seemed, to govern their economies, Marshall Aid provided the wherewithal to the extent of $12 000 million, and Keynes, in his *General Theory* had shown them how. It was simply a matter of matching demand to potential supply. If demand languished then it must be boosted in any one or more of a number of ways. The Organization for European Economic Co-operation (OEEC) had been established to oversee Marshall Aid; in September 1959 this was reformed into the OECD, with Canada and the United States as full members. At about that time Nikita Krushchev, then in power in the Soviet Union, challenged the capitalist world to a race – not in armaments but in economic growth, and a further political dimension was added to the efforts at economic management of the members of the OECD.

In the 1950s and 1960s the OECD countries did remarkably well and their governments appeared to have succeeded in their efforts at management. There was more international co-operation than ever before: the General Agreement on Tariffs and Trade (GATT) was effective in dismantling tariffs and restrictive practices; the International Monetary Fund was keeping some sort of order in indebtedness and rates of exchange; regional economic commissions were functioning under the United Nations, and the OECD was busy with advice and the promotion of co-operation.

There was much talk of 'fine-tuning' the economy, and many outward signs of success: GNP at constant prices was rising steadily, averaging 5.2 per cent per year in the six nations of the EEC from 1955 to 1965 and a bit less in the seven nations of the European Free Trade Association (EFTA) (3.6 per cent) and in the United States (3.4 per cent). The annual average for 1965–70 continued the process:

	%
EEC	5.5
EFTA	3.4
USA	3.9

Growth at 3.9 per cent, if sustained, would double real income in a little over 18 years; at 5.5 per cent, in 13 years.

Unemployment in the 1960s was down to levels that would have astonished Lord Keynes: an average of 2.0 per cent in the United Kingdom; in France, Germany and Switzerland guest-workers were being imported to meet labour shortages; in the United States, with its more inclusive method of counting the unemployed, unemployment averaged 4.7 per cent. Of course, prices were rising too, at a rate thought to be excessive by the members of the OECD. Between 1955 and 1970 consumer prices in France doubled, and in Japan and Denmark rose by about 90 per cent. In the United States the rise was 45 per cent, in Germany a bit less and the other countries ranged between 37 and 82 per cent. But this was spread over fifteen years and, in retrospect, seems extraordinarily moderate.

After 1968 the vision of order and control vanished. The rate of price increase more than doubled. With 1971 = 100 the average for consumer price indexes in the OECD countries in October 1982 was 275. Then, in 1973, the phenomenon appeared that, by the rules of all the textbooks, should have been impossible: the co-existence of unused capacity and rising prices, stagnation and inflation, inelegantly named stagflation.

In Samuel Johnson's *Rasselas, Prince of Abyssinia*, the Prince's friend, Imlac, comes upon a wise man who has discovered that he is able to control the Nile floods by the exercise of his magical powers. This is a fearful responsibility, but he settles down to perform his spells and incantations, for there was really no other option for a conscientious philosopher.

I suggest governments of capitalist states are in a similar position *vis-à-vis* the economies of their countries. They have more equipment than the wise man: in their treasuries, departments of finance and industry and in their central banks there are enormous staffs of highly educated people operating computer programmes with hundreds or even thousands of economic variables that, by an examination of what an economy has just done are supposed to forecast what it will do next. The finance ministers then select a tool from their tool-kit to persuade it not to (if the forecast suggests an adverse trend) or encourage it to augment it, if the forecast shows something good. But, as the statistics show, the response to government policies in the past ten years has been most perverse.

In such circumstances, enough voters are likely to change their minds, or float from one party to the other, to occasion a change of government. The new governments, in Britain in 1979 and the United States in 1980, tried out a different set of tools, with disastrous results.

I invite you now to enter the realm of policy analysis, where assertion is substituted for evidence and where it is difficult or impossible to separate cause from effect or identify either, because *ceteris* refuses to remain *paribus*. So please scrutinise critically what I am about to say.

I assert, to begin with, that long observation of governments at work has led me to conclude *that governments are effective at restraining hyperactivity and very bad at alleviating depression*. When the patient enters his manic phase they bang him on the head with a mallet and let blood; in his depressive phase they are quite unable to cheer him up. Thus the full-employment of the 1950s and 1960s was not the result of government skill at economic control; they were too busy applying the brakes to worry much about where they were being taken. Then, when boom had been converted into recession, governments relaxed their pressure on the brakes. But even in this negative method of control, great skill is required in the timing of changes: if relaxation comes too late, it may convert a recovery into a boom; if restraint is applied too early, it may convert recession into a slump. Thus J. C. R. Dow: 'The analysis also suggests that the fluctuations in the growth of demand in the years 1952–60 were due in large part to fluctuations in policy.... However well demand had been managed, it would, too, have been difficult to eliminate fluctuations in investment in stocks. But so far from countering such basic causes of instability, the influence of policy seems rather to have exaggerated their effects.' (J. C. R. Dow, *The Management of the British Economy 1945–60*, Cambridge University Press, 1964. Students' ed., 1970, pp. 391–2. See, too, C. D. Cohen, *British Economic Policy 1960–1969*, London: Butterworth, 1971; Samuel Brittan, *The Treasury under the Tories 1951–1964*, Harmondsworth: Penguin Books, 1964; and Frank T. Blackaby (ed.), *British Economic Policy, 1960–74*, Cambridge University Press, 1978.)

Capitalist economies display cumulative disequilibrium, or positive feedback. But at some stage, when a number of phenomena appear simultaneously, the process will go into reverse and become cumulative in the opposite direction. There are abundant references to these processes from observers of the last three hundred years. There are some economic entities that we can identify whose presence contributes to the change: the reduction of stocks, elimination of enterprises through insolvencies, accumulation of liquid capital, fall in interest rates, build-up of purchases whose execution has been postponed. But finally, the change of direction depends on a change in the state of mind of consumers, investors and entrepreneurs, who get bored by prolonged inaction and forbearance, as well as from hyperactivity, spending and expansion. Whereas governments can force people to curtail expenditure or investment by raising taxes and restricting credit, they cannot compel them to spend or invest by reversing the process.

Governments attempt to affect events by remote-control, by changing a few elements that are within their range of regulation. They can, for instance, use the market for consumer durables as a means of deflating or inflating the whole economy. They can change interest rates, limit the length of hire-purchase agreements or require higher deposits. The result is that producers of consumer durables have been confronted by augmented fluctuations in the demand for their goods.

Another difficulty is that some of their most often-used instruments may have the intended effect – or its opposite. To discourage expenditure in a period of inflation, and reduce the pressure of demand, purchase tax or value-added-tax or sales tax may be raised. The side-effect of this is to further raise prices, thus provoking a reaction in greater pressure for pay rises. Restricted sales also brings about a rise in prices as manufacturers compensate for their rise in costs.

Governments react to an outflow of funds arising from a run on their currency by acting through the Central Bank to raise interest rates. If the managers of these funds are satisfied as to the stability of the currency they will reverse the flow in order to profit by the rise in interest. This, too, has in it elements that will deepen the problem that it is supposed to solve: in so far as the funds are controlled from abroad there will be an augmented flow of interest out of the country; and the cost of public sector borrowing will be raised, thus increasing government expenditure for no useful purpose. In addition, the reaction of fund managers may not accord with the intentions of government: when, in 1964, the Bank of England raised bank rate (as it was then called) by 2 whole per cent instead of $\frac{1}{2}$ per cent, and this happened on a Monday and not a Thursday, the outflow of funds doubled.

I have been writing about 'governments' and the management of capitalist economies: because in these economies decision-making is atomised, they are confronted by the same range of options whatever their political complexion. But there can be great differences in what options they choose to use and how vigorously they use them. Though the Social Democrats have been in power in Sweden for most of the last fifty years, their policy has been to leave decision-making to employers and trade unions, and use their own discretion to pay very high social benefits financed by very high taxation. In Britain Labour

Governments nationalise and Conservative Governments 'privatise'. In France a variety of governments have pursued a French variety of planning, dependent on factors peculiar to France. (See Martin Cave and Paul Hare, *Alternative Approaches to Economic Planning*, London: Macmillan, 1981, chap. 4.) All sorts of governments are ready to momentarily discard their loyalty to market forces when confronted by the awful consequences of the collapse of some great company: the United States Government rescued Chrysler and Lockheed; the British (Conservative) Government Rolls-Royce. But still more paradoxical is their willingness to heap vast sums of public aid on corporations willing to invest in their countries, some of which, like the millions bestowed by the British Government on DeLorean, is lost for ever. As I write a complaint has been lodged to the EEC Commission against the French Government, who are alleged to have offered Timex finance of £52 million to persuade them to move one of their factories from Dundee in Scotland to Besançon in France.

The problem may be stated thus: the making of economic decisions is in the hands of the management teams of a limited number of giant corporations, fund managers, bankers and trade unions. They make decisions relating to expansion, contraction, relocation and incomes. Millions of households make decisions about consumption. Governments make decisions peripheral to this economic activity. Hundreds of economists in government, universities, research institutions and business have for many years sought ways of eliminating the faults in the system. They have failed. The answer may simply be that it cannot be done.

So the Radcliffe Committee on the Working of the Monetary System mildly concluded: 'when all has been said on the possibility of monetary action and of its likely efficacy, our conclusion is that monetary measures cannot alone be relied upon to keep in nice balance an economy subject to major strains from both without and within. Monetary measures can help, but that is all.' (*Report*, Aug. 1959, para. 514.) Mr G. E. P. Thorneycroft, the Conservative Chancellor who had appointed the Committee, afterwards recalled: 'I remember telling Lord Radcliffe how the monetary system appeared to us at the Treasury – at least at the Ministerial level. It appeared like an antiquated pumping machine, creaking and groaning, leaking wildly at all the main valves, but still desperately attempting to keep down the level of water in the mine. There was, I observed, quite a lot of water in the mine at the time and more was seeping in.' (Quoted in J. C. R. Dow, *The Management of the British Economy*, p. 109.)

11 Socialism

11.1 PREPARATIONS

How does one set about the conversion of a country to socialism? Marx and his disciples did not seem to anticipate any special problem. The proletariat seizes power as the last act of an immense historical process, classes are abolished, since the State (instrument of oppression by one class of another) is no longer needed, it withers away. All is harmony and, since expropriation of surplus value has ended, well-being. One would expect some guidance from the mature Frederick Engels, *Socialism Utopian and Scientific*, first published in 1882, but this does not go much beyond suggesting an immense release of energy by which social problems will be resolved:

> Active social forces work exactly like natural forces; blindly, forcibly, destructively, so long as we do not understand and reckon with them....
> But when once their nature is understood, they can, in the hands of the producers working together, be transform 1 from master demons into willing servants. The difference is as that between the destructive force of electricity in the lightning of the storm, and electricity under command in the telegraph and the voltaic arc; the difference between a conflagration, and fire working in the service of man. With this recognition at last of the real nature of the productive forces of today, the social anarchy of production gives place to a social regulation of production upon a definite plan, according to the needs of the community and of each individual....
> *The proletariat seizes political power and turns the means of production into state property.*
> But, in doing this, it abolishes itself as proletariat, abolishes all class distinctions and class antagonisms, abolishes also the state as state.... The first act by virtue of which the state really constitutes itself the representative of the whole of society – the taking possession of the means of production in the name of society – this is, at the

same time, its last independent act as a state. (Engels, *Socialism Utopian and Scientific*, New York: International Publishers, 1935, pp. 68–70.)

There had been many utopias published in the eighteenth and nineteenth centuries – indeed, Sir Thomas More's *Utopia*, that gave its name to this type of literature, was published in 1516 – and communes had been established in various parts of the world to put their ideas into effect (see Albert Fried and Ronald Sanders, *A Documentary History of Socialist Thought*, Edinburgh University Press, 1964). One of the most celebrated was established by Robert Owen in New Harmony, Indiana, in 1824, and has existed to this very day. The best-known of the socialist blueprints is probably Edward Bellamy's *Looking Backward*, published in America in 1888. But Marks and Engels regarded these works as unscientific and did not attempt to emulate them.

The withering away of the State has not yet occurred, though the Russian Revolution took place two-thirds of a century ago, and the system operating in the Union of Soviet Socialist Republics is known as 'mature socialism', its slogan 'from each according to his ability, to each according to the work done'. Still in the future lies the stated aim of communism, with the slogan, 'from each according to his ability, to each according to his needs'.

So it was in a state of some innocence that the Bolsheviks came to power in Russia in 1917. If they had known the ordeals that lay ahead, would any of them have dared? Certainly, Tsarist Russia was a very unlikely place for a proletariat to seize power. There were very few of them, since 85 per cent of the population were peasants, many of whom were at the stage of subsistence farming. Russia was at an early stage of capitalism and the Revolution was supposed to come at the end of the most advanced stage, when the instruments of production had become too big for capitalist institutions to handle. Instead of a release of creative energies the Revolution and the years following were marked by chaos and confusion. The ramshackle Tsarist State, struggling to wage war against Germany, was enduring fearful losses. It was partly because of the state of disorganisation that the first Revolution of 1917 took place and was succeeded by the second. The Bolsheviks were successful in mobilising the fervour of soldiers and workers, while they won the support of the peasants by enacting a law entitling them to take over their land. (Alec Nove, *An Economic History of the U.S.S.R.*, Harmondsworth: Penguin Books, 1982, p. 61.)

And then what? Fortunately for those who would wield power, the training of public servants is such as to condition them to go on doing their job, and the Tsarist administrative machine saved the country from falling apart. I have seen the same phenomenon on a small scale in Uganda where, through coups, revolution and war, government departments have continued to operate, the salaries of civil servants paid by a miracle of routine.

Peace with Germany was followed by the war of intervention, which was followed, in 1921, by famine. Rescue came from the American Relief Administration (ARA), under the direction of Herbert Hoover. Desperate methods were to be taken to avoid catastrophe. The sowing and harvesting of 20 million peasant holdings were to be directed by decree. Industry had to be revived, food provided. 'We must concentrate all our efforts on this task', Lenin told the Soviets. 'It has to be solved by military methods, with absolute ruthlessness, and by the absolute suppression of all other interests.' (Nove, *An Economic History*, p. 77.)

Then, in 1923, aspirations were trimmed in conformity with reality. The New Economic Policy (NEP) was introduced: private trade and production were encouraged, money was reformed (with the new gold rouble exchanging for 50 000 million old roubles!), coercion of the peasants relaxed, prices for agricultural produce raised so that they became more consistent with manufactured goods. By 1926 pre-war levels of production had been restored, and the way was clear, in 1929, for the introduction of the first five-year plan.

How does one plan the economy of so vast, variegated and populous a country as the USSR? There were about 150 million people at that time, in nearly a dozen republics, including 169 ethnic groups of which about half were non-Russians, spread over an area of more than 20 million km^2. Part of the plan was the conversion of the peasantry to collective farms, the disastrous results of which have been well documented (see Nove, *An Economic History*, chap. 7).

11.2 FIRST FIVE-YEAR PLAN

A state planning commission (Gosplan) had been established in 1921, its first task to implement a long-term plan for electrification. (See Raymond Hutchings, *Soviet Economic Development*, Oxford: Basil Blackwell, 1971, p. 49.) Thus, by 1928, when the first five-year plan was formulated, there was some administrative infrastructure in operation. It was, none the less, the Party that devised the objectives, with Gosplan ultimately instructed to carry them out. From a planning viewpoint the task was simplified by the emphasis on heavy industry, and especially on a few giant projects: the creation of a new metallurgical centre, Magnitogorsk; the enormous dam and hydroelectric project of Dnepropetrovsk on the Dnieper; the Volga–White Sea canal. The plan was received in Russia with enthusiasm and, on Stalin's bidding, it was resolved to complete it in four years instead of five. To achieve the necessary foreign exchange to pay for imports of machines and technicians, primary products were 'dumped' on international markets – that is, sold at less than cost price. Internal prices were controlled by means of rationing and subsidies.

The difficulties may easily be imagined. Between 1927–8 and 1932 the number of industrial workers doubled, from 11.3 million to 22.8 million. Peasants who had previously handled nothing more complicated than a spade flocked from the newly formed collective farms to the construction sites and factories. Craftsmen and engineers hired from the rest of Europe or North America were appalled to see the resulting neglect and destruction of machinery. Many workers lived in barracks, with food and sanitation inadequate.

The achievement was so unlike the aim that one can scarcely call the process one of planning; it was a matter of improvisation, a desperate attempt to allocate limited resources to the most urgent purposes. These were defined by Stalin's premonition of the cataclysm to come. Nevertheless there were important achievements, measurable in real terms:

	1927–8	1932
Electricity (milliard kWh)	5.05	13.4
Hard coal (million tons)	35.4	64.3
Oil (million tons)	11.7	21.4
Iron ore (million tons)	5.7	12.1
Steel (million tons)	4.0	5.9

Source: Nove, *An Economic History*, p. 192.

While unemployment was mounting in the capitalist world it disappeared in the USSR, never to appear again. (I leave aside questions of underemployment and low productivity that have been persistent problems.) There were more jobs than available workers. 'Certain professions, notably medicine and teaching, became almost feminine preserves, while tough ex-peasant women provided a large part of the unskilled labour force.' (Nove, p. 199.) This has remained a conspicuous feature of the Soviet Union to the present day.

When people are attempting the impossible they can blame their failure either on themselves, the nature of the task, or on the wickedness of those who wish them ill. It was unthinkable to blame the Party for the failures of the 1930s, and so there began that series of trials which, by their destructive absurdity, did much to contribute to the difficulties with which the country was beset. The paranoia of these times was subsequently blamed on Stalin, but it became easy for much less important people to attribute their own failures to 'class enemies, white-guardists, kulaks...'. (Nove, pp. 217–8.)

These were the circumstances in which the planning process was conceived. With no relevant experience on which to draw and in the face of enormous difficulties, man-made and natural, the Russians learnt by their blunders, failures and successes, until they reached the methods of the present day.

11.3 DEVELOPMENTS IN PLANNING

Frightful ordeals lay ahead, some inflicted by the authorities, some by enemies from abroad. Paranoia, in its social manifestations, is highly infectious and can affect a whole society. In the Russia of the 1930s it reached lethal proportions.

> It swept away a high proportion not only of leading party cadres, but also of army officers, civil servants, managers, technicians, statisticians, planners, even foremen. Everywhere there were said to be spies, wreckers, diversionists. There was a grave shortage of qualified personnel, so the deportation of many thousands of engineers and technologists to distant concentration camps represented a severe loss. But perhaps equally serious was the psychological effect of this terror on the survivors. With any error or accident likely to be attributed to treasonable activities, the simplest thing to do was to avoid responsibility . . . to obey mechanically any order received.... (Nove, p. 237.)

In these unpropitious circumstances the planning system was developed. The plan itself was formulated by the Party to achieve politically-devised objectives. Gosplan had the task of co-ordinating its various parts, matching outputs to inputs so that the end-result could be achieved. This was done first in general terms for the five years of the plan, and then year-by-year in detail for each ensuing year. Specifications were in quantitative terms, not forecasts as in indicative planning, but orders: instructions to each industry as to what was required of it. Enterprises were grouped under ministries (People's Commissariats) by industry, plans for the industry would go to the appropriate ministry, from where they would be allocated to enterprises.

Activities were financed by sales, the differences between costs and prices providing the funds required to operate the system. Food and other agricultural products were obtained by 'procurement quotas' imposed on the collective farms. From 1935 these managed themselves, to the extent of electing a mangement committee and chairman, who supervised and organised the work of the farm. Farm workers were paid, in cash or kind, according to the work units that they earned. In 1935 each household was given an allocation of land that they could work for themselves and whose produce they could consume or sell.

Workers' wages were set along with the plan, so that trade unions did not undertake collective bargaining but operated as welfare organisations or took up the grievances of individual workers. In the 1930s incentive systems were devised in terms of which higher pay could be earned by greater efficiency or effort.

The Second Five-Year Plan was for the years 1933–7 inclusive. Nove quotes the following figures as indicating its achievements:

	1932 (Actual)	1937 (Plan)	1937 (Actual)
Electricity (milliard kWh)	13.4	38.0	36.2
Coal (million tons)	64.3	152.5	128.0
Oil (million tons)	22.3	46.8	28.5
Pig iron (million tons)	6.2	16.0	14.5
Steel (million tons)	5.9	17.0	17.7
Machine tools (thousands)	15.0	40.0	45.5
Cement (million tons)	3.5	7.5	5.5
Cotton fabrics (million metres)	2720	5100	3448
Wool fabrics (million metres)	94.6	226.6	108.3
Sugar (thousand tons)	828	2500	2421
Tractors (thousands) (15 h.p. units)	51.6	166.7	66.5

Source: Nove, *An Economic History*, p. 226.

The plan's guiding principles had been *consolidation, mastering technique* and *improving living standards*. Certainly, immense effort was put into education, secondary and technical. In 1928 there were less than a million pupils in secondary schools, in 1934 more than two million (Nove, p. 197). The number of graduates in employment multiplied by four between 1928 and the beginning of 1941, 'secondary specialists' and technicians by five.

But in 1933, with the accession to power in Germany of the Nazis, whose declared intention was to stamp out communism, the imminence of war became evident, and production was diverted from peaceful purposes in preparation. This explains the great shortfall shown above in the production of tractors, now replaced by tanks and planes.

That the country survived the German onslaught is one of the wonders of the age. 'By the end of November 1941 the Soviets in their retreat had lost vast territories, which contained 63 per cent of all coal production, 68 per cent of pig iron, 58 per cent of steel, 60 per cent of aluminium, 41 per cent of railway lines, 84 per cent of sugar, 38 per cent of grain, 60 per cent of pigs.' (Nove, p. 271.) 'Yet by redeployment and improvisation, and the imposition of ruthless priorities, even in 1942 the arms industry managed to produce 25 436 aircraft, 60 per cent more than in 1941, and 24 688 tanks, or 3.7 times more than 1941.' (Nove, p. 274.)

11.4 PLANNING TODAY

Some of the elements listed above remain in operation. The Party, specifically the Politbureau, lists major objectives. For five- or fifteen-year plans they have a wider area of choice, for in such a time-span substantial changes can be made, but for the year ahead much has already been decided, so that choice is restricted. Here, Gosplan plays the major role.

Requests and schemes pour in from the ministries, representing the aspirations and needs of the industries under their jurisdiction, and republican or regional bodies put up their proposals. The Ministry of Foreign Trade will seek information on import needs, and give information on requirements of products for export.

Gosplan must fit this multitude of needs and offerings into a coherent whole. They have also the task of matching household income to the price of goods and services available for consumption. They deal all the time with material input and output: the resources required to expand output of this or that to specified levels.

Gosplan prepares balances for about two thousand products, while the supply committee, dealing with the requisite inputs, about eighteen thousand. Allocations are given to the ministries, who, in turn, allocate them to the enterprises under their control.

A decree of July 1979 aimed at increasing the feedback between the various strata in the planning process. Gosplan is instructed to submit an outline plan 1¼ years in advance of the five-year period. When this has been approved 'control figures' will be submitted to the ministries. The ministries interpret them into requirements for their enterprises, who in turn make their own proposals, broken down by years, and enter into preliminary negotiations with their suppliers. The resulting information is returned to the ministries, who co-ordinate it and submit it to Gosplan. (Alec Nove, *The Soviet Economic System*, 2nd ed., London: Allen & Unwin, 1980, p. 61.)

Wages and salaries are laid down by decrees issued on the authority of the Council of Ministers, on the advice of the State Committee on Labour and Wages. They are changed infrequently, and so are the prices attached to products in the planning process. The 1967 price revision took seven years' work by thousands of specialists. (Nove, *The Soviet Economic System*, p. 182.) Nove quotes the head of the Prices Committee: 'Market prices are, in our view, alien to our economy and contradict the task of centralized planning. It is ... incorrect to imagine that prices should balance supply and demand. The balance between demand and supply . . . is the task of the planning organs.' (Ibid. p. 184.)

In other socialist countries there have been attempts at decentralisation, pre-eminently in Yugoslavia which, in 1964, took the syndicalist path. Here enterprises have considerable autonomy and can formulate plans for their own development, in conjunction with local authorities and the Central Bank. Profits are divided between local needs, social services, further investment, interest on bank loans and bonuses.

In Hungary reforms were instituted in 1968. Instead of the output of each industry, and hence each enterprise, being laid down by the plan, enterprises were now required to produce their own plans, with the decisions of the central-planners replaced by price signals. Costs were to remain the basis for prices, but the actual costs of the enterprise not those laid down in the rule book. To these costs specified margins were to be added: a 25 per cent mark-up on the enterprise's wage bill, to include social-security contributions and wage tax (a similar tax was applied in the United Kingdom for a few years on the advice of Sir Harold Wilson's advisers, who, by coincidence, were Hungarian by birth); capital charges of 5 per cent and a further 6.5 per cent return on capital. (Martin Cave and Paul Hare, *Alternative Approaches to Economic Planning*, p. 52.) If the same product were produced by more than one enterprise they would agree on the price, and differences evened-out by taxes or subsidies to avoid excess profits or losses.

Thus far the difference from the Soviet method has been that enterprises instead of the central planners determined output and prices. Rules were included for adjusting prices, with products placed in three categories: fixed-price products whose prices could be changed only by central decision; free price products whose prices could be changed by the enterprises themselves; an intermediate category requiring joint decisions. Prices of raw materials, power and basic foods were generally fixed. Free prices applied to about a third of all transactions.

Profits remaining after deduction of the taxes mentioned above are also taxed. They are divided between the 'sharing fund', to be distributed amongst the employees, and the development fund. Wage increases and production bonuses come from the first, while the second, together with credits and grants, is used for investment in the enterprise. Taxes are then exacted of development fund profits at a rate of 70 per cent, and on sharing-fund profits at progressive rates.

Annual increases in basic pay are laid down each year by the national plan, and increases above this come from the sharing-fund. Bonuses from this fund are limited to 10 per cent, though managers may receive bonuses of up to 30 per cent as well as additions from ministry funds. But managers' salaries may be cut by as much as 25 per cent if the enterprise does badly.

Influenced, perhaps, by the ideas of bourgeois economics, the designers of the new system envisaged the payment of higher wages by successful firms, which would attract workers from those less successful and in due course eliminate them. But things did not work out that way. 'When it became clear that enterprises which were not really economic were going to survive for an extended period, something had to be done about the wages they could pay; gradually a system of so-called "wage preferences" developed which enabled many of the less successful firms to pay at least the wage increases specified in the annual plan.' (Cave and Hare, p. 55.)

Two-thirds of industrial investment is now undertaken on the initiative of enterprises, but, since credits and subsidies are linked to the priorities of the central planners, enterprises have increasingly linked their own investments to the plan. Indeed, Cave and Hare

Socialism   281

remark the tendency towards recentralisation since the reforms of 1968. (*Alternative Approaches*, p. 56.)

11.5 ACHIEVEMENTS

There is a curious paradox in Soviet achievements: in some things they have been brilliant innovators, and in many others have displayed a marked tendency to lag. I have already referred to their astonishing output of arms in the Second World War. Their tanks, aircraft and rocketry were highly effective and produced on a massive scale. (See Nove, *An Economic History*, p. 275.)

Eugen Loebl, until 1968 director of the Czechoslovakian State Bank, then a professor at Vassar College in the United States, explains the contrast thus:

> It is only in the fields of war production and space production that the Soviets are equal to the Americans, but it is significant that in these two fields there is no central planning. More precisely, the scientists, engineers, and managers in these industries have a free hand to devise their own methods for production and can dictate to the planning body how they will produce and what materials they will need. If the planned task is to reach the moon, they are free to work out whatever plans are necessary to reach this goal. In these areas, the scientists have freedom equal to, and possibly even greater than, the scientists in the United States, with the same or better working conditions. Despite their importance in the national defense and the secrecy involved, there are much smaller political demands on these experts than, for instance, those in the textile industry. For the war industries, a man's expertise is the decisive factor in his assignment to a particular position. It is in the consumer industries that expertise is ignored for political considerations....
> (*Humanomics*, New York: Random House, 1976, p. 88.)

It is often remarked that Soviet enterprises are preoccupied with the need to fulfil the current one-year plan, and therefore neglect the research and development required for the introduction of new products in the years ahead. By contrast, giant capitalist firms spend excessive amounts on research and development (R & D). They do so in self-defence, because technical competition is more stringent than price competition: in their product-development they are continually trying to get ahead of the competition or catch up with the competition. The results are not always socially beneficial.

The Russians are free of this pressure and are compelled, instead, to buy-in techniques from capitalist corporations. Does this indicate a weakness in their research effort?

There has undoubtedly been a high rate of technical change in the socialist countries and, associated with this, a massive expansion of technical education and investment in research and development and in many other scientific and technical services. However, it is still open to the critics of socialist societies to point to the high rate of import of foreign technology into the socialist countries and the continuing world leadership of the capitalist countries in many branches of technology. Advocates of 'convergence' hypotheses can argue that each system is gradually coming to resemble the other. There has been substantial decentralisation of research and development activities to enterprise and university level in the socialist countries and a growing use of contract techniques, whilst public investment and involvement has increased in the capitalist countries. Moreover, essentially similar technologies are now being developed and applied on a world-wide scale, which provides a strong continuing basis for convergence. (Christopher Freeman, Charles Cooper and Keith Pavitt, 'Policies for Technical Change', in Christopher Freeman and Marie Jahoda, eds, *World Futures*, Oxford: Martin Robertson, 1978, chap. 7, p. 215.)

Soviet agriculture seems to suffer not so much from antiquated technology as from an absence of zeal, derived perhaps from the trauma of fifty years ago. In Britain and North America there are large capitalist farms producing meat and eggs by battery methods and crops by chemical processes. But there are also substantial numbers of farms of more modest size, run with the greatest dedication by the families who own them. These people are self-selected: they choose farming as a way of life and thus put their madness to good use, in the way suggested by Fourier a century and a half ago. In the Soviet Union, by contrast, the farms are of enormous size, with 500 million acres of cropland divided in roughly equal amounts between 20 800 state farms and 26 000 collective farms, the former averaging just over 13 000 acres and the latter 9000. (Lester R. Brown, 'The U.S.–Soviet Food Connection', *Challenge*, Jan.–Feb. 1983, p. 42.)

In 1970 the United States exported 38 million tons of grain and the

Soviet Union 8 million. In 1981, however, the United States exported 115 million tons and the Soviet Union *imported* 46 million. Lester Brown comments:

> Support for Soviet agriculture from the nonfarm sector is generally inadequate. Despite the accelerated investment in farm equipment over the past three Five-Year Plans ... Soviet agriculture is still plagued by defective equipment and poor maintenance. This helps explain the frequent Soviet press reports of planting or harvesting delays caused by equipment breakdown. To compensate for equipment defects Soviet farmers have become expert at cannibalizing one piece of equipment for the spare parts needed to keep a similar piece running, leading to the sprawling equipment 'boneyards' observed on state farms. Among the most revealing numbers published in Soviet statistical yearbooks are those showing that the number of tractors in use at the end of 1981 was only marginally greater than the number delivered to farms between 1976 and 1981, indicating a short life expectancy.
>
> The situation contrasts sharply with that in the United States, where farm tractors are often still in use after 20 years. When a U.S. farmer buys a tractor from a farm equipment dealer, he purchases a package that includes servicing and maintenance.   (Ibid. p. 44.)

Reports, letters and articles in the Soviet press testify to the general awareness of these defects. Soviet citizens can hardly fail to be aware of them, but their existence is publicly discussed, complaints are aired and explanations demanded. In an article in the monthly *Kommunist* Mr Andropov remarks on the need for change, local initiative and material incentives. 'What is holding us up? Why do we not get the right return from massive capital investment? Why are scientific and technological achievements not being applied to production fast enough?' The economy could not be run by 'communist decrees', but required 'measures which give broad freedom of action to the colossal creative forces latent in our economy'. (*The Times*, 24 Feb., 1983, p. 7.)

There does indeed appear to be a need to release colossal creative forces, and such a transformation might well occur in a state of detente, whose institution will itself require a colossal feat of political engineering. Capitalism has many contradictions of which socialism is free; some contradictions they share, but socialism has others peculiar to itself. It should not be necessary to offer financial rewards to induce enterprises to operate efficiently, nor to establish proper maintenance services.

The restraint on travel is a continual reminder of the lack of detente, illustrative of a contradiction in the present political system. It results in a form of claustrophobia that compels some people to engineer escape or to defect from official delegations. They can then claim asylum in whatever country they happen to be. If there were freedom to come and go it is probable that fewer people would wish to emigrate, while those that did could no longer claim asylum, but would have to take their chances along with all the other applicants for status as 'landed immigrants' and citizens.

But however one frames the balance-sheet of advantages and disadvantages, the Soviet system shows itself clearly superior to capitalism in two respects: the absence of inflation and the absence of unemployment, effects achieved not by chance but by design. Prices are what the planners determine them to be and there are great advantages, for planning purposes, to maintaining their stability. The growth in employment, too, is determined in the planning process. More generally, these economies are free from the booms and slumps that afflict the capitalist world and, indeed, exert a steadying effect on world trade.

12 The Third World

12.1 PROBLEMS OF POVERTY

The World Bank, in its annual development reports, divides the world into five:

	Percentage of world	
	Population	Area
Low-income countries	30.5	20.1
Middle-income countries	20.6	25.3
Industrialised countries	15.7	23.3
Capital-surplus oil exporters	1.4	4.6
Centrally planned economies	31.8	26.7
All	100	100

There are 38 low-income and 52 middle-income countries. The poorest country shown in the 1981 *World Bank Atlas* is Bhutan. In 1979 its population was 1 267 000, to whom was attributed a GNP of $80 per head. In the years 1970–9 its population had grown at the rate of 2.2 per cent a year, while GNP per head had declined by 0.1 per cent per year. The *Atlas* lists no fewer than 19 countries whose real per capita GNP fell in the decade of the 1970s.

Growth of output per head and growth of population are often presented as in opposition to one another, but the relationship is not merely arithmetical: the number of children in the family affects the effort exerted by the parents, technical advances may cause output per hectare to rise faster than the reduction in hectares per household, and in sparsely populated areas an increase in population density may bring about economies of scale that reduce the costs per head of transport, health and education, power and water supply.

Even so, it is a daunting thought, presented in *The Global 2000 Report to the President* (Harmondsworth: Penguin Books, 1982), that world population is likely to increase by 55 per cent between 1975 and 2000, from 4100 million to 6350 million. Of these, 5000 million will live in the Third World: 79 per cent of the whole, 92 per cent of the increase. Daunting, too, is the projected size of Third-World cities in the year 2000:

	Millions
Mexico City	31.6
Calcutta	19.7
Greater Bombay	19.1
Seoul	18.7
Jakarta	16.9
Greater Cairo	16.4
Karachi	15.9

Source: *The Global 2000*, p. 12.

The World Bank's projections postulate some fall in the rates of population increase for China and India, but all the same by the year 2000 they would between them account for 37 per cent of world population. The Indian Government continues to make strenuous efforts to reduce the birth-rate, though they have retreated somewhat from their more drastic policies, but indications are that the Chinese will succeed in reducing theirs. Their present policy of only one child per married couple that will take them below zero-population-growth (ZPG) would be ineffective in any other country, but might succeed in China. The precept is reinforced by financial sanctions: withdrawal of free education and family allowances from couples with more than one child.

There is an inverse correlation between birth-rate and the rise in income. In India GNP per head rose by 1.6 per cent per head in the 1970s, but this carries two effects: reduction in births, but rise in survival rate. Since in India life-expectancy at birth in 1978 was only 51 years (compared with 74 for industrialised countries) there is plenty of scope for improvement.

Study the World Bank Tables, or the UN *Year Book of National Accounts Statistics* and you will note the great range in national income per head (Switzerland $15 360 in 1979; Bhutan $80), likewise in population growth (-0.2 in the German Democratic Republic, 5.7 in the Ivory Coast), and in the growth of GNP (6.7 per cent for Singapore, -3.7 for Jamaica). (1981 *World Bank Atlas*, pp. 6 and 8.) The Brandt Commission described the problem:

We see a world in which poverty and hunger still prevail in many huge regions; in which resources are squandered without consideration of their renewal.... (p. 13.) Pollution and exploitation are all-embracing, whether of the atmosphere or soil.... The grave consequences of increasing soil erosion and desertification should concern all of us. Unchecked deforestation at its present rate would halve the stock of usable wood by the end of this century (and deprive more than one billion poor people of their essential fuel for cooking). The 'absorption capacity' of trees, which checks carbon dioxide pollution, would be reduced to a dangerous level.... (pp. 19–20.) Food production in all the developing countries rose by over two and a half per cent annually between 1950 and 1975; but demand for food has grown by well over three per cent a year as population and incomes have gone up. As a result the developing countries have rapidly increased their imports of cereals, from relatively low levels in the 1950s to 20 million tons in 1960 and 1961, to over 50 million tons in the early 70s, and nearly 80 million by 1978–9.... (p. 91.) In the countries of the South the great majority of people have a life expectancy of closer to fifty years; in the poorest countries one out of every four children dies before the age of five; one-fifth or more of all the people in the South suffer from hunger and malnutrition; fifty per cent have no chance to become literate. (p. 32.) (*North–South: a Programme for Survival*, London: Pan Books, 1980.)

We have been talking about average income per head by country; but distribution within countries is also uneven. John Whalley, in the *Review of Income and Wealth* (Series 25, no. 3, Sept. 1979), has attempted to estimate a world income distribution from which national boundaries have been eliminated. 'The basic data are potentially very unreliable', he warns, but offers a tentative conclusion:

> The indications from calculations reported in this paper are that the top 1 per cent of the world's population may receive 10–15 per cent of world income, the top 10 per cent, 45–65 per cent, and the bottom 20 per cent, 1–4 per cent. Domestic inequality (in contrast to inequality across countries) appears to approximately double the share of the top 1 per cent and to halve the share of the bottom 10 per cent.

Michael Lipton ascribes this persistence of poverty to urban bias, observing that the disparity between urban and rural welfare is much greater in poor countries now than it was in rich countries during their early development. There has been little change since 1965, 'mainly because less than 20 per cent of investment for development has gone to the agricultural sector'. (Michael Lipton, *Why Poor People Stay Poor*, London: Temple Smith, 1977, p. 16.)

In the days before the industrial revolution famine occurred occasionally owing to harvest failures; now, at least, famine-relief organisation is able to alleviate the worst effects. We have noticed that wealth grew very slowly during the process of industrialisation but, through persistence over 1½ or 2 centuries, brought the countries concerned to a state of affluence. If in India GNP per head continues to grow at 1.6 per cent a year, in 25 or 26 years it will have increased by 50 per cent; in 43 or 44 years it will have doubled. The population of India, if it continues to grow at its present rate, would then be approaching 1500 million, and in GNP per head the country would have just reached the *present* status of a country near the bottom of the World Bank list of middle-income countries – say Egypt or Ghana. That is a long time to wait, especially since a high proportion of the people even of middle-income countries suffer from primary poverty.

12.2 CAUSES

In the days of hope before the withdrawal of the colonial powers, the issues seemed very clear. We read in Lenin of the extraction of super-profits from the colonial empires; when the colonies threw off the imperial yoke, these super-profits would revert to their rightful owners who would then enjoy modest but growing wealth.

In fact it was stagnation rather than exploitation that typified the colonial presence. 'The colonial economy utilized a tiny proportion of Africa's natural resources. Only in exceptional enclaves such as the Katanga–Zambia copper belt, the Maghreb coastal plain, and the Ghana cocoa belt was anything like full exploitation of land and mineral resources attained. In no case were the Africans themselves permitted to achieve anything like full development of their own resources.' (Reginald H. Green and Ann Seidman, *Unity or Poverty? The Economics of Pan-Africanism*, Harmondsworth: Penguin Books, 1968, pp. 31–2.)

The presence of European or American companies was marked by the appearance of enclaves – mines or plantations – once the slave trade had been abolished (or almost abolished) and the elephant herds reduced. By the 1920s and 1930s the imperial powers had lost their appetite for imperialism and limited their aims to ensuring that the colonies paid for their own administration. Trading companies continued to flourish, but they were minor elements in the metropolitan economies.

Peace was maintained, tribal wars suppressed and traditional modes of justice and administration maintained, with appeals to the district commissioner, in cases of importance, from traditional courts. During the Second World War various parts of colonial empires assumed a sudden strategic importance, and the colonial powers were suddenly overtaken by humanitarian impulses. In Britian a Colonial Development and Welfare Act was passed and, in 1946, £140 million granted to be spent on colonial development over the ensuing ten years. The wind of change assumed gale force, the spirit of the time was against fighting colonial wars, so independence was hurried through, and the grants became a golden-handshake in more senses than one.

The ex-colonies were left with some infrastructure, a modest system of education, some hospitals, and an administrative service. What would have happened if the territories had never been annexed in the first place? It may be interesting to speculate, but not very profitable. In the colonial service were some devoted souls whose service had been their vocation: agronomists, doctors and teachers, as well as administrators. Some of them were accorded the honour of being asked to stay on after independence. Others left curious scars derived from their extraordinary sense of ethnic superiority.

After independence the newly liberated countries failed to blossom in the way expected. The early 1960s were years of excitement when, travelling in Africa, one could listen to innumerable discussions as to the manner in which countries should be transformed. In the main the choice was of some sort of socialist path, along which there were some initial advances. Foreign firms were nationalised or invited into partnership with industrial development corporations, but soon difficulties were encountered, hopes disappointed. For some the change brought rapid promotion in business or government, accession to power and wealth, but to the mass of the population little change. Towards the end of the 1960s agricultural prices fell and, while workers in industry won or were accorded rapid increases in pay, new jobs lagged behind the rapid influx of job-seekers who began to converge on the towns.

There was no shortage of well-meaning advisers from Europe and North America. They came confident of their ability to teach the new governments how to achieve economic growth. They used Harrod-Domar models and incremental capital–output ratios (ICORs). The savings ratio must be increased, savings converted into investment, the capital-labour ratio raised and hence the productivity of labour. Great reserves of labour, in the form of under-employment on peasant farms were identified. These must be absorbed by rising urban employment before (according to the Lewis model) the marginal productivity of farm labour could be raised. Mobilisation could be effected by transmission of price-signals: the production of cash-crops raised and the resulting export earnings used for the purchase of capital goods from abroad with their effect on the growth of industrial jobs.

National plans were hurriedly concocted that purported to apply these theories, but the plans bore little recognisable resemblance to actual events. Walter Elkan commented on the instability of ICORs, even in advanced industrial countries. 'It is of even more doubtful value for planning in the low income countries. First, it must be immediately obvious that the capital cost of a given increase in output must vary greatly from industry to industry and between directly productive activities and social overhead capital projects.' (*An Introduction to Development Economics*, Harmondsworth: Penguin Books, 1973, p. 75.) A. P. Thirlwall concludes his review of the causes of growth: 'it should be said again that these aggregate models which have produced the results above are rough tools. They do, however, give an important idea of the forces at work and a rough idea of the likely quantitative significance of different factors. If one overriding conclusion emerges it is probably that developing countries ignore capital accumulation at their peril if they are to increase their rate of growth significantly.' (*Growth and Development with Special Reference to Developing Economies*, London: Macmillan, 2nd ed., 1978, p. 71.) And on E. F. Denison's attempt to identify the reasons for differences in rates of growth: 'His attempt to quantify the sources of increases in output per unit of input, however, falls short of complete success, and some of his conclusions must be considered of doubtful worth. As much as one admires his attention to detail the present state of our knowledge does not permit some of the sweeping assumptions that Denison is forced to rely on. The residual factor in economic growth remains the "coefficient of our ignorance".' (*Why Growth Rates Differ: Postwar Experiences in Nine Western Countries*, Washington: Brookings Institution, 1967, p. 80.)

Disappointed in the results, the advisers gave up trying to engineer *growth* and turned their attention instead to *development*. Even though a country might not be growing with much speed it might still be developing if literacy was increasing, crops being diversified, women liberated and so on. Later, aims became still more modest (let us think in terms of 'basic needs') or abstract: let us create a new World Economic Order.

At the same time, from Latin America, theories were circulated to explain that, while colonial empires had been dissolved, the malign influence of the metropolitan powers lingered on in the form of neo-colonialism, the colonial heritage and, arising from the continued dependence of the peripheral countries on the metropolitan powers, *the development of underdevelopment.* Peripheral societies remain in servitude as exporters of primary products, or as labour-intensive departments in the productive processes of foreign corporations, incapable of breaking into the fields of advanced technology. Debt interest and dividends drain productive surpluses from peripheral countries, augmented by the savings of their own bourgeoisie who prefer to preserve their wealth in the safety of the United States or Europe. These theories are reviewed in the introduction of Manfred Bienefeld and Martin Godfrey, eds, *The Struggle for Development* (Chichester: John Wiley, 1982).

12.3 THE NATURE OF THIRD WORLD COUNTRIES

Both advisers and advised have suffered from a serious disability in respect of the Third World: their Euro–North American preconceptions. These are implanted in the elite of the Asian, African and Latin American countries in the course of their education, essential ingredients for the achievement of honours in European or North American universities. They are taken for granted by the experts supplied by the World Bank and UN Agencies. Paradoxically, they are also at the basis of Marxist thought.

They assume the primacy of material desires; that other sentiments are subordinate to the desire for wealth. One saw this most clearly in respect of the assumption that peasants were underemployed and suffered greatly on this account. My own researches into the life of peasant farmers in Tanzania in 1967 and 1968 revealed a different picture:

> on the comparative advantages of town and country: country people were independent with regard to food, while in towns even wild spinach had to be bought. On the other hand, towns had social amenities, good roads, easier work, more abundant money.

'Townspeople are richer with many modern things such as electricity. The town is good for making money through business. The townspeople are the ones who control the government and hence favour themselves.' But with all this, the consensus was that life in the country was better, both for the parents and for their children, except for the boys and then only if they could get good jobs. 'The weather in town is very uncomfortable. Townspeople live amidst all evils. No good children can be reared in the town.' (Guy Routh, 'Development Paths in Tanzania', in Ukandi G. Damachi *et al.*, eds, *Development Paths in Africa & China*, London: Macmillan, 1976, p. 25.)

The households had few material possessions and limited ambitions. They had to work in order to feed themselves and make a little cash for shop goods, clothes and a few other things. But after work, in the early afternoon, came the real pleasures of life: social intercourse, with much talk and the drinking of home-brewed beer. It was these hours of recreation that the experts were proposing to take away. Those most in need of relief were the women, and this has been given by the provision of piped water, for the fetching and carrying of water was one of their most onerous tasks.

It has long been accepted that, to peasant households, children are an investment as well as a pleasure. In poor countries the transmission of money from town to country, children to parents, eliminates some of the income disparities otherwise observable. One observes, too, that large families are so highly valued that, even with a declining infant mortality rate, the number of births is not much reduced. The opposition of the men to birth-control is particularly strong: perhaps the liberation of women might bring about a change.

These are examples of cultural differences that the 'western mind' and the western-educated non-western mind have the greatest difficulty in comprehending. By such minds it is taken for granted that everybody in the world wants nothing more than to achieve the status of inhabitants of medium-sized European or North American industrial towns. They do not. It requires a great deal of education to change them in this respect, and the education does not, as a rule, include the sort of defences needed to protect them from the temptations to which they are then subjected.

Nearly all countries in Africa and Asia have cultures with which the minds of their inhabitants are deeply imbued: in some – Japan, Korea, Taiwan, Singapore – these cultures act as a catalyst in the process of economic change. In others they may hinder the process while at the same time enabling those who subscribe to them to survive; in still others, there may be a combination of the worst features in the indigenous and the imported culture, to produce disastrous results.

One should mention in this context that there are strict limits to the meaning that may be attached to the national income (or GNP) scoreboards published by the World Bank or in the UN *Year Book of National Accounts Statistics*. The calculation of GNP for any country is itself beset by many inaccuracies and unreal assumptions, while the conversion of local currencies into dollars, for purposes of international comparison, is an exercise in 'stylised facts' (data accepted as factual for econometric purposes only). The German Federal Statistical Office has for many years been converting currencies on the basis of the cost of baskets of consumables, and published the results in the Federal statistical yearbook (*Statistisches Jahrbuk für die Bundesrepublik Deutschlauf*. The relevant table is 10.5 on pp. 720–2.) Pioneering work was done, too, by Milton Gilbert and I. B. Kravis in *An International Comparison of National Products and the Purchasing Power of Currencies* (Paris, OEEC, 1954). One may thus assess the purchasing power of currencies relative to one another, but there remain questions such as the evaluation of expenditure necessary in one country (for example, for heating bills, warm clothes, transport) that is unnecessary in another country.

Greed, cruelty and corruption are conspicuous in many of the poor countries to an extent that is not tolerated in industrially developed countries with more effective protective institutions and more critical elements amongst the mass media. In most countries at some time and some countries at most times the populace is held powerless by military groups or dictators who, regrettably, are sometimes sustained or brought to power by foreign governments or multinational corporations playing their own political or business game. Knowing, perhaps, that their days are numbered the dictators and their allies generally take the precaution of misappropriating vast funds that are then kept in some haven beyond the reach of those by whom they may be overthrown.

12.4 DEVELOPMENT PROGRAMMES

In this, as in other respects, there are marked differences between countries. The 1981 *World Bank Atlas* shows a great range between countries in their annual average rate of economic growth for the 1970s, for example:

	%
Republic of Korea	8.1
Malaysia	5.4
Ecuador	5.4
Morocco	3.5
Congo	−0.2
Zimbabwe	−1.9
Egypt	5.3
Sudan	1.5
Kenya	2.6
Tanzania	0.8
China	3.8

Source: *World Bank Atlas*, p. 6.

Of course, different countries are very differently endowed with natural resources, and natural resources are of great importance at the beginning of industrialisation when primary products play a predominant part, but this affects total production rather than the rate of growth. The discovery of new resources may indeed cause a jump in output, but growth is generally a matter of improving output per worker by labour-saving or capital-saving innovations, or the introduction of new crops or products that yield higher values per unit of labour or capital. Why are some countries so much better at this than others?

One thing is clear: that those theorists were foredoomed to disappointment who, in the 1950s and 1960s, sought or offered a formula guaranteed to hit the jack-pot. The records of those years give ample instances of the hit-and-run tactics of those consultants who came, prescribed and disappeared, leaving the country concerned to apply the formula and discover, the hard way, that it did not work, or brought with it secondary effects of a damaging kind. Panaceas of the left or right emerged from planning offices, not infrequently bringing with them aid from a politically interested metropolitan government.

When General Mohammed was President of Nigeria he was asked by Ukandi Damachi to tell him his ideology. 'I have no time for an ideology,' he replied, 'I am too busy trying to govern the country.' Whether or not he had an ideology, he did have a morality, in terms of which he began stamping our corruption – a campaign that ended in his own assassination. The bullet-riddled limousine in which he died is displayed in the national museum in Lagos.

But most governments and political parties have pretensions to ideologies, from which their programmes and policies are supposedly drawn. They may not be aimed at the growth of national wealth, but only at its redistribution. Frances Stewart writes of Kenya: 'One of the prime aims of post-independence policy has been to take over the positions of power and privilege from the Europeans and Asians. The immediate takeover was that of the government itself. By 1967 it was estimated that 90 per cent of the civil service was Kenyanised. The settlers on the White Highlands were rapidly bought out and the land distributed to African smallholders. Subsequently, using a variety of methods, non-Kenyans have been gradually replaced in the army, education and business.' ('Kenya: Strategies for Development', in Ukandi G. Damachi et al., eds, *Development Paths in Africa and China*, p. 84.)

The first and immediate gain of independence is the 'indigenisation' of power, and the jobs and salaries that go with it. Sometimes from the gaols, the guerrilla bands, from exile or, in more tranquil circumstances, from the unofficial groups in advisory councils, the new rulers converge on the cabinet offices and parliament buildings. Names of streets, towns and, sometimes, countries are changed, new flags are waved, new anthems sung.

Then the process is extended to the subsidiaries of foreign companies. They are given a date by which 51 per cent of their shares must be owned by nationals, or they are offered partnerships in terms of which the new government will take over a majority of the shares, with an agreement, perhaps, for the continuing management of the company by the foreign firm. Programmes are instituted by which nationals are trained to take over the posts still held by non-nationals. It is a slow process, fraught with tension for, to their subordinates, other people's jobs often look easier than they are, and most decisions are a matter of routine. The real test is, 'Would he or she know what to do in an emergency?'

In this process of redistribution of power, ownership and jobs, powerful political forces are seen to operate. Those who cried out against ethnic discrimination are curiously insensible to their own prejudices so that it becomes difficult to distinguish, in the moral hierarchy, between the countries of East Africa, Zimbabwe, India, Indonesia, Israel and South Africa.

The subordination of national interests to sectional interests results in a reduction of national product and a slow-down of growth that may take years to correct. Engineers, doctors and teachers take many years to become fully operational, but this can be done according to well-established programmes; skilled craftsmen present a more difficult problem, because so much of their training, including their industrial conditioning, can take place only on the job; still more difficult is the reproduction of a class of entrepreneurs. When the Asians were turned out of Uganda by Idi Amin the economy relapsed into stagnation and decay.

These are subjects whose rationale can be found only in politics; in economic terms they are *ipso facto* irrational, and it is this that gives an air of unreality to much of the economic theorising about Third-World affairs. Bernard Schaffer and Geoff Lamb present one of the rare books confronting the problem (*Can Equity be Organized?*, Farnborough: Gower; Paris: UNESCO, 1981). They comment on A. Nozick, *Anarchy and Utopia* (Oxford University Press, 1974), 'State distributive interventions will always be unfair. The only answer then can be to have as few of them as possible. That is particularly true in relation to redistributive procedures. Their themes might be merit, justice, etc. These are not the outcomes.' They refer approvingly to Nozick's 'sense of history and irony, of unanticipated consequences, of the institutional record'. (Ibid. p. 52.) These 'unanticipated consequences' are conspicuous in much of the agricultural reorganisation to which, with inadequate consultation, the peasants of various countries have been subjected.

Part of the first act of independence has been the establishment of national development corporations. They are provided with funds and called upon to perform various functions. They act as holding companies for the public interest in partially-nationalised concerns; they may engage foreign corporations to advise on or participate in the establishment of new concerns; they may support local entrepreneurs or they may set up new enterprises of their own.

Another early programme has been one of import-substitution. All countries have departments of customs and excise and it is easy to see, from their records, what imported products are in demand. The government of Mauritius publishes lists of imported products suitable for local production, with offers of finance for those willing to manufacture them. Import-substitution is not infrequently made difficult by lack of the economies of large-scale production which would make the local product unacceptably expensive. The import-content of the newly produced product is another critical factor. At the break-even point for local manufacture the venture may result in an increase in import costs rather than their reduction.

Another device is the substitution of subsistence crops by cash crops: tea, coffee, cocoa, sisal, jute or other commodities that enter into world trade, or, as part of a programme of 'export-led growth' the enactment of agreements with multinationals for the establishment of labour-intensive assembly departments as part of their process of manufacture.

The production of national development plans is regarded as an essential concomitant to all this. Early examples are almost always hastily produced and inadequately prepared by experts imported specially for the occasion. They are expressions of intent with little resemblance to what afterwards occurs. Later, they cover shorter periods – one year, perhaps, instead of five, and limit themselves to projects already planned and ready financed.

Since 80 or 90 per cent of Third-World people have been rural dwellers, rural development programmes have formed part of national plans. The Green Revolution was enthusiastically received, but its benefits offset by the high cost of fertiliser, need for irrigation, susceptibility of new strains to pests and viruses. Roads, water-supplies, schools, health centres and agricultural extension services have been instituted and are slowly helping to improve the countryside.

Some countries have been transformed and have performed successful invasions of the markets of the industrially advanced countries; most retain the characteristics of economic backwardness, with more than half their populations still engaged in subsistence agriculture, and modern sectors growing slower than population.

The solutions having proved inadequate, it was decided to change the problems. Growth, as already noted, became development; development became modernisation. Transformation was dropped in favour of the provision of basic needs. By the end of the 1960s a dangerous phenomenon had appeared: the failure of job-creation to keep place with population growth. The desire for modern-sector jobs sent wave upon wave of young men and women into the towns, encouraged by the spread of education to seek income and work superior to the prospects of the family farm. In the 1980s unemployment has affected the whole non-socialist world, but in those days it appeared peculiarly virulent in Third-World countries, as severe in Latin America as in Africa and Asia. It was with this in mind that the International Labour Organization launched its World Employment Programme in 1969. Countries could apply to the ILO for an inter-agency team to study their employment problems and produce a report. See, for instance, *Employment, Incomes and Equality: A Strategy for Increasing Productive Employment in Kenya* (Geneva: ILO, 1972) that attributed importance to the development of 'the informal sector' whose importance has more recently been discovered in the 'black economy' in Italy and other industrialised countries.

A central difficulty has been the way in which capital/labour ratios rise in the course of industrial development. Thus job-creation lags behind investment. This results in the rise of the labour/output ratio, which is not counteracted by a sufficiently fast rise in effective demand. The result has been that Third-World countries have frequently been unable to fully use even that capital that they have.

Planning is a much slower and more laborious matter than had been initially thought. To decide what additional products to produce requires long and careful study and market research; almost as difficult is the decision of what production methods to apply. Firms of consultants and manufacturers will by this time have been drawn into the discussions and will be pressing for those techniques that suit their own convenience. Once decisions have been taken they are difficult to reverse or adapt. Thus, while some government-sponsored enterprises have been markedly successful, others have been dogged by difficulties and a few have been disastrous.

12.5 CASE STUDIES

Why do some countries grow fast, some slowly, some not at all and others grow poorer? To complicate things still further, one must also ask why does the rate of growth fluctuate for the same country over time?

The second question is much easier to answer than the first in the case of Third-World countries (though not for the capitalist or socialist world). Fluctuations are caused by weather, and thus harvests, on the one side, and by fluctuations in commodity prices on the other. If these two factors are favourable, then possibilities arise that themselves may lead to accelerated development.

We noted above that the World Bank had attributed to Kenya a growth rate of 2.6 per cent per year in the seventies, and to Tanzania 0.8 per cent. In Tanzania banking, insurance, the import-export trade and the major manufacturing enterprises were nationalised (or partly nationalised) in 1967. Minimum wages were raised, jobs legally secured and joint-consultation instituted. Farmers' houses had been widely dispersed until, first voluntarily, then by law, *ujamaa* (socialist or communal) villages were established. Salaries were severely limited, no one in the government allowed to have more than one paid job or to own a second house for purposes of letting. (See Guy Routh, 'Development Paths in Tanzania', in Damachi, *Development Paths in Africa and China*.)

It is not surprising, then, that wealth, where it exists, is much more conspicuous in Kenya than Tanzania. Kenya has a flourishing professional/entrepreneural class, its towns have supermarkets, their streets are thronged with cars. Tanzania, by contrast, presents a picture of dilapidation. If I were rich, I would choose to live in Kenya; if I were poor, in Tanzania.

One might hope that one could compare the level of achievement of each country by comparing the assessments in Damachi, op. cit. (1976) with those in Bienefeld and Godfrey, *Struggle for Development* (1982). (Martin Godfrey, 'Kenya: African Capitalism or Simple Dependency?' and Manfred Bienefeld, 'Tanzania: Model or Anti-model?' in the latter volume.)

Godfrey notes increasing poverty for the poorest sectors in Kenya (ibid. p. 286), and populist moves by President Moi, who came to power in 1978. Otherwise, he cites the writings of other analysts who differ from one another in their interpretations. R. Kaplinsky found that 'local capitalists already tend to shift their surplus abroad and are more guilty of transfer pricing than are foreign subsidiaries. If the 1980s see Kenyan dynamism running out of steam, against a background of international recession and labour-saving technical change, this tendency will become even stronger.' (Ibid. p. 289.) Colin Leys seeks an alternative pattern that might accelerate the expansion of productive forces, without undermining the living standards of the masses, but finds it difficult to believe that there is such an alternative. Godfrey leaves this for the future to decide.

Bienefeld finds even greater differences of interpretation amongst those assessing Tanzanian achievements. Balance-of-payments deficits have caused acute difficulties. 'In the context of just such a situation of external imbalance political forces in Tanzania seeking a fundamental policy change have now grown very strong. With large sections of the bureaucracy disillusioned and antagonized; with much of the population no longer mobilized, either politically within the Party, or ideologically; with substantial sections of the left wing vying with the right as to who can paint a starker picture of internally generated unmitigated failure....' (Ibid. p. 315.) Despite all this, perhaps indicating that the whole African predicament is gloomy, Bienefeld finds that, 'To date Tanzania's strategy has, under difficult circumstances, produced a pattern of economic and social development which compares favourably with most other African economies, and which is in many respects better placed to meet the challenges of the 1980s, so that there is a clear case for continued critical but constructive support of that strategy....' (Ibid. p. 313.)

Problems of a different sort are involved in comparing and explaining the achievements of North and South Korea. Here are two countries whose development strategies have been brilliantly successful, and have yet been in stark contrast to one another. The North is communist, the South capitalist; the North trades with China and the Soviet Union, the South with the United States and Japan; the North has pursued autarky, the South export-led growth.

The products of South Korea may be inspected in the clothing and electronic shops of Europe and America; they have succeeded, too, in shipbuilding, mechanical, chemical and civil engineering. By the 1970s North Korea was producing large power presses, heavy trucks, tractors, bulldozers, electric and diesel locomotives, 5000-ton ships and precision machines, and complete sets of plant equipment for power stations, metallurgical and chemical factories. (Ibid. p. 345.)

12.6 SECRETS OF SUCCESS?

There may be no formula for success, but can we at least discern some of the underlying causes behind the very different fortunes of different countries? I have made reference to the negative characteristics to which some people fall prey when they get access to wealth and power: the effect of greed, cruelty and corruption is to disrupt productive processes as well as injure the quality of life. Islamic law prohibits alcoholic drink, but in non-Islamic Africa drunkenness is a serious problem. It is noteworthy, and gives hope for the future, that amongst the first targets of the Soweto school-children were the municipal beerhalls. The children are wiser than the parents. It gives some hope, too, that the poor have few illusions about the rich. They are better informed, or at least more informative, about the defects of a country than those who are doing well out of it.

National characteristics are not quantifiable, so that economists have been inclined to ignore them in favour of variables that are. Harvey Leibenstein is to be applauded for his attempt to correct economic theories for their omission of non-economic factors. Multiple correlation explains some of the change in a dependent variable by the movements of independent variables, but there is generally an unexplained residual. In productive processes Leibenstein calls this residual 'X-efficiency'. One must seek non-economic causes for the extraordinary economic successes of the Japanese. When, as a young man, Laurens van der Post visited Japan in 1926, he observed 'the profound passion of commitment of the totality of the person to his allotted task is natural to the Japanese'. (*Yet Being Someone Other*, London: The Hogarth Press, 1982, p. 234.) In *British Factory–Japanese Factory* (London: Allen & Unwin, 1973) Ronald Dore studies behavioural modes in the 'organization-orientated' productive system of Japan, towards which, he suggests, the British 'market-orientated' system is evolving.

Tony Mitchell in his chapter on South Korea (in Bienefeld and Godfrey's book) describes activities that suggest great enterprise and an egalitarian ethos. He does not devote much space to motivation, but remarks that 'the whole economic structure is based heavily on central direction which the various ministries will not give up easily ...' and adds, 'to the Korean administrator, unconscious heir to 500 years of neo-confucianism, market forces look like anarchy in which no faith should beplaced'. He also asks, 'How could a docile labour force evolve in a society without neo-confucian traditions?' (Ibid. pp. 213–14.)

In the same volume Gordon White emphasises the importance in North Korea of the concept of *juche* (self-reliance). The Korean Workers' Party leadership has succeeded in mobilising the general population for the national goals of independence and economic development. 'It is important to note the unprecedented degree of mass involvement in political organizations ...; the ideological appeal of *juche* as an expression of both national and individual aspirations; "mass line" leadership theory and practice; and the distinctive role of Kim Il-song as the supreme leader and national symbol'. As the Party's contributions to rapid development Gordon White lists the use of the Korean Han'gul writing instead of Chinese characters to improve literacy, free and well-equipped medical system, compulsory technical education up to and including senior high school, the rapid increase of technicians and others with tertiary qualifications, 'and a stress on education as a lifetime task for the individual, not merely as a transient stage of one's youth'. (Bienefeld and Godfrey, *Struggle for Development*, p. 341.)

Oil-wealth is not a substitute for morality, incorruptibility and dedication. I am not suggesting that these are the only requirements. Development is a matter of hard and patient work sustained over many years, and the maintenance of this state is as much a political as an economic matter.

12.7 AID

There are some problems of poverty that only wealth can cure. Malnutrition in infancy may have a permanent effect on physical and mental development; lack of hygiene spreads debilitating diseases that impair the ability to work; lower birth-rates are associated with higher standards of living. Considerations of this kind led John Stuart Mill in the middle of last century to suggest a doubling of wages as a cure for poverty.

The Brandt Report, with its 1983 addendum (*Common Crisis*) presents a full and well-reasoned programme in terms of which the industrialised world can contribute, in part by removing restrictions on trade, in part by increased aid. The aid-lobby in the United States and other countries is confronted by an anti-aid lobby that has gathered strength from the failures of the past. This comes at a time when the OPEC countries, who provide about a quarter of all aid, are themselves in financial difficulties. In 1981 they contributed 1.46 per cent of their GNP in public aid to the third world, the European Community and its Member States 0.53 per cent, Japan 0.28 per cent, the United States 0.20 per cent and the USSR and Eastern Bloc 0.14. (*The Community and Developing Countries, European File*, 3/83, Feb. 1983, p. 9.) The target has been raised to 0.7 per cent, and this the EEC Commission hopes to achieve and, over the next ten years, increase to 1.0 per cent. The very smallness of these contributions gives hope in so far as it indicates the great scope for improvement. But the knowledge that aid has been misapplied prompts the Commission, with great delicacy, to suggest some changes:

> to be truly effective such a concentration on the well-springs of development must be linked to a change of method. The Community, while seeking to increase the quantity of its aid, should not ignore ways of improving its quality. To this end, the Community must seek a new form of political dialogue with Third World Leaders. This dialogue must go beyond mere haggling and technical discussions of

which projects to finance. It must lead to a genuine development 'contract' between rich and poor countries. This is not a question of attaching conditions to aid. Third World governments have a sovereign right to determine their own priorities. It is a question of achieving more coherence between external aid efforts and internal policies.   (Ibid. p. 6.)

It is noteworthy that the UN Conference on Trade and Development (UNCTAD) has been trying for twenty years to promote the export of manufactures from the Third World, with indifferent results, while its Integrated Programme for Commodities (IPC) has failed to stabilise the prices of commodities at satisfactory levels. The EEC, by contrast, through the Lomé Convention has accorded duty-free entry to almost all the products of sixty African, Caribbean and Pacific (ACP) countries.

I am aware that this chapter has presented a somewhat gloomy picture of the Third World, where wealth is squandered while children go hungry to sleep. As you will know if you have travelled in Third World countries, they are a mixture of appalling squalor and immense vitality. One cause for encouragement amidst the gloom is the improvement in understanding that has revealed itself in what is now called 'development studies' rather than 'development economics'. There has been a decline in the unreal assumptions, premature theories and naïve models made complex by mathematical superstructures. There cannot now be many institutes or university departments concerned with these studies that still impose disciplinary blinkers, that do not identify the problems by empirical research, and who do not call on all the social sciences to contribute to solutions.

Conclusion

In this book I have invited you to follow the path of history into the modern world, with stops amongst the hunter-gatherers, herdsmen and cultivators, through slave-owning kingdoms and republics and the feudal system, to the despotisms by which European States were unified, and the great explorations from which capitalism was born, by which the despots were replaced by the bourgeois democracies that dominate the world of today.

Why this long prelude when it is the world of today that we wish to understand? Because we cannot understand any world, modern or otherwise, unless we understand the nature of the people who have created it, who day by day recreate it, and who have been struggling, over the millennia, to perfect it.

It has been mankind's earnest wish to become master of their destiny. The price of Eden was to ask no questions and seek no answers, and it was an impossible price to pay. So our ancestors moved to many countries and tried out many sorts of society. They accumulated knowledge, at first imperceptibly, then less slowly. The more knowledge they had, the faster it grew despite all that was done to fossilise it. Today scientific knowledge is mass-produced in great research establishments, though for many different motives: for money to beat competitors to a new drug or video or car, for the easing of pain and the preservation of human life, or the creation of pain and the destruction of human life.

Thus it becomes important that we cultivate a capacity to step outside our society so that we may understand its dynamics. One way of stepping outside it is to observe other societies of previous epochs, in which people also survived and earned their living.

One of the features of pre-capitalist societies was the integration of work and social life, in which music and dancing, religion and magic were essential parts. Under industrial capitalism the link between working life and social life is the cash nexus, but now attempts are being made to reintegrate work and social life so that work is rehumanised. Japanese society was held to be marked by survivals of the past; now it is being reexamined as a possible model for the future.

Conclusion

Chapters 3 and 4 were devoted to the origins of capitalism and the industrial explosion that followed it. Affluence, undreamt-of in previous epochs, has engulfed some countries of the world, but much of the world has remained embedded in its pre-capitalist, pre-industrial mode, while another part has opted out of capitalism and is experimenting with various forms of socialism. There are important interconnexions between all these countries; what happens in one part has repercussions in others. If we are to understand capitalist economies, we must see them in their world setting.

But we must also subdivide them, not into discrete departments, but by facets or viewpoints, whose interactions we may then observe. Having examined the physiology of the system in Chapter 5, we then turn to the decision-making unit of the productive system: the firm, the dominant form of which is the giant, transnational corporation. They share common characteristics, but in important respects each of them is different. Hence case studies are essential, for we must learn to distinguish the similarities from the differences. There is a whole branch of learning – organisation studies or organisation theory – that deals with this subject.

Then we look at the same phenomena but with a change of aspect: those who work in firms, the nature of work, its design and its evaluation. The links between worker and job, job and household and society, appear to be more immediate and more intricate than the 'cash nexus' had led us to believe. There is a great deal of relevant material now available, based on empirical research, for outside economics departments, labour and industrial relations studies have forged ahead.

In Chapter 8 we consider the material needs of men and women and how, having obtained their income, they proceed to satisfy them. In orthodox economics consumers are also maximisers, though what it is they maximise we are no longer told. Yet there is really no way of evaluating a system unless we know what motivates people in their consumer role, and how worthwhile their satisfactions have turned out to be. These studies are of necessity an alliance between economics and psychology, long since pioneered by George Katona.

Chapter 9 takes another facet: the money that is pumped into the banking system and pumped out again, in part energising the productive system, in part leading a life of its own in a realm of finance and speculation that is generally esoteric and sometimes lurid. Here again the case studies give indispensable insights into the nature of the institutions and their modus operandi.

Of course governments are deeply involved in the economic activities of their countries and in economic relations between countries. In democracies, parties with different economic policies alternate: the public sector may expand or contract, welfare be increased or reduced. But in capitalist societies decision-making is decentralised into dozens of giant firms and thousands of little ones, so that the capacity of governments to manage economies is minimal and responses to government measures often perverse.

Chapters 11 and 12 are concerned with countries most of which have economic systems markedly different from the capitalist democracies of the OECD. Some in the Third World have made their breakthrough and qualify for classification amongst the industrialised countries of the world; others are desperately experimenting; many are in the grip of dictators or military juntas. Ten years ago job-creation was regarded as their peculiar problem, second only to nutrition. Now job-creation has become a problem for OECD countries too.

Fortunately for the capitalist democracies, their economic systems are flexible enough for experiment. We are far away from the days when the firm was managed by the man who owned it. Nowadays, pension and insurance societies, unit trusts and mutual funds have a preponderance of power, and the private investor, however wealthy he may be, has not much say in the operation of business enterprises. They are ruled, instead, by professional managers whose salaries are far more important sources of income than their dividends.

Some of the largest enterprises have no private shareholders at all. They were drawn, by various means, into the public sector: Renault and the major banks in France, the Institute for Industrial Reconstruction (IRI) in Italy. British Leyland still have some private shareholders (I am one), but they have been overwhelmed by the massive government share. For a number of years after the Second World War, Volkswagen in Germany flourished with no owners at all, then was divided amongst so many that each is powerless.

In Switzerland, that redoubt of private property and free enterprise, we find one of the most fascinating and successful experiments in co-operation and co-ownership: the multiple grocery store, Migros, that, forty years ago, was given by its owner to the customers. Gottlieb Duttweiler returned to Switzerland in the 1930s determined to help his fellow countrymen survive the depression by providing them with good-quality food at 'semi-wholesale' prices. This he did against the opposition of powerful retailing interests, backed by local authorities. When his warehouses were prohibited from selling milk, he gave it away until the prohibition was revoked. He combated drunkenness by offering subsidised fruit-juices instead of wine or spirits.

Migros now has twelve regional co-operative societies, linked in a federation. It members participate vigorously in its affairs; the proceedings of its conferences are of intellectual interest, with moral issues ranking high – no foods grown with the use of injurious chemicals; the substitution of indestructible plastic containers by sorts that will disintegrate by natural process. Their adult-education and youth programmes, libraries and cultural centres flourish. Their trading activities flourish too and have spread to co-operative housing, petrol stations, *bureaux de change*, restaurants. It is a sound business that gives its members a great deal of fun.

Migros is a consumers' co-operative. The Mondragon enterprises, in the Basque country of Spain, are producers' co-operatives. In the civil war the Basques had been staunchly republican. After Franco came to power they suffered from government discrimination and neglect. A Jesuit priest, Father Jose Maria Arismendiarrieta, set about devising ways by which they could help themselves. The first Mondragon cooperative enterprise was established in 1956, after a long period of planning, training and preparation. In 1982 there were 91 industrial co-operatives, with another 60 or 70 institutions including banking, research, management consultancy, agriculture, housing and education. Their elegant buildings stand on the hills of Mondragon; their factories are spread over the surrounding country.

The Ularco group (the largest of the constituents) includes co-ops employing over 6000 people. 'The core of the group is the original 23-man workshop, Ulgor, which now employs 2780. Ulgor is the Spanish market leader in washing machines, cookers, dish-washers and fridges under the Fagor trademark.' (David Gardner in the *Financial Times*, 10 June 1982.) Peter Hildrew wrote in *The Guardian* (1 Dec. 1981):

> The cooperative principle pops up in every facet of Mondragon life. The bank itself is a co-op, the members being its staff and the other co-ops it finances. The schools are run by an education co-op, teenagers can work their way through college by part-time manufacturing work at a student co-op, linked to courses at the co-op polytechnic. There is a catering and cleaning co-op, a consumer co-op embracing 105,000 families, a research and development co-op and numerous housing co-ops. Cooperators are treated as self-employed, and so they have their own social security and pensions co-op.

Some of the enterprises have suffered from the depression of the early 1980s. Those that need financial help are given it by the bank and the others. The management consultants look for ways to better their performance. The workers have granted themselves very moderate increases in pay. Each worker is also part-owner and must, on entry, contribute the equivalent of almost £3000 to the capital of the enterprise (but he can borrow from the Co-operative bank and repay in instalments).

The first 10 per cent of profits goes into an educational and social fund, a minimum of 20 per cent is added to reserves and the remainder is credited to the worker's stake in the enterprise, in proportion to his or her wages. When workers retire they may withdraw their capital. New co-ops may be formed by non-members with a good idea and a will to work together, with advice and financial aid from the organisation.

The Basques have a strong sense of national identity. They are united by language, culture and religion: these were essential ingredients for the success of their venture. But the point that I am making is that people may have more latitude than at first appears to experiment with new forms of ownership and control, a latitude that will have to be exercised if we are not to remain helpless victims of economic instability, inflation and unemployment.

But, you may object, this book is too far-ranging. Does an *economist* have to know all this? Why can we not be left to our ordinary courses and textbooks, where we are taught a dozen or so inapplicable but simple economic models, the refutations of which the texts and teachers also candidly present? This, after all, is a straightforward way of getting an economics degree. We can then get jobs teaching it to future generations of students, or go into banking, industry or government where we can quite rapidly forget it all and learn on the job how the real world works.

These are powerful arguments and, if that is really what you want I would no sooner try to discourage you than I would try to rob someone of his or her religion. My aim has been to show that there is an alternative world-view or paradigm in terms of which the puzzles of economic behaviour become more intelligible. And it is presented, too, as an attempt to turn economics into an operational discipline that may be applied to the solution of economic problems, in which respect I can do no better than quote Sismondi's judgement of 1819: 'This has never been more necessary than at the present time when business has been afflicted by a universal langour, when all industrial arts are in distress and, at least in some countries, agriculture itself seems to be menaced.'

Index

Aaronovitch, Sam 65
Abbot, Wilbur Cortes 28
Abegglen, James C. 71
Adams, Brooks 47
advertising 197–201
African societies 9–10
Agnelli, Giovanni 75
Alem, André 34
Allende, Salvadore 98
American Telephone and Telegraph Company 95
Anderson, Jack 97–8
Andrews, Kenneth R. 12
Andrews, P. W. S. 83
Anglo-American Corporation 52
Anti-Trust Act 62, 100
Aquinas, St. Thomas 22
Arismendiarrieta, Fr Jose Maria 307
Aristotle 17
arms, sales of 3
Arnold, Sir Edwin 119
Aryans 15
Asia Minor 9
asset-stripping 108–9, 232
Athens 17
Austin, M. M. 11, 16–17
Avis 95–6, 97, 99
Azurare, Gomes Eannes de 27

Babeuf, François Noel 35
Bakhshi 19
balance of payments 245–6
balance-sheet 63
Bamfield, J. A. N. 197
banking 31, 211–18
Bank of England 218, 233
Barnet, Richard J. 106
barrel, oil 89, 244
Basham, A. L. 16
Bastiat, Frédéric 172
Baumol, W. J. 82
Beazley, Charles Raymond 27
Behn, Sosthenes 95, 98
Beit, Alfred 50–1

Bell, Daniel ix
Bengal, conquest of 46–7
Bentham, Jeremy 164
Berkeley, Bishop George 199–200
Berle, Adolf A. 76, 77, 104
Bessemer, Sir Henry 38
Béteille, André 16
Beveridge, William H. 255, 267
Bhagavadgita 118–19
Bienefeld, Manfred 291, 299–301
bills of exchange 31
binocular vision 5
birth-spacing 8
Bismarck, Otto von 254
Black Death, bubonic plague 25–8
black economy 67
Blackaby, Frank T. 269
Bloch, Marc 19–20
Boer Republics 49–50
Bobongiari, Dino 22
Boisguillebert, Pierre le Pesant 36, 132, 180
booms *see* trade cycle
Boulding, Kenneth 165
Boulton, Matthew 37
bounded rationality 79, 104
Bourbons 34
bourgeoisie 34–7, 112
Brandt Commission 2, 3, 286–7, 302–3
Brown, Lester R. 282–3
Brown, W. A. 144
Brummer, Alex 111
Buddha 14
bureaucracy 76–7, 113–14
Burnett, John 210
Bushmen 6
business cycle *see* trade cycle

Cairnes, J. E. 165
Cammack, Diana 50–1
Campbell, R. H. 152, 171
Canaan 15
Cape of Good Hope 25

309

Index

Cantillon, Richard 35, 139–40, 163, 171
capital 55, 56
 consumption 55, 58
capitalism 24, 25
car prices 202
Carlbach, Julius 208
Carnegie, Andrew 85–7, 88, 94
Cartier, Jacques 25
cash and carry 194
castes 16
Cathay 19
Cave, Martin 271, 279–81
Caxton, William 28
Cayman Islands 220
central banks 217–18
Ceuta, capture by Portuguese 25
Ch'ien, Sse 13–14
Charles I 36
Chile 97–8
Chinese 13
 Opium War 47–8
Christianity 20, 21
Christians 13
Church 21, 26
 Catholic 20, 28–9
chrysomilid beetles 8
Cipolla, Carlo M. 20, 21
Civil War 35–6
Clark, John Bates 153
Clay, Henry 220–1
Clayton Act 62
Clean Air Act 261
Clovis 20
Cobbett, William 44
Cohen, C. D. 269
Cole, Charles Woolsey 35
Cole, W. A. 39, 40, 52
collective bargaining 158–62
Collins, Wilkie 121
Colonial Development and Welfare Act 289
Columbus, Christopher 25
Combination Acts 253
Committee on Industry and Trade 265
commodity prices 242–4
Companies Act 63
concentration 64–6
conditioned reflex 198
Confucius 13–14
conglomerates 64, 95, 98, 107
Congo 44–5, 48–9, 52–3
Cooper, Charles 282
Cornfeld, Bernard 226–30
Cornford, F. M. 13, 17, 131

Consolidated Gold Fields 52
Constantine 18
Constantinople 18, 25
consumer associations 203–6, 257–8
 behaviour 178–83, 257
 expenditure 41
 protection 257–62
consumption 54, 178–83
 conspicuous 171, 176
correlation 155
cost of living 210–11
 see also price index
cost push 238–9
costs 58
Cotton, Sir Henry 47
Counter Information Services 224–5, 242, 245
Crassus 18
Crises 31
 see also trade cycle
Cromwell, Oliver 36
Crusades 26
cultures, hand-axe 5
cuneiform 4
custom and practice 157–8
Cyert, Richard M. 80

Daire, Eugene 132
Damachi, Ukandi G. 292, 294, 295, 299
Dark Ages 26
Daubigny, J. P. 149
Davidson, Basil 10
Davis, Dorothy 184
Dawson, John A. 186
De Beers 51, 52
Deane, Phyllis 39, 40, 52, 126–7
debt, of poor to rich countries 2
deflation 236
demand pull 238–9
Denison, E. F. 290
depression see also trade cycle
Dewhurst 109
Diaz, Bartholomew 25
Dietrich, Noah 92
differentials 147–50
discretionary expenditure 60, 179–81, 207
Distribution of Income and Wealth, Royal Commission on 149–50, 152, 162–3
distributive trade 56
division of labour 131–2
Doeringer, Peter B. 163
domestication of animals 11
double-entry 68–9

Douty, H. M. 163
Dow, J. C. R. 269, 271
Drake, Francis 25, 29, 30, 31
Dubos, René 2
Duff, Euan 116-7
Duignan, Peter 49
Dunlop, John T. 158
Dutt, R. Palme 46

East India Companies 24, 26, 29, 31, 44, 46-7, 51, 52, 63
Eastern Empire 18
Economic Man 1, 9
Edgeworth, Francis Ysidro 175
Eels, Richard 106
Egypt 10, 15
Ehrenberg, A. S. C. 183
Einzig, Paul 239, 249, 250
elasticity 167
Eldridge, C. C. 53
Elkan, Walter 290
employers 123
employment of children 42-3
Engels, Friedrich 41, 272-3
Environmental Quality, Council on 3
Environmental Protection Agency 261
Equal Pay Act 148-9
evolution 4
exploitation 11

Factories Acts 253
   Inquiry Commission of 1832 41
Fagan, Brian M. 9
farming, sedentary 11
Federal Trade Commission 259-60
Feinstein, Charles H. 40, 129
Ferguson, Wallace K. 26
Ferry, John William 184
Ferris, Paul 215, 223, 225
feudal system 19-23
fiat 75
Fisher, Mel 28
Fogarty, Michael 23
Fogg, Phileas 2
Food and Drug Administration 259-60
Frank, Tenney 18
Frankel, S. Herbert 51
Frazer, Sir James George 12
Freeman, Christopher 282
French Revolution 36
Freud, Sigmund 120
Frick, H. C. 86-7
Fried, Albert 272
Friedman, Milton 237-8, 249
Friedmann, Georges 117, 120, 132

Frommel, S. N. 264

Galbraith, John Kenneth 77, 79, 175-8, 194, 255, 257-8
Galenson, Walter 158
Gama, Vasco da 25
Gann, L. H. 49
Gardner, David 307
GATT 267
Geneen, Harold Sydney 95-9, 103
General Motors 205
Gestalt psychology 183
Getty, J. Paul 88-92, 94
Gibbon, Edward 21
Gibbons, Henry de Beltgens 37-8, 52
Gibbs, James L. 10
Gilbert, Milton 293
Gilbreth, Frank and Lillian 138
Gill, Jack 107
Gladstone, William Ewart 48
Godfrey, Martin 291, 299-301
Goodman, George J. W. 220, 224
Gordon, Robert Aaron 72-3
Gosplan 275, 276-9
Gower, L. C. B. 264
Grade, Lew 107-8
Granada, recapture of 25
Granger, Clive W. J. 222-3
Gray, John 15
Greece, Ancient 11, 16-18
Green, Reginald H. 288
Griffin, C. E. 82
Grose, Daphne 204
gross domestic product 41, 286-7, 288, 293
gross national product, 286-7, 288, 293
Grousset, René 26
guilds 20
Guinea, conquest of 27
Gutenberg, Johann 25, 28

Habsburgs 34
Hammond, J. L. and Barbara 41-2
Hare, Paul 271, 279-81
Hargreaves, James 37
Haskins, J. S. 204
Haw Par 232-4
Hawkins, Sir John 29, 30
Heilbroner, Robert L. 65, 111
Hell's Angels 92
Henry VIII 25
Henry the Navigator 25, 27
herdsmen and cultivators 9
Herodotus 18
Hess, Moses 208

Hildrew, Peter 307
Hobson, J. A. 45-6, 53
Hodgson, Godfrey 226-30
Holmes a'Court, Robert 107
Holt, Edgar 47, 48
Homestead strike 86-7
hominids 4, 5, 6
homo erectus 5
homo sapiens 4, 6
Hoover, Herbert 265-6, 274
Hopkins, Sheila V. 157
household surveys 133
Howard, Philip 112
Hughes, Howard Robard 92-4
   Aircraft Corporation 93, 94
   Tool Company 92-3
Huguenots 29-30
Human Environment, UN Conference on 2
Hume, David 24
hunters and gatherers 5-9
Hutchings, Raymond 274-5
Hyman, Richard 143, 159

Ice Age 9
import-substitution 296
incentive systems 142-4
income 55
   and expenditure account 63
incremental capital-output ratios 289-90
India, Ancient 15-16
industrial classification 126-31
   engineering 138
   fluctuations *see* trade cycle
   production, index of 127-9
   Revolution 37-44
   rise in real incomes from 40-4
inflation 23, 234-50
Inglis, Brian 41
institutional shareholders 104-5
insurance companies 218-19
interest 55, 245-6
interlocking directorates 62, 64
internal labour markets 162-3
International Business Machines 99-102
International Telephone and Telegraph Company 94-9, 105, 108
investments 55, 60
   private foreign 3
Investors Overseas Services 226-30
Iron Age 9
irrigation 15
Islam 20

Israel, Ancient 15
Italy 18

Jaffé, William 153
Jahoda, Marie 282
James II 36
Jameson, Dr Leander Starr 49-50, 51
Jardine, Matheson 47, 52
Jefferys, James B. 184
Jenghiz Khan 18
Jesus 14, 27
Jevons, W. Stanley 115-16, 154
Jews 20
job evaluation 139-42
   at Lever Brothers 140-1
   grading 142
John Lewis Partnership 185
Johnson, Samuel 268
joint-stock companies 29, 32, 69
just price 22, 208, 230
just wage, 23, 208, 230

Kahn, Richard 240
Kalahari 6
Kaplinsky, Rafael 299
Kassarjian, Harold H. 179, 183
Katona, George 82, 178-82, 305
Kautilya 16
Kay, John 37
Keats, John 92
Kenya, development in 298-300
Kerr, Clark 154, 155, 157-8, 163
Keynes, John Maynard 58, 61, 169, 180, 182, 212
   Drake's booty 31
   involuntary unemployment 153
   on stock market 221-2, 224
Kim, Il-song 301
Knightly, Phillip 109
Korea, development in 300-2
Kosambi, D. D. 14-15
Kravis, I. B 293
Kristol, Irving ix
Kruger, President Paul 50-1
Krushchev, Nikita 267
Kublai Khan 18-19, 26
Kuic, Vukan 115

labour theory of value 115
laissez-faire 41, 44, 112, 251
Lamb, Geoff 296
landlords 24
Lanning, Greg 52
Lassalle, Ferdinand 254

Index

Latham, Ronald 18
Law, John 32
Lazards 15, 96
Le Godd, Jacques 21
Leaky, L. S. B. 5, 6, 9
Lee, Richard Borshay 6, 8
Lee, William 37
Leibenstein, Harvey 300-1
Lekachman, Robert 221
Lenin, V. I. 46, 53, 274, 288
Leontief, Wassily 154-5
Leopold II 48-9, 52
Lesley, Cliffe 154
Lester, R. A. 154, 155, 157
Lewin, Kurt 183
Lewin, Roger 6, 9
Lewis, Ray 73
Leys, Colin 299
limited liability 56, 63-4
Lipton, Michael 287-8
Livesey, Frank 194
Llewellyn, David T. 217
Locke, John 169
Loebl, Eugen 115, 281
Logan, J. P. 82
Lomé Convention 303
Lonrho 107
Louis XIV 35
Luther, Martin 25, 28, 29

McAnally, Patrick 185, 188-9
McCarry, Charles 205
Macaulay, Lord 48
McCone, John 98
McCormick, B. J. 155
McCulloch, J. R. 169
Machiavelli, Niccolo 85
Mackay, Donald 163
McLaren, Richard 97
McLellan, David 119
Magellan, Ferdinand 25
magic 11, 12
Magnuson, Warren G. 258-9
Major, John 265-6
Majumdar, R. C. 16
Malibu 91, 92
Malthus, Thomas Robert 168, 169
managers, origins and education 71-4
Mandeville, Bernard de 169
Mangold, Tom 258
manorial system *see* feudal system
Mantoux, Paul 37
Mao Tse-tung 119
Maquet, Jacques 10

marginal productivity 153
 utility 175
markets, early 11
Marks & Spencer 193-5
Marquand, John P. 75
Marsden, David 162-3
Marsden, Dennis 116-17
Marshall, Alfred 153, 154, 167, 188, 221
Marx, Karl 24, 46, 119, 132, 208
 Marxism 103
Matthew, St. 171
Mayer, Martin 200
Mayhew, Kenneth 163
Means, Gardner C. 76, 77, 104
Meinhardt, P. 264
merchants 21, 24, 26, 27
merit rating 144
Mesopotamia 4, 9, 11, 14
Metal Age 5
methodology 2
Mexico, capture of 25
Middle Ages 20, 21
 see also feudal system
Migros 197, 306-7
Miles, Raymond E. 83-4
Mill, James 46
Mill, John Stuart 58-9, 61, 70, 76-7, 302
Miller, Walter 132
Milner, Sir Alfred 50
Ming dynasty 25
Mintz, Morton 111
Mississippi Company 32
Mitchell, B. R. 39, 126-7, 252-3
Mitchell, Jeremy 204
Mitchell, John 97
Mitchell, R. L. 138
Mitchell, Tony 301
Mogul, Mongol Empire 18-19, 25, 26, 28
Mohammed, President 294
Mohomet 19
Mondragon 307-8
Mongols 18
Mongongo plant 8
money 58
 fiat 19
 love of 24
 supply of 247-9
More, Sir Thomas 45-6
Morel, E. D. 45, 48-9
Morgan, E. Victor 209
Morgenstern, Oskar 222-3
Morgan, J. Pierpont 87

Moslems 13
Mueller, Marti 52
Müller, Ronald E. 106
multinational corporations 53, 98, 103–7, 109
mutual funds 227–8

Nader, Ralph 205
National Cash Register 99–100
national development corporations 296
natural selection 6
Neale, A. D. 62
Neanderthal Man 5
Netherlands, independence of 26
Nevins, Allan 88
Newcomen, Thomas 37
Newcomer, Mabel 71–2
Newman, W. H. 82
Nixon, President 97
North, Sir Dudley 169
Nove, Alec 273–81
Nozick, A. 296

occupational classification 131–7
OECD 123–4, 267, 268
Office of Fair Trading 260
oil 244–5
Olduvai Gorge 5
OPEC 244–5, 302
Opium War 47–8, 52
organisation theory 75–85
Orr, Sir David 69
Osiris 11, 12
Ottoman Turks 27
  Empire 28
output per head 41
overheads 58
overproduction 58
Owen, Robert 44
Owen Smith, Eric 155

Pacioli, Luca 69
Packard, Vance 200–1
Page, Bruce 226–30
Page, Kevin 230
paired comparisons 142
Pakenham, Thomas 50–1
Palmerston, Lord 48
parasites, class of 11
Parry, J. H. 25, 27
pastoralists 10
participation rates 123–5
pattern bargaining 160
Patterson, John Henry 99–100
Paul, Eden and Cedar 26

Paul, Lewis 37
Paul, St. 24, 207–8
Pavitt, Keith 282
Pavlov, Ivan Petrovitch 198
pay structure and dispersion 145–52
payment by results 142–4
pension funds 218–19
perfect competition 164–5, 257
Persia 19
Petty, Sir William 238, 251
Phelps Brown, Sir Henry 149, 156, 157
Phillips curve 154
Physiocrats 251
pictograph 4
Pigou, A. C. 178
Pilgrim Fathers 26
Pindar 13
Piore, Michael J. 162–3
Pires, Thomá 25
Pizarro, Francisco 25
Place, Francis 44
Plato 12–13, 17, 131
Polo, Marco 18–19
Pompey 18
Pope, Maurice 17
population 8, 10, 20, 34, 252–3, 285–7
Post, Laurens van der 6, 7, 301
Prais, S. J. 65
Prawdin, Michael 26
prehensile thumb 5
Prestage, Edgar 27
price index 210, 235
priesthood 12, 16, 21
primary products 56
printing 28
Priouret, Roger 74
production 55
profit 58, 61, 68, 246–7
  maximisation 79, 103
profit and loss account 63
Protestantism 29
Public Citizen 205
purchasing power of currencies 293
Pyatt, F. G. 183

quantity theory of money 237–9

Radcliffe Committee 217, 218, 271
Ramos, Alberto Cuerreiro 84–5
Rand Mines 51
ratchet effect 172
rationality, instrumental and substantive 84–5
Raw, Charles 226–30
Rayfield, Joan 10

Reddaway, W. B.   155
Rees, Goronwy   194–5
Reformation   28–9
Rehoboam   15
religion   11–14, 16, 19–23
Renaissance   28
Renourd, Yves   27
research and development   282–3
restrictive practices   138–9
Rhodes, Cecil John   49–50, 51
Riches, E. J.   138
riverine states   14
RKO   93–4
Roberts, D. R.   82
Robertson, James   156
Robertson, Thomas S.   179, 183
Rockefeller, John Davidson   87–8, 94
Rodgers, William   99–102
Rohatyn, Felix   95, 97
Roman Empire   18, 19, 21, 26
Roosevelt, Franklin Delano   90, 102, 220, 265–6
Ross, Alexander   215–16
Rotwein, Eugène   24
roustabout   89
Rowland, Tiny   107
Runciman, W. G.   77
Ruskin, John   45
Russell, J. C.   20

Sadler, Michael Thomas   44
Sahara   10
Sampson, Anthony   91–2, 94–9, 245
Samuelson, Paul A.   176, 224
San   6
Sanders, Ronald   273
Santa Margarita   28
satisficing   79
Saunders, Christopher   162–3
saving   181–2
Sawyer, Malcolm   65
Sayers, Dorothy   200
Scarborough, John   17, 18
Schaffer, Bernard   296
scientific management   83–4, 138
Scott, William Robert   31–2
secondary industry   56
Securities and Exchange Commission   229, 230–2, 262–3
Seidman, Ann   288
self-employed   123
selling short   231
Sen, Benoy Chandra   16
Sesostris   15

Seven Sisters   90, 92
sex   4
Shaftesbury, Lord   44
Sherman, John   62
Silvestre, J. J.   149
Simon, Herbert A.   78–80, 83, 85, 104, 114
Simon, Yves   115
Sintra, Pedroda   25
Sismondi, Simonde de   308
Sinuhe   15
Skinner, A. S.   152, 171
Slade, Ruth   48
Slater, Jim   232–4
slavery   17–18, 25, 42, 44
   origin of   11
slumps   *see* trade cycle
slush-money   111
Smith, Adam   38, 58, 119, 163, 171, 253
   conspiracy to raise prices   62
   human mind   152
   immobility of labour   153
   indeterminacy of wages   145
   indolent careless application   137
   job evaluation   140
   monopolising spirit   110
   public expenditure   251–2
   rigidity of wages   157
   saving and consumption   168
Smith, Robert S.   158
Snow, Charles C.   83–4
social security   19, 252–7
Société Générale   52
socio-economic groups   134–7
socio-technical systems   80
Sofer, Cyril   73
Solomon, King   15
Sombart, Werner   68–9
South Sea Bubble   32
South-West Africa   6, 7
Spanish Armada   26
Sparta   16–17
species   4, 5
Springbett, David   2
stagflation   235, 236
Stalin, Joseph   275, 276
Stakhanov, Aleksei   138
Standard Oil   62–3, 87–8
Standard Telephones and Cables   95
Stanley, Sir Henry Morton   44
Starbuck, W. H.   81–3, 104
Stark, W.   164
steam-engine   37–8
   ships   38

Stephenson, George 38
Stewart, Frances 295
stock exchanges 220-4
stock-watering 88
Stone Age 5
Strumpel, Burkhard 182
subsistence theory of wages 115
supernatural 20
Swann, Dennis 260

Taft, Philip 86
Tanzania 5
  development in 298-300
Tartars *see* Mongols
Tawney, R. H. 23, 118
tax havens 220
Taylor, D. W. 80
Taylor, F. W. 138
tea 52
technostructure 77, 94
terms of trade 52, 244
Thirlwall, A. P. 290
Thomas, Elizabeth Marshall 6-8
Thompson, J. H. 264
Thomson, George Malcolm 30-1
Thorneycroft, G. E. P. 271
Tiger Balm 232-4
time-and-motion study 137-9
Timm, Bernhard 74-5
Timur, Toghan 25, 26
tools 5
Tourtellot, Arthur Bernon 88
Town and Country Planning Act 261
Townsend, Robert 99, 105
towns, origins of 10-11, 21
trade cycle 31, 60-1, 180, 182, 215, 268-71
trade-unions 44, 158-62, 237, 240, 253-4
Trans-World Airlines 93
Tucker, K. A. 69
Tugendhat, Christopher 102, 106
Turnbull, Colin M. 10

Ulman, Lloyd 156
unemployment 116-17, 255-6, 257, 264-71
Unilever 69
Union Minière du Haut-Katanga 52, 53
unit trusts 227-8
US Department of State 3
usury 22, 23, 28

Vandivier, Kermit 111
Veblen, Thornstein 67, 170-5, 176-7, 178
Verne, Jules 2
Vesco, Robert 230
Vestey family 109
Vidal-Naquet, P. 11, 16-17

wage leadership 160-1
Wakeman, Frederic 47
Wall, Joseph Frazer 87
Walker, Geoffrey 162
Walmsley, Keith 264
Walras, Leon 153, 154
war 34
  of the Roses 25, 35
Ward, Barbara 2
Ward, Scott 183
Warner, W. Lloyd 71
Watson, Thomas John 99-102, 103
Watt, James 37
We-Chi, Liu 13
Webb, Sidney and Beatrice 260-1
Weber, Max 28, 68, 77
Welsch, Lawrence A. 80
Werner, Julius 50-1
Western Electric 95
Whaley, John 287
Whately, Archbishop 154
Wheatcroft, Patience 108
White, Gordon 301
Wiles, Peter x
Wilhelm, Richard 14
Wilson Committee 218, 219
Wilson, Edmund 254-5
Winchester, Simon 220
witchcraft 10
Wolff, P. de 156
Woodward, Joan 80-1, 104
Woolworth, F. W. 108-9
Wootton, Barbara 158, 237
work study 137-9
workmen's compensation 254
World Bank 3
World Employment Programme 297-8
Wragg, Richard 156
writing, earliest 14
Wyatt, John 37
Wynne-Roberts, C. R. 138

Xenophon 131-2

Yamey, Basil S. 69

GPSR Compliance
The European Union's (EU) General Product Safety Regulation (GPSR) is a set of rules that requires consumer products to be safe and our obligations to ensure this.

If you have any concerns about our products, you can contact us on

ProductSafety@springernature.com

In case Publisher is established outside the EU, the EU authorized representative is:

Springer Nature Customer Service Center GmbH
Europaplatz 3
69115 Heidelberg, Germany

www.ingramcontent.com/pod-product-compliance
Ingram Content Group UK Ltd.
Pitfield, Milton Keynes, MK11 3LW, UK
UKHW041415180426

11947UKWH00007B/152